MARVEL VOICES
IDENTITY

Read more and listen at MARVEL.COM/VOICES.

START HERE

MARVEL'S VOICES: IDENTITY

INTRODUCTION by RINA AYUYANG

"WHAT IS VS. WHAT IF"
GENE LUEN YANG // writer
MARCUS TO // artist
SUNNY GHO // colorist

"THAT ONE THING"
CHRISTINA STRAIN // writer & coloris
JASON LOO // artist

"JIMMY WOO 1959"
GREG PAK // writer
CREEES LEE // artist
BRIAN REBER // colorist

"SEEING RED"
SABIR PIRZADA // writer
MASHAL AHMED // artist
NEERAJ MENON // colorist

"PERSONAL HEROES"
ALYSSA WONG // writer
WHILCE PORTACIO // artist
JAY DAVID RAMOS // colorist

"SINGULAR/PLURAL"
JEREMY HOLT // writer
ALTI FIRMANSYAH // artist
IRMA KNIIVILA // colorist

"TRADITIONAL PINK SUSH
KEN NIIMURA //
writer, artist & colorist

"NEW YORK STATE OF MIND"
MAURENE GOO // writer
LYNNE YOSHII // artist
SEBASTIAN CHENG // coloris
LINDSEY COHICK // co-edito

AN INTERVIEW WITH MARVEL CREATIVE LARRY HAMA
"WHAT DOES IDENTITY MEAN TO YOU?"

VC's JOE SABINO // letterer
JIM CHEUNG & ROMULO FAJARDO JR. // cover art
ANGÉLIQUE ROCHÉ // consulting editor
KAT GREGOROWICZ // assistant editor
DARREN SHAN // editor

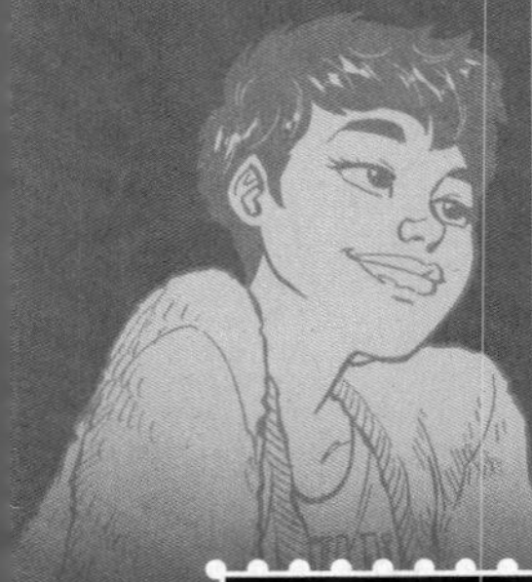

AMAZING FANTASY #15

"MASTERMIND EXCELLO"
GREG PAK // writer
TAKESHI MIYAZAWA // artist
CHRISTINA STRAIN // colorist
DAVE LANPHEAR // letterer
PETE WOODS // cover art
NATHAN COSBY // assistant edi
MARK PANICCIA // editor

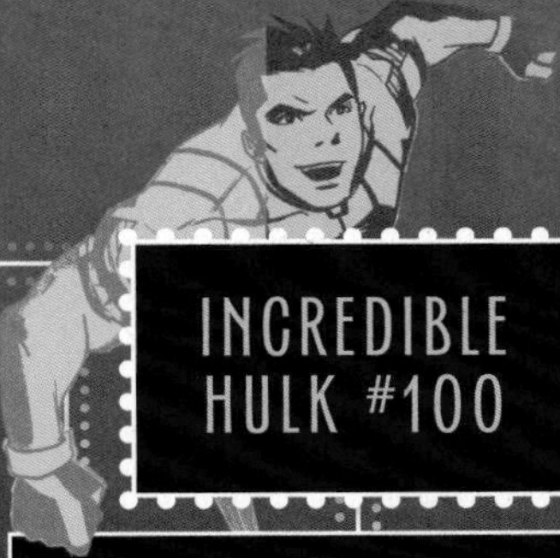

INCREDIBLE HULK #100

"PLANET CHO"
GREG PAK // writer
GARY FRANK // penciler
JON SIBAL // inker
CHRIS SOTOMAYOR // colorist
VC's RANDY GENTILE // letterer
NATHAN COSBY // assistant editor
MARK PANICCIA // editor

MARVEL #5

"A DAY IN THE MYSTICAL LIFE OF WONG"
GENE HA & ZANDER CANNON // writers
GENE HA // artist & colorist
ZANDER CANNON // letterer
MARTIN BIRO // assistant editor
ALANNA SMITH // associate editor
TOM BREVOORT // editor

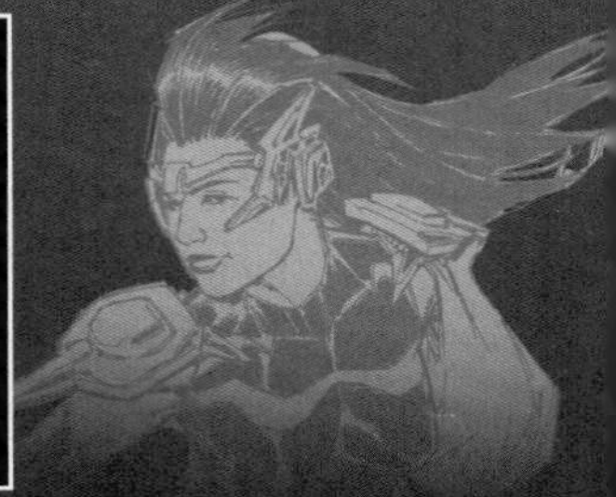

MARVEL'S VOICES: IDENTITY. Contains material originally published in magazine form as MARVEL'S VOICES: IDENTITY (2021) #1, AMAZING FANTASY (2004) #15, INCREDIBLE HULK (2000) #100, MAGNIFICENT MS. MARVEL (201 SHANG-CHI (2020) #1, MARVEL (2020) #5, DEMON DAYS: X-MEN (2021) #1 and SILK (2021) #1. First printing 2022. ISBN 978-1-302-94597-8. Published by MARVEL WORLDWIDE, INC., a subsidiary of MARVEL ENTERTAINMENT, LLC. OF PUBLICATION: 1290 Avenue of the Americas, New York, NY 10104. © 2022 MARVEL No similarity between any of the names, characters, persons, and/or institutions in this book with those of any living or dead person or instit intended, and any such similarity which may exist is purely coincidental. **Printed in Canada.** KEVIN FEIGE, Chief Creative Officer; DAN BUCKLEY, President, Marvel Entertainment; JOE QUESADA, EVP & Creative Director; DAVID BOGART, As Publisher & SVP of Talent Affairs; TOM BREVOORT, VP, Executive Editor; NICK LOWE, Executive Editor, VP of Content, Digital Publishing; DAVID GABRIEL, VP of Print & Digital Publishing; MARK ANNUNZIATO, VP of Planning & Forecastin YOUNGQUIST, VP of Production & Special Projects; ALEX MORALES, Director of Publishing Operations; DAN EDINGTON, Director of Editorial Operations; RICKEY PURDIN, Director of Talent Relations; JENNIFER GRÜNWALD, Director of Pro & Special Projects; SUSAN CRESPI, Production Manager; STAN LEE, Chairman Emeritus. For information regarding advertising in Marvel Comics or on Marvel.com, please contact Vit DeBellis, Custom Solutions & Integrated Advertising M at vdebellis@marvel.com. For Marvel subscription inquiries, please call 888-511-5480. **Manufactured between 1/28/2022 and 3/1/2022 by SOLISCO PRINTERS, SCOTT, QC, CANADA.**

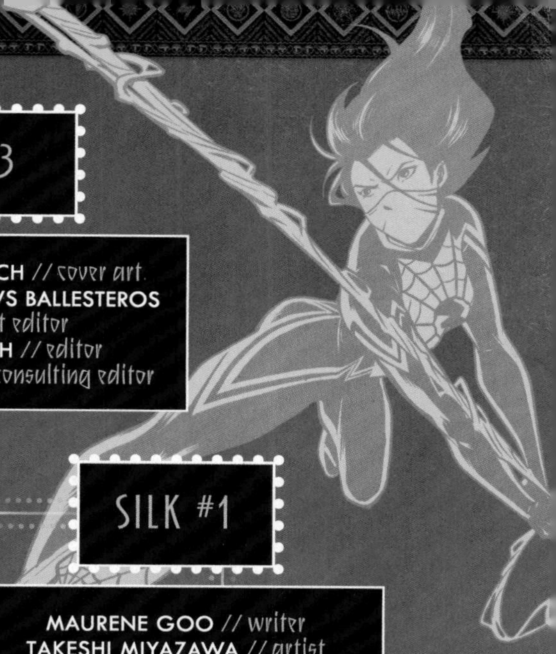

MAGNIFICENT MS. MARVEL #13

SALADIN AHMED // writer
JOEY VAZQUEZ // penciler
JUAN VLASCO // inker
IAN HERRING // colorist
VC's JOE CARAMAGNA // letterer

EDUARD PETROVICH // cover art
SHANNON ANDREWS BALLESTEROS // assistant editor
ALANNA SMITH // editor
SANA AMANAT // consulting editor

SHANG-CHI #1

"BROTHERS & SISTERS PART ONE"
GENE LUEN YANG // writer
DIKE RUAN // artist
PHILIP TAN // flashback artist
SEBASTIAN CHENG // colorist
VC's TRAVIS LANHAM // letterer
JIM CHEUNG & LAURA MARTIN // cover art
LAUREN AMARO // assistant editor
DARREN SHAN // editor
special thanks to MARK BASSO

SILK #1

MAURENE GOO // writer
TAKESHI MIYAZAWA // artist
IAN HERRING // colorist
VC's ARIANA MAHER // letterer
STONEHOUSE // cover art
LINDSEY COHICK // assistant editor
JAKE THOMAS // editor
NICK LOWE // executive editor

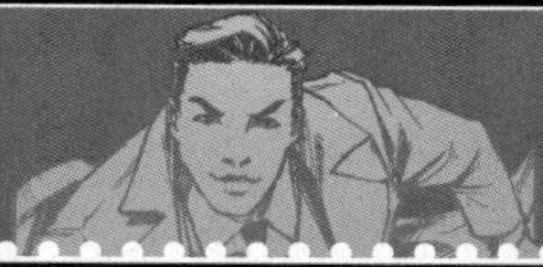

DEMON DAYS: X-MEN

PEACH MOMOKO // writer, artist & colorist
ZACK DAVISSON // english adaptation
VC's ARIANA MAHER// letterer
PEACH MOMOKO // cover art
LINDSEY COHICK // assistant editor

"MARVEL'S VOICES" ESSAYS

INTRODUCTION BY PAUL BAE
AFTERWORD BY GREG PAK
ESSAY BY ALYSSA WONG
ESSAY BY CHRISTINE DINH
ESSAY BY PREETI CHHIBBER
MARVEL'S VOICES PODCAST INTERVIEWS WITH
RONNY CHIENG, SALADIN AHMED,
KIMIKO GLENN & JACINDA CHEW

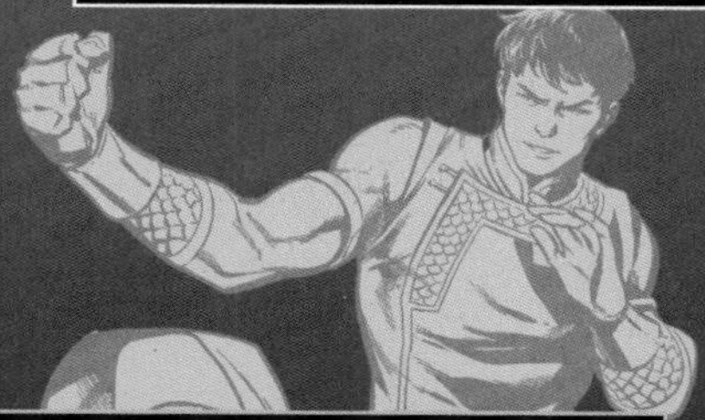

ANGÉLIQUE ROCHÉ // consulting editor
JENNIFER GRÜNWALD // collection editor
DANIEL KIRCHHOFFER // assistant editor
MAIA LOY // assistant managing editor
LISA MONTALBANO // associate manager, talent relations
JOE HOCHSTEIN // associate manager, digital assets

JEFF YOUNGQUIST // vp production & special projects
JESS HARROLD // research
STACIE ZUCKER // book designer
DAVID GABRIEL // svp print, sales & marketing
C.B. CEBULSKI // editor in chief

Special thanks to SARAH AMOS, BRAD BARTON, ROBYN BELT, BRENDON BIGLEY, ANTHONY BLACKWOOD, TIM CHENG, HALEY CONATSER, PATRICK COTNOIR, ADRI COWAN, MR DANIEL, CHRISTINE DINH, JILL DUBOFF, JON-MICHAEL ENNIS, JASMINE ESTRADA, HARRY GO, BRANDON GRUGLE, MARIKA HASHIMOTO, TUCKER MARKUS, RON RICHARDS, ISABEL ROBERTSON, LARISSA ROSEN, WALT SCHWENK, STEPHEN WACKER, ALEXIS WILLIAMS & PERCIA VERLIN

END HERE

INTRODUCTION

BY PAUL BAE

Flight is for white people. Super-strength is not for Asians. Super heroes come to rescue people like me, but they're never me.

— Paul Bae, Age 7

It was 1976. Mississauga, Ontario. I was 7 years old when the neighbourhood kids voted me captain of our imaginary pirate ship one day at the local playground. I was elated. In our lower-middle-class district, that meant that in the eyes of my peers, I was the ass-kickingest of the ass-kickers. In times of nautical strife, whatever dangers our young minds could throw at ourselves, they would put their collective trust in me. It was quite the honour.

Then my friend's mother interrupted our play session by informing me that, "captains are never Chinese." I told her I was Korean but to her, that was beside the point. She calmly and patiently explained that if I paid closer attention to stories and television shows, I would have noticed that captains of ships are always white. I remember being confused, but this was an adult educating me on things of which I was not aware. So I climbed down from our jungle gym/ pirate ship while her daughter took over as captain (even though none of us voted for her).

That was the day I learned I was not white. I had always had a hunch something was different about me, but I was too young to fully allow that truth to wash over me. I didn't even know what *white* was until that day. But I started to notice the differences, the things that set me apart. My grandmother did not speak English

Our house smelled differently, likely from the kimchi and Korean stews constantly being heated in the kitchen. And my father didn't know how to teach me hockey like the other fathers on our block. My friend Carl's father had to show me how to skate and handle a stick on the pond that covered the field across the street.

And when you are a 7-year-old boy, suddenly learning that you are not like other boys is a destabilizing experience. I felt unmoored and needed something to attach my identity to or risk floating away.

That is when my friends got into comic books. One series in particular: *Fantastic Four*. I don't recall exactly who brought them over to my house (probably Joey — Joey always stole stuff from his older brother to share with us despite the constant retributive ass whuppings), but I stared at those covers, slowly turned the pages, allowing the images to seep into my brain to forever find a home there. I was mesmerized by the Galactus trilogy, the vibrant Jack Kirby artwork, the unimaginable stakes.

But what I fell in love with was the Thing's pain. Ben Grimm had returned from space forever changed, ugly in the eyes of his fellow citizens. But this orange monster was a hero, even if many people couldn't see it.

Then came my next comic obsession: the

Hulk. Those comics landed in my lap just as the original TV series launched on televisions across North America. Banner's sense of alienation and loneliness became something like a source of power in my eyes. It was as though my weakness was transformed into my power. The qualities that made me different *made a difference*.

Then came the X-Men. Daredevil. Iron Man. Spider-Man. And a pattern built itself like a web in my psyche: This is what heroes look like. They were all different and often castigated for it, but they were different to an acceptable degree due to one crucial element: all of them were white. And that early lesson sunk its way deeper into my psyche: I was different; super heroes were set apart. These are not the same thing.

And in this way, heroism was equated with whiteness to my adolescent, developing mind. White people are the ones who can fly, who have super-strength, who are burdened with the task of righting wrongs. Asians had martial arts. We had Bruce Lee — nearly superhuman in his abilities, but considered foreign at the time.

This is why I am honoured to be invited to contribute an introduction to this collection of Asian stories by Asian creators. As a former public educator, my hope is that you pass this on to your children, your nieces and nephews and your neighbours' kids, so that they can see heroes like Jubilee, Shang-Chi and Aero written and drawn by incredible creators like Christina Strain, Gene Luen Yang, Marcus To, Alyssa Wong and Whilce Portacio (to name only a few). My wish is that these stories be woven into their subconscious so that the ceilings on their dreams vanish.

I only have one regret: I wish that 7-year-old Korean kid at that playground in Mississauga had grown up with these stories. Maybe it wouldn't have taken so long for him to realize that we can all be heroes, no matter what we look like.

We can all fly.

PAUL BAE — a former high school English teacher and stand-up comedian — is an author (*You Suck, Sir*) and award-winning audio drama creator-producer of *The Black Tapes* and *The Big Loop*. Paul is the director of Marvel Entertainment's critically acclaimed hit series *Marvels*.

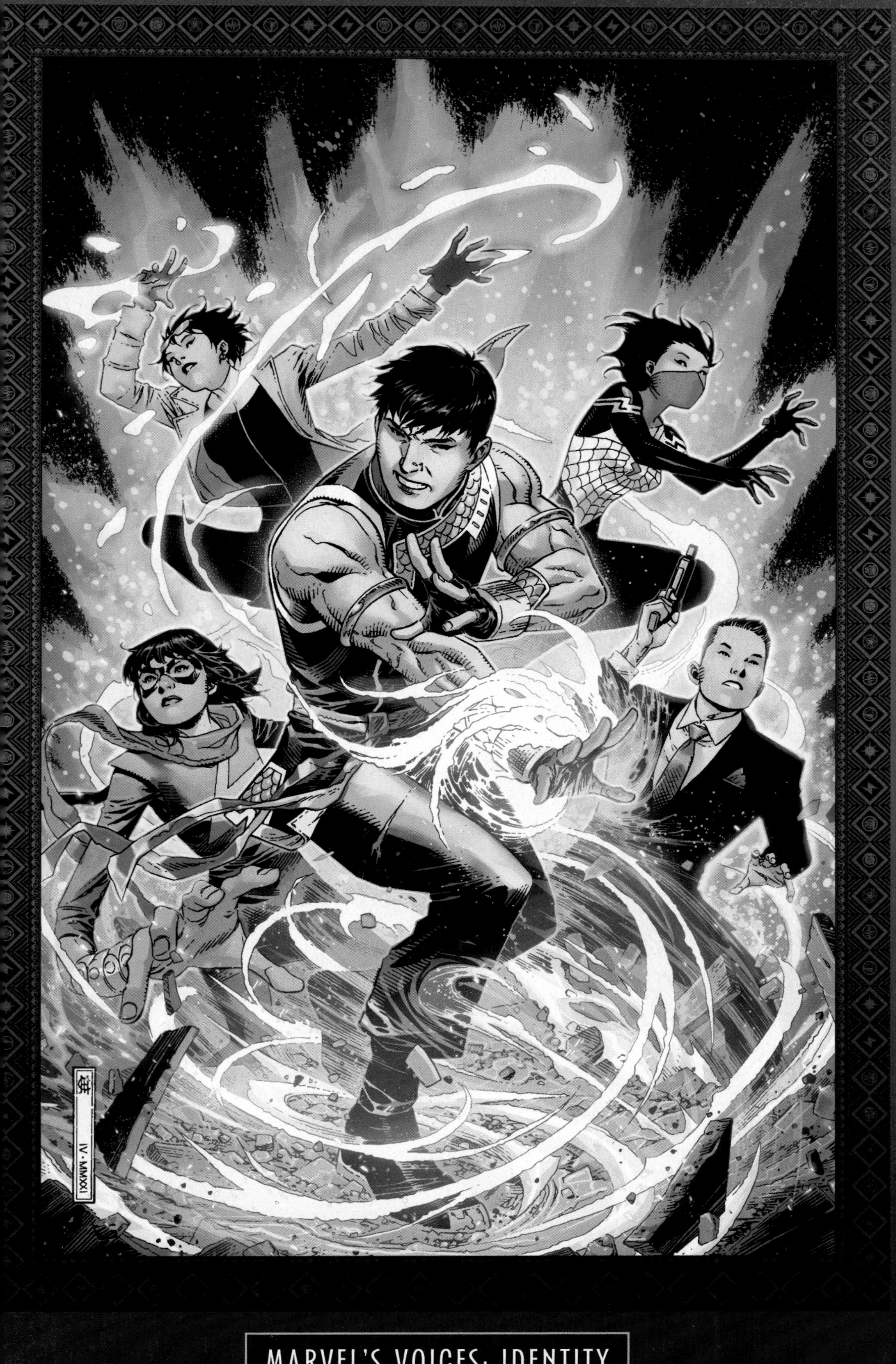
IV · MMXXI

MARVEL'S VOICES: IDENTITY

INTRODUCTION BY RINA AYUYANG

My humble initiation into the Marvel Universe consisted of 9-year-old me in Pittsburgh, Pennsylvania, watching *Spider-Man and His Amazing Friends* on Saturday mornings and reading random super hero comics from my brother's collection.

While writing this introduction, I reflected on one particular episode focused on Spider-Man's "amazing friend" Firestar. She begins a fiery (pun intended) romance with a smart, charismatic Japanese businessman named Shiro Yoshida (A.K.A. Sunfire). In the last scene of the episode, Sunfire has to go back to Japan to help with his villainous uncle's rehabilitation. While saying their goodbyes, Firestar asks Sunfire what the cure is for missing someone. Sunfire responds, "...knowing he will return!" I still remember how emotional I got while watching that heartfelt scene, wondering if Sunfire would ever come back!

Even with my love of the Marvel animation, I must admit that it was hard for me to relate to super heroes in the comics. They seemed intense, larger than life, and (sometimes literally) out of this world — everything that I felt I was not. I instead gravitated to the humor of the Sunday "funnies." I attribute my love of comic strips like *Peanuts* and *Nancy* to why I became part of the small-press indie comics community, mainly reading about people's real-life experiences. Through this community, I was eventually empowered to share my own stories about being Filipino American — a core part of my identity as a creator and fan.

As an adult, I have come to appreciate Marvel comics in a different way. I realized that those intense and larger-than-life storylines I read as a kid — which are still sometimes overwhelming for me — focus a great deal on the relatable human side of being a super hero. Sure, the heroes fought the bad guys, but they also had day jobs, family issues, and even relationship troubles. Beyond the super-powers and super villains, their stories explored vulnerabilities like self-doubt, grief, and fear — all things I can relate to on a very personal level.

But this isn't anything new — throughout the over eighty years of Marvel, its characters have grappled with the notion of their own identities, including their humanity. I connected with the stories that highlighted their

feeling the need to hide instead of being able to celebrate what makes them unique. Growing up as an Asian American and Pacific Islander kid in a predominantly white suburb, it seemed easier to just fit in than to call attention to the things that made me different, even at the risk of feeling less like myself.

I struggled with my own identity. How American was I if I preferred adobo over cheeseburgers? Was I still Filipino if I didn't know how to speak Tagalog? How much of myself was enough to belong? Fast forward to the year 2021, when racial tensions and violence against the Asian American and the Pacific Islander community have increased. The parallels of the community's current anxieties and the themes found in many Marvel storylines — with characters struggling to embrace their identity, and fighting things like alienation, discrimination, fearmongering, and scapegoating — are not lost on me. These stories are not only relatable, but they are also powerful and necessary.

When I became a cartoonist, I finally understood all the work that went into creating a comic. I was inspired by the skill and artistry involved in making even just a single Marvel comic book page and grew to admire the incredible artists behind their creation. There are two particular Marvel covers from my brother's collection that are etched in my mind forever: *Conan the Barbarian #72* and *Captain America #222*. I later discovered that Ernie Chan worked on both of those covers. Ernie was part of a group of Filipino artists like Tony DeZuniga, Alex Niño, Alfredo Alcala, and Nestor Redondo who were recruited by Marvel in the '70s and '80s. To know that Filipinos

like me played a huge part in Marvel's legacy made a significant impact on me as a cartoonist and fan.

Now, decades later, we have a whole new generation of Asian, Asian American, and Pacific Islander artists and writers who are not only writing for Marvel but are also bringing Asian American and Pacific Islander characters to the forefront. Though Asian, Asian American, and Pacific Islander artists and writers have been integral to the artistry and storytelling of the Marvel Universe for decades, the opportunity to share their talents to tell the stories of Asian, Asian American, and Pacific Islander Marvel characters like Shang-Chi, Jimmy Woo, Silk, Jubilee, Ms. Marvel, Wave, Silhouette, Silver Samurai, and Armor makes people like me — folks who once felt like these stories didn't and couldn't "belong to me" — get excited by the possibilities and power of the super hero comics genre as a whole.

That is why this moment and the book you have in your hands is so important. Today, I think about that moment from decades ago when I watched Firestar and Sunfire, the first time I remember seeing an Asian super hero, and then look at where we are now. There is a feeling of hope that we will see more Asian, Asian American, and Pacific Islander characters stepping out of the shadows and finally into the spotlight, written in ways that reflect their communities, with the potential to empower and to finally celebrate their true identity.

Rina Ayuyang

RINA AYUYANG is a Filipino American cartoonist based in Oakland, CA. Her latest graphic novel, *"Blame This on the Boogie,"* explores family, Filipino identity, and American pop culture fandom. She has been nominated for the Eisner and Ignatz Awards and has been honored with a MoCCA Arts Festival Awards of Excellence silver medal. She co-hosts an alt-comics podcast called *The Comix Claptrap,* and is currently working on her upcoming graphic novel, *"The Man in the McIntosh Suit,"* a film noir inspired by the 1920s Filipino American immigration experience.

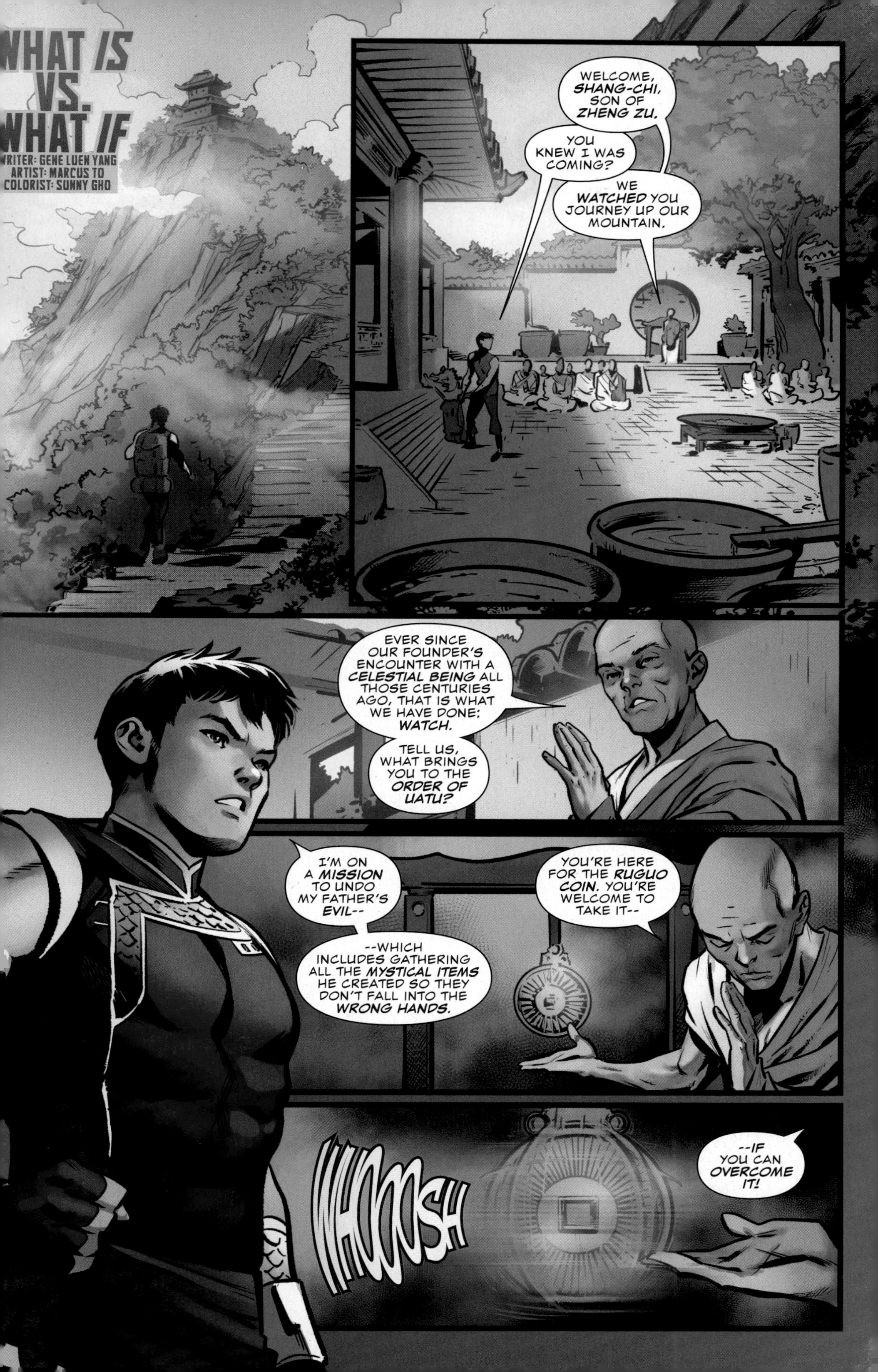
WHAT IS VS. WHAT IF
WRITER: GENE LUEN YANG
ARTIST: MARCUS TO
COLORIST: SUNNY GHO
WELCOME, SHANG-CHI, SON OF ZHENG ZU.
YOU KNEW I WAS COMING?
WE WATCHED YOU JOURNEY UP OUR MOUNTAIN.
EVER SINCE OUR FOUNDER'S ENCOUNTER WITH A CELESTIAL BEING ALL THOSE CENTURIES AGO, THAT IS WHAT WE HAVE DONE: WATCH.
TELL US, WHAT BRINGS YOU TO THE ORDER OF UATU?
I'M ON A MISSION TO UNDO MY FATHER'S EVIL--
--WHICH INCLUDES GATHERING ALL THE MYSTICAL ITEMS HE CREATED SO THEY DON'T FALL INTO THE WRONG HANDS.
YOU'RE HERE FOR THE RUGUO COIN. YOU'RE WELCOME TO TAKE IT--
WHOOOSH
--IF YOU CAN OVERCOME IT!

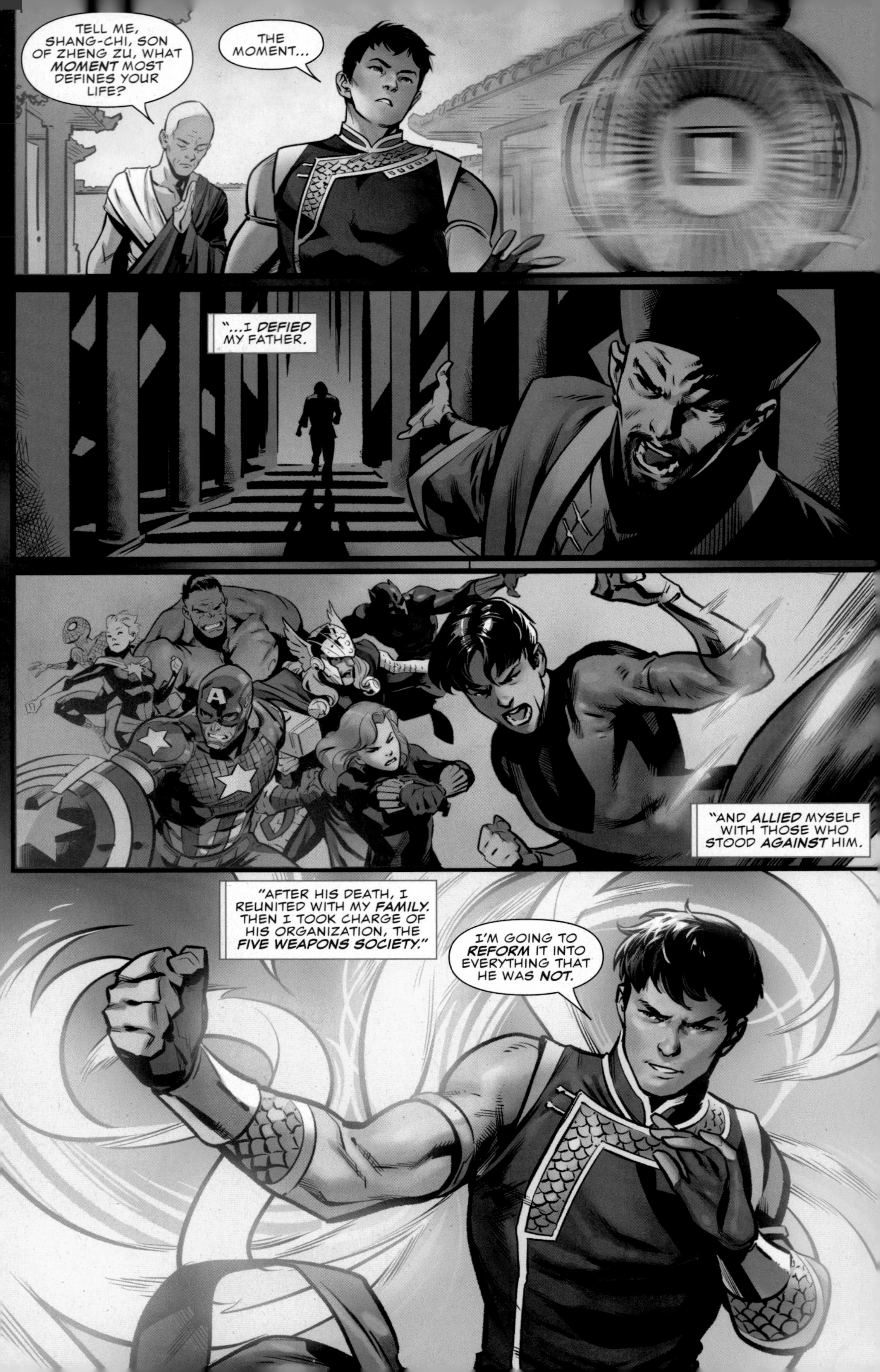
TELL ME, SHANG-CHI, SON OF ZHENG ZU, WHAT MOMENT MOST DEFINES YOUR LIFE?
THE MOMENT...
"...I DEFIED MY FATHER.
"AND ALLIED MYSELF WITH THOSE WHO STOOD AGAINST HIM.
"AFTER HIS DEATH, I REUNITED WITH MY FAMILY. THEN I TOOK CHARGE OF HIS ORGANIZATION, THE FIVE WEAPONS SOCIETY."
I'M GOING TO REFORM IT INTO EVERYTHING THAT HE WAS NOT.

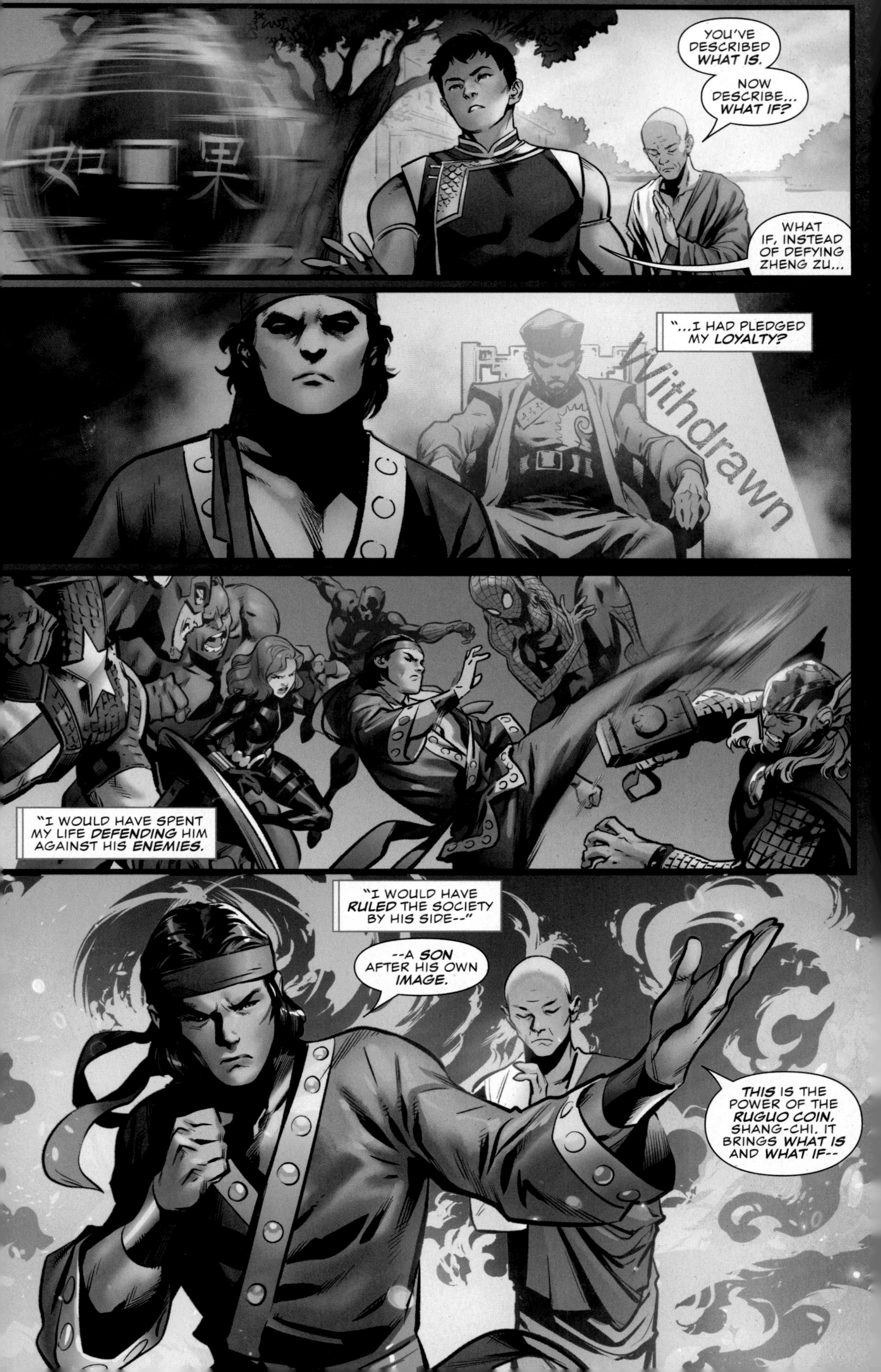
如果
YOU'VE DESCRIBED WHAT IS.
NOW DESCRIBE... WHAT IF?
WHAT IF, INSTEAD OF DEFYING ZHENG ZU...
"...I HAD PLEDGED MY LOYALTY?
Withdrawn
"I WOULD HAVE SPENT MY LIFE DEFENDING HIM AGAINST HIS ENEMIES.
"I WOULD HAVE RULED THE SOCIETY BY HIS SIDE--"
--A SON AFTER HIS OWN IMAGE.
THIS IS THE POWER OF THE RUGUO COIN, SHANG-CHI. IT BRINGS WHAT IS AND WHAT IF--

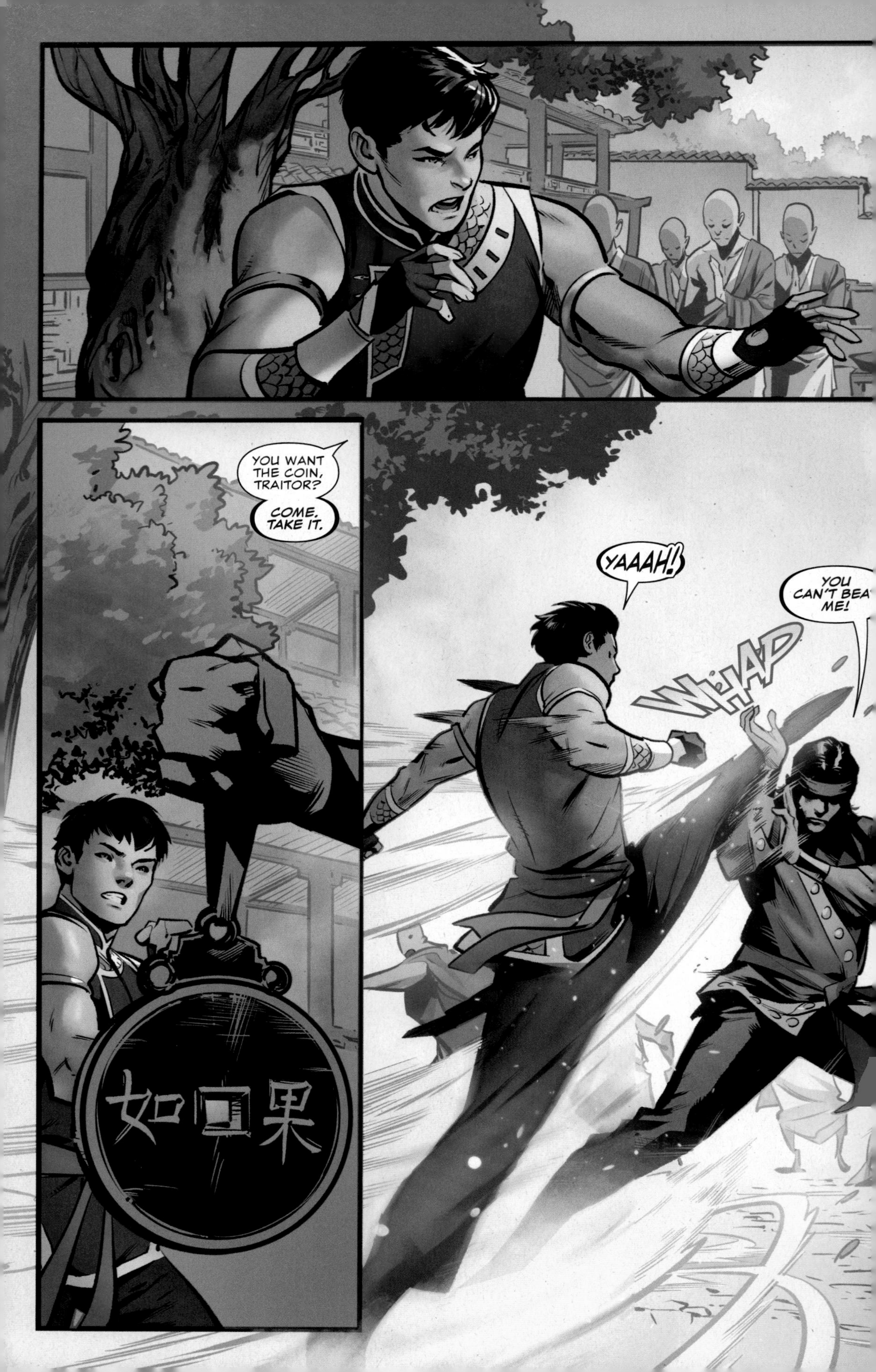
YOU WANT THE COIN, TRAITOR?
COME. TAKE IT.
YAAAH!
WHAP
YOU CAN'T BEAT ME!
如果

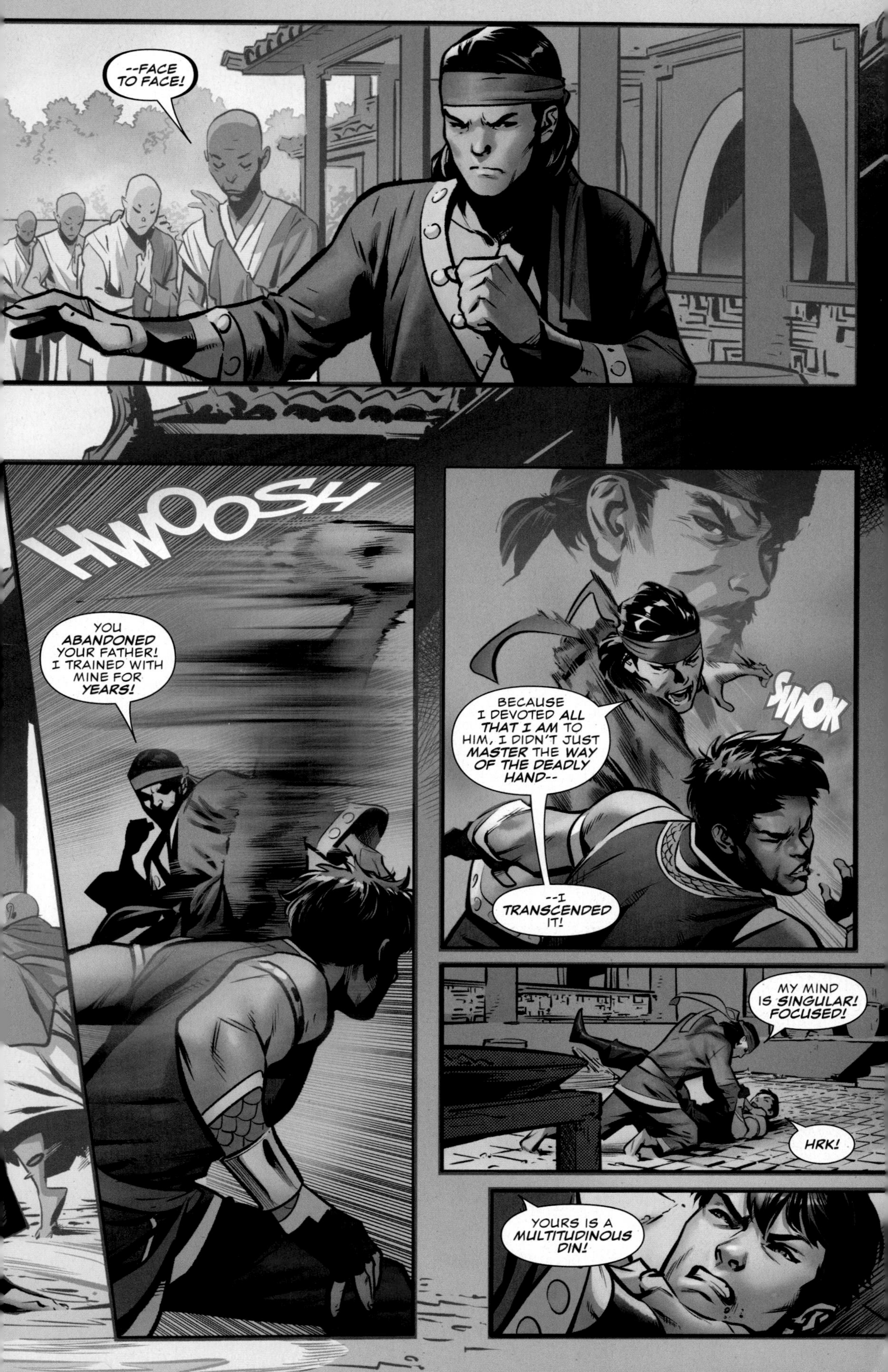
--FACE TO FACE!
HWOOSH
YOU ABANDONED YOUR FATHER! I TRAINED WITH MINE FOR YEARS!
SWOK
BECAUSE I DEVOTED ALL THAT I AM TO HIM, I DIDN'T JUST MASTER THE WAY OF THE DEADLY HAND--
--I TRANSCENDED IT!
MY MIND IS SINGULAR! FOCUSED!
HRK!
YOURS IS A MULTITUDINOUS DIN!

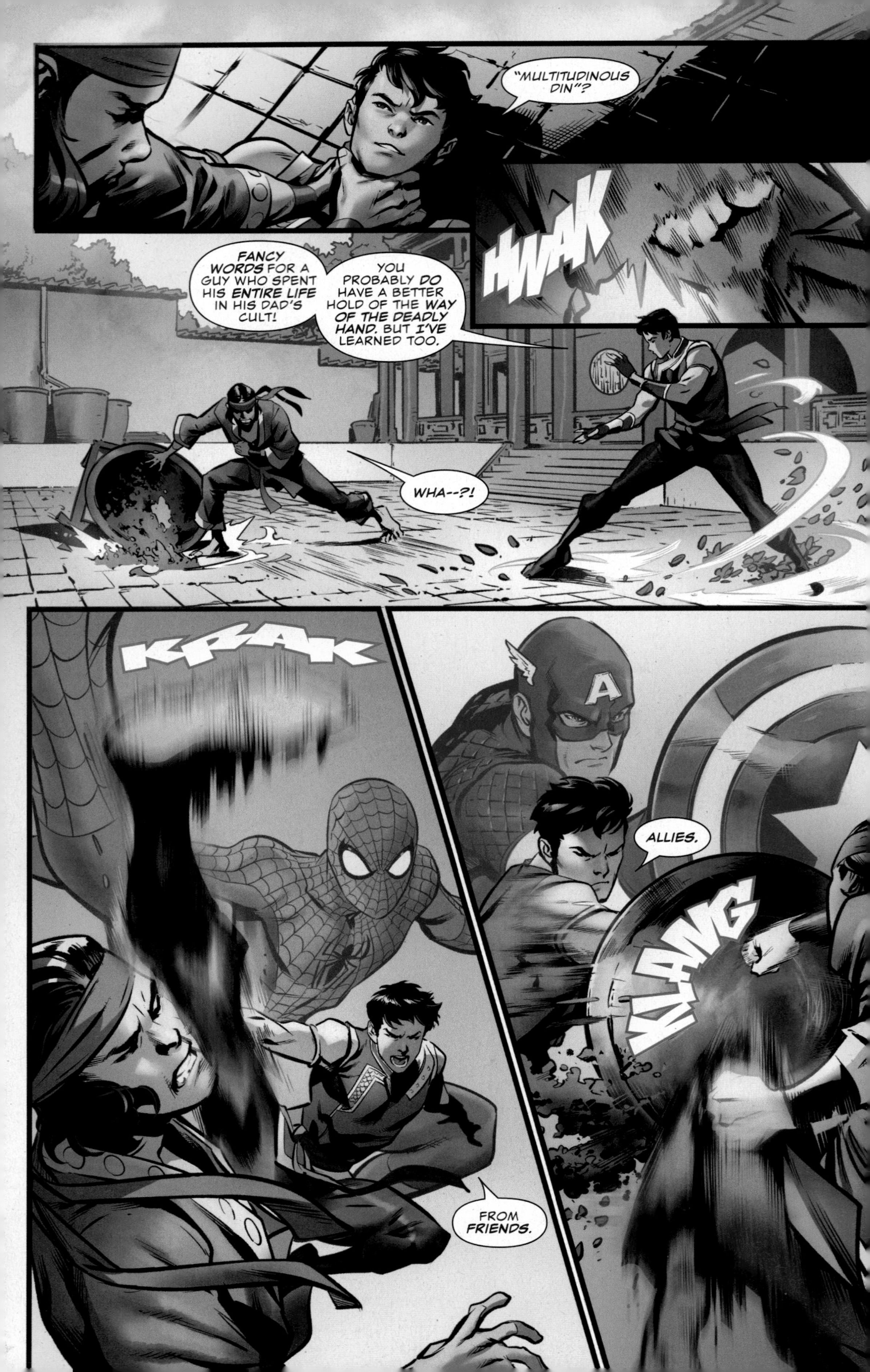
"MULTITUDINOUS DIN"?
HWAK
FANCY WORDS FOR A GUY WHO SPENT HIS ENTIRE LIFE IN HIS DAD'S CULT!
YOU PROBABLY DO HAVE A BETTER HOLD OF THE WAY OF THE DEADLY HAND. BUT I'VE LEARNED TOO.
WHA--?!
KRAK
FROM FRIENDS.
ALLIES.
KLANG

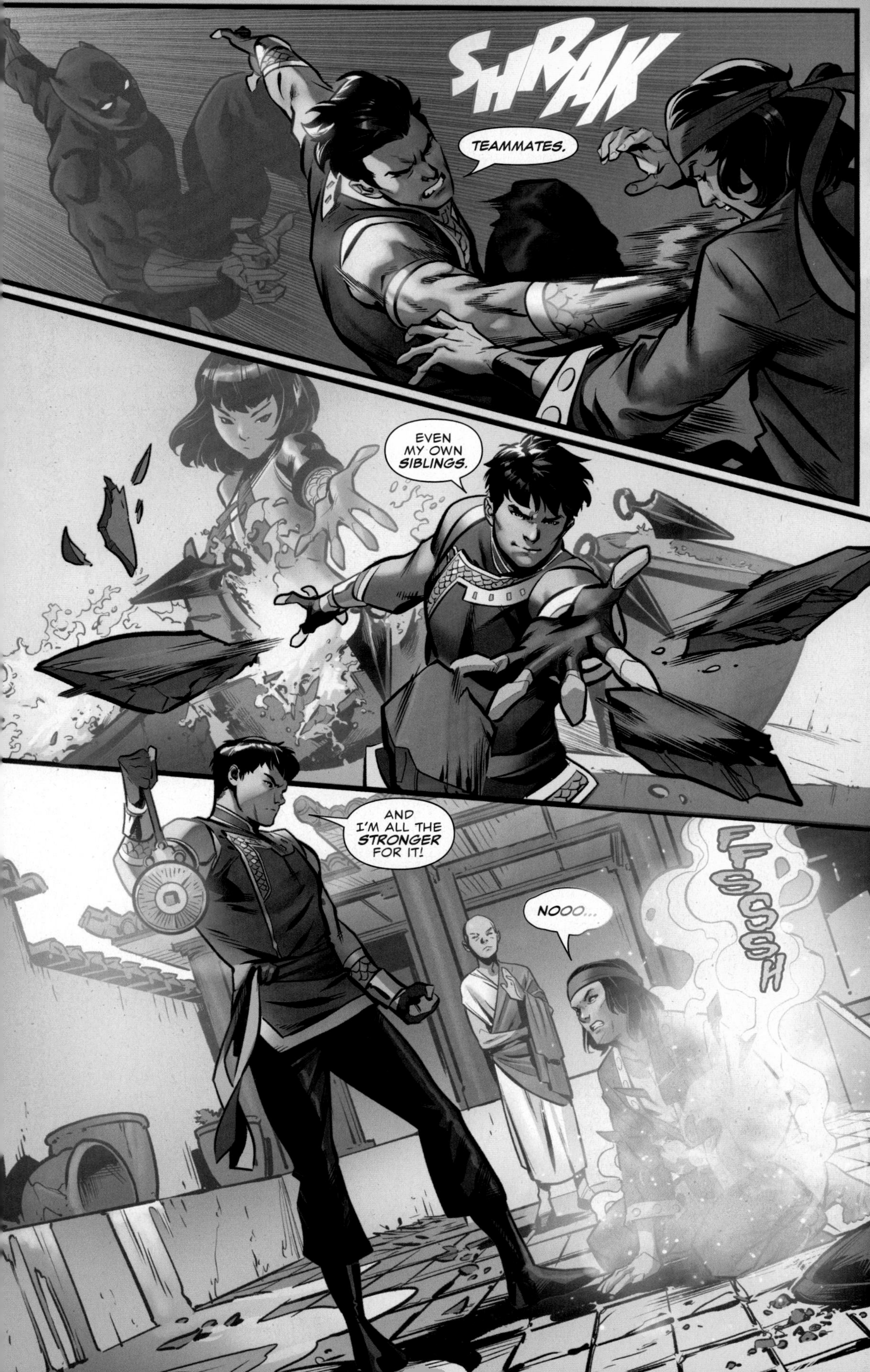
SHRAK
TEAMMATES.
EVEN MY OWN SIBLINGS.
AND I'M ALL THE STRONGER FOR IT!
NOOO...
FFSSSH

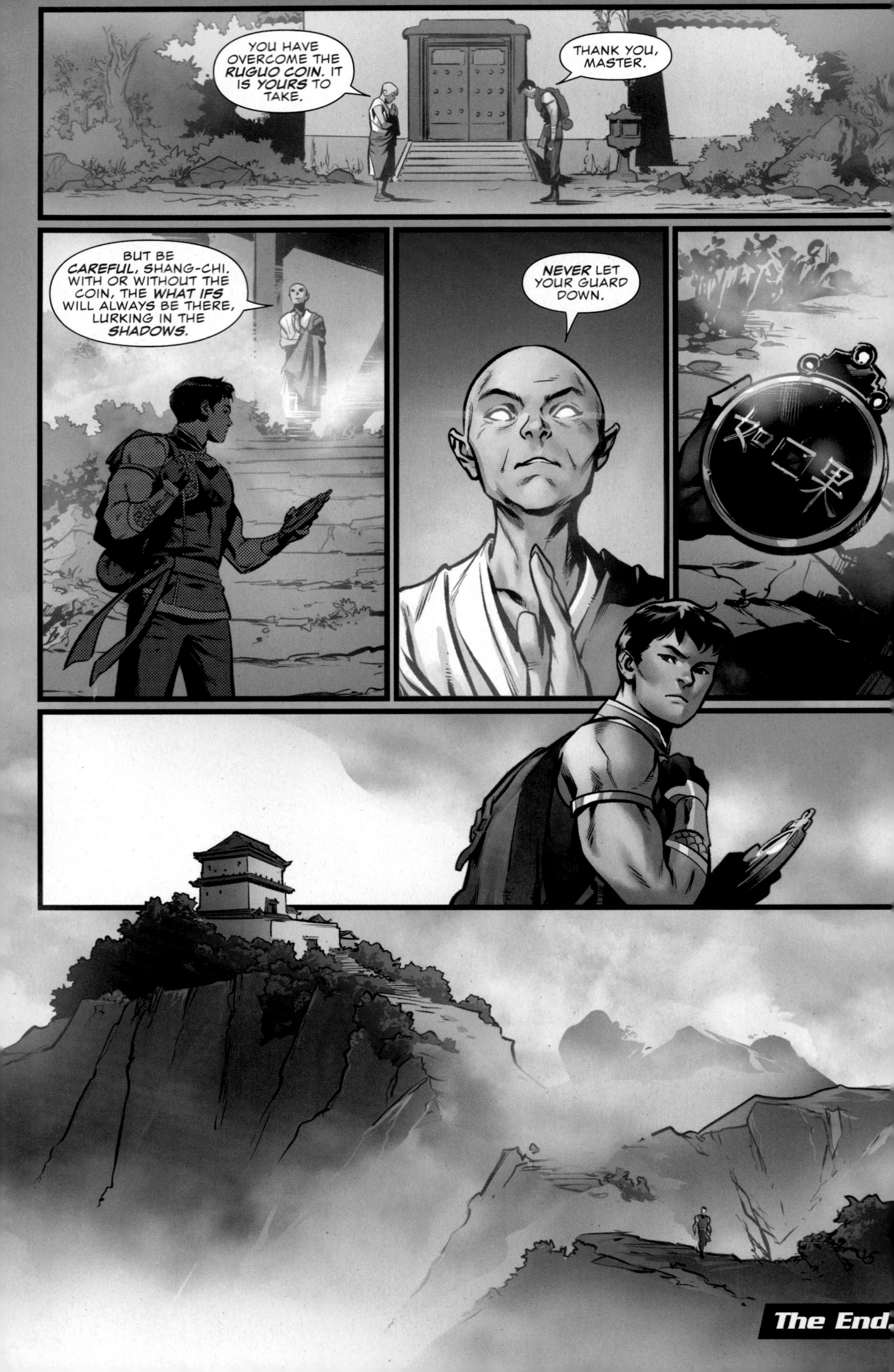
YOU HAVE OVERCOME THE RUGUO COIN. IT IS YOURS TO TAKE.
THANK YOU, MASTER.
BUT BE CAREFUL, SHANG-CHI. WITH OR WITHOUT THE COIN, THE WHAT IFS WILL ALWAYS BE THERE, LURKING IN THE SHADOWS.
NEVER LET YOUR GUARD DOWN.
如果
The End.

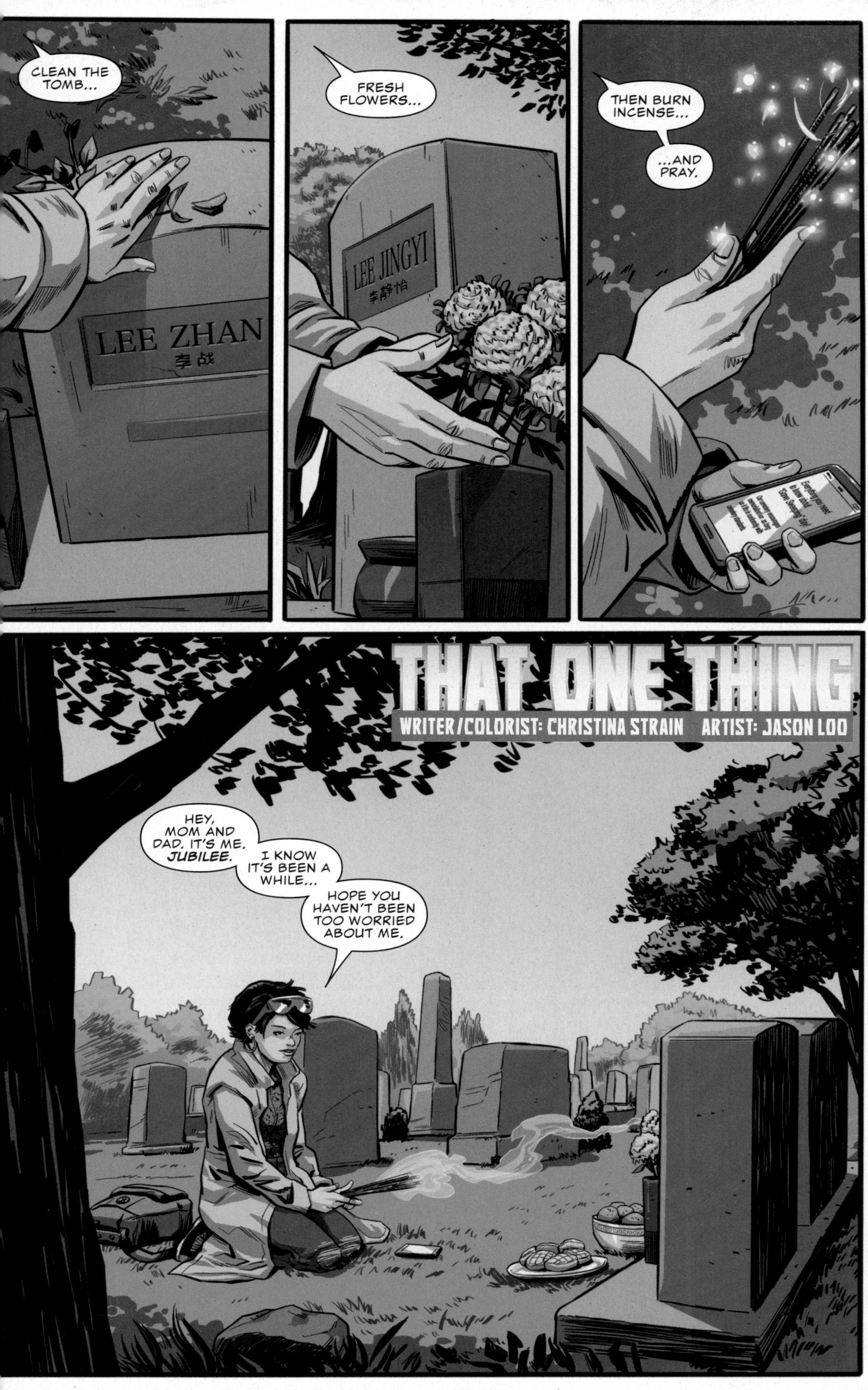
CLEAN THE TOMB...
LEE ZHAN
李战
FRESH FLOWERS...
LEE JINGYI
李静怡
THEN BURN INCENSE...
...AND PRAY.
THAT ONE THING
WRITER/COLORIST: CHRISTINA STRAIN ARTIST: JASON LOO
HEY, MOM AND DAD. IT'S ME. JUBILEE.
I KNOW IT'S BEEN A WHILE...
HOPE YOU HAVEN'T BEEN TOO WORRIED ABOUT ME.

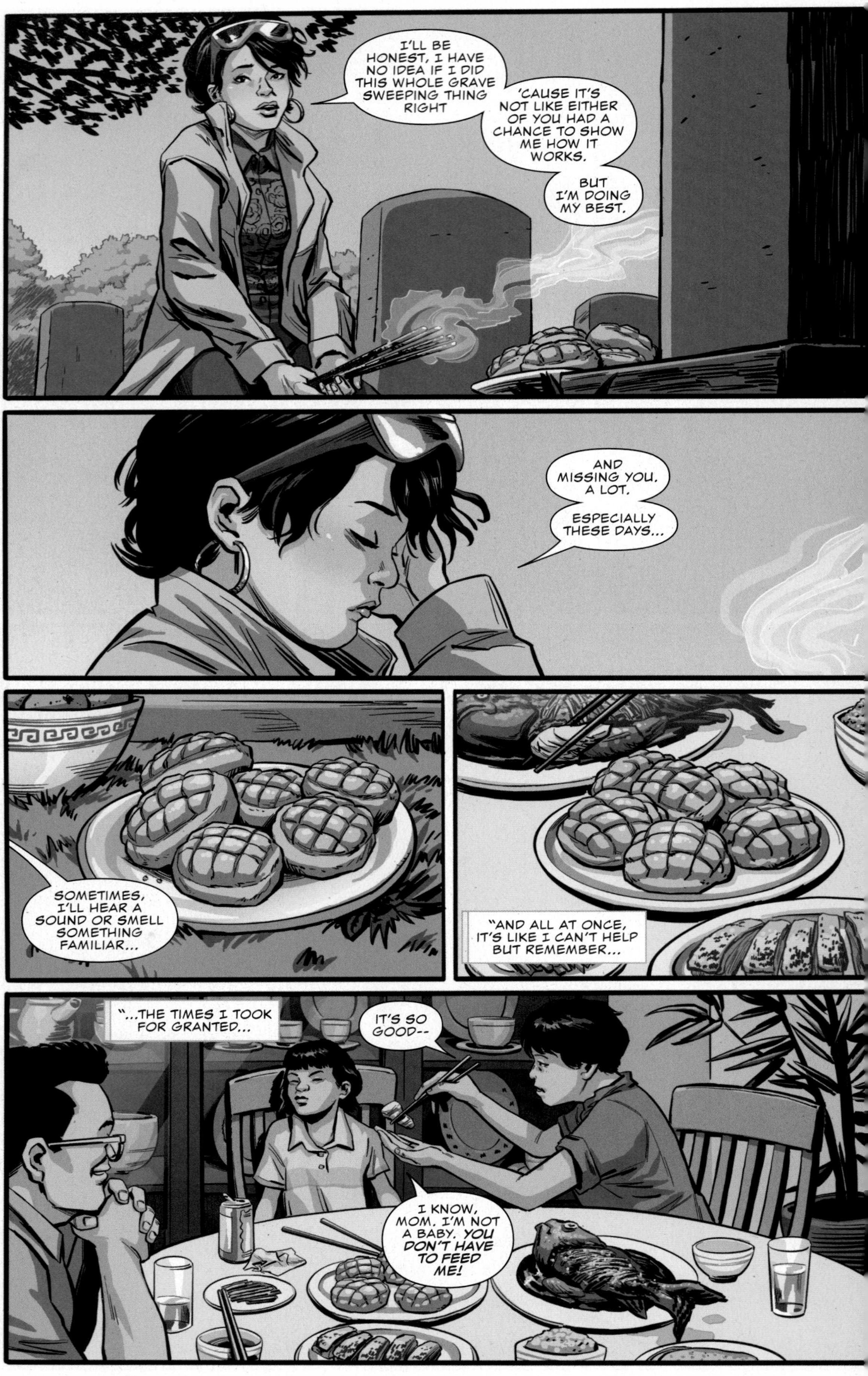
I'LL BE HONEST, I HAVE NO IDEA IF I DID THIS WHOLE GRAVE SWEEPING THING RIGHT
'CAUSE IT'S NOT LIKE EITHER OF YOU HAD A CHANCE TO SHOW ME HOW IT WORKS.
BUT I'M DOING MY BEST.
AND MISSING YOU. A LOT.
ESPECIALLY THESE DAYS...
SOMETIMES, I'LL HEAR A SOUND OR SMELL SOMETHING FAMILIAR...
"AND ALL AT ONCE, IT'S LIKE I CAN'T HELP BUT REMEMBER...
"...THE TIMES I TOOK FOR GRANTED...
IT'S SO GOOD--
I KNOW, MOM. I'M NOT A BABY. *YOU DON'T HAVE TO FEED ME!*

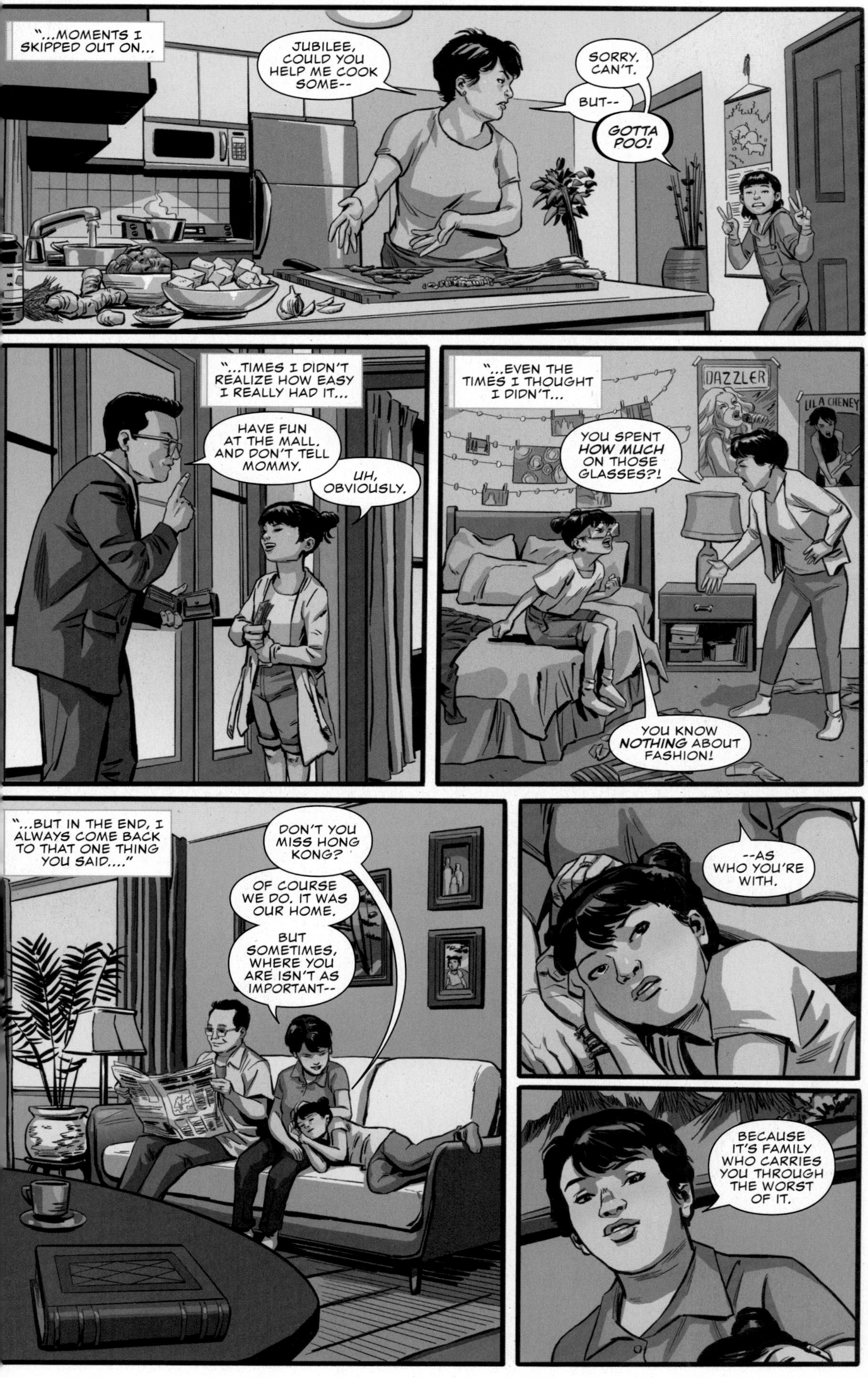
"...MOMENTS I SKIPPED OUT ON...
JUBILEE, COULD YOU HELP ME COOK SOME--
SORRY. CAN'T.
BUT--
GOTTA POO!
"...TIMES I DIDN'T REALIZE HOW EASY I REALLY HAD IT...
HAVE FUN AT THE MALL. AND DON'T TELL MOMMY.
UH, OBVIOUSLY.
"...EVEN THE TIMES I THOUGHT I DIDN'T...
DAZZLER
LILA CHENEY
YOU SPENT HOW MUCH ON THOSE GLASSES?!
YOU KNOW NOTHING ABOUT FASHION!
"...BUT IN THE END, I ALWAYS COME BACK TO THAT ONE THING YOU SAID...."
DON'T YOU MISS HONG KONG?
OF COURSE WE DO. IT WAS OUR HOME.
BUT SOMETIMES, WHERE YOU ARE ISN'T AS IMPORTANT--
--AS WHO YOU'RE WITH.
BECAUSE IT'S FAMILY WHO CARRIES YOU THROUGH THE WORST OF IT.

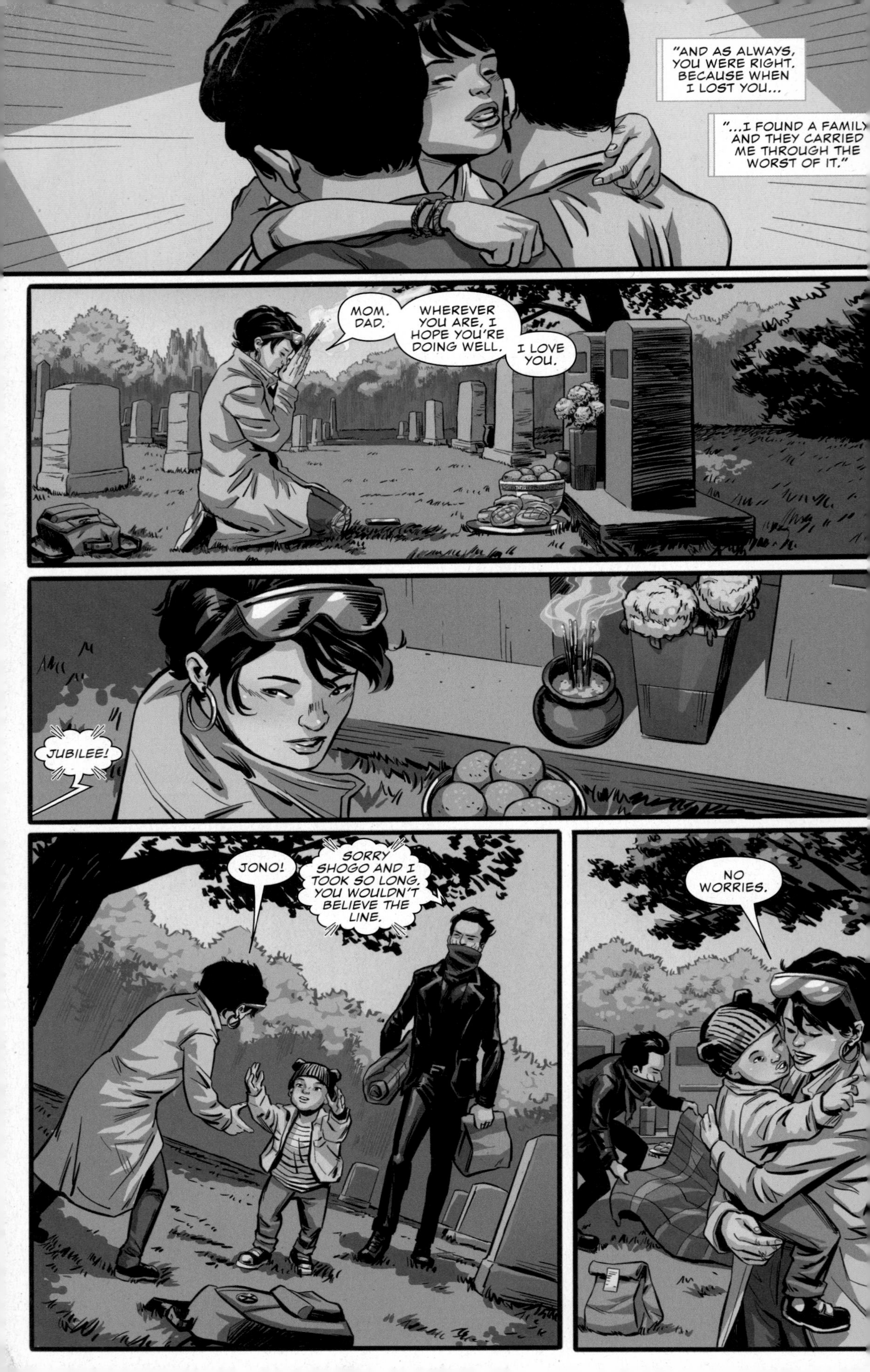
"AND AS ALWAYS, YOU WERE RIGHT. BECAUSE WHEN I LOST YOU...
"...I FOUND A FAMILY AND THEY CARRIED ME THROUGH THE WORST OF IT."
MOM. DAD.
WHEREVER YOU ARE, I HOPE YOU'RE DOING WELL.
I LOVE YOU.
JUBILEE!
JONO!
SORRY SHOGO AND I TOOK SO LONG. YOU WOULDN'T BELIEVE THE LINE.
NO WORRIES.

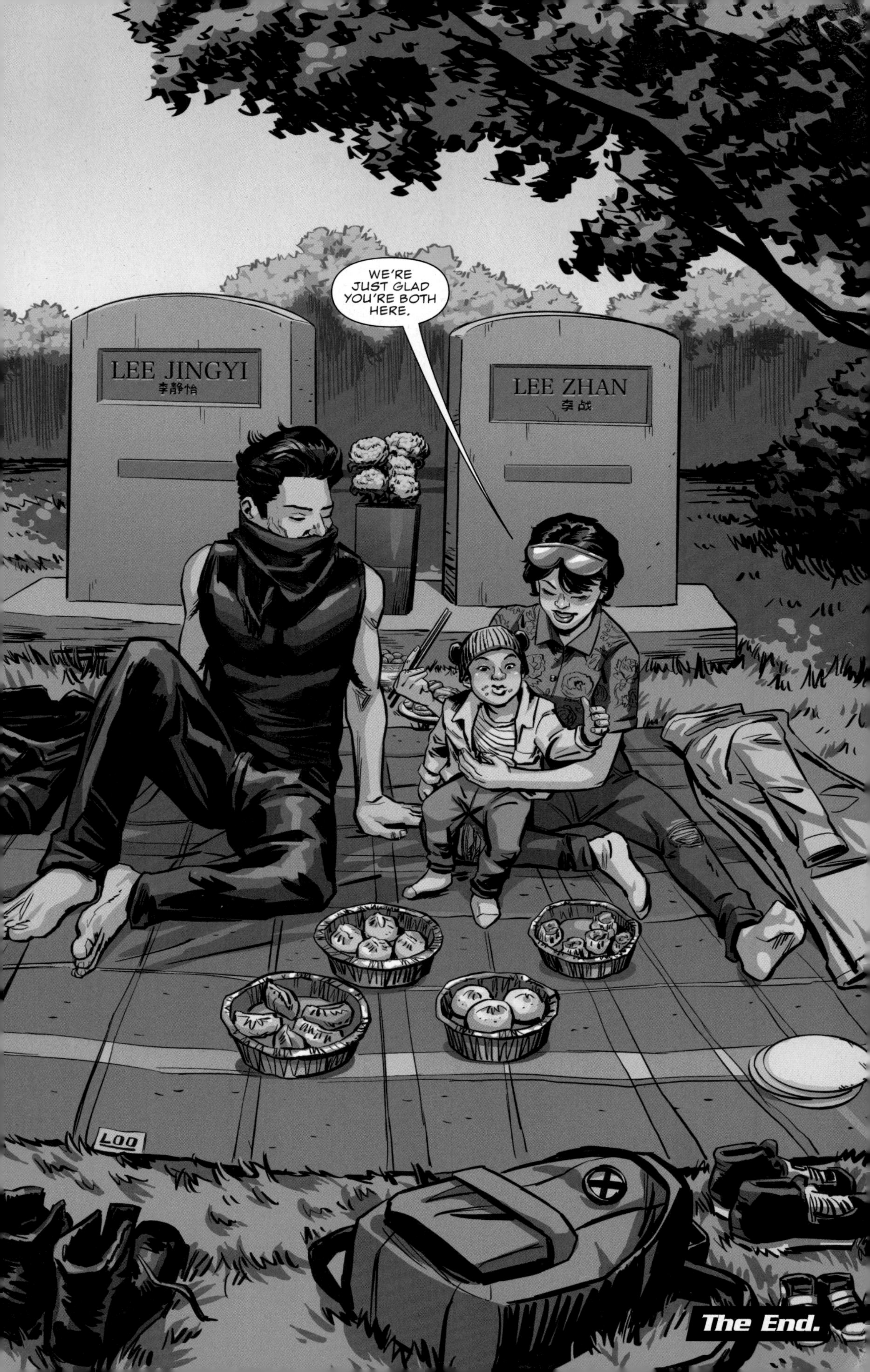
LEE JINGYI
李静怡
LEE ZHAN
李战
WE'RE JUST GLAD YOU'RE BOTH HERE.
LOO
The End.

San Francisco.

JIMMY, I FOUND THAT *SECRET GOVERNMENT WAREHOUSE*...

...BUT I HAVEN'T SEEN THIS *MONSTER* EVERYONE'S TALKING ABOUT. ARE YOU *SURE*--

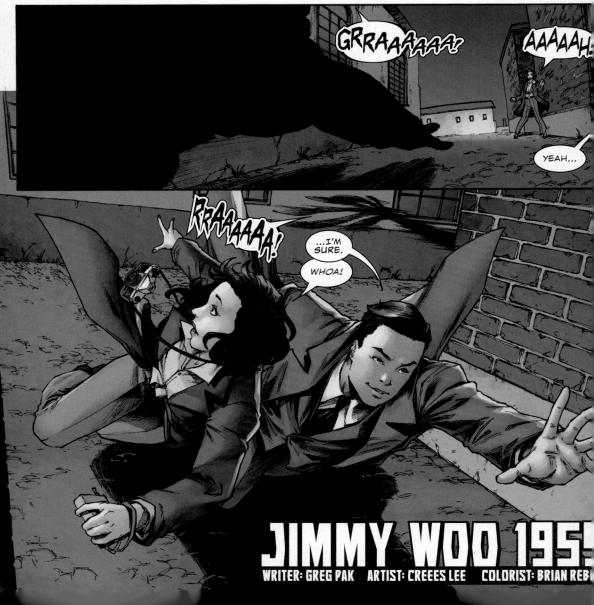

GRRAAAAAA!

AAAAAH!

YEAH...

RRAAAAAA!

...I'M *SURE*.

WHOA!

JIMMY WOO 195!

WRITER: GREG PAK   ARTIST: CREEES LEE   COLORIST: BRIAN REB

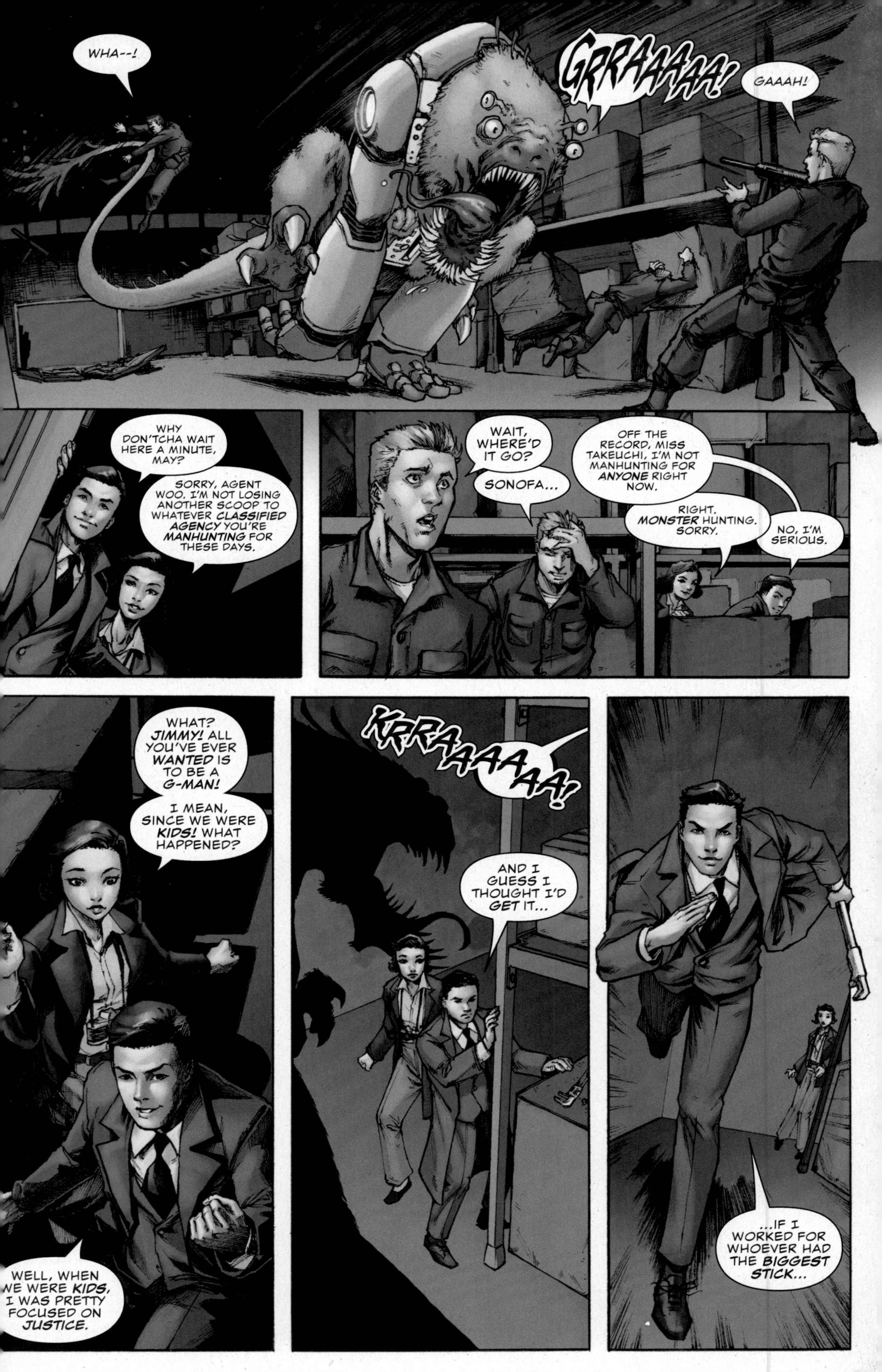
WHA--!
GRRAAAAA!
GAAAH!
WHY DON'TCHA WAIT HERE A MINUTE, MAY?
SORRY, AGENT WOO. I'M NOT LOSING ANOTHER SCOOP TO WHATEVER CLASSIFIED AGENCY YOU'RE MANHUNTING FOR THESE DAYS.
WAIT, WHERE'D IT GO?
SONOFA...
OFF THE RECORD, MISS TAKEUCHI, I'M NOT MANHUNTING FOR ANYONE RIGHT NOW.
RIGHT. MONSTER HUNTING. SORRY.
NO, I'M SERIOUS.
WHAT? JIMMY! ALL YOU'VE EVER WANTED IS TO BE A G-MAN!
I MEAN, SINCE WE WERE KIDS! WHAT HAPPENED?
WELL, WHEN WE WERE KIDS, I WAS PRETTY FOCUSED ON JUSTICE.
KRRAAAAAAA!
AND I GUESS I THOUGHT I'D GET IT...
...IF I WORKED FOR WHOEVER HAD THE BIGGEST STICK...

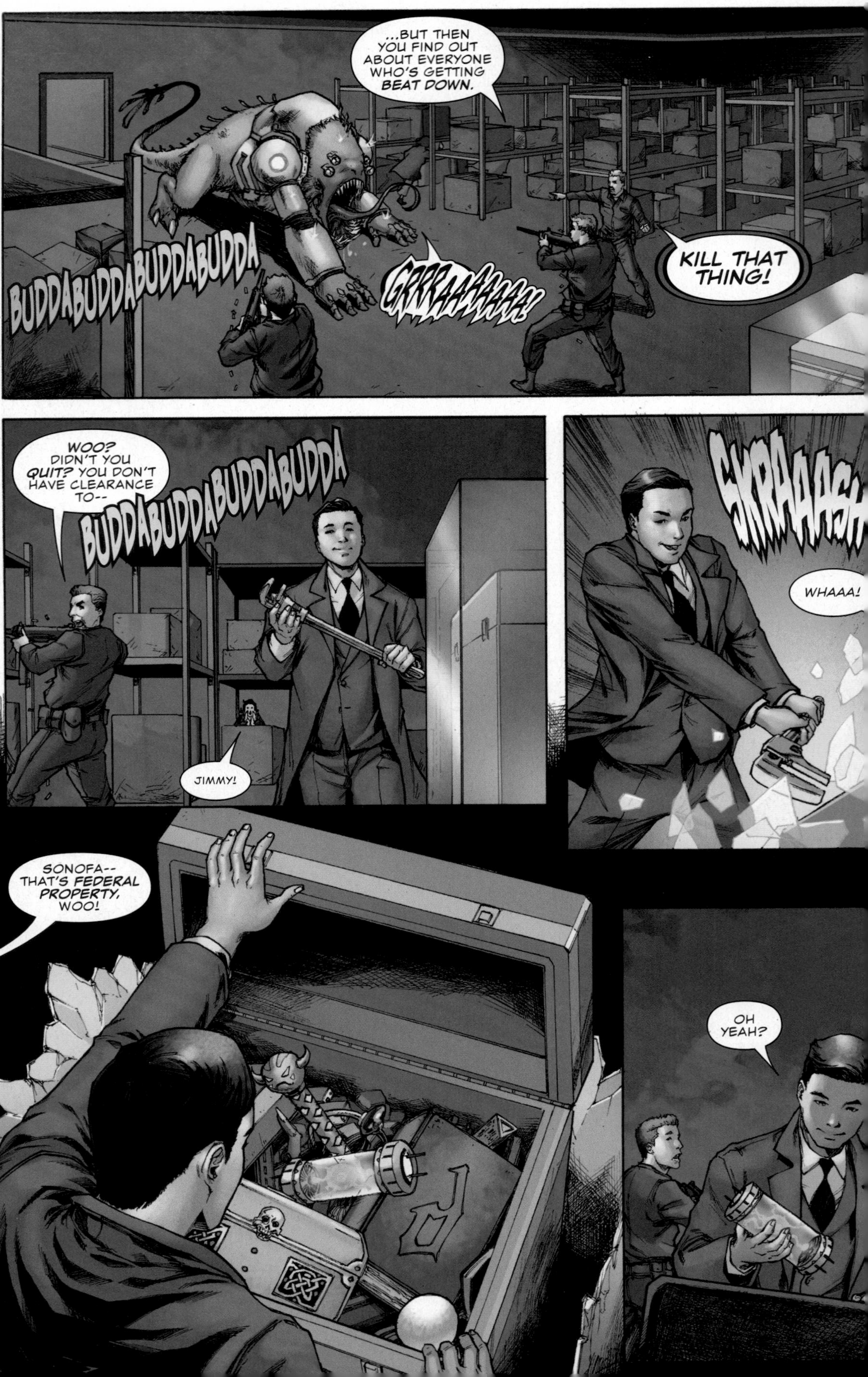

...BUT THEN YOU FIND OUT ABOUT EVERYONE WHO'S GETTING BEAT DOWN.
BUDDABUDDABUDDABUDDA
GRRRAAAAAAAA!
KILL THAT THING!
WOO? DIDN'T YOU QUIT? YOU DON'T HAVE CLEARANCE TO--
BUDDABUDDABUDDABUDDA
JIMMY!
SKRAAASH
WHAAA!
SONOFA-- THAT'S FEDERAL PROPERTY, WOO!
OH YEAH?

TELL THAT TO THE **VENUSIAN** YOU **STOLE** IT FROM.

RRRR?

THIS **IS** YOUR **ALIEN POWER REACTOR**, ISN'T IT?

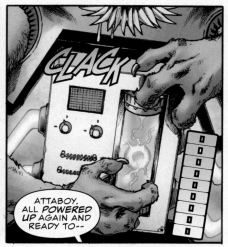

CLACK

ATTABOY, ALL **POWERED UP** AGAIN AND READY TO--

NO!

HA!

FWWOOOOOMP

I HATE THAT GUY.

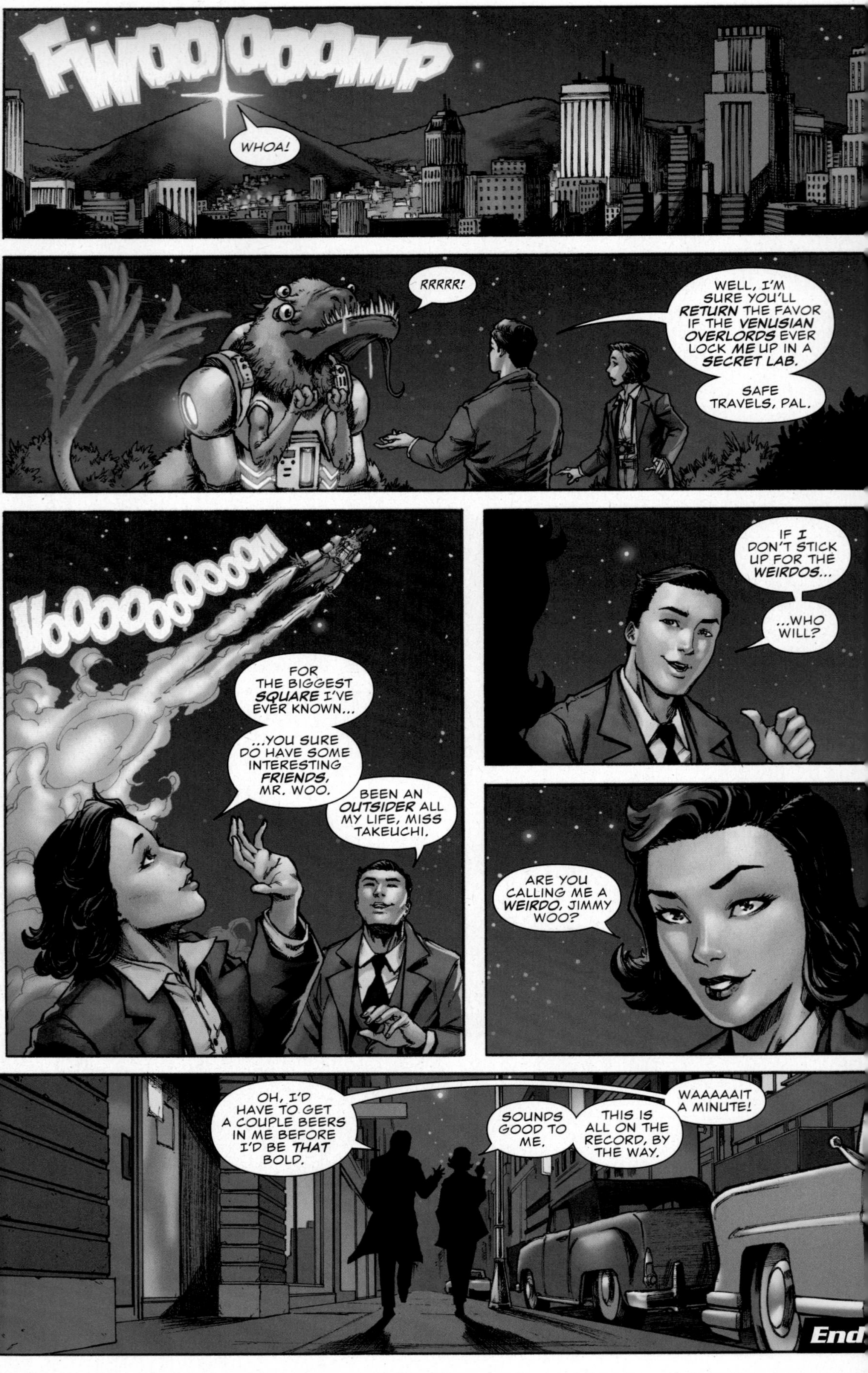
FWOOOOOOMP
WHOA!
RRRRR!
WELL, I'M SURE YOU'LL RETURN THE FAVOR IF THE VENUSIAN OVERLORDS EVER LOCK ME UP IN A SECRET LAB.
SAFE TRAVELS, PAL.
VOOOOOOOOOOM
FOR THE BIGGEST SQUARE I'VE EVER KNOWN...
...YOU SURE DO HAVE SOME INTERESTING FRIENDS, MR. WOO.
BEEN AN OUTSIDER ALL MY LIFE, MISS TAKEUCHI.
IF I DON'T STICK UP FOR THE WEIRDOS...
...WHO WILL?
ARE YOU CALLING ME A WEIRDO, JIMMY WOO?
OH, I'D HAVE TO GET A COUPLE BEERS IN ME BEFORE I'D BE THAT BOLD.
SOUNDS GOOD TO ME.
THIS IS ALL ON THE RECORD, BY THE WAY.
WAAAAAIT A MINUTE!
End

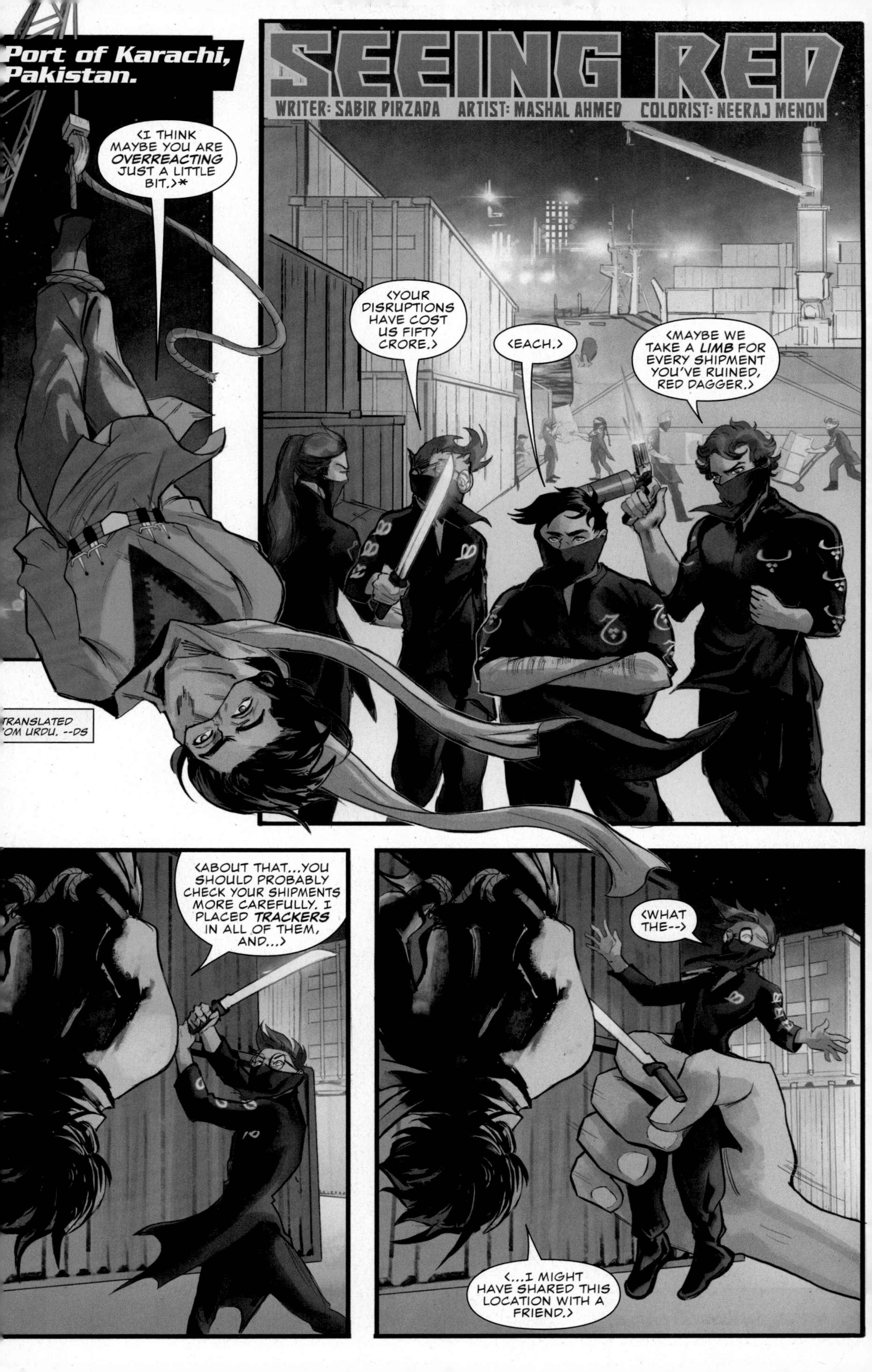

Port of Karachi, Pakistan.
SEEING RED
WRITER: SABIR PIRZADA ARTIST: MASHAL AHMED COLORIST: NEERAJ MENON
<I THINK MAYBE YOU ARE OVERREACTING JUST A LITTLE BIT.>*
<YOUR DISRUPTIONS HAVE COST US FIFTY CRORE.>
<EACH.>
<MAYBE WE TAKE A LIMB FOR EVERY SHIPMENT YOU'VE RUINED, RED DAGGER.>
*TRANSLATED FROM URDU. --DS
<ABOUT THAT...YOU SHOULD PROBABLY CHECK YOUR SHIPMENTS MORE CAREFULLY. I PLACED TRACKERS IN ALL OF THEM, AND...>
<WHAT THE-->
<...I MIGHT HAVE SHARED THIS LOCATION WITH A FRIEND.>

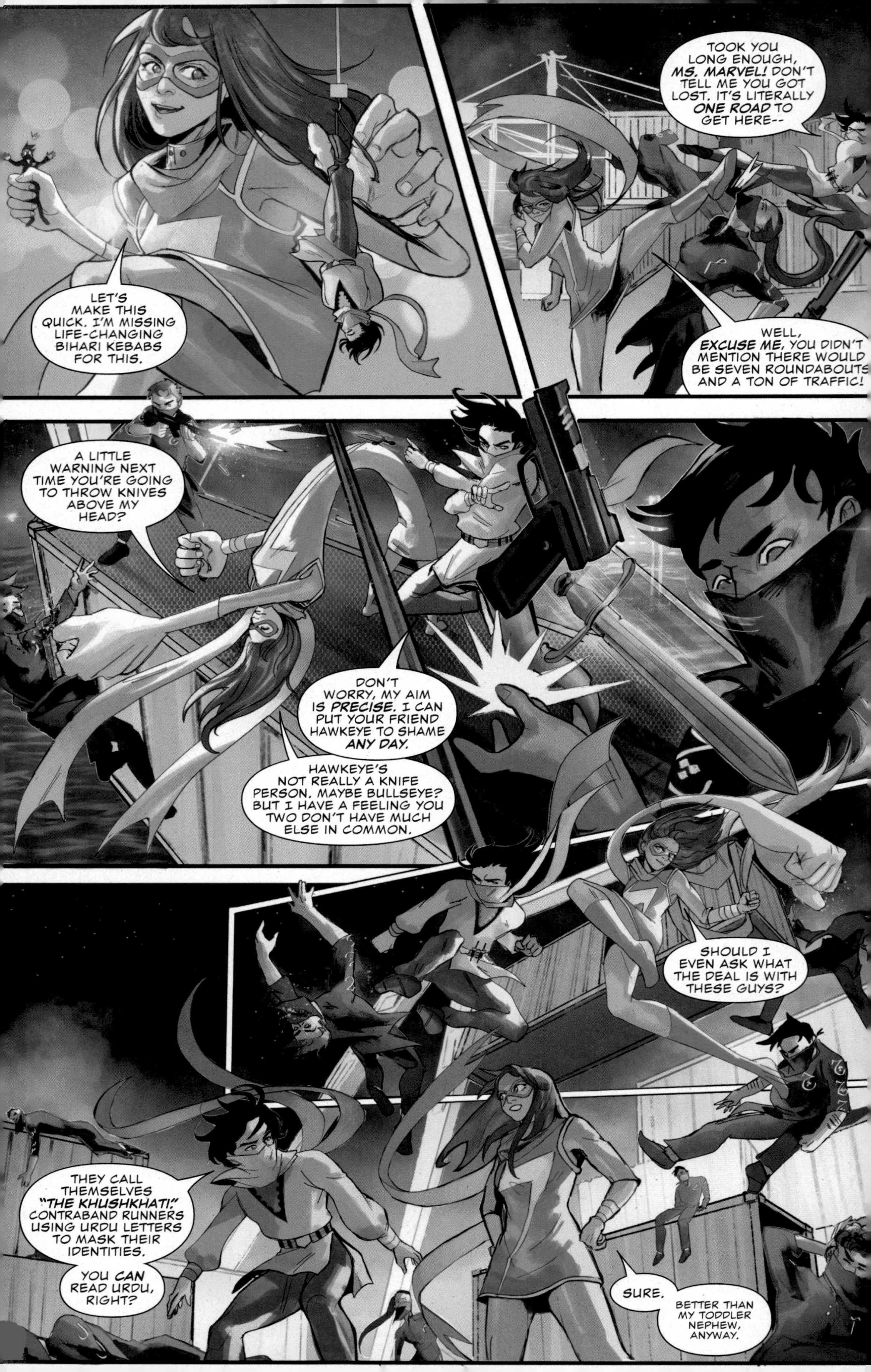
LET'S MAKE THIS QUICK. I'M MISSING LIFE-CHANGING BIHARI KEBABS FOR THIS.
TOOK YOU LONG ENOUGH, MS. MARVEL! DON'T TELL ME YOU GOT LOST. IT'S LITERALLY ONE ROAD TO GET HERE--
WELL, EXCUSE ME, YOU DIDN'T MENTION THERE WOULD BE SEVEN ROUNDABOUTS AND A TON OF TRAFFIC!
A LITTLE WARNING NEXT TIME YOU'RE GOING TO THROW KNIVES ABOVE MY HEAD?
DON'T WORRY, MY AIM IS PRECISE. I CAN PUT YOUR FRIEND HAWKEYE TO SHAME ANY DAY.
HAWKEYE'S NOT REALLY A KNIFE PERSON. MAYBE BULLSEYE? BUT I HAVE A FEELING YOU TWO DON'T HAVE MUCH ELSE IN COMMON.
SHOULD I EVEN ASK WHAT THE DEAL IS WITH THESE GUYS?
THEY CALL THEMSELVES "THE KHUSHKHATI." CONTRABAND RUNNERS USING URDU LETTERS TO MASK THEIR IDENTITIES.
YOU CAN READ URDU, RIGHT?
SURE.
BETTER THAN MY TODDLER NEPHEW, ANYWAY.

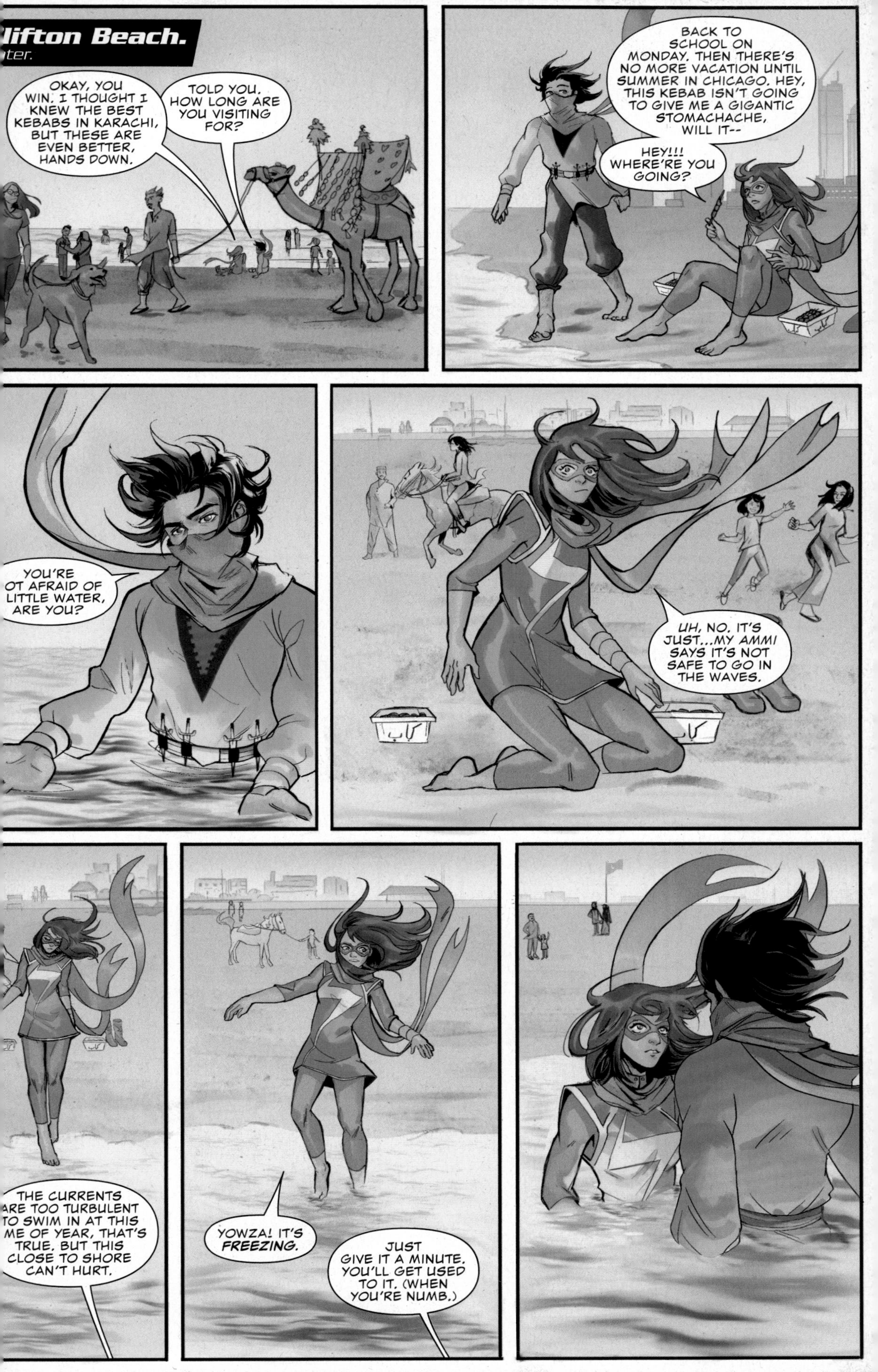
lifton Beach.
ter.
OKAY, YOU WIN. I THOUGHT I KNEW THE BEST KEBABS IN KARACHI, BUT THESE ARE EVEN BETTER, HANDS DOWN.
TOLD YOU. HOW LONG ARE YOU VISITING FOR?
BACK TO SCHOOL ON MONDAY. THEN THERE'S NO MORE VACATION UNTIL SUMMER IN CHICAGO. HEY, THIS KEBAB ISN'T GOING TO GIVE ME A GIGANTIC STOMACHACHE, WILL IT--
HEY!!! WHERE'RE YOU GOING?
YOU'RE OT AFRAID OF LITTLE WATER, ARE YOU?
UH, NO. IT'S JUST...MY AMMI SAYS IT'S NOT SAFE TO GO IN THE WAVES.
THE CURRENTS ARE TOO TURBULENT TO SWIM IN AT THIS ME OF YEAR, THAT'S TRUE. BUT THIS CLOSE TO SHORE CAN'T HURT.
YOWZA! IT'S FREEZING.
JUST GIVE IT A MINUTE. YOU'LL GET USED TO IT. (WHEN YOU'RE NUMB.)

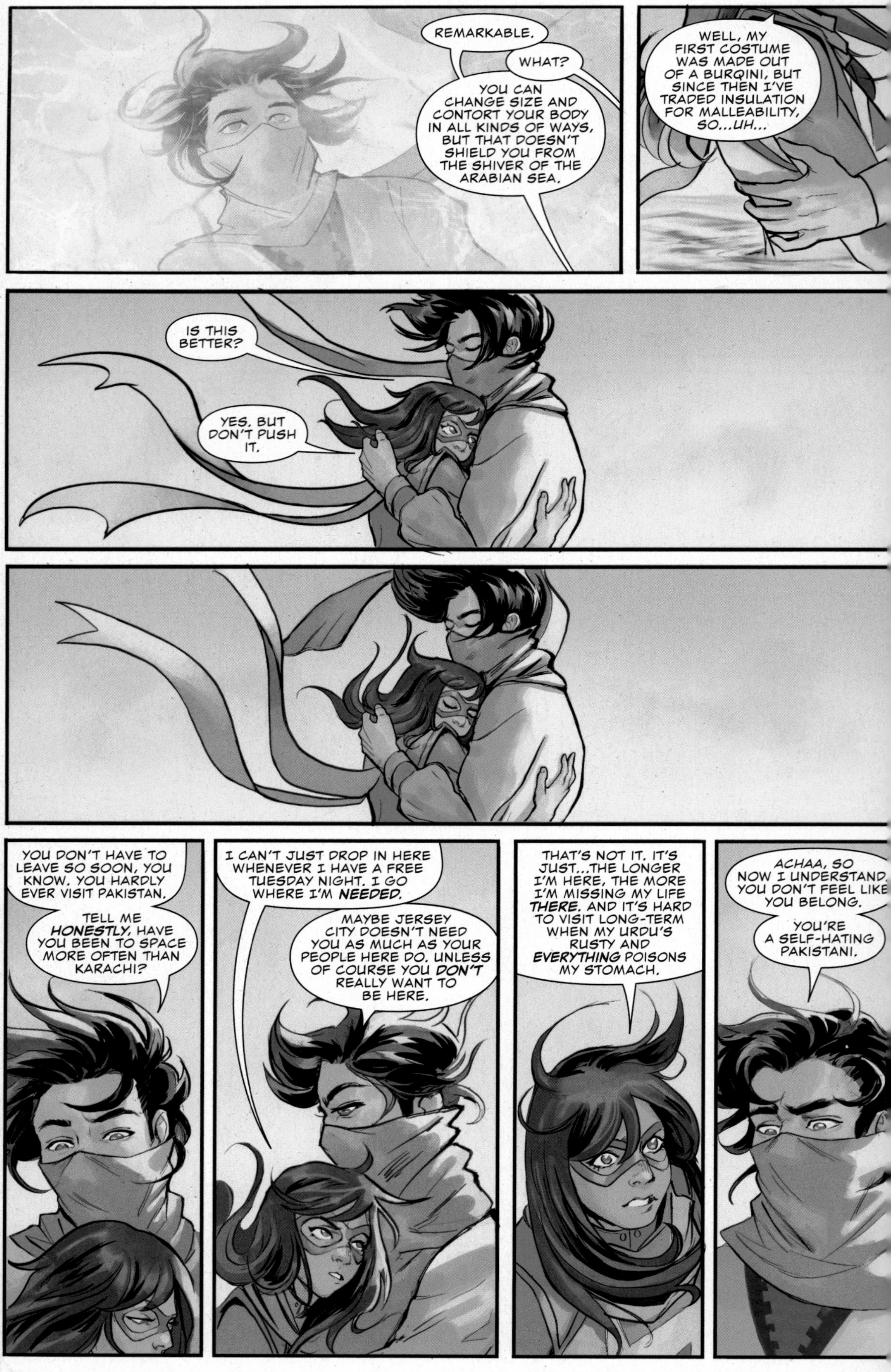
REMARKABLE.
WHAT?
YOU CAN CHANGE SIZE AND CONTORT YOUR BODY IN ALL KINDS OF WAYS, BUT THAT DOESN'T SHIELD YOU FROM THE SHIVER OF THE ARABIAN SEA.
WELL, MY FIRST COSTUME WAS MADE OUT OF A BURQINI, BUT SINCE THEN I'VE TRADED INSULATION FOR MALLEABILITY, SO...UH...
IS THIS BETTER?
YES. BUT DON'T PUSH IT.
YOU DON'T HAVE TO LEAVE SO SOON, YOU KNOW. YOU HARDLY EVER VISIT PAKISTAN.
TELL ME *HONESTLY*, HAVE YOU BEEN TO SPACE MORE OFTEN THAN KARACHI?
I CAN'T JUST DROP IN HERE WHENEVER I HAVE A FREE TUESDAY NIGHT. I GO WHERE I'M *NEEDED*.
MAYBE JERSEY CITY DOESN'T NEED YOU AS MUCH AS YOUR PEOPLE HERE DO. UNLESS OF COURSE YOU *DON'T* REALLY WANT TO BE HERE.
THAT'S NOT IT. IT'S JUST...THE LONGER I'M HERE, THE MORE I'M MISSING MY LIFE *THERE*. AND IT'S HARD TO VISIT LONG-TERM WHEN MY URDU'S RUSTY AND *EVERYTHING* POISONS MY STOMACH.
ACHAA, SO NOW I UNDERSTAND. YOU DON'T FEEL LIKE YOU BELONG.
YOU'RE A SELF-HATING PAKISTANI.

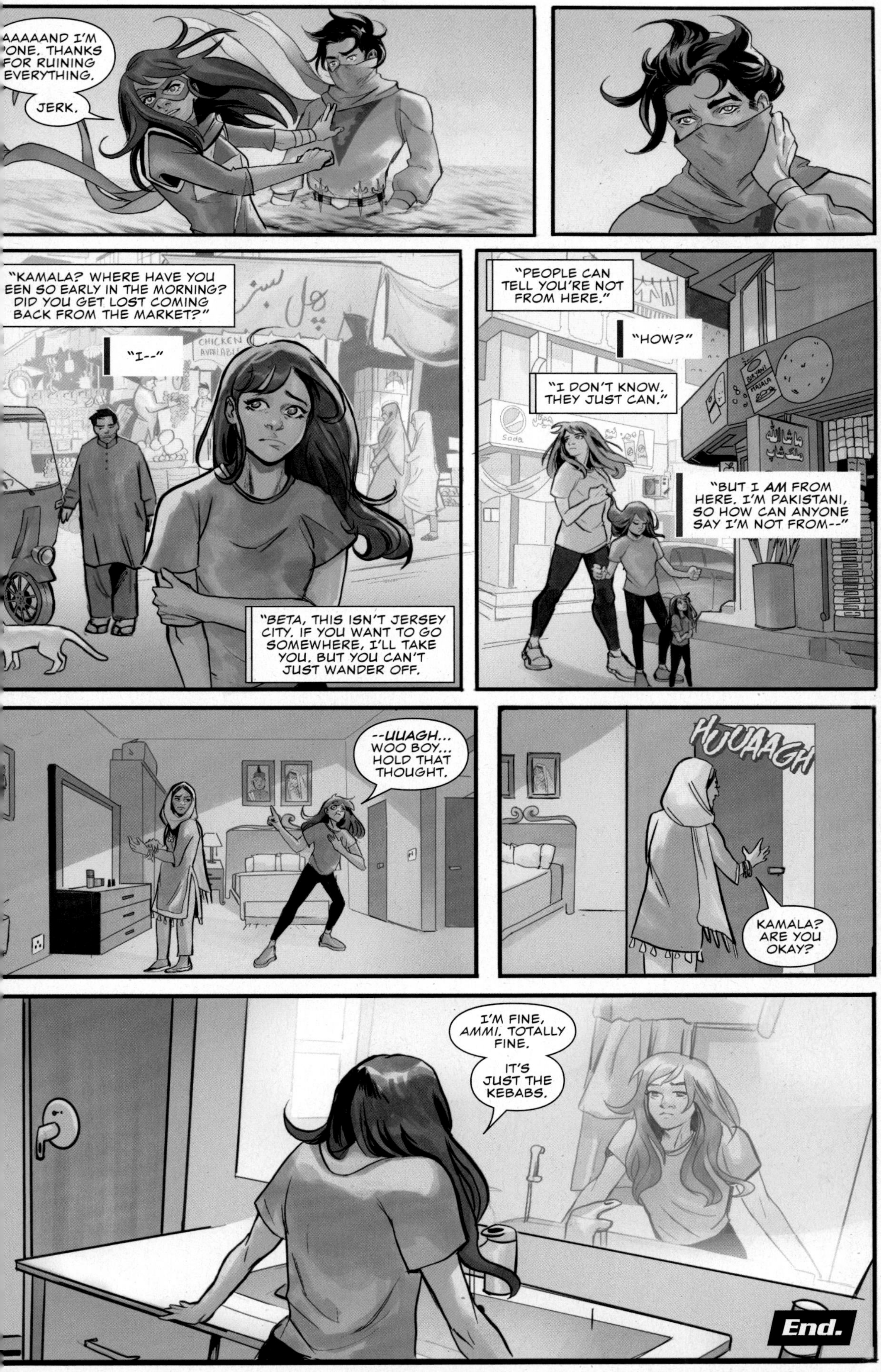
AAAAAAND I'M DONE. THANKS FOR RUINING EVERYTHING.
JERK.
"KAMALA? WHERE HAVE YOU BEEN SO EARLY IN THE MORNING? DID YOU GET LOST COMING BACK FROM THE MARKET?"
"I--"
"BETA, THIS ISN'T JERSEY CITY. IF YOU WANT TO GO SOMEWHERE, I'LL TAKE YOU. BUT YOU CAN'T JUST WANDER OFF.
"PEOPLE CAN TELL YOU'RE NOT FROM HERE."
"HOW?"
"I DON'T KNOW. THEY JUST CAN."
"BUT I AM FROM HERE. I'M PAKISTANI, SO HOW CAN ANYONE SAY I'M NOT FROM--"
--UUAGH... WOO BOY... HOLD THAT THOUGHT.
HUUAAGH
KAMALA? ARE YOU OKAY?
I'M FINE, AMMI. TOTALLY FINE.
IT'S JUST THE KEBABS.
End.

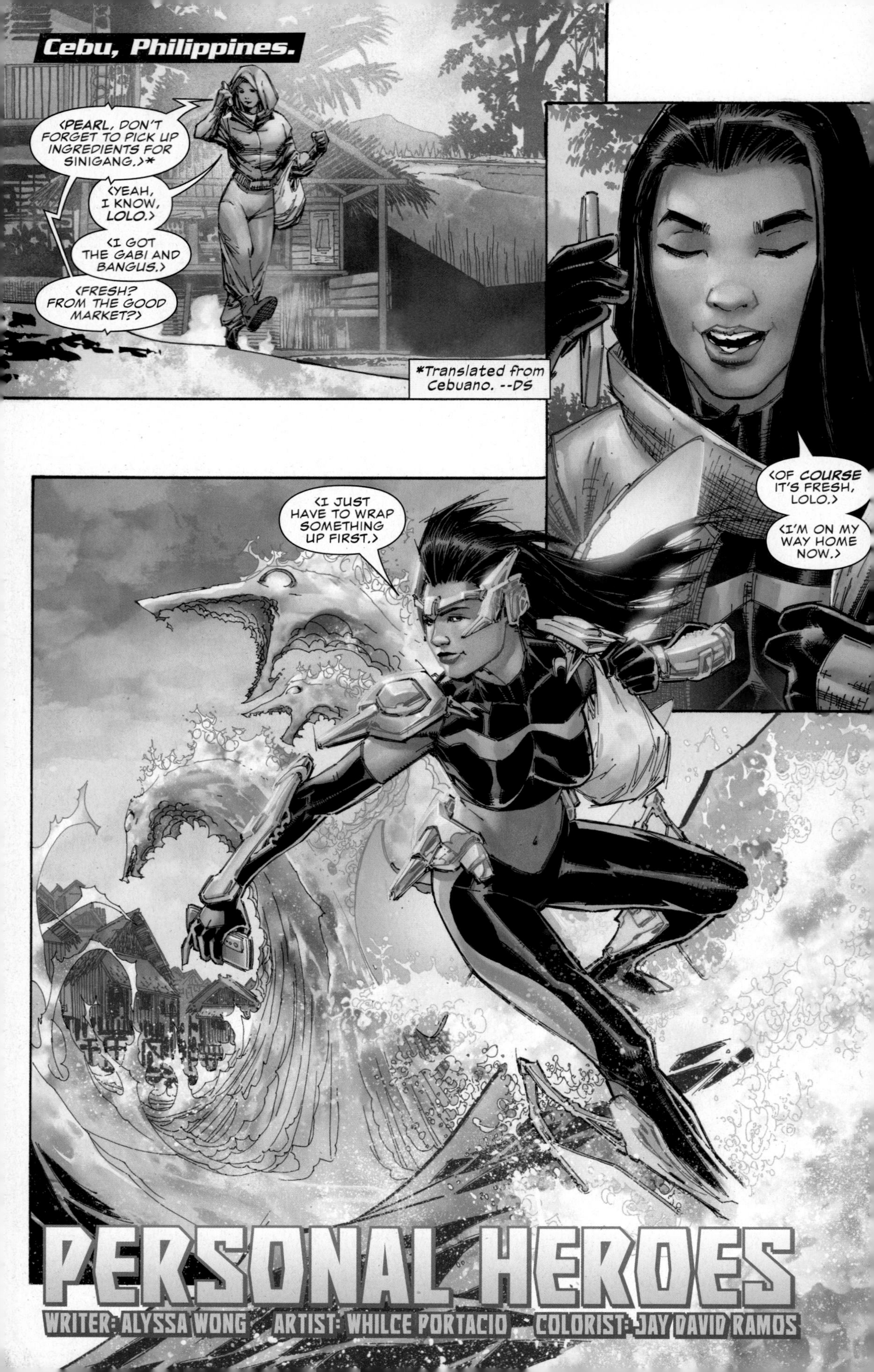
Cebu, Philippines.
<PEARL, DON'T FORGET TO PICK UP INGREDIENTS FOR SINIGANG.>*
<YEAH, I KNOW, LOLO.>
<I GOT THE GABI AND BANGUS.>
<FRESH? FROM THE GOOD MARKET?>
*Translated from Cebuano. --DS
<OF COURSE IT'S FRESH, LOLO.>
<I'M ON MY WAY HOME NOW.>
<I JUST HAVE TO WRAP SOMETHING UP FIRST.>
PERSONAL HEROES
WRITER: ALYSSA WONG ARTIST: WHILCE PORTACIO COLORIST: JAY DAVID RAMOS

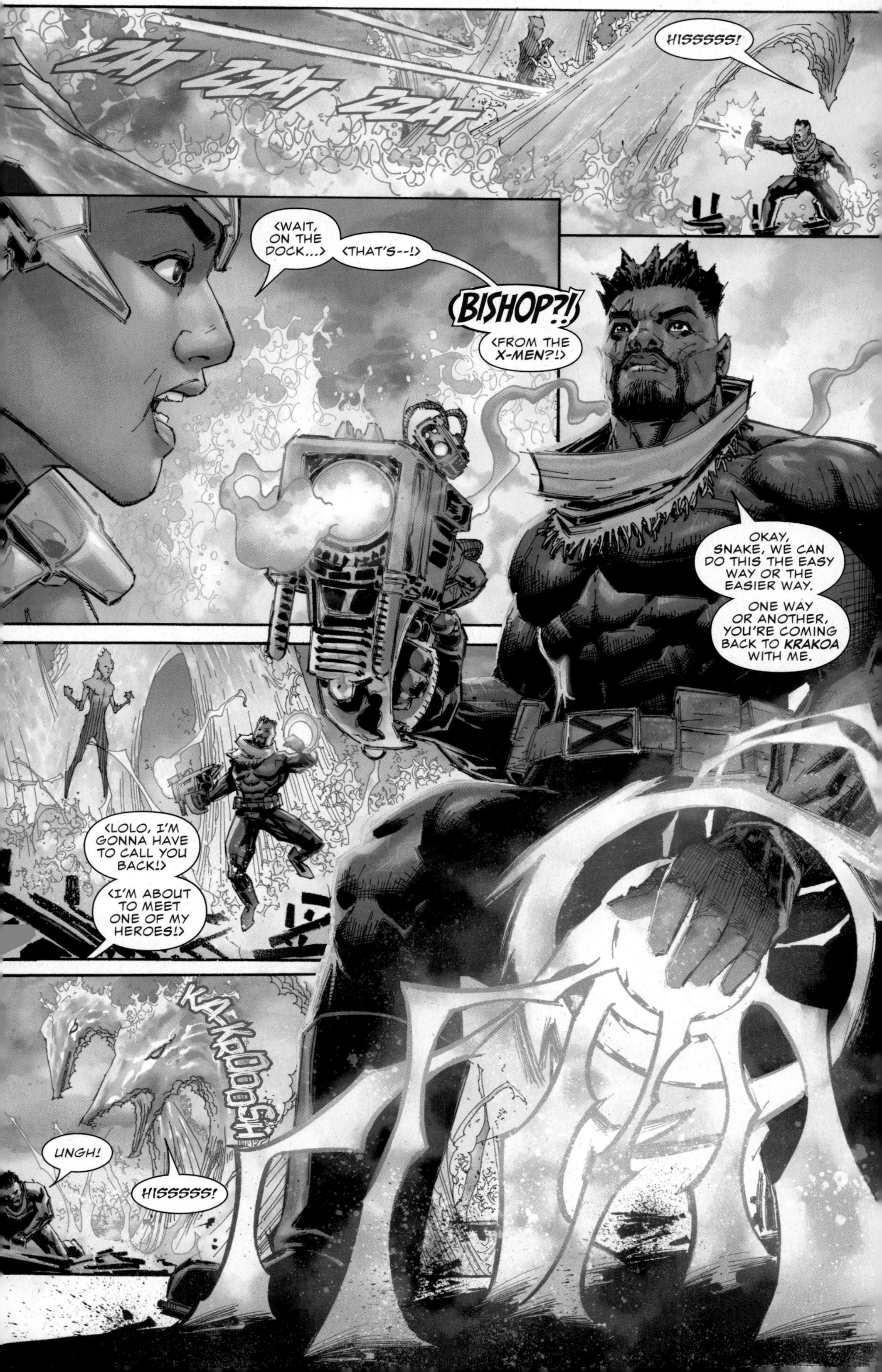
ZZAT ZZAT ZZAT
HISSSSS!
<WAIT, ON THE DOCK...>
<THAT'S--!>
<BISHOP?!>
<FROM THE X-MEN?!>
OKAY, SNAKE, WE CAN DO THIS THE EASY WAY OR THE EASIER WAY.
ONE WAY OR ANOTHER, YOU'RE COMING BACK TO KRAKOA WITH ME.
<LOLO, I'M GONNA HAVE TO CALL YOU BACK!>
<I'M ABOUT TO MEET ONE OF MY HEROES!>
KAKROOOSH
UNGH!
HISSSSS!

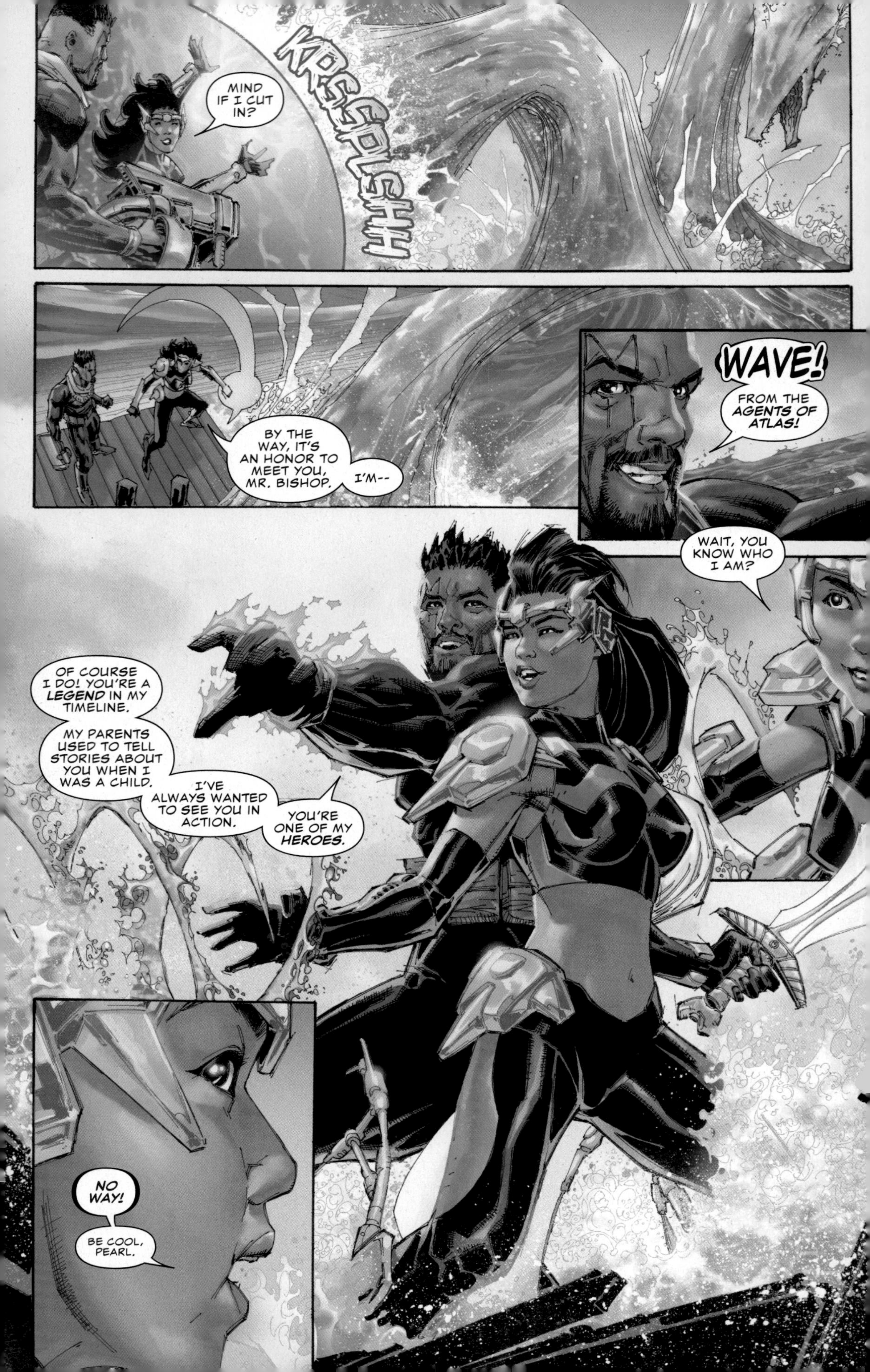
KRSPLSHH
MIND IF I CUT IN?
BY THE WAY, IT'S AN HONOR TO MEET YOU, MR. BISHOP.
I'M--
WAVE!
FROM THE AGENTS OF ATLAS!
WAIT, YOU KNOW WHO I AM?
OF COURSE I DO! YOU'RE A LEGEND IN MY TIMELINE.
MY PARENTS USED TO TELL STORIES ABOUT YOU WHEN I WAS A CHILD.
I'VE ALWAYS WANTED TO SEE YOU IN ACTION.
YOU'RE ONE OF MY HEROES.
NO WAY!
BE COOL, PEARL.

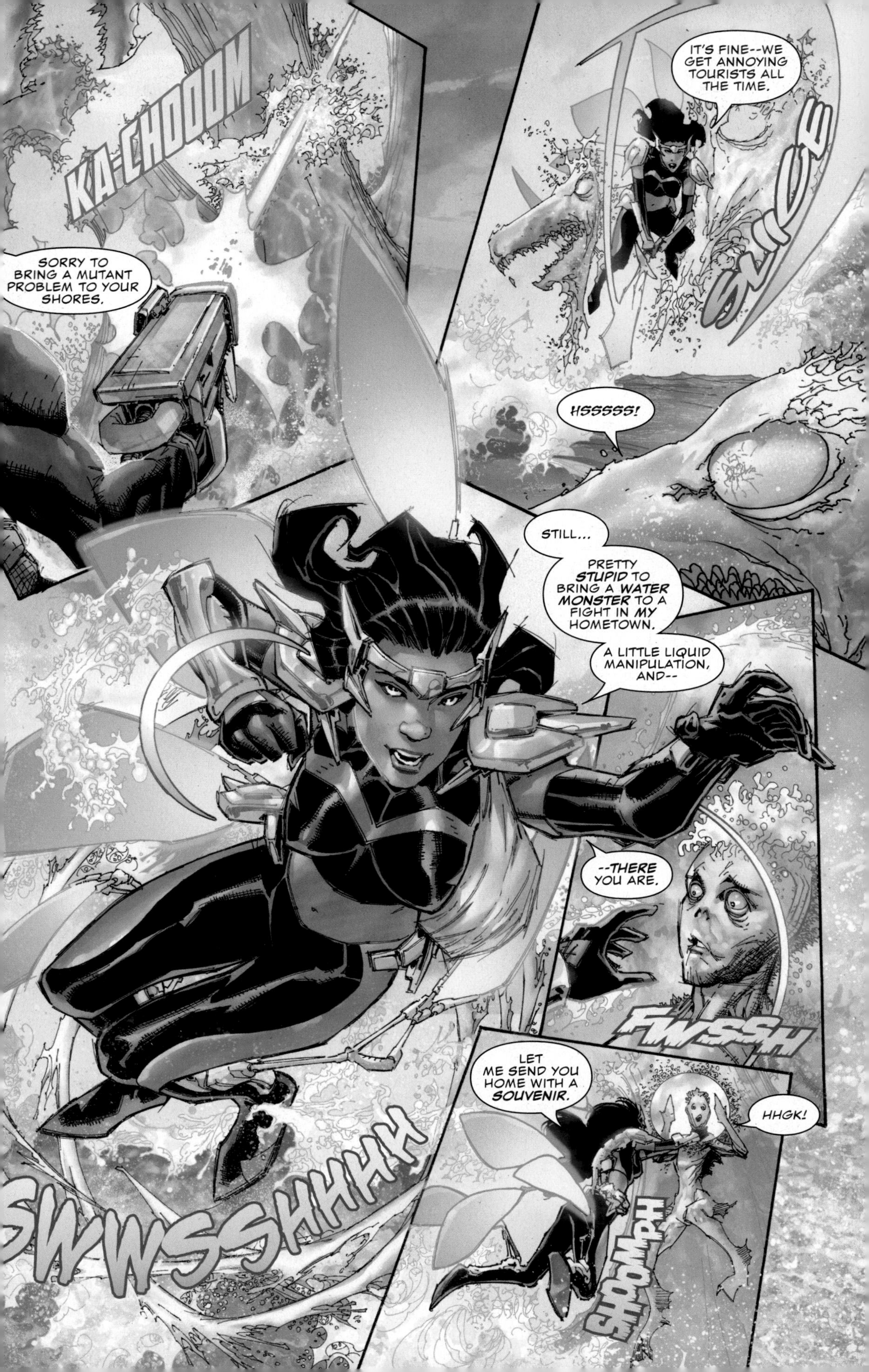
KA-CHOOOM
SORRY TO BRING A MUTANT PROBLEM TO YOUR SHORES.
IT'S FINE--WE GET ANNOYING TOURISTS ALL THE TIME.
HSSSSS!
STILL...
PRETTY STUPID TO BRING A WATER MONSTER TO A FIGHT IN MY HOMETOWN.
A LITTLE LIQUID MANIPULATION, AND--
--THERE YOU ARE.
FWSSH
LET ME SEND YOU HOME WITH A SOUVENIR.
HHGK!
SWWSSHHHH
SHOOMPH

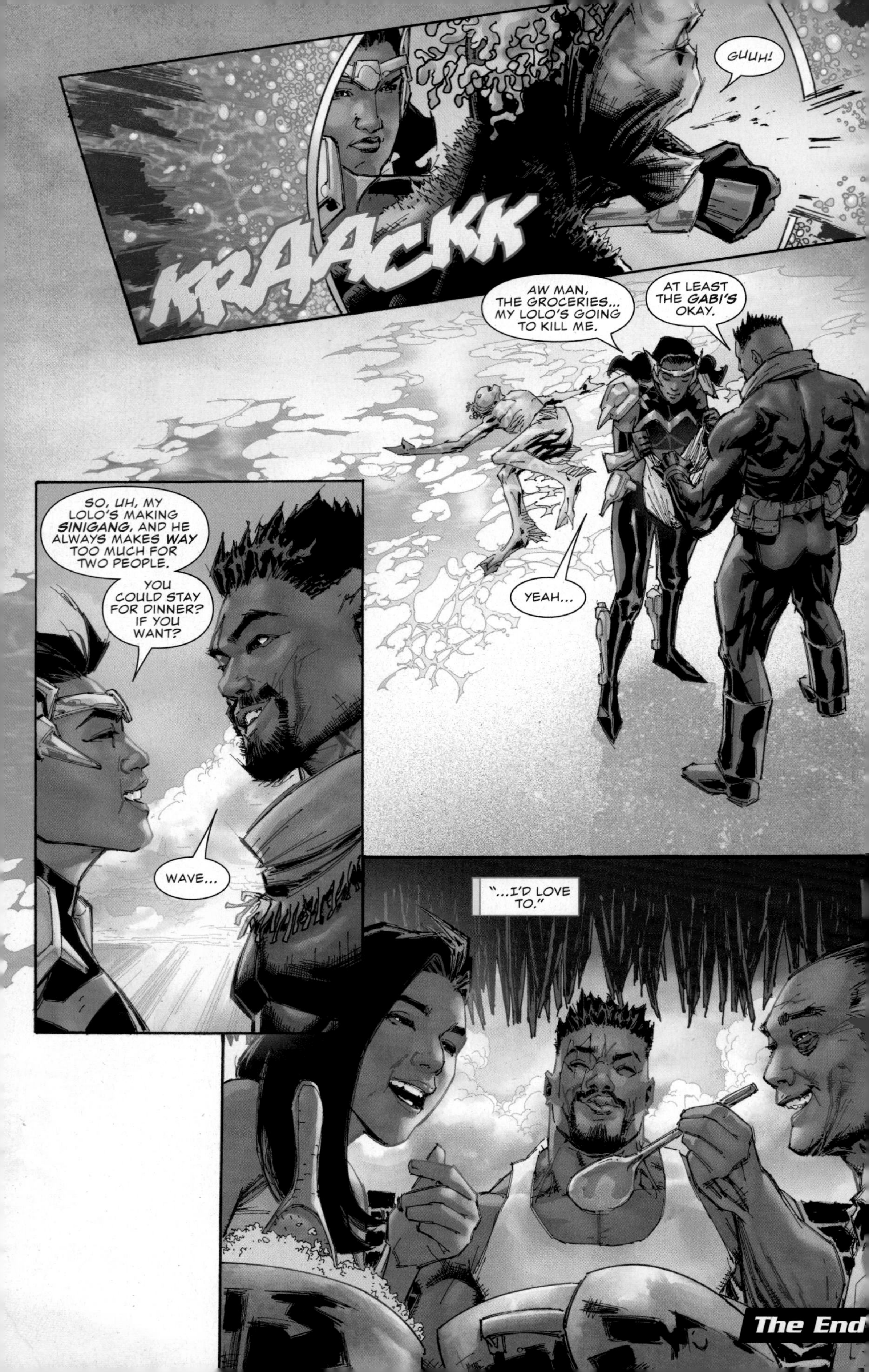
GUUH!
KRAACKK
AW MAN, THE GROCERIES... MY LOLO'S GOING TO KILL ME.
AT LEAST THE GABI'S OKAY.
YEAH...
SO, UH, MY LOLO'S MAKING SINIGANG, AND HE ALWAYS MAKES WAY TOO MUCH FOR TWO PEOPLE.
YOU COULD STAY FOR DINNER? IF YOU WANT?
WAVE...
"...I'D LOVE TO."
The End

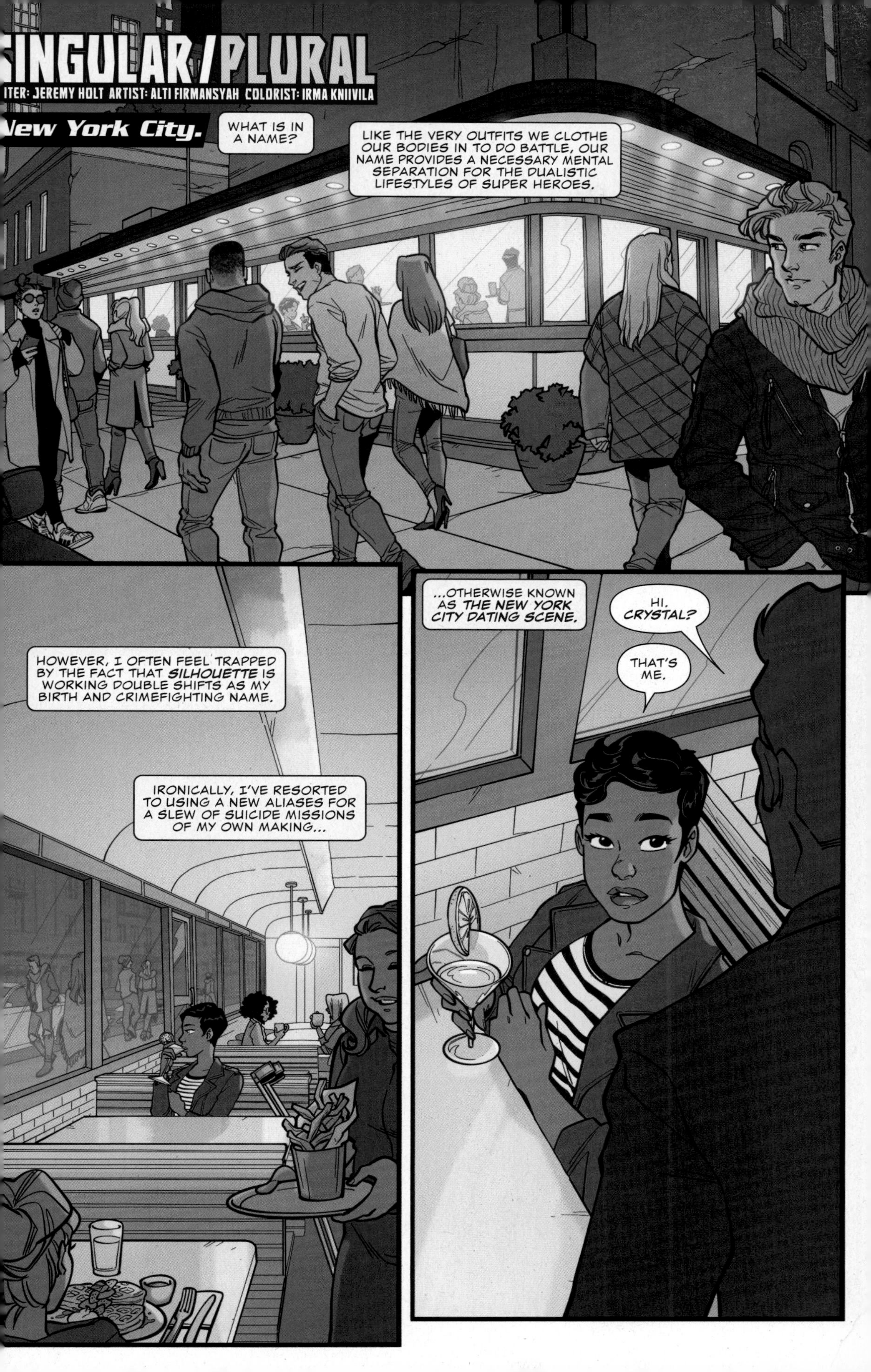

SINGULAR/PLURAL
WRITER: JEREMY HOLT ARTIST: ALTI FIRMANSYAH COLORIST: IRMA KNIIVILA
New York City.
WHAT IS IN A NAME?
LIKE THE VERY OUTFITS WE CLOTHE OUR BODIES IN TO DO BATTLE, OUR NAME PROVIDES A NECESSARY MENTAL SEPARATION FOR THE DUALISTIC LIFESTYLES OF SUPER HEROES.
HOWEVER, I OFTEN FEEL TRAPPED BY THE FACT THAT SILHOUETTE IS WORKING DOUBLE SHIFTS AS MY BIRTH AND CRIMEFIGHTING NAME.
IRONICALLY, I'VE RESORTED TO USING A NEW ALIASES FOR A SLEW OF SUICIDE MISSIONS OF MY OWN MAKING...
...OTHERWISE KNOWN AS THE NEW YORK CITY DATING SCENE.
HI. CRYSTAL?
THAT'S ME.

"YOU'RE SO EXOTIC-LOOKING. WHERE ARE YOU FROM?"

"I'M FROM HERE."

"NO, I MEAN WHERE ARE YOU *FROM FROM*?"

WHILE YOUR REAL NAME ONCE BELONGED TO AN ASS-KICKING MEMBER OF THE NOW-DEFUNCT *NEW WARRIORS*...

"SO, MONICA... ABOUT YOUR HANDICAP. WHEN IT COMES TO...*INTIMACY*, HOW DOES IT WORK DOWN THERE?"

...YOUR ALIAS HAS TO ENDURE EXCRUCIATING CONVERSATIONS LIKE THESE.

"I'M SO SORRY, *JANELL* I'LL BE TWO SECONDS."

I USED TO BELIEVE MY NAME SERVED AS METAPHORIC ARMⓞ OVER MY FRAGILE PSYCHE.

OR SHOWCASED MY EXTRAORDINARY ABILITY TO USE ANY SHADOW AS MY OWN PERSONAL TELEPORTER,

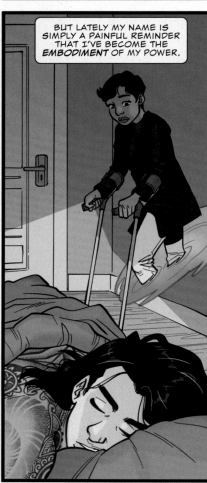

BUT LATELY MY NAME IS SIMPLY A PAINFUL REMINDER THAT I'VE BECOME THE *EMBODIMENT* OF MY POWER,

TRUTH IS, I NO LONGER FEEL LIⓚ I'M MANIPULATING DARKFORCEⓔ RATHER, DARKFORCE HAS RELEGAⓣ ME TO A *DISEMBODIED* EXISTENⓒ

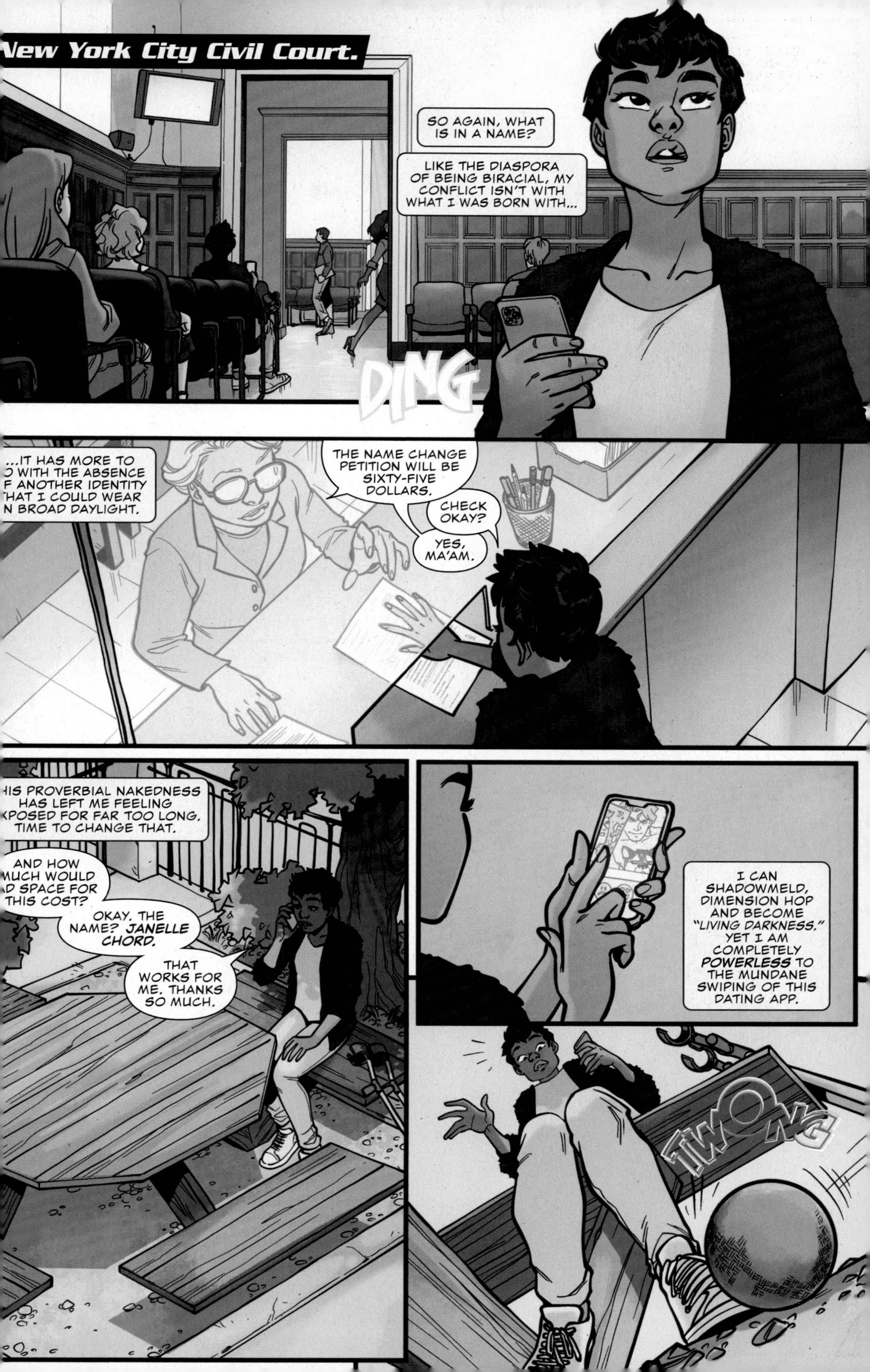
New York City Civil Court.
SO AGAIN, WHAT IS IN A NAME?
LIKE THE DIASPORA OF BEING BIRACIAL, MY CONFLICT ISN'T WITH WHAT I WAS BORN WITH...
DING
...IT HAS MORE TO O WITH THE ABSENCE F ANOTHER IDENTITY THAT I COULD WEAR N BROAD DAYLIGHT.
THE NAME CHANGE PETITION WILL BE SIXTY-FIVE DOLLARS.
CHECK OKAY?
YES, MA'AM.
HIS PROVERBIAL NAKEDNESS HAS LEFT ME FEELING XPOSED FOR FAR TOO LONG. TIME TO CHANGE THAT.
AND HOW MUCH WOULD D SPACE FOR THIS COST?
OKAY. THE NAME? JANELLE CHORD.
THAT WORKS FOR ME. THANKS SO MUCH.
I CAN SHADOWMELD, DIMENSION HOP AND BECOME "LIVING DARKNESS," YET I AM COMPLETELY POWERLESS TO THE MUNDANE SWIPING OF THIS DATING APP.
TWONG

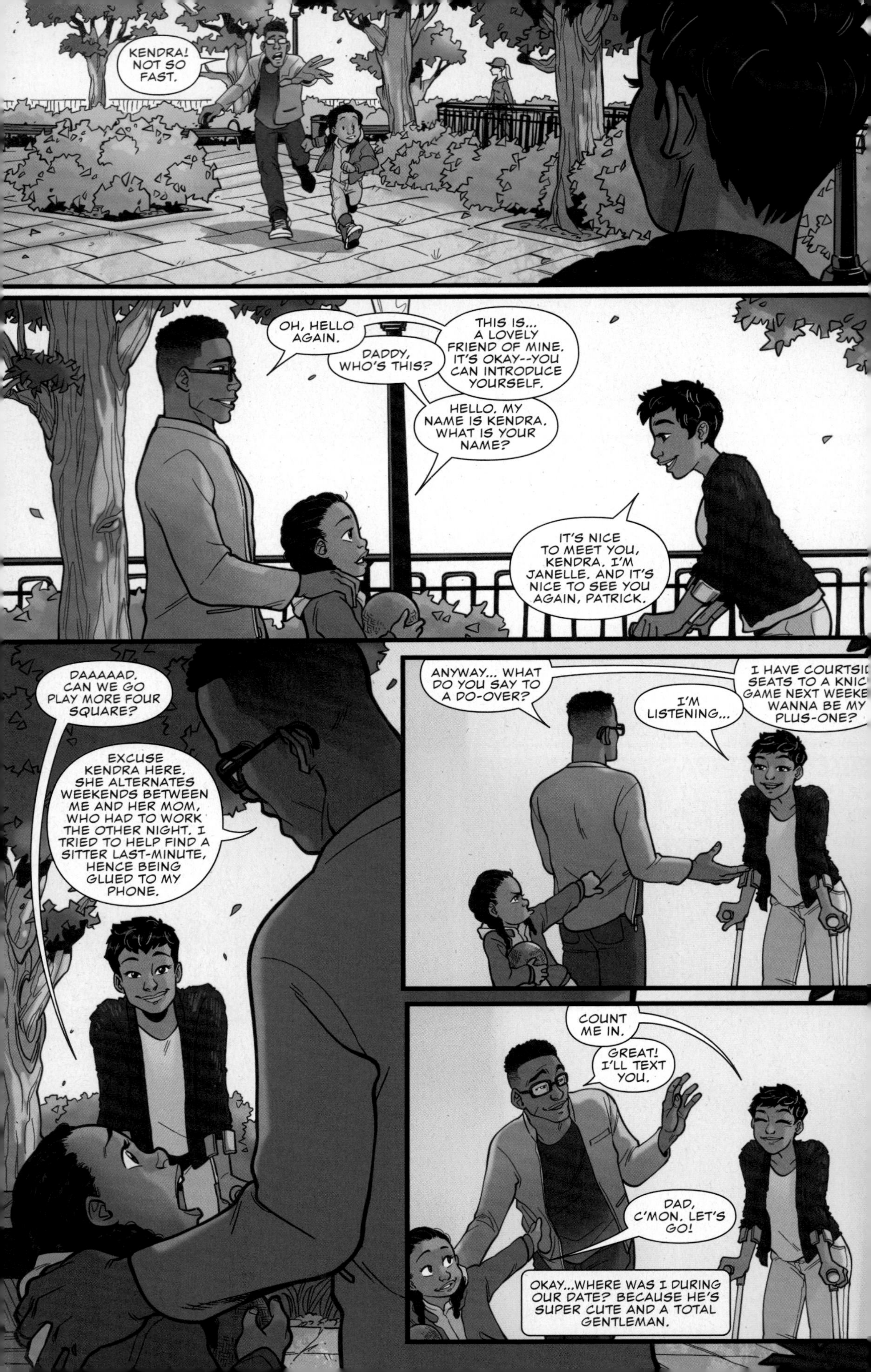
KENDRA! NOT SO FAST.
OH, HELLO AGAIN.
THIS IS... A LOVELY FRIEND OF MINE. IT'S OKAY--YOU CAN INTRODUCE YOURSELF.
DADDY, WHO'S THIS?
HELLO. MY NAME IS KENDRA. WHAT IS YOUR NAME?
IT'S NICE TO MEET YOU, KENDRA. I'M JANELLE. AND IT'S NICE TO SEE YOU AGAIN, PATRICK.
DAAAAAD, CAN WE GO PLAY MORE FOUR SQUARE?
EXCUSE KENDRA HERE. SHE ALTERNATES WEEKENDS BETWEEN ME AND HER MOM, WHO HAD TO WORK THE OTHER NIGHT. I TRIED TO HELP FIND A SITTER LAST-MINUTE, HENCE BEING GLUED TO MY PHONE.
ANYWAY... WHAT DO YOU SAY TO A DO-OVER?
I'M LISTENING...
COUNT ME IN.
GREAT! I'LL TEXT YOU.
DAD, C'MON. LET'S GO!
OKAY...WHERE WAS I DURING OUR DATE? BECAUSE HE'S SUPER CUTE AND A TOTAL GENTLEMAN.

PERHAPS I'M NOT GIVING JANELLE ENOUGH CREDIT.

IF SHE HAD THE WHEREWITHAL TO ESTABLISH NEW BOUNDARIES FOR HERSELF...

...THEN THE LEAST SILHOUETTE CAN DO IS SUPPORT HER BY STEPPING OUT IN FRONT OF HER OWN SHADOW.

Remove "Kindling"?

Removing from home screen will keep the...

Delete A

Remove from Home Screen

Cancel

End.

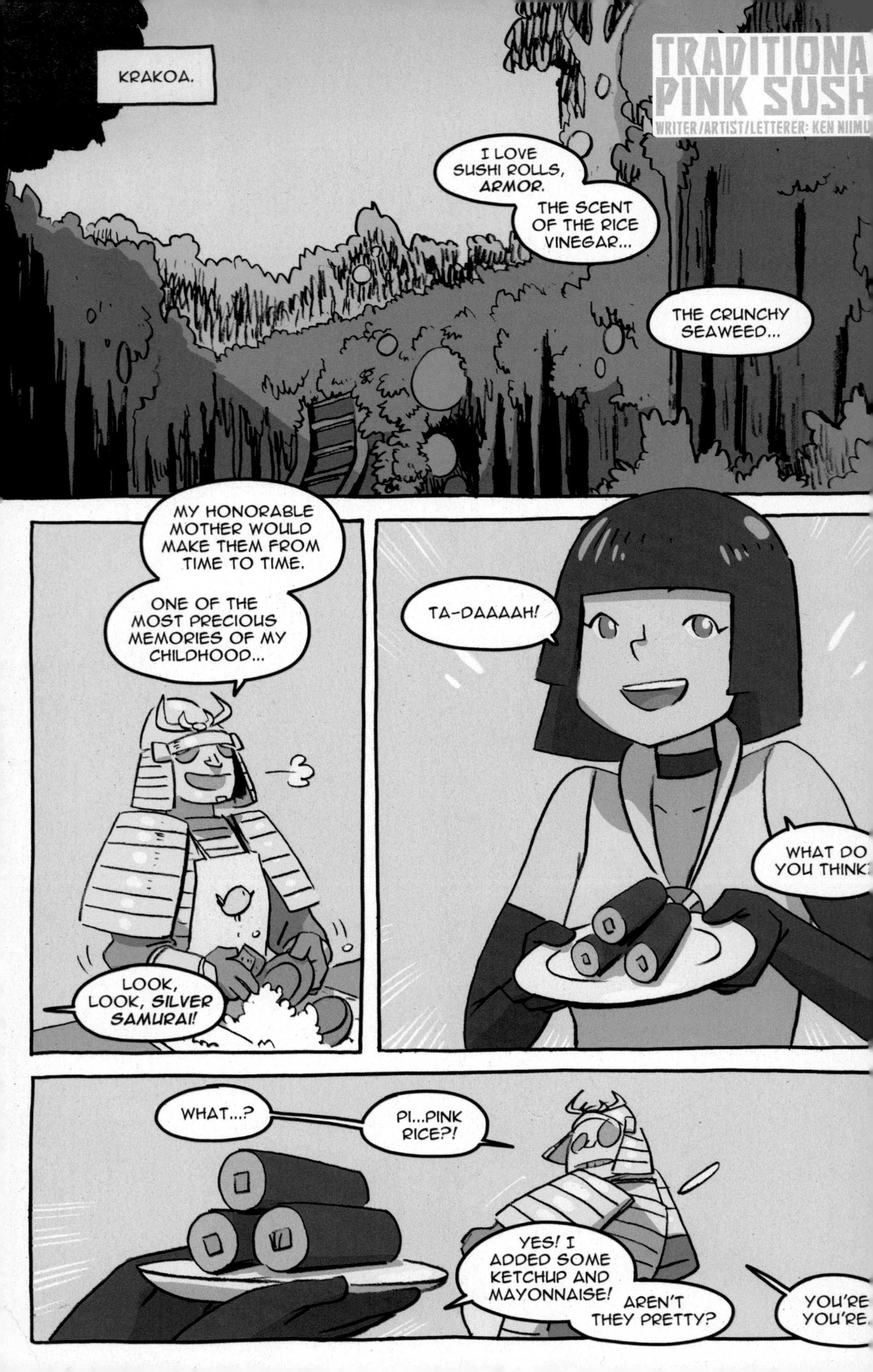
TRADITIONA
PINK SUSH
WRITER/ARTIST/LETTERER: KEN NIIMU
KRAKOA.
I LOVE SUSHI ROLLS, ARMOR.
THE SCENT OF THE RICE VINEGAR...
THE CRUNCHY SEAWEED...
MY HONORABLE MOTHER WOULD MAKE THEM FROM TIME TO TIME.
ONE OF THE MOST PRECIOUS MEMORIES OF MY CHILDHOOD...
LOOK, LOOK, SILVER SAMURAI!
TA-DAAAAH!
WHAT DO YOU THINK
WHAT...?
PI...PINK RICE?!
YES! I ADDED SOME KETCHUP AND MAYONNAISE!
AREN'T THEY PRETTY?
YOU'RE YOU'RE.

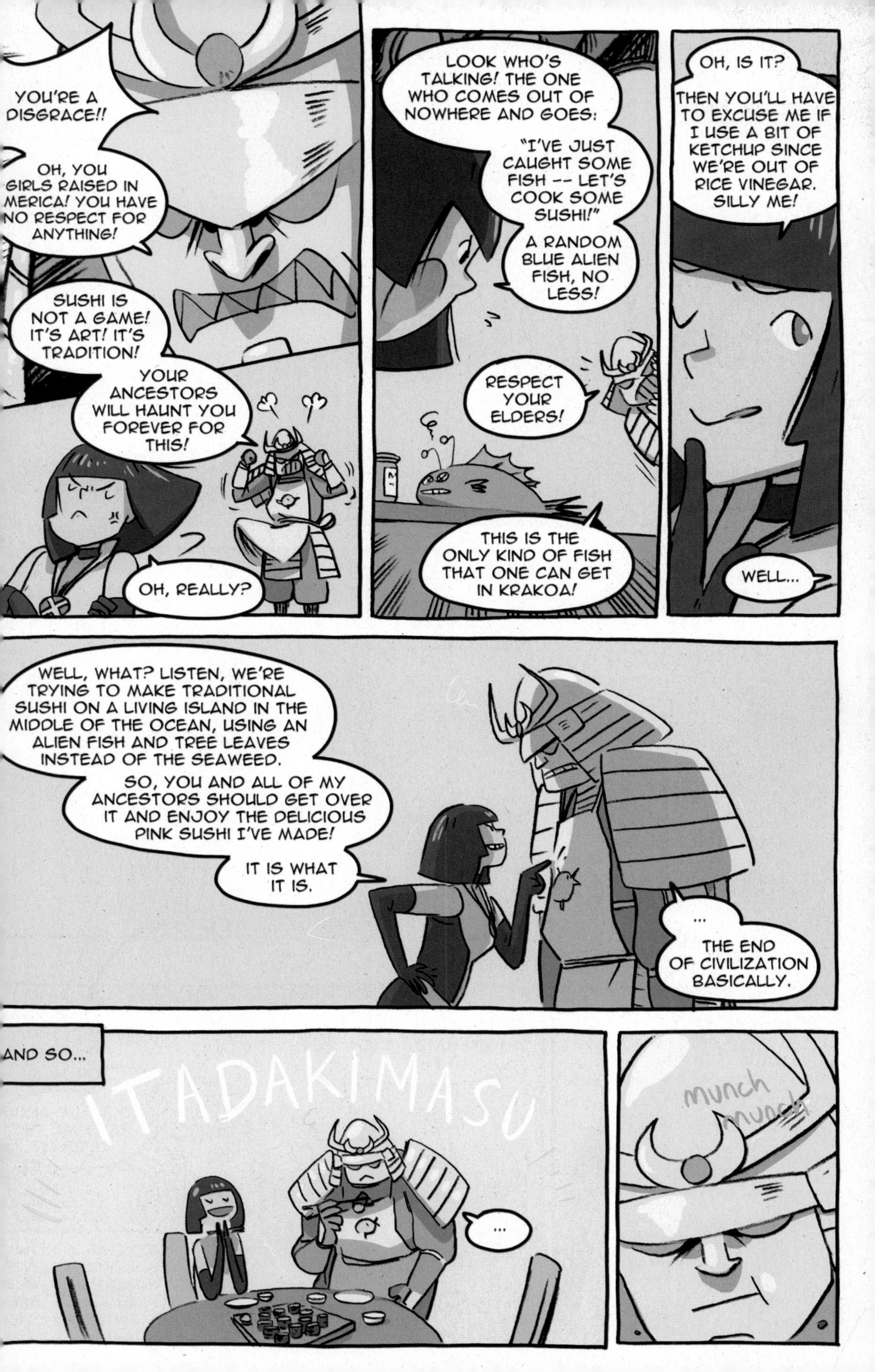
YOU'RE A DISGRACE!!
OH, YOU GIRLS RAISED IN MERICA! YOU HAVE NO RESPECT FOR ANYTHING!
SUSHI IS NOT A GAME! IT'S ART! IT'S TRADITION!
YOUR ANCESTORS WILL HAUNT YOU FOREVER FOR THIS!
OH, REALLY?
LOOK WHO'S TALKING! THE ONE WHO COMES OUT OF NOWHERE AND GOES:
"I'VE JUST CAUGHT SOME FISH -- LET'S COOK SOME SUSHI!"
A RANDOM BLUE ALIEN FISH, NO LESS!
RESPECT YOUR ELDERS!
THIS IS THE ONLY KIND OF FISH THAT ONE CAN GET IN KRAKOA!
OH, IS IT?
THEN YOU'LL HAVE TO EXCUSE ME IF I USE A BIT OF KETCHUP SINCE WE'RE OUT OF RICE VINEGAR. SILLY ME!
WELL...
WELL, WHAT? LISTEN, WE'RE TRYING TO MAKE TRADITIONAL SUSHI ON A LIVING ISLAND IN THE MIDDLE OF THE OCEAN, USING AN ALIEN FISH AND TREE LEAVES INSTEAD OF THE SEAWEED.
SO, YOU AND ALL OF MY ANCESTORS SHOULD GET OVER IT AND ENJOY THE DELICIOUS PINK SUSHI I'VE MADE!
IT IS WHAT IT IS.
...
THE END OF CIVILIZATION BASICALLY.
AND SO...
ITADAKIMASU
...
munch munch

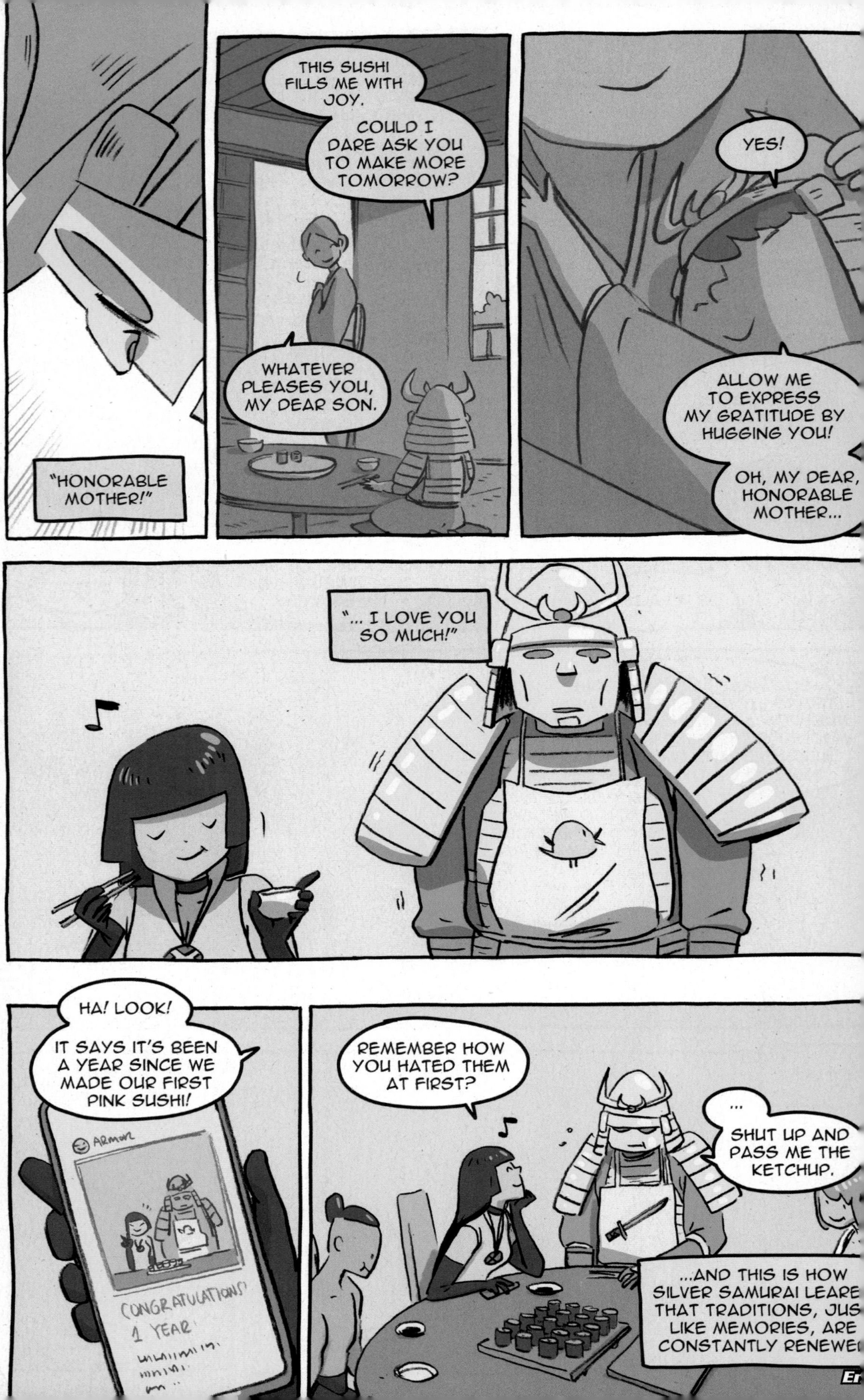

"HONORABLE MOTHER!"
THIS SUSHI FILLS ME WITH JOY.
COULD I DARE ASK YOU TO MAKE MORE TOMORROW?
WHATEVER PLEASES YOU, MY DEAR SON.
YES!
ALLOW ME TO EXPRESS MY GRATITUDE BY HUGGING YOU!
OH, MY DEAR, HONORABLE MOTHER...
"... I LOVE YOU SO MUCH!"
HA! LOOK!
IT SAYS IT'S BEEN A YEAR SINCE WE MADE OUR FIRST PINK SUSHI!
ARMOR
CONGRATULATIONS! 1 YEAR
REMEMBER HOW YOU HATED THEM AT FIRST?
...
SHUT UP AND PASS ME THE KETCHUP.
...AND THIS IS HOW SILVER SAMURAI LEARE THAT TRADITIONS, JUS LIKE MEMORIES, ARE CONSTANTLY RENEWE

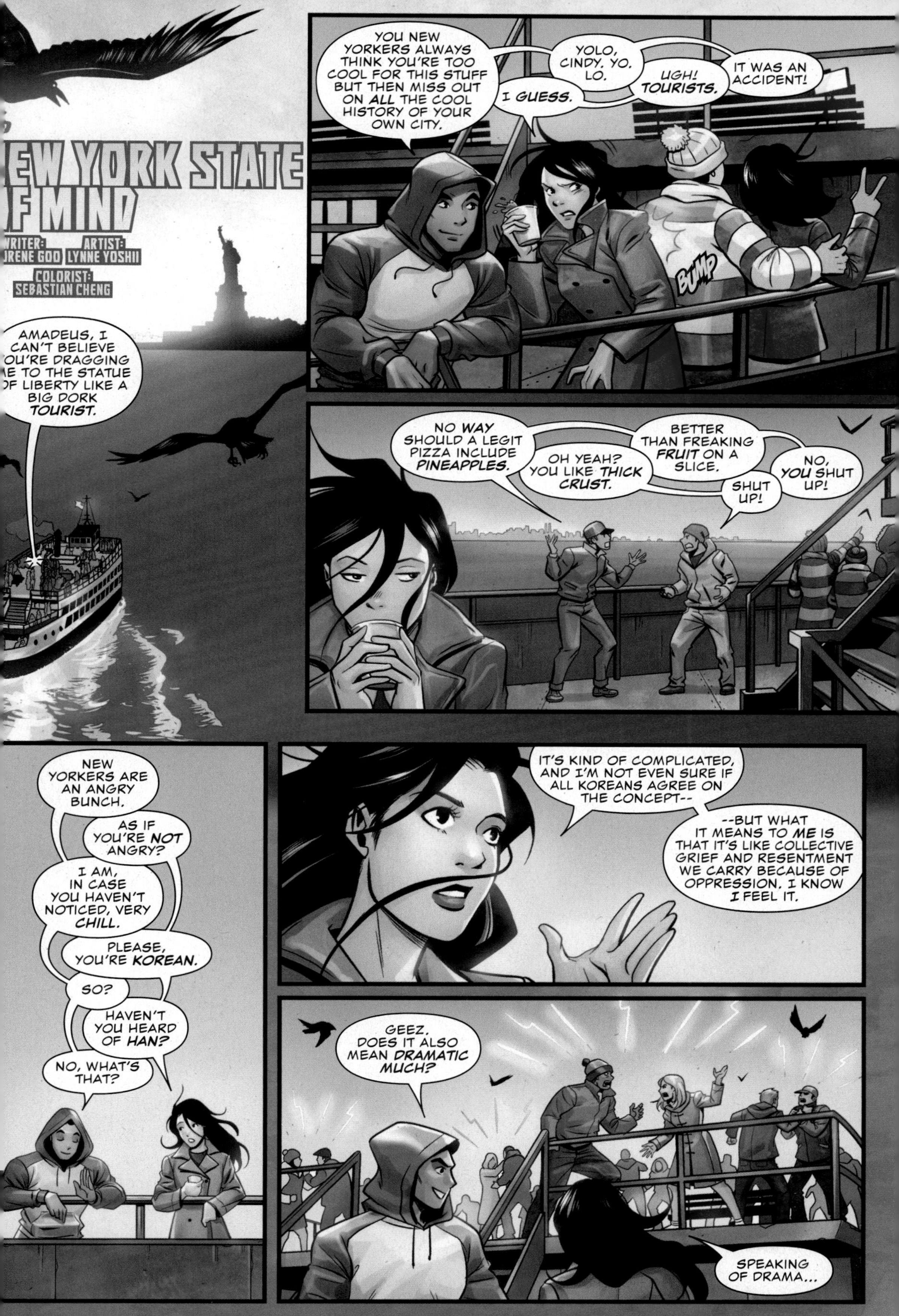
NEW YORK STATE OF MIND
WRITER: IRENE GOO
ARTIST: LYNNE YOSHII
COLORIST: SEBASTIAN CHENG
AMADEUS, I CAN'T BELIEVE YOU'RE DRAGGING ME TO THE STATUE OF LIBERTY LIKE A BIG DORK TOURIST.
YOU NEW YORKERS ALWAYS THINK YOU'RE TOO COOL FOR THIS STUFF BUT THEN MISS OUT ON ALL THE COOL HISTORY OF YOUR OWN CITY.
YOLO, CINDY. YO. LO.
I GUESS.
UGH! TOURISTS.
IT WAS AN ACCIDENT!
BUMP
NO WAY SHOULD A LEGIT PIZZA INCLUDE PINEAPPLES.
OH YEAH? YOU LIKE THICK CRUST.
BETTER THAN FREAKING FRUIT ON A SLICE.
SHUT UP!
NO, YOU SHUT UP!
NEW YORKERS ARE AN ANGRY BUNCH.
AS IF YOU'RE NOT ANGRY?
I AM, IN CASE YOU HAVEN'T NOTICED, VERY CHILL.
PLEASE, YOU'RE KOREAN.
SO?
HAVEN'T YOU HEARD OF HAN?
NO, WHAT'S THAT?
IT'S KIND OF COMPLICATED, AND I'M NOT EVEN SURE IF ALL KOREANS AGREE ON THE CONCEPT--
--BUT WHAT IT MEANS TO ME IS THAT IT'S LIKE COLLECTIVE GRIEF AND RESENTMENT WE CARRY BECAUSE OF OPPRESSION. I KNOW I FEEL IT.
GEEZ. DOES IT ALSO MEAN DRAMATIC MUCH?
SPEAKING OF DRAMA...

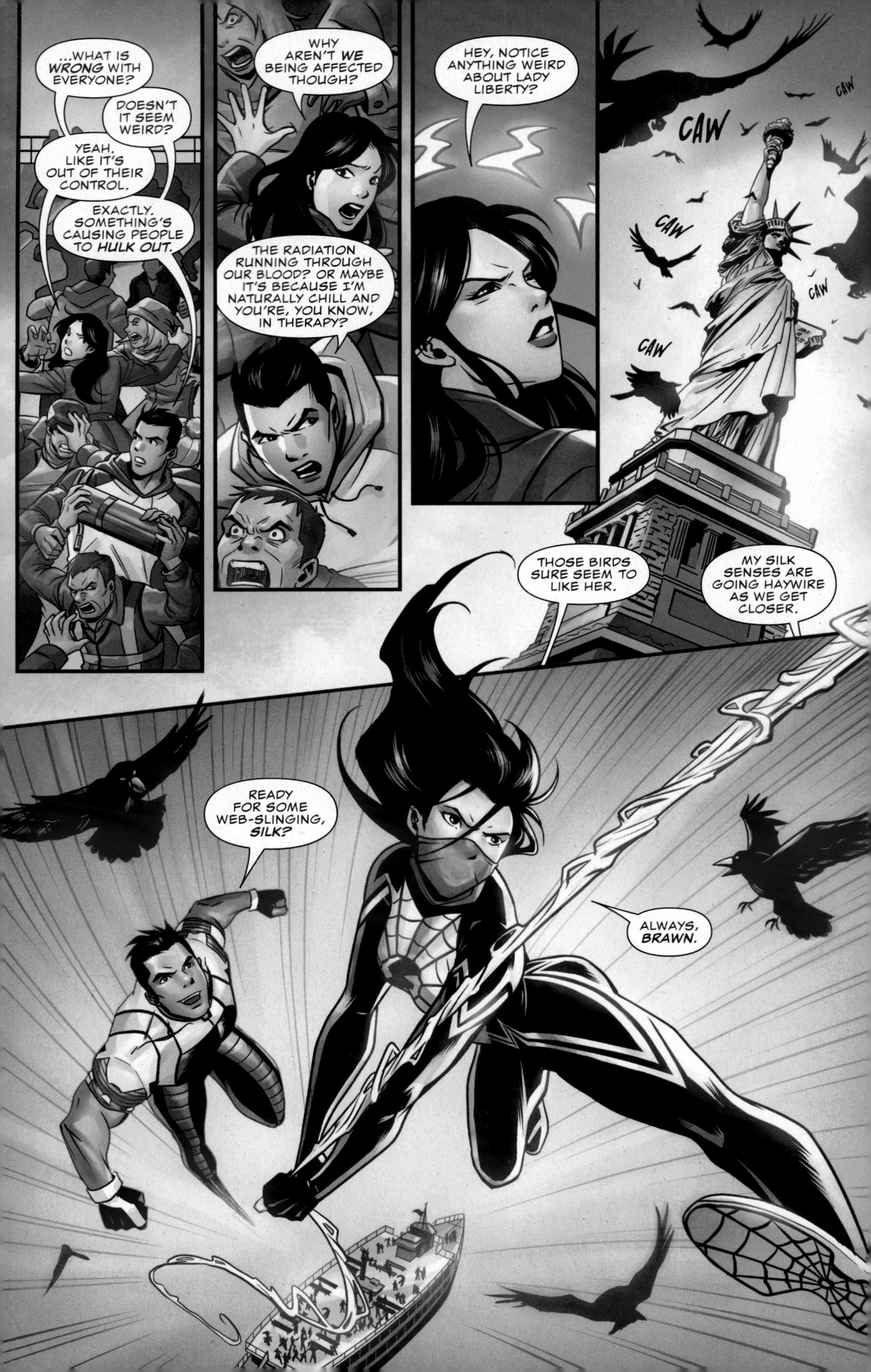

...WHAT IS WRONG WITH EVERYONE?
DOESN'T IT SEEM WEIRD?
YEAH, LIKE IT'S OUT OF THEIR CONTROL.
EXACTLY. SOMETHING'S CAUSING PEOPLE TO HULK OUT.
WHY AREN'T WE BEING AFFECTED THOUGH?
THE RADIATION RUNNING THROUGH OUR BLOOD? OR MAYBE IT'S BECAUSE I'M NATURALLY CHILL AND YOU'RE, YOU KNOW, IN THERAPY?
HEY, NOTICE ANYTHING WEIRD ABOUT LADY LIBERTY?
CAW
CAW
CAW
CAW
CAW
THOSE BIRDS SURE SEEM TO LIKE HER.
MY SILK SENSES ARE GOING HAYWIRE AS WE GET CLOSER.
READY FOR SOME WEB-SLINGING, SILK?
ALWAYS, BRAWN.

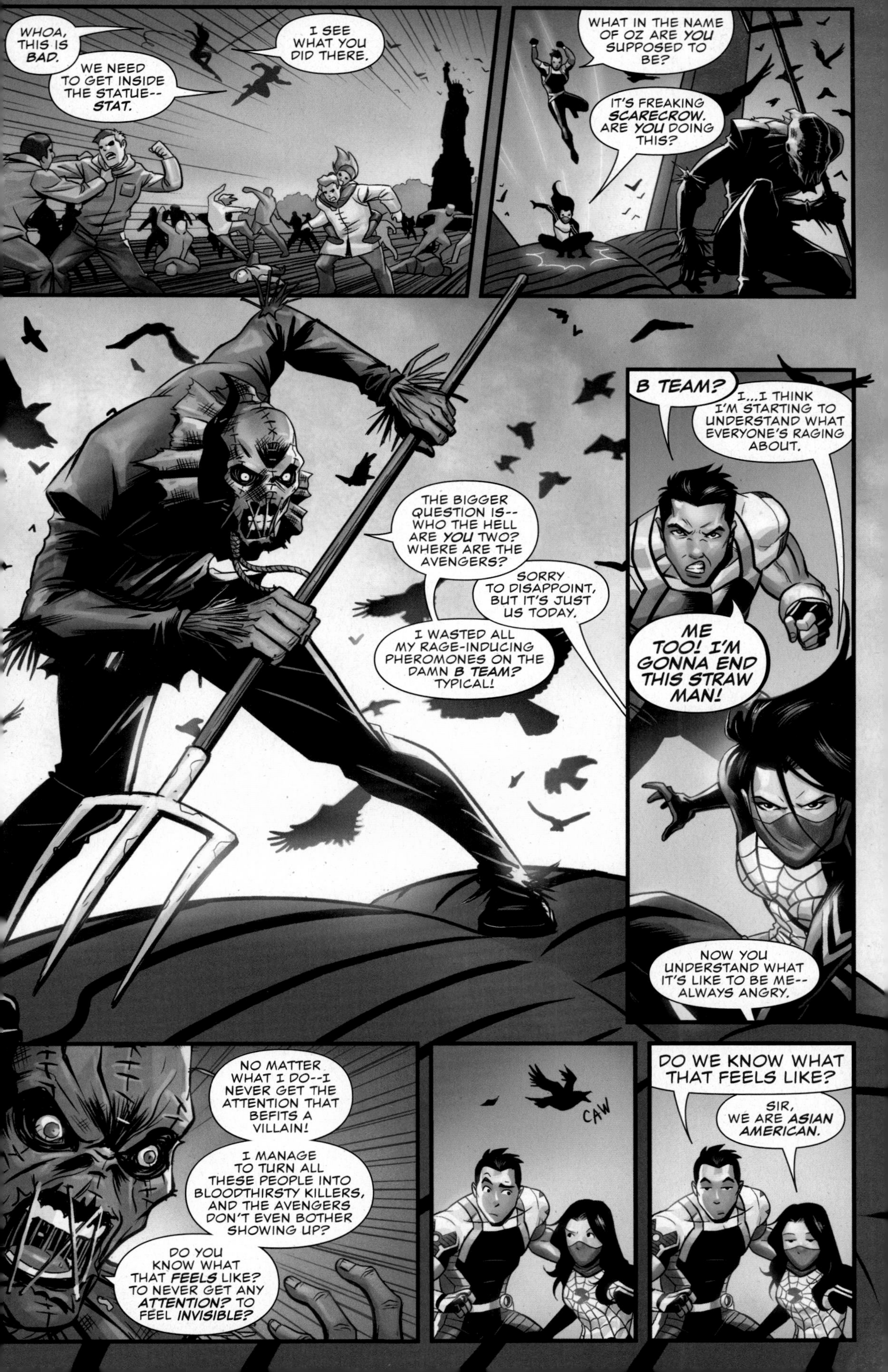
WHOA, THIS IS BAD.
WE NEED TO GET INSIDE THE STATUE-- STAT.
I SEE WHAT YOU DID THERE.
WHAT IN THE NAME OF OZ ARE YOU SUPPOSED TO BE?
IT'S FREAKING SCARECROW. ARE YOU DOING THIS?
THE BIGGER QUESTION IS-- WHO THE HELL ARE YOU TWO? WHERE ARE THE AVENGERS?
SORRY TO DISAPPOINT, BUT IT'S JUST US TODAY.
I WASTED ALL MY RAGE-INDUCING PHEROMONES ON THE DAMN B TEAM? TYPICAL!
B TEAM?
I...I THINK I'M STARTING TO UNDERSTAND WHAT EVERYONE'S RAGING ABOUT.
ME TOO! I'M GONNA END THIS STRAW MAN!
NOW YOU UNDERSTAND WHAT IT'S LIKE TO BE ME-- ALWAYS ANGRY.
NO MATTER WHAT I DO--I NEVER GET THE ATTENTION THAT BEFITS A VILLAIN!
I MANAGE TO TURN ALL THESE PEOPLE INTO BLOODTHIRSTY KILLERS, AND THE AVENGERS DON'T EVEN BOTHER SHOWING UP?
DO YOU KNOW WHAT THAT FEELS LIKE? TO NEVER GET ANY ATTENTION? TO FEEL INVISIBLE?
CAW
DO WE KNOW WHAT THAT FEELS LIKE?
SIR, WE ARE ASIAN AMERICAN.

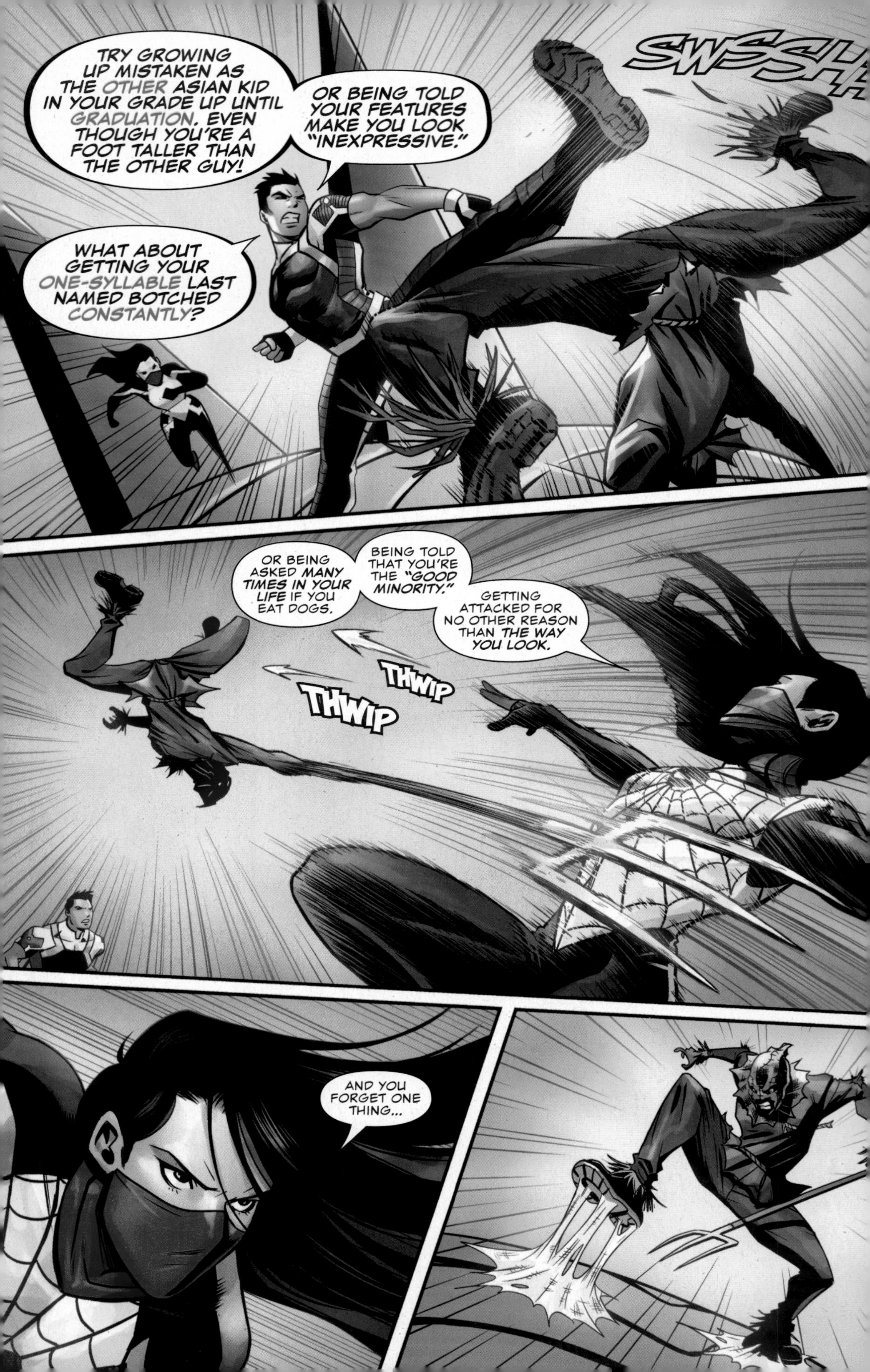

SWSSH
TRY GROWING UP MISTAKEN AS THE OTHER ASIAN KID IN YOUR GRADE UP UNTIL GRADUATION. EVEN THOUGH YOU'RE A FOOT TALLER THAN THE OTHER GUY!
OR BEING TOLD YOUR FEATURES MAKE YOU LOOK "INEXPRESSIVE."
WHAT ABOUT GETTING YOUR ONE-SYLLABLE LAST NAMED BOTCHED CONSTANTLY?
OR BEING ASKED MANY TIMES IN YOUR LIFE IF YOU EAT DOGS.
BEING TOLD THAT YOU'RE THE "GOOD MINORITY."
GETTING ATTACKED FOR NO OTHER REASON THAN THE WAY YOU LOOK.
THWIP
THWIP
AND YOU FORGET ONE THING...

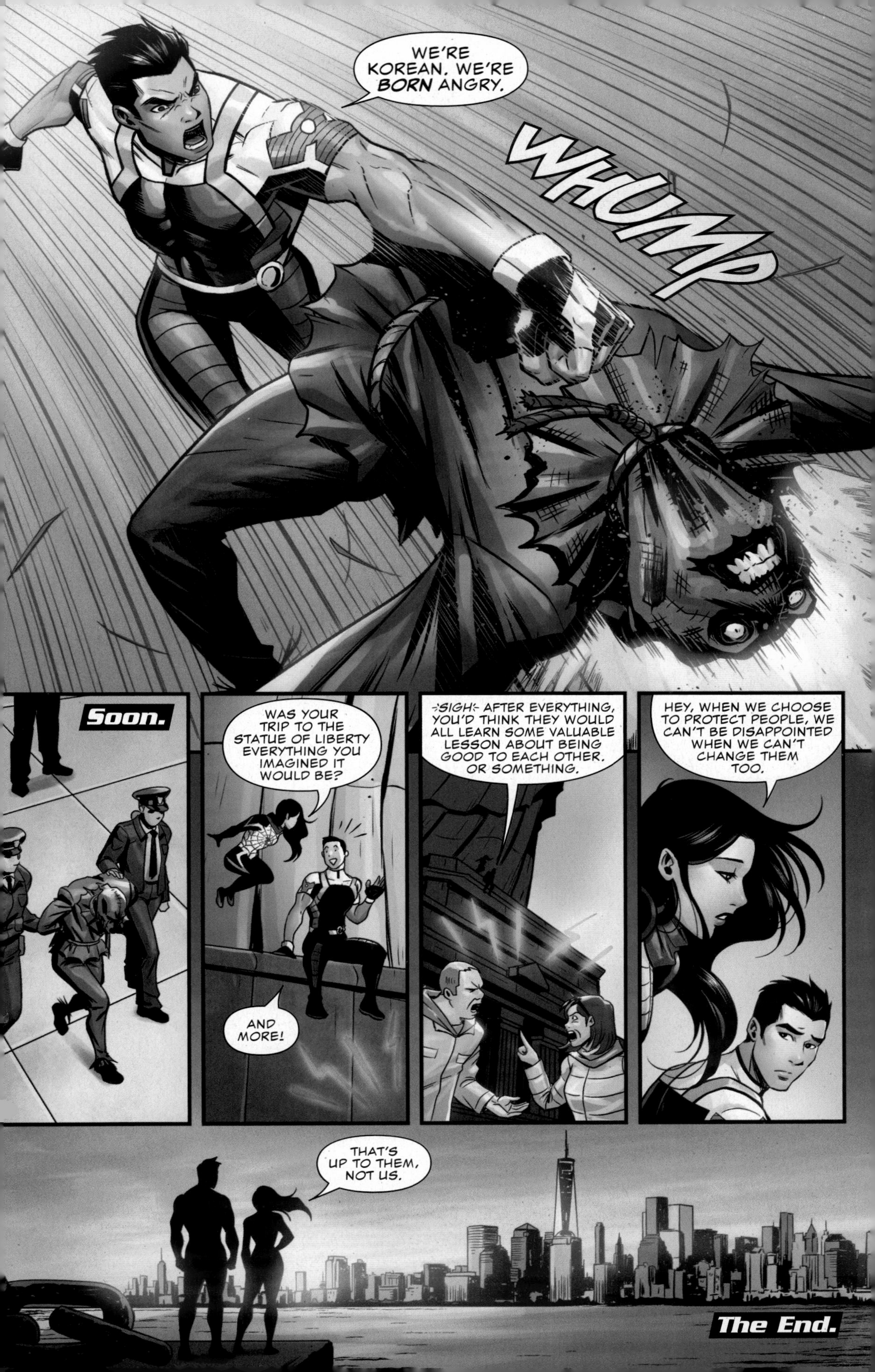
WE'RE KOREAN. WE'RE BORN ANGRY.
WHUMP
Soon.
WAS YOUR TRIP TO THE STATUE OF LIBERTY EVERYTHING YOU IMAGINED IT WOULD BE?
AND MORE!
-SIGH- AFTER EVERYTHING, YOU'D THINK THEY WOULD ALL LEARN SOME VALUABLE LESSON ABOUT BEING GOOD TO EACH OTHER. OR SOMETHING.
HEY, WHEN WE CHOOSE TO PROTECT PEOPLE, WE CAN'T BE DISAPPOINTED WHEN WE CAN'T CHANGE THEM TOO.
THAT'S UP TO THEM, NOT US.
The End.

AN INTERVIEW WITH MARVEL CREATIVE LARRY HAMA

BY ANGÉLIQUE ROCHÉ

Over Marvel's eight-plus decades, the characters and creatives in the Marvel Universe have continued to evolve. As we celebrate the amazing stories in *Marvel's Voices: Identity #1*, we also want to take a look back to spotlight one of Marvel's Asian American creators, Larry Hama. I sat down to chat with Larry about his career, the evolution of the comics industry, and his time at Marvel. The lifelong creative has served as the writer and artist for many series including but not limited to *G.I. Joe* (1982) and *Wolverine* (1988), and he was also an editor for *Conan*, *Crazy Magazine*, and *Fumetti*. But his credits outside of the comics industry run just as long—fashion designer, performing as a cast member of the Stephen Sondheim-directed Broadway play *Pacific Overtures*, playing a soldier on *M*A*S*H*, serving as a soldier in the United States Army during the Vietnam War.

You've done so many incredible things in your life—comics, musical theater, television writing, and even an appearance on *SNL*—is this what you set out to do as a kid? I learned very early in life that, when the train comes to the station, if you don't get on it, it might never stop there again.

When were you first introduced to comics? The first comics I remember were *Uncle Scrooge* comics. In those days [1950s], every kid had a stack of comics.

How did comics feel for you at that time? I was really fascinated by Carl Barks' *Uncle Scrooge*. I loved the concept of the Junior Woodchucks — this fascinating fantasy of being a part of something where the kids were empowered. The very fact that there was this funny animal universe, meant that I could fantasize about being part of it. It didn't matter if I didn't look like everybody else.

What was it about comic books that followed you through your life? It's what I could do. It's not something I started out wanting to. I never thought I'd be a writer. I still don't consider myself a writer or an artist. I'm a person who draws. I think the word "artist" is an acclamation, not a job description. Calling yourself an artist is a little pretentious. It self-assumes that what you do is art.

So what about acting and Broadway? It all goes back to getting on that train. All these things that I've done, I had absolutely no idea how to do them. I never went to college. I had a full New York State Regents scholarship to Pratt but dropped out on registration day. I went downtown and got a job drawing shoes for the Sears Roebuck catalogs. I got my first acting job completely by accident. I was in the elevator, and a woman gets on. She looks at me and asks, "Are you an actor?" I said, "No." She says, "Well, do you want to be one?" She was producing an off-Broadway production of *Moby Dick*. So, I went the next day, and I got the part.

You got on the train. I got on the train, man. Somebody saw me in that show, and I started getting gigs. A year later, I got a call to audition for a Broadway musical. I neither sang nor danced, but she liked my look.

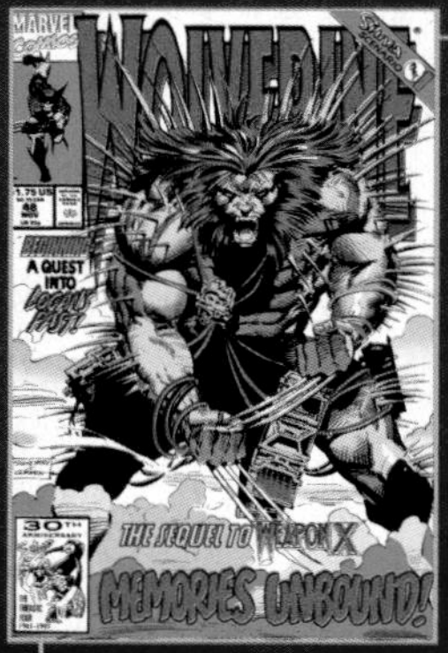

MARVEL COMICS
WOLVERINE
BEGINNING A QUEST INTO
THE SEQUEL TO WEAPON X
MEMORIES UNBOUND!

Wolverine #48, cover by Marc Silvestri & Dan Green

You got on the train. I walk over. Hal Prince looks at me and says, "I want to see him in the theater tomorrow." The next day I give them the first two verses of "Just Like a Woman," by Bob Dylan, because I knew a nifty guitar riff for it. Hal Prince, Stephen Sondheim, Paul Gemignani, and Patricia Berg — these are the top musical theater people in the country — are looking back at me slack-jawed. It was later that I signed an Equity Broadway Producers principals' contract.

How did you end up at Marvel? I got a job offer at DC as an editor. I remember walking in, sitting down at my editor's desk and thinking, "What the heck does an editor do?" I had no idea. So, I just sort of started making it up as I went along.

Almost exactly a year later, DC had a major sales drop, and Al Milgrom — another artist — and I were let go. Al Milgrom landed on his feet at Marvel. A month later, Al calls me and says, "Hey! The water's fine! Why don't you come over here!" So I did — I got a gig at Marvel being in charge of *Crazy Magazine*.

How did the industry look at that time? In the early '70s, in my opinion, the comic book industry was pretty damn color-blind. They did not care if you were, white, purple, pink, brown or chartreuse. If you could do the the work, you were golden.

There were vestiges of things left over from previous generations, the conceptual stuff. The ingrained sort of prejudice that people didn't notice anymore, like coloring Asian people bright yellow. It wasn't like this was a policy — it was because that's the way it had always been done. That was the way that they/we were trained to do these things. So they just kept on doing that. Even if the people that were doing them themselves were Asian.

Do you feel like you were able to change this? I thought stuff had to change, but the only way that was gonna happen was for people of color to come into editorial. That was gonna make a big difference.

Marvel was structured differently at this time, right? It was a real bullpen, We had real wooden drawing tables there and big pots of rubber cement and pieces of paper being glued together to make the pages. There wasn't a computer in sight.

Yeah? The offices at Marvel were completely open at that time. There was no signing in at the door. A freelancer would come in and go sit in one office for an hour, then stroll down the hall and sit in another office. That's how a lot of work was sort of acquired.

People networked, and they socialized outside the office. At the first *Star Wars* movie, Chris Claremont was the first one in line. He just let everybody else in the comic book industry come in front of him, much to the chagrin of the rest of the line.

What was it about the stories at Marvel that you were able to draw and tell that made you stay? At that time, there were two styles of writing for comics. The DC method and the Marvel method. DC was more like a full screenplay. The Marvel method was plot and dialogue. The Marvel method gave most of the creative freedom to the artists. I always thought that the Marvel method was one of the main things that led to Marvel taking the lead away from DC.

How do you find your voice in all of this? It takes a while to find your own voice. Doing comics takes a very bizarre combination of chops. I craft a story by trying to visualize the whole thing in my head as a visual sequence rather than thinking of it in words. I don't think of it in terms of words. I'm dyscalculic, which means I can't do simple arithmetic, sort of like dyslexia. For instance, the only way I can remember that Christmas is on December 25 is I have a mental picture in my head of a calendar page with a red 25 on it.

So I have had to come up with little tricks like that 'cause I can't remember numbers as abstractions. I can see numbers as their visual symbols.

My thinking is that every aspect of a character is important — the gestures, the slightest movement in the facial features, are part of the acting. You combine that with the lighting and the framing and the pace.

I'm pretty good at doing visual storytelling and getting down a basic story, but I'm not a very good finish artist. I'm not a

terrific renderer. My anatomy chops are very sketchy. But I try to concentrate on what I know I can do and what I know I'm good at. So that's what I work at. At the same time, I'm always aware of this really important thing that Gail Adams told me years ago, in the '70s that I had to stop settling. And he said that when I was working on my drawings.

He said, "You're settling." And I said, "Well, what do you mean?" He said, "I can tell that you see something in your head that's ten times better than what you're drawing there on the board. Instead of settling, you should try to draw that really difficult thing, and you have to accept that the first time you do that, it's probably gonna suck. And even the second or third or fourth time, it's gonna suck. But the magic happens on the day that it stops sucking."

But you don't get to that day when it stops sucking unless you have all those other days before when it sucked.

I would imagine that that was helpful on that journey, being able to take those risks. Yeah, you have to take the risks, and you also have to understand the reality of what you're doing.

What was it for you that kept you going? You have to have thick skin, have faith in yourself and not care what other people are saying. I went to a specialized art high school, and there were dozens of people there that could draw rings around me. And they never went anywhere with it because they got shot down the first time, they got rejected. You know, 90% of getting ahead in any of the arts — in drawing, writing, acting, music — is getting past the incredible amount of rejection that you have to wade through to get your foot on the shore.

You have written G.I. JOE, you've written IRON FIST, and you've drawn across the board. How do you approach "authentic storytelling" and bringing the voice out of these characters, whether it is writing or image-wise? It's Stanislavski. You have to walk in their shoes. You just can't create this mannequin and assign it attributes. You have to construct a character that's as real as you can make it and then inhabit the character and walk around as the character. And, like you said, sometimes I get to the point where I realize the plot is

dictating what the characters do.

The plot should never trump the characters. If the story doesn't come out of the true interactions of the characters, then it's just flat choreography, and soulless creatures are just marching through this choreography that you've created. You have to have the characters interacting and being themselves, and then, all of a sudden, fate throws a monkey wrench into it. And then you have to deal with that as a story element.

That's all there is to it. That's why I've never written an outline. I write everything literally page-by-page. I don't know what comes on page seven until I get to page six. I just make it up as I go along. You know, I'm up to 287 issues of G.I. JOE, and I have no idea how I got there.

Now we have MARVEL'S VOICES IDENTITY #1. When you started making comics at Marvel, did you think this would happen? I thought it was going to be an eventuality. I looked around and I saw where the new talent was coming from. We were getting second-generation Chinese Canadians, an influx of Filipinos, folks from Argentina — including García-López — Mexico, and China. And, you know, it was on the wall.

As the writers and the artists moved up the ladder and moved into editorial, more changes happened. Because there was a voice at the editorial meeting.

Wolverine #90, cover by Adam Kubert, Greg Hildebrandt & Tim Hildebrandt

Do you think it makes a difference when there is a voice in the room? Well, absolutely. And it brings a whole new dimension to it.

Check out an extended version of this interview in Season 5 of the *Marvel's Voices* podcast, coming this fall to SiriusXM and everywhere you listen to podcasts.

IDENTITY

If you are familiar with *Marvel's Voices* books, each individual anthology is unique not just because of the incredible writers and artists (and the stories they tell), but also the additional spotlights, essays, and interviews in the books that celebrate BIPOC perspectives, stories, and the characters we love.

For *Marvel's Voices: Identity #1*, the team decided to create a space for each of the writers, artists and members of the Marvel staff to contribute a little extra. We asked each of them, "What does identity mean to you?" Here are their answers.

GENE LUEN YANG, writer

I have a friend named Marsha Qualey who is the author of young adult books. She says that at the heart of every young adult novel is an equation:

Belonging + Power = Identity

Where do I belong? What is my power? These questions plagued me when I was a young Asian American. Super hero comics did help me find answers, but the stories they told often missed the particulars of my life.

That's why I'm so thankful to be part of this anthology. These stories give distinctively Asian American answers to those questions. They give the answers that I was so desperate for when I was a kid.

MARCUS TO, artist

For me, identity is a journey. I've spent a lot of my life trying to figure out just who I am, and it seems to change every so often. The combination of where I grew up, my cultural heritage from my ethnicity, as well as my country of birth. To my love of sports and comics and the search for what all of that means to me. But at the end of the day, I guess all of that is what makes me, me.

CHRISTINA STRAIN, writer/colorist

For me, identity means understanding where you come from and how that helped shape who we are. Be it your family, heritage, or culture — all of these things have a hand in informing who you are as a person. And for those of us who feel like outsiders, having a better understanding of those foundations helps us better understand ourselves in a way that makes us feel less alone. Because it helps us understand we're part of a bigger whole.

JASON LOO, artist

As a Jubilee fan from the '90s *X-Men* cartoon, it was refreshing to see an Asian character on one of the most popular Marvel teams who wasn't a martial arts expert. Though I wished we got to see her roots shine through a little more. Like Jubilee, I also grew up with Asian immigrant parents. So when I was drawing her story, I could totally relate to her relationship with her mom and dad, and her mixed feelings on food from her culture as a kid. I'm so thrilled we got to tell her true origin story!

BRIAN REBER, colorist

I used to really struggle with my identity growing up. I come from a mixed family where my father is American and my mother is Vietnamese. I grew up with very few other Asians in my community. Outside of my family I had to look to comics, TV, and movies to discover more things about my heritage. I feel representation plays a big role in helping people learn more about what makes up their own identities. I hope that I'm able to provide that for readers, fans, and other creators through my actions and my work.

SABIR PIRZADA, writer

For me, identity is the perpetual reconciliation of how I see myself with how I'm perceived by others. It's the ownership I attempt to have when I describe myself as "American," "Pakistani," "Muslim" or any other descriptor when I know those words mean vastly different things to other people. Identity is the most challenging concept to confine into words, and perhaps the most important.

MASHAL AHMED, artist

I feel like identity is a result of a process of self-actualization. Because when it comes to discovering my identity, the world tunes out for me. It is a process that has led to the discovery of pursuits that are authentic to me such as enjoyment in creating art and the pursuit of understanding self and world through philosophy. Through philosophy, I have also discovered a self-authentic Islamic tradition. All of these things sit right with me, and so I feel that identifying with something lies solely in how it sits with a person at a fundamental level, rather than in how others value it.

ALYSSA WONG, writer

You are what you eat, and when it comes to family and heritage, I immediately think about food. What do you eat? How do you eat it? With whom do you eat it?

When I was a kid, my mom often made Filipino food. My favorite dish was fish sinigang, because it was one of her favorite dishes. It was something she grew up eating, and something she loved enough to pass down to me. When I met her family in Manila, we bonded over food and coming together for big meals. It didn't matter that we were an ocean apart. Eating with them felt like coming home.

I write about food a lot! It's deeply ingrained in the way I understand family, community, and communication. Putting my mom's sinigang in this Wave story is a delicious nod to her — and to everything she's given me. (Thanks, Mom.)

WHILCE PORTACIO, artist

Identity is the whole of what makes up who you are. In my case I grew up here in America, detached from my Filipino roots because society told me I had to assimilate. Turns out I was really good at it. I was incomplete and didn't even know it.

Comic book fans in Manila allowed me to explore my Pinoy roots. There, I discovered that I've always had little feelings, desires, and attractions which I had felt were not quite American, were actually Pinoy.

I was denying parts of myself from myself. I am now in my 26th year of my journey to discover my complete self...and am happy.

JAY DAVID RAMOS, colorist

When I got the assignment to color Wave's story, I was ecstatic! She's a character I can truly identify with — she is a Filipino who speaks Cebuano and lives in a coastal town in the Philippines! Filipinos are all about family — we call anybody "kuya" (brother), "ate" (sister), "tito" (uncle), and "tita" (auntie); even if there is no relation at all! In our story, after a fierce battle, Wave invites Bishop to dinner with her and her grandfather, welcoming him to her family! And that perfectly captures what it means to identify as a Filipino.

JEREMY HOLT, writer

Identity, to me, is a never-ending journey inward. How I present myself to the world is a culmination of experiences and choices that are constantly evolving. Embracing this change gives me the permission to live my life as authentically as possible, based on no one else's rules but my own.

MAURENE GOO, writer

The word identity and labels like "identity politics" are unnecessarily fraught. I've seen comments that *Silk* is "just another identity-driven comic sure to bore readers," and though *Silk* is doing just fine, thanks, it's annoying when terms that help us define our experiences get co-opted and denigrated. I think identity is something every single person living in a society can understand; it's how we view and define ourselves. It doesn't have to focus on your race, religion, no denying all of that factors into who you are when you live in a world that constantly challenges people with those definitions. I don't shy away from writing about identity in my work — it's an inextricable part of who my characters are.

PEACH MOMOKO, artist

Honestly, I do not know what my identity is in life. But I do know that I love my home country, Japan, and its history and fairy tales. And I would love to keep representing Japan.

RIAN GONZALES, artist

An identity is something that seeps through every little thing you do that no one can ever take away from you! Especially in the digital age when social acceptance is paraded on billboards and commercials, there are times when we trade bits of ourselves to please others. I used to do it — believe me, it wasn't fun! I only felt a sense of fulfillment when I stayed true to myself and my art. By being myself, I was able to attract amazing people (and hey, I even got Marvel to notice my work!).

INHYUK LEE, artist

It is what allows me to exist as myself. It is to make InHyuk Lee exist as InHyuk Lee.

PHILIP TAN, artist

We are all connecting in many different ways, and here, how our hearts speaks to each other is through comic books. The never-ending drive to create an insatiable hunger to absorb this special kind of art is what ties us together. For me, identity is here to tell others what beautiful experiences and stories they have yet to see, and at the same time that we all connect with the same intense emotions that colors our worlds.

Identity is what makes us different and alike at the same time. That we are unique individuals and also human beings that laugh, cry, and love the same way.

ASHLEY CHOY,
Merchandising & Promotions Production Designer

To me, identity means how I am represented in life and among others. Growing up as an Asian American, I was afraid of being different from the majority of people, but I grew to understand that my identity is what makes me unique. Identity to me is everything that I am as a person, how I perceive myself, and what makes me special as an individual. And that is something that I take pride in.

MARIKA HASHIMOTO,
Associate Editor, Digital Media

In the world of super heroes, having a secret identity could be what protects you. Or, like so many super heroes, it could also eat away at you if you can't strike a balance between where your two (or three or four...) lives intersect. To me, identity is not necessarily something that has to be revealed or performed. Your true self always has those special powers that lie within you — those qualities are only waiting for the right time, space, or opportunity to come out. Once it does, like any good story, it's the moment we've all been waiting for.

HARRY GO, Director, Creative & Content, Digital Media

As an immigrant with Chinese, Japanese and Filipino heritage, learning how to embrace my identity at an early age was a necessity. I flew on a one-way ticket to New Jersey at the age of 8 with one suitcase, a head full of information about the X-Men and a love for super hero comics. I remember going to my first day of school, a kid from another place, and finding myself in a lively conversation about Wolverine vs. Cyclops. That was an important lesson early on. That who I was, was more than what I looked like or where I came from. My identity was partly that, yes, but it's also what's in my head and what's in my heart. As long as I'm able to show people what's on the inside along with what's on the outside, somehow it will always work.

CHRISTINE DINH, Editor, Marvel.com

For my entire life, I knew myself to be Vietnamese American, but I only identified as American. From a young age, I knew I didn't want to be othered. Identity is how we relate ourselves to the world; if we're unable to see ourselves reflected back, it's painful to not feel important enough to be represented. Accepting others begins with accepting yourself. I've come to embrace my full identity; we all deserve to be seen. But it's no longer enough to just be seen; it's time we now see each other.

TIM CHENG, Executive Director, Communications

As a second-generation Asian American, I learned over time to embrace both sides of my identity

to create something special. For me, that growth was deeply impacted by seeing myself in stories — both through authentic representation and the universal values we live by. My parents and older brother were the first to shape my identity by telling me their stories and embodying them by example, and in a way, seeing these stories and heroes on the page or screen is no different. And that's what identity means to me: it's telling a living story, which Marvel does in spades.

DARREN SHAN, Editor

Identity is a tough one for me. Am I Asian enough? Am I American enough? It's something that I struggled with as a kid, a teenager and an adult. I used to deny my heritage growing up. Who wants to stand out when you could fit in? But as I get older, I realize: identity is ever-evolving. You're never going to be just one thing your whole life. And at the end of the day, only you should decide who you're going to be, not anyone else.

We'd like to thank all of the creators and staff who took the time to respond. Our identities are not just something personal and particular, but are ever-evolving parts of who we are and our journey. Identities bring us together, set us apart, and make us stronger. From cultural origins and geographic regions to our families and the food we love, identity is not just who we are, but the stories we know and love.

ANGÉLIQUE ROCHÉ
Consulting Editor

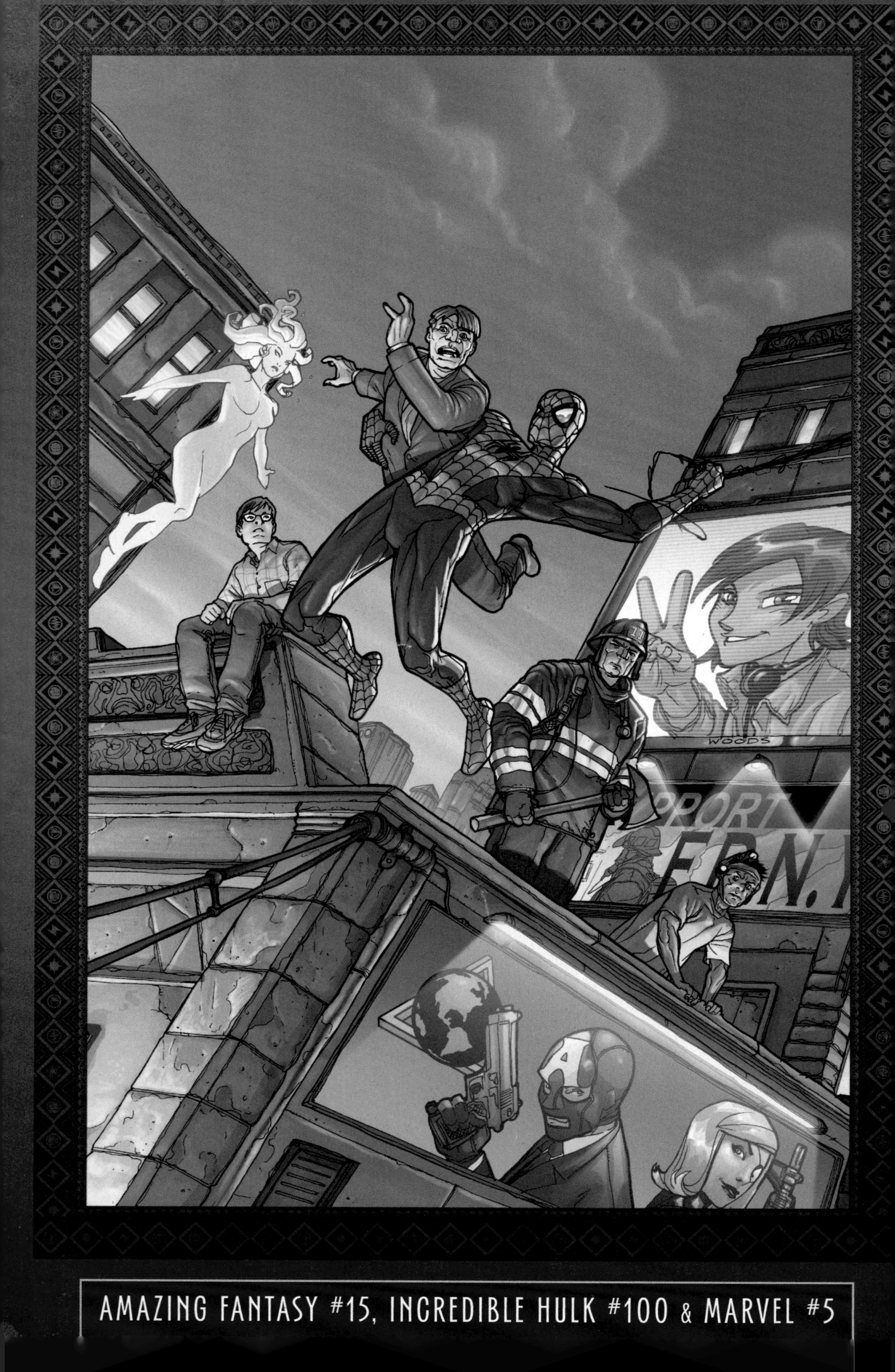
WOODS

AMAZING FANTASY #15, INCREDIBLE HULK #100 & MARVEL #5

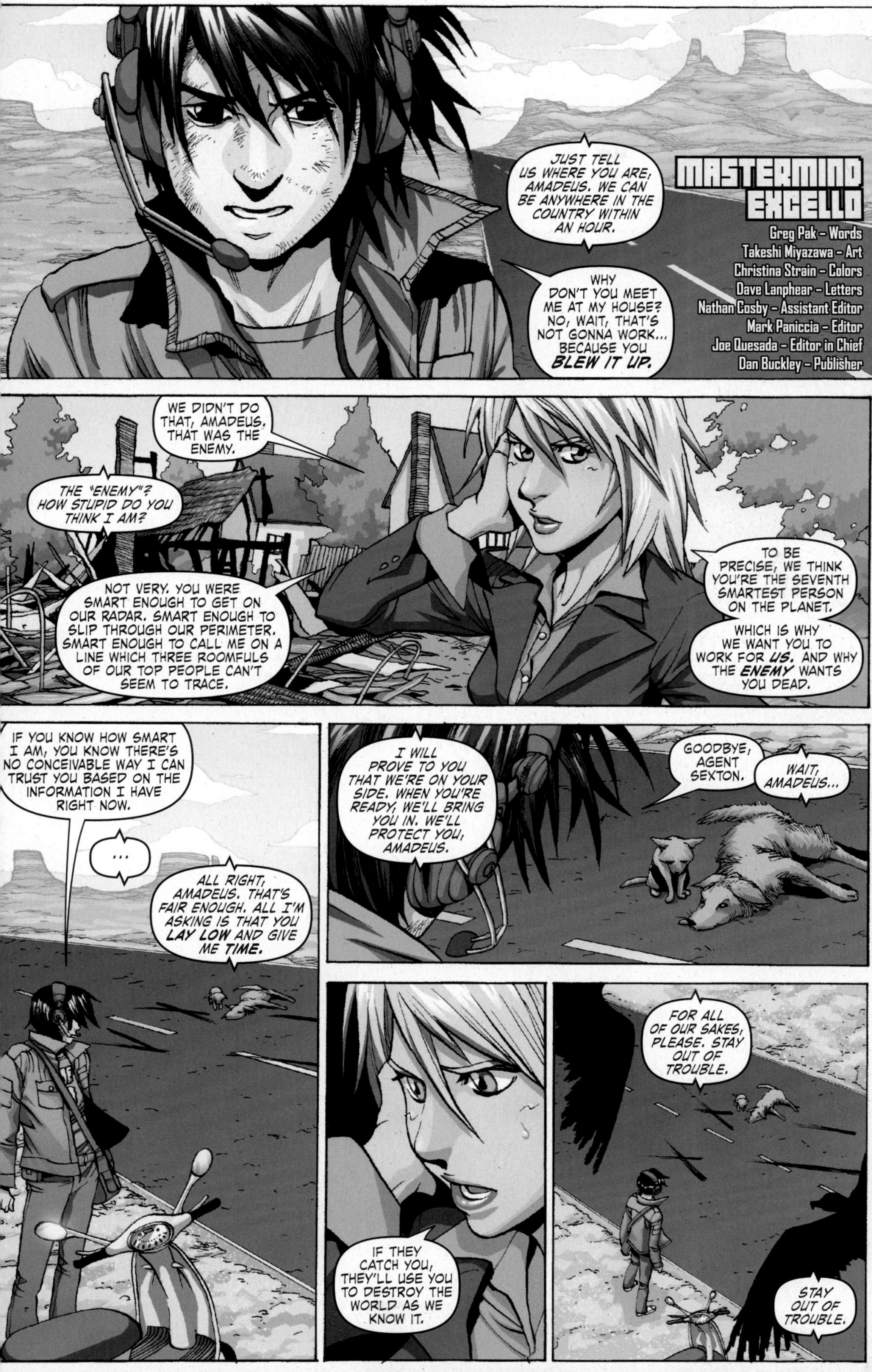
MASTERMIND EXCELLO
Greg Pak – Words
Takeshi Miyazawa – Art
Christina Strain – Colors
Dave Lanphear – Letters
Nathan Cosby – Assistant Editor
Mark Paniccia – Editor
Joe Quesada – Editor in Chief
Dan Buckley – Publisher
JUST TELL US WHERE YOU ARE, AMADEUS. WE CAN BE ANYWHERE IN THE COUNTRY WITHIN AN HOUR.
WHY DON'T YOU MEET ME AT MY HOUSE? NO, WAIT, THAT'S NOT GONNA WORK... BECAUSE YOU BLEW IT UP.
WE DIDN'T DO THAT, AMADEUS. THAT WAS THE ENEMY.
THE "ENEMY"? HOW STUPID DO YOU THINK I AM?
NOT VERY. YOU WERE SMART ENOUGH TO GET ON OUR RADAR. SMART ENOUGH TO SLIP THROUGH OUR PERIMETER. SMART ENOUGH TO CALL ME ON A LINE WHICH THREE ROOMFULS OF OUR TOP PEOPLE CAN'T SEEM TO TRACE.
TO BE PRECISE, WE THINK YOU'RE THE SEVENTH SMARTEST PERSON ON THE PLANET.
WHICH IS WHY WE WANT YOU TO WORK FOR US. AND WHY THE ENEMY WANTS YOU DEAD.
IF YOU KNOW HOW SMART I AM, YOU KNOW THERE'S NO CONCEIVABLE WAY I CAN TRUST YOU BASED ON THE INFORMATION I HAVE RIGHT NOW.
...
ALL RIGHT, AMADEUS. THAT'S FAIR ENOUGH. ALL I'M ASKING IS THAT YOU LAY LOW AND GIVE ME TIME.
I WILL PROVE TO YOU THAT WE'RE ON YOUR SIDE. WHEN YOU'RE READY, WE'LL BRING YOU IN. WE'LL PROTECT YOU, AMADEUS.
GOODBYE, AGENT SEXTON.
WAIT, AMADEUS...
IF THEY CATCH YOU, THEY'LL USE YOU TO DESTROY THE WORLD AS WE KNOW IT.
FOR ALL OF OUR SAKES, PLEASE. STAY OUT OF TROUBLE.
STAY OUT OF TROUBLE.

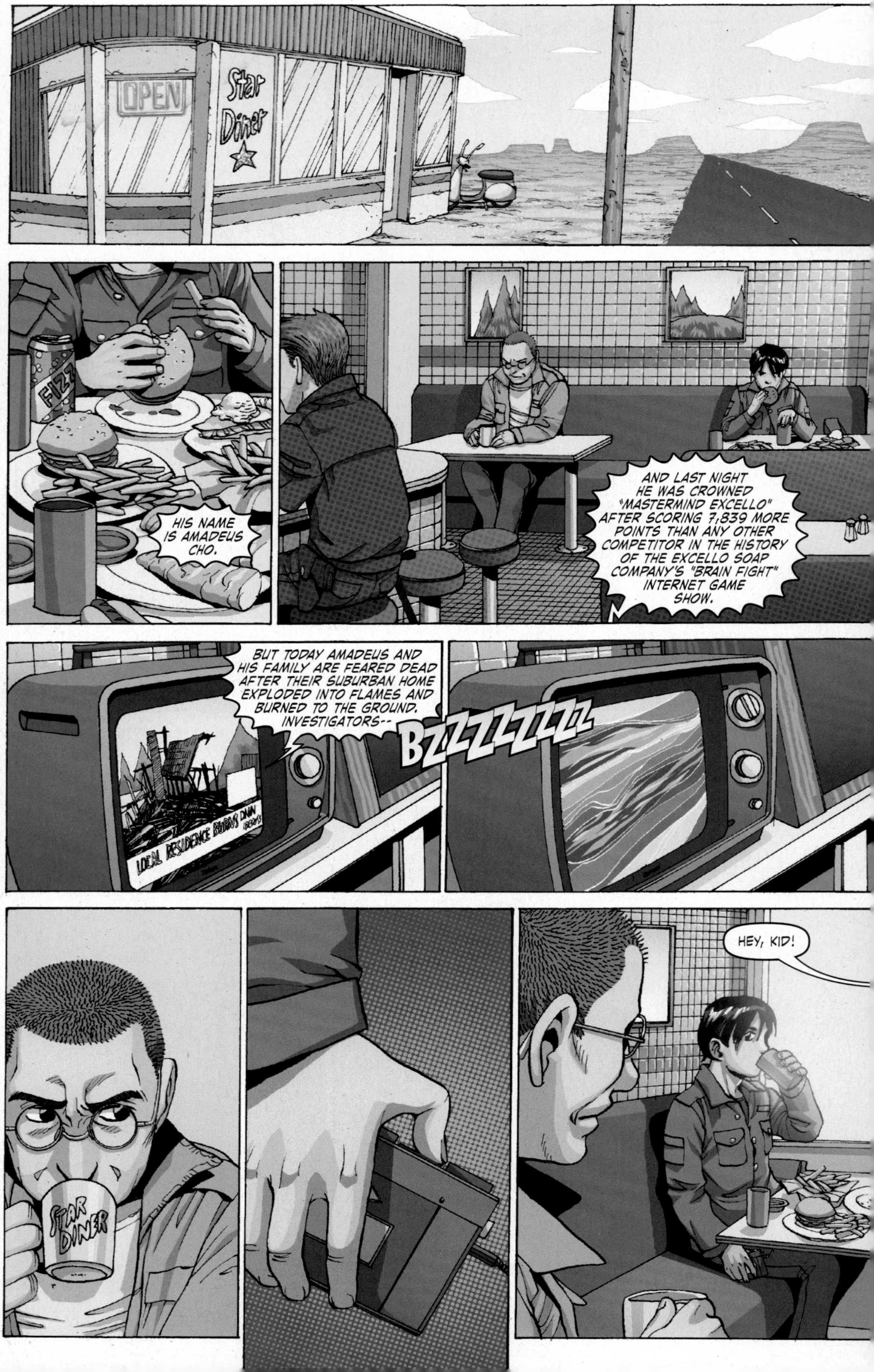
OPEN
Star Diner
FIZZ
HIS NAME IS AMADEUS CHO.
AND LAST NIGHT HE WAS CROWNED "MASTERMIND EXCELLO" AFTER SCORING 7,839 MORE POINTS THAN ANY OTHER COMPETITOR IN THE HISTORY OF THE EXCELLO SOAP COMPANY'S "BRAIN FIGHT" INTERNET GAME SHOW.
BUT TODAY AMADEUS AND HIS FAMILY ARE FEARED DEAD AFTER THEIR SUBURBAN HOME EXPLODED INTO FLAMES AND BURNED TO THE GROUND. INVESTIGATORS--
LOCAL RESIDENCE BURNS DOWN
BZZZZZZZZ
STAR DINER
HEY, KID!

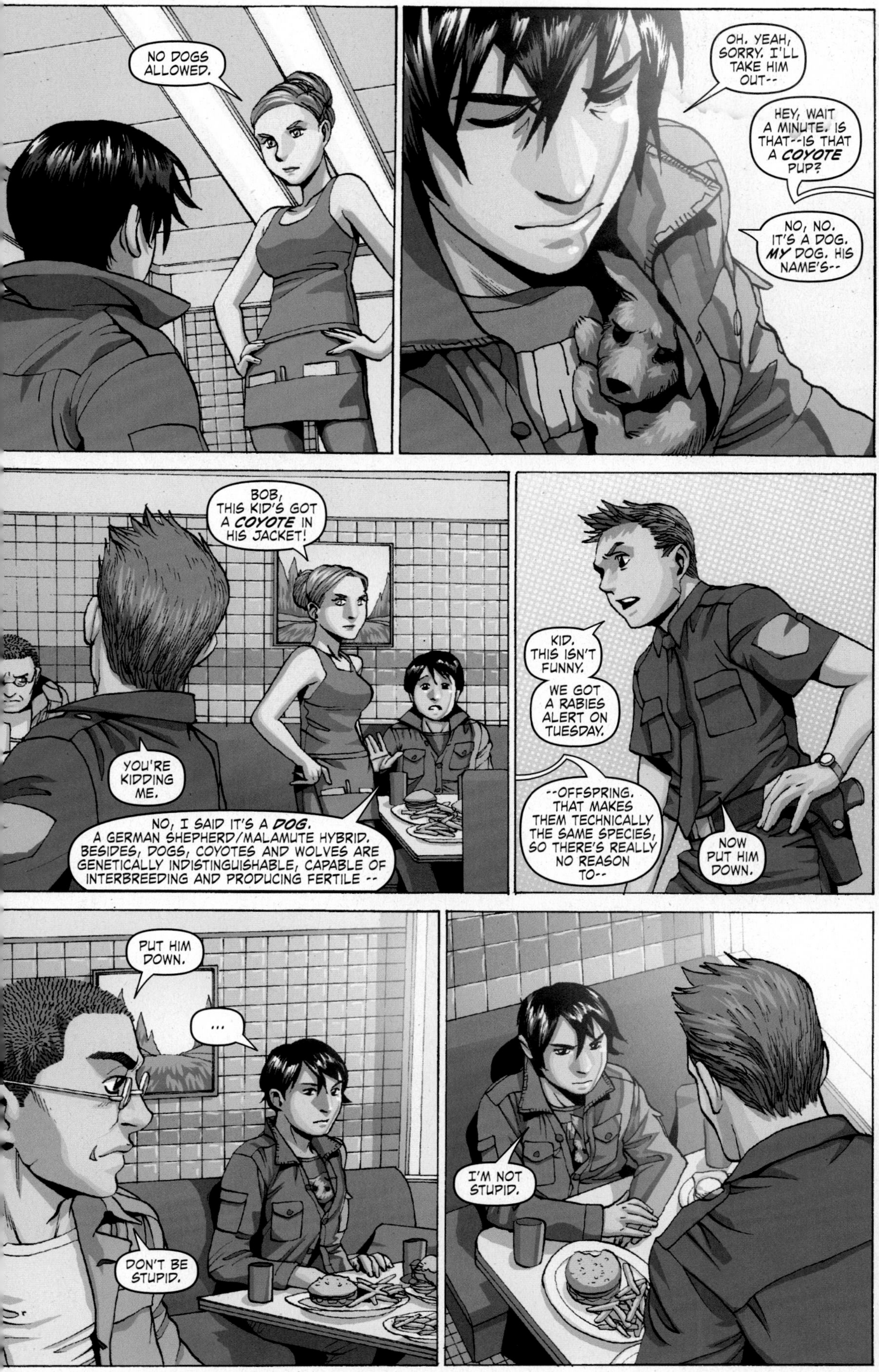
NO DOGS ALLOWED.
OH. YEAH, SORRY. I'LL TAKE HIM OUT--
HEY, WAIT A MINUTE. IS THAT--IS THAT A *COYOTE* PUP?
NO, NO. IT'S A DOG. ***MY*** DOG. HIS NAME'S--
BOB, THIS KID'S GOT A *COYOTE* IN HIS JACKET!
YOU'RE KIDDING ME.
NO, I SAID IT'S A *DOG.* A GERMAN SHEPHERD/MALAMUTE HYBRID. BESIDES, DOGS, COYOTES AND WOLVES ARE GENETICALLY INDISTINGUISHABLE, CAPABLE OF INTERBREEDING AND PRODUCING FERTILE --
KID. THIS ISN'T FUNNY.
WE GOT A RABIES ALERT ON TUESDAY.
--OFFSPRING. THAT MAKES THEM TECHNICALLY THE SAME SPECIES, SO THERE'S REALLY NO REASON TO--
NOW PUT HIM DOWN.
PUT HIM DOWN.
...
DON'T BE STUPID.
I'M NOT STUPID.

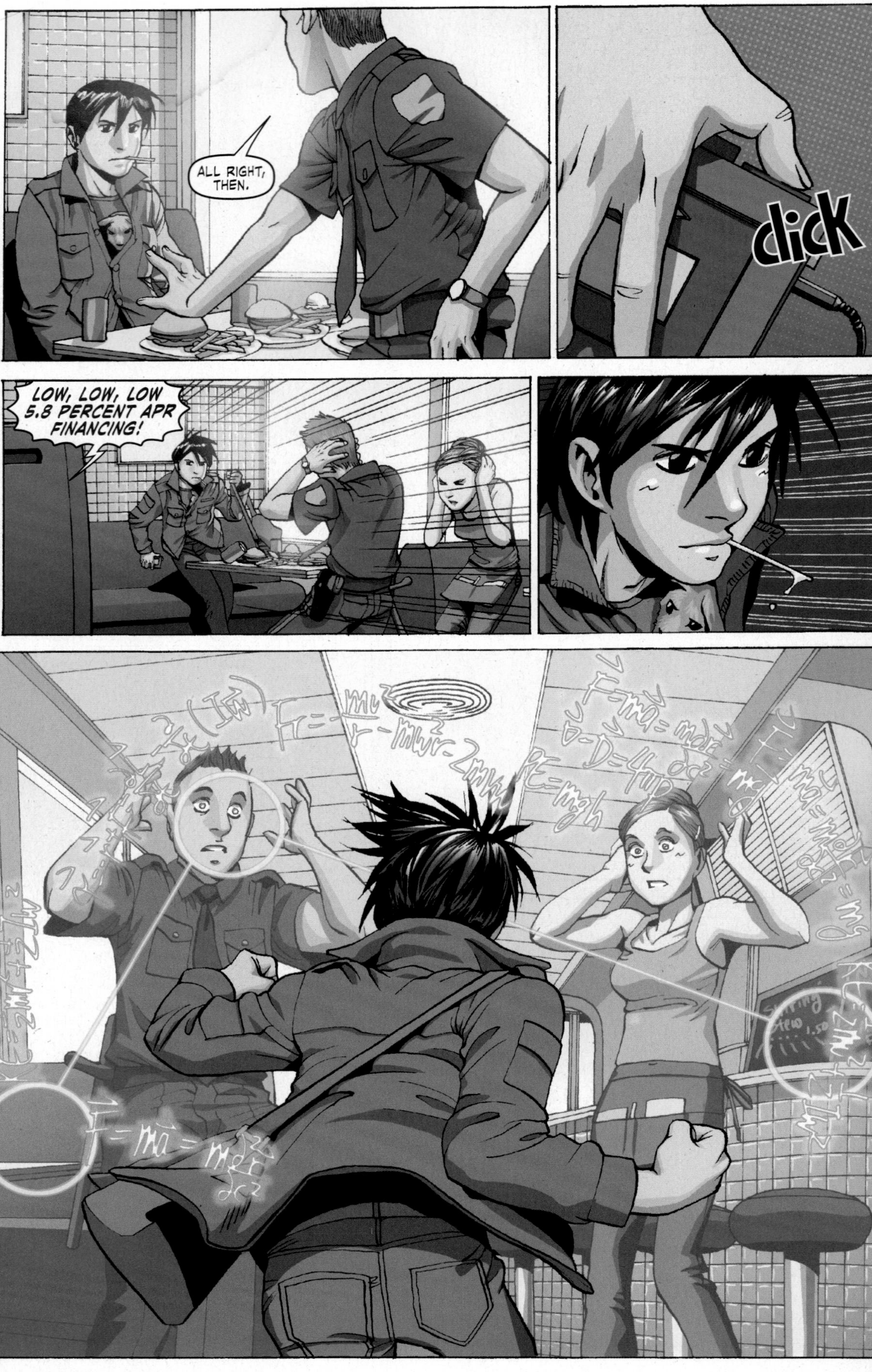
ALL RIGHT, THEN.
CLICK
LOW, LOW, LOW 5.8 PERCENT APR FINANCING!

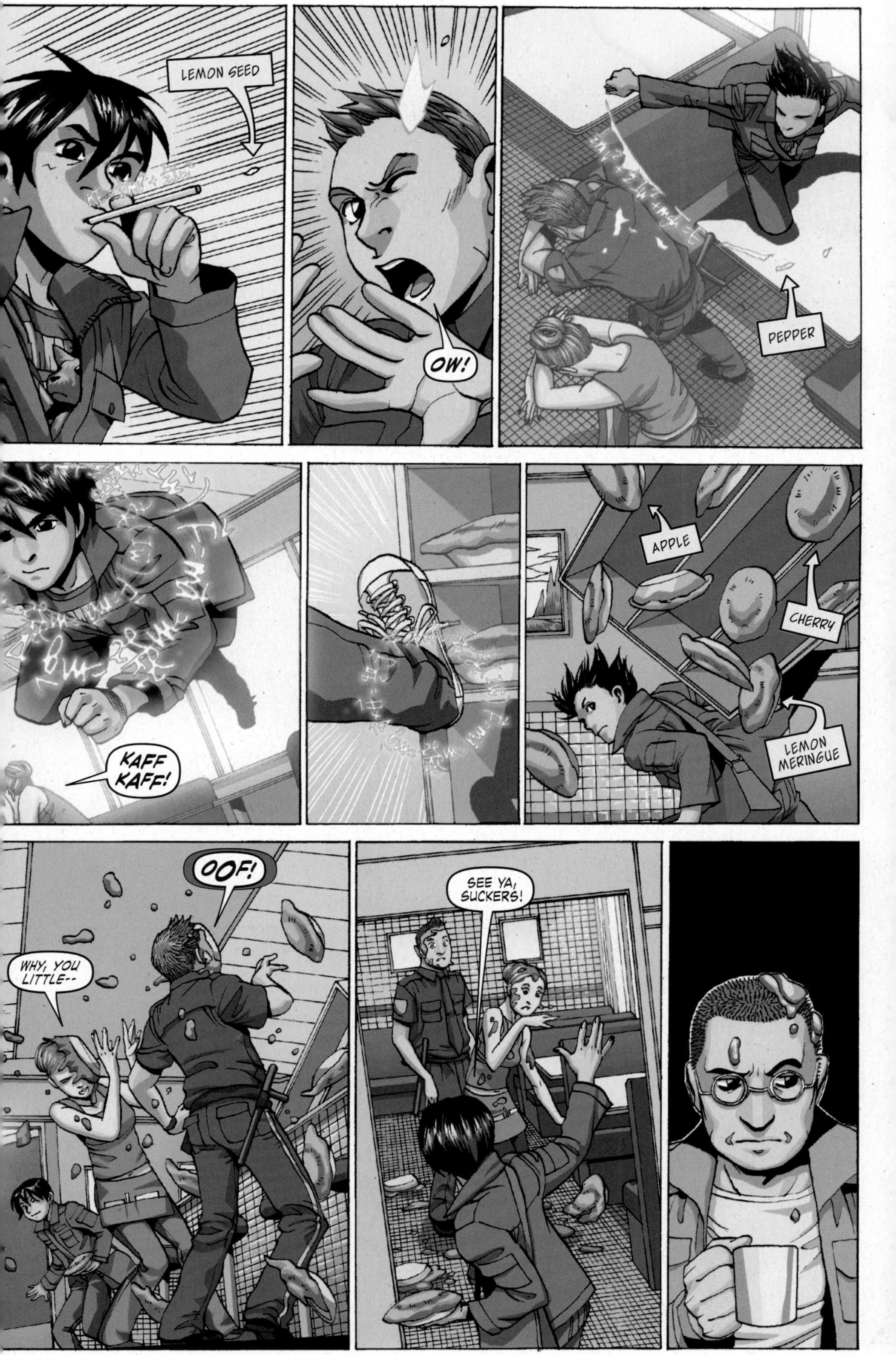
LEMON SEED
OW!
PEPPER
KAFF KAFF!
APPLE
CHERRY
LEMON MERINGUE
OOF!
WHY, YOU LITTLE--
SEE YA, SUCKERS!

STAR DINER

YEAH, EXACTLY, A SKINNY ASIAN KID...

... JUST LIKE ON THE TEE VEE.

THAT'S THE LOCAL POLICE BAND. SHOULD BE CLOSE--

GOT HIM.

UH OH...

LASER SIGHT.

REARVIEW MIRROR

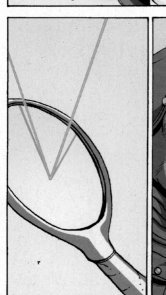

WHA--

PANICCIA 135mm M72 PORTABLE WARHEAD

GAH!

AW, MAN...

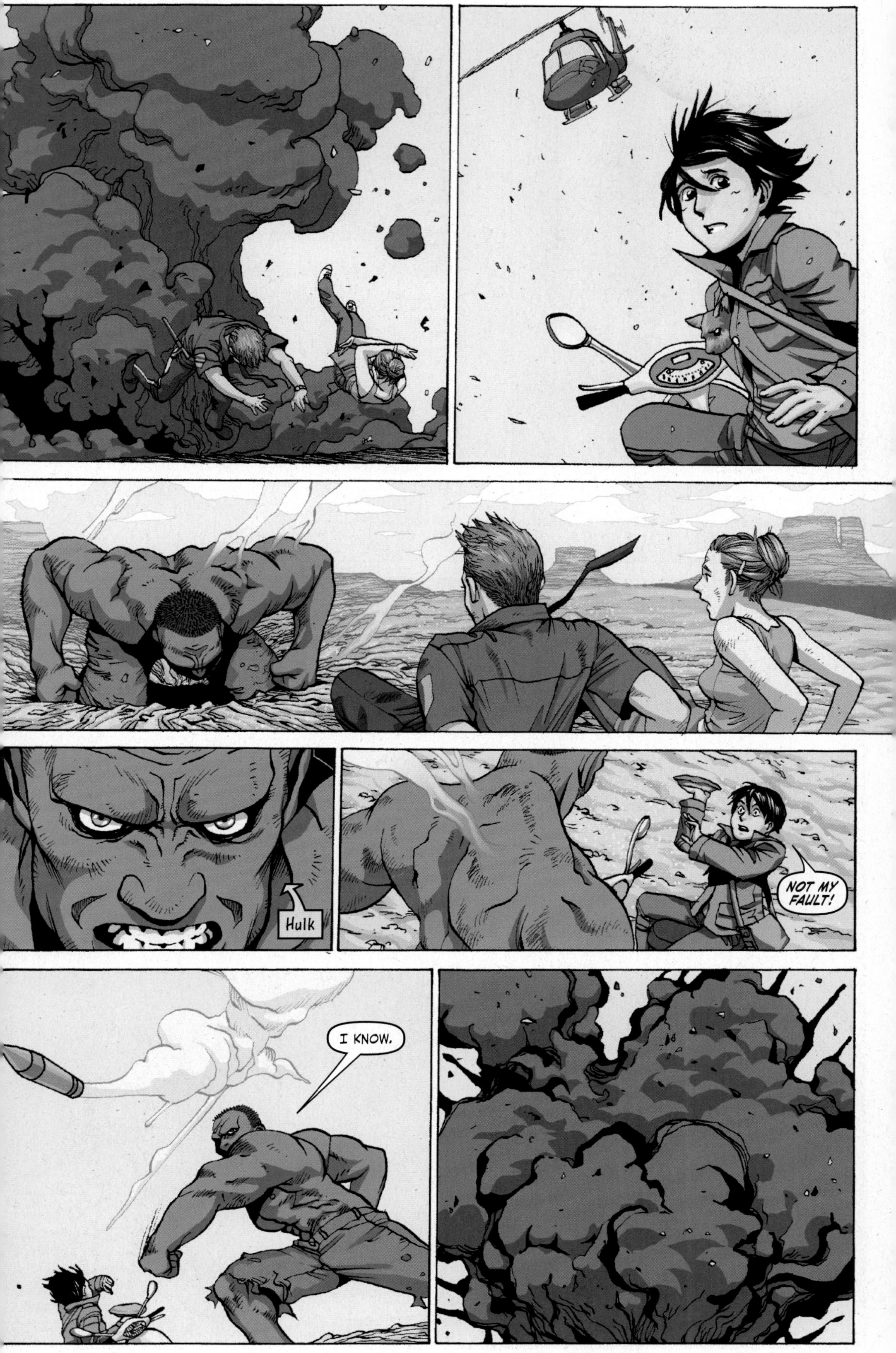
Hulk
NOT MY FAULT!
I KNOW.

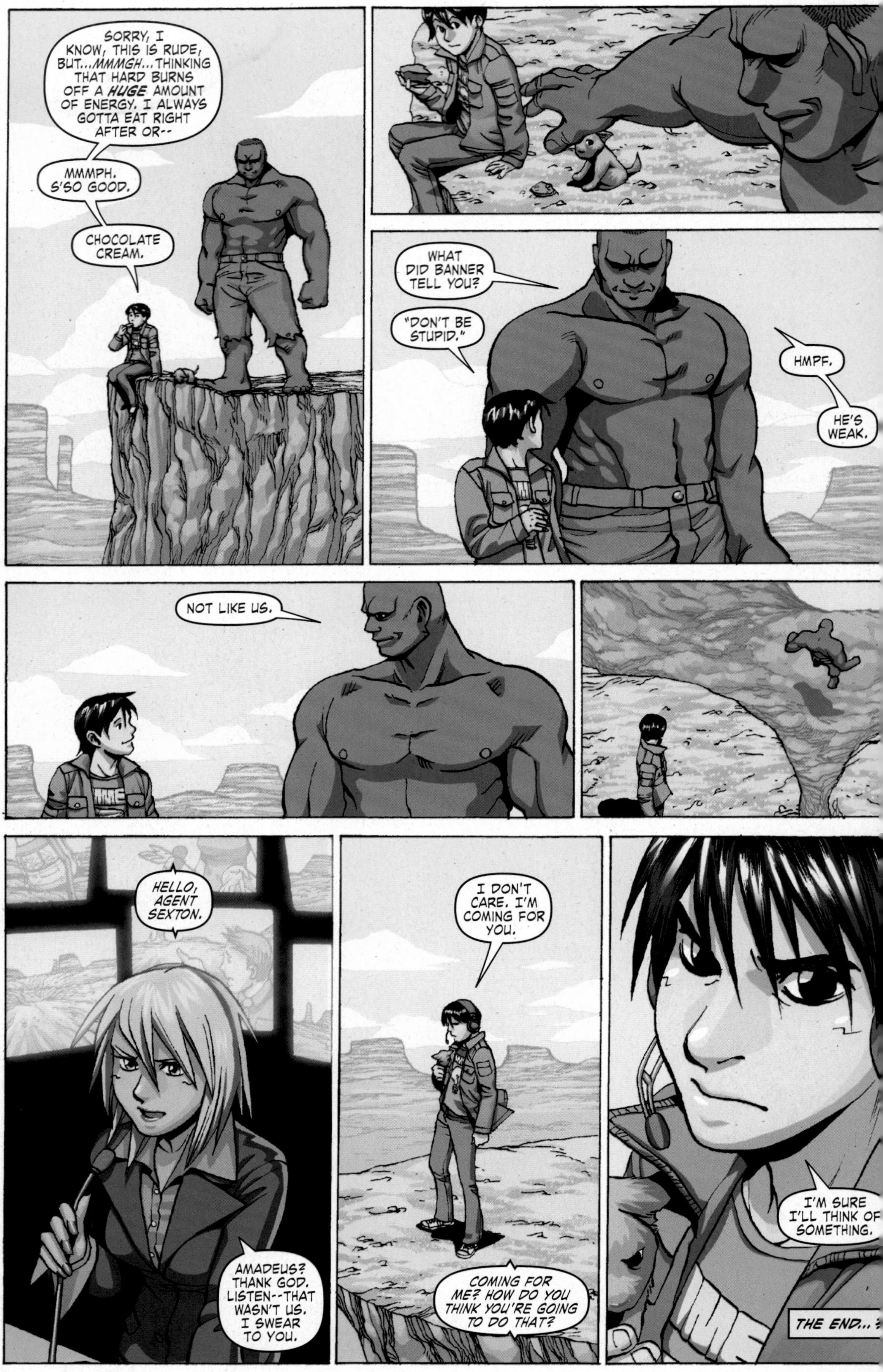
SORRY, I KNOW, THIS IS RUDE, BUT...MMMGH...THINKING THAT HARD BURNS OFF A HUGE AMOUNT OF ENERGY. I ALWAYS GOTTA EAT RIGHT AFTER OR--
MMMPH. S'SO GOOD.
CHOCOLATE CREAM.
WHAT DID BANNER TELL YOU?
"DON'T BE STUPID."
HMPF.
HE'S WEAK.
NOT LIKE US.
HELLO, AGENT SEXTON.
AMADEUS? THANK GOD. LISTEN--THAT WASN'T US. I SWEAR TO YOU.
I DON'T CARE. I'M COMING FOR YOU.
COMING FOR ME? HOW DO YOU THINK YOU'RE GOING TO DO THAT?
I'M SURE I'LL THINK OF SOMETHING.
THE END...

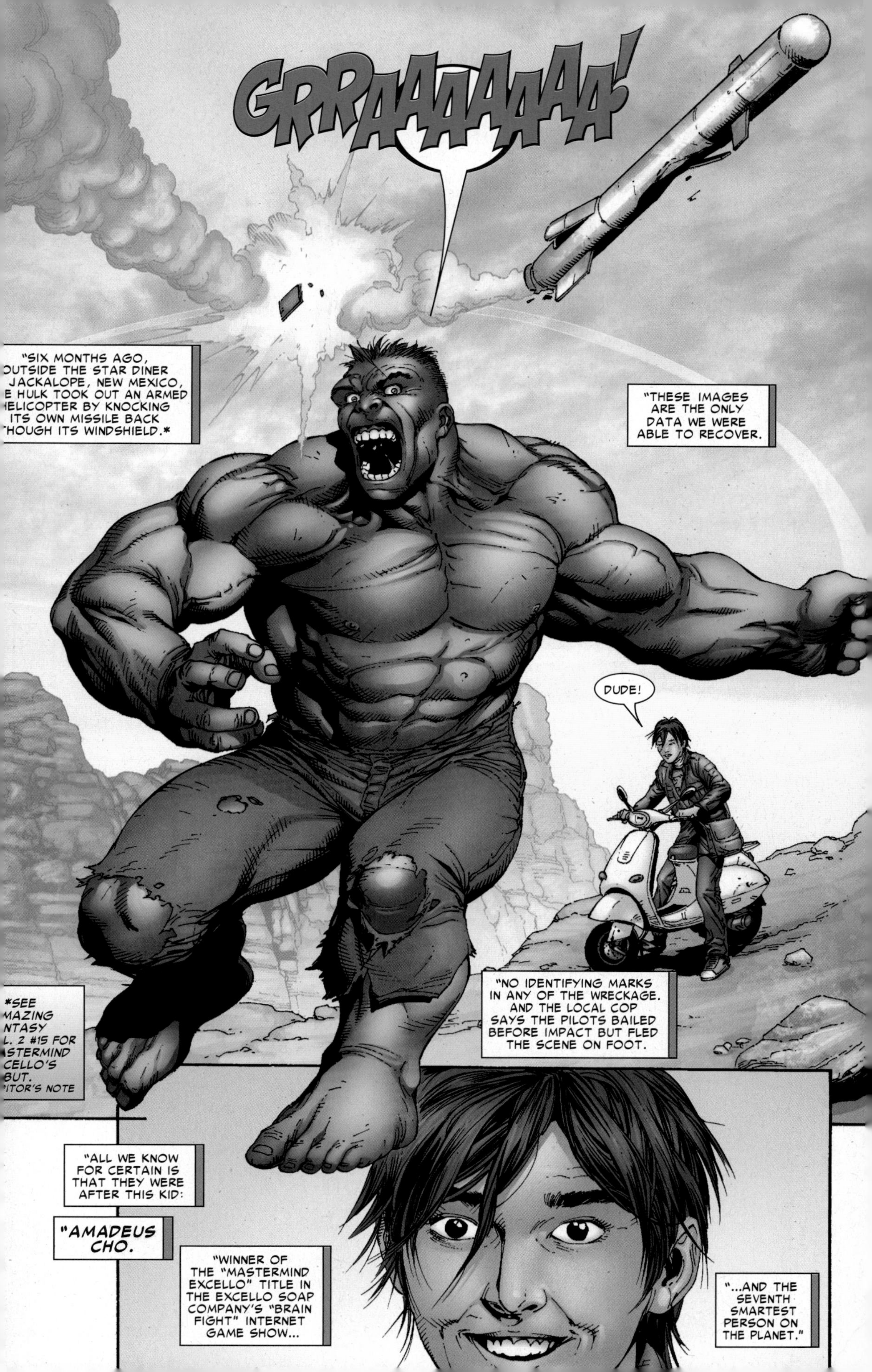

GRRAAAAAAA!
"SIX MONTHS AGO, OUTSIDE THE STAR DINER JACKALOPE, NEW MEXICO, E HULK TOOK OUT AN ARMED HELICOPTER BY KNOCKING ITS OWN MISSILE BACK THOUGH ITS WINDSHIELD.*
"THESE IMAGES ARE THE ONLY DATA WE WERE ABLE TO RECOVER.
DUDE!
"NO IDENTIFYING MARKS IN ANY OF THE WRECKAGE. AND THE LOCAL COP SAYS THE PILOTS BAILED BEFORE IMPACT BUT FLED THE SCENE ON FOOT.
*SEE MAZING NTASY L. 2 #15 FOR STERMIND CELLO'S BUT. ITOR'S NOTE
"ALL WE KNOW FOR CERTAIN IS THAT THEY WERE AFTER THIS KID:
"AMADEUS CHO.
"WINNER OF THE "MASTERMIND EXCELLO" TITLE IN THE EXCELLO SOAP COMPANY'S "BRAIN FIGHT" INTERNET GAME SHOW...
"...AND THE SEVENTH SMARTEST PERSON ON THE PLANET."

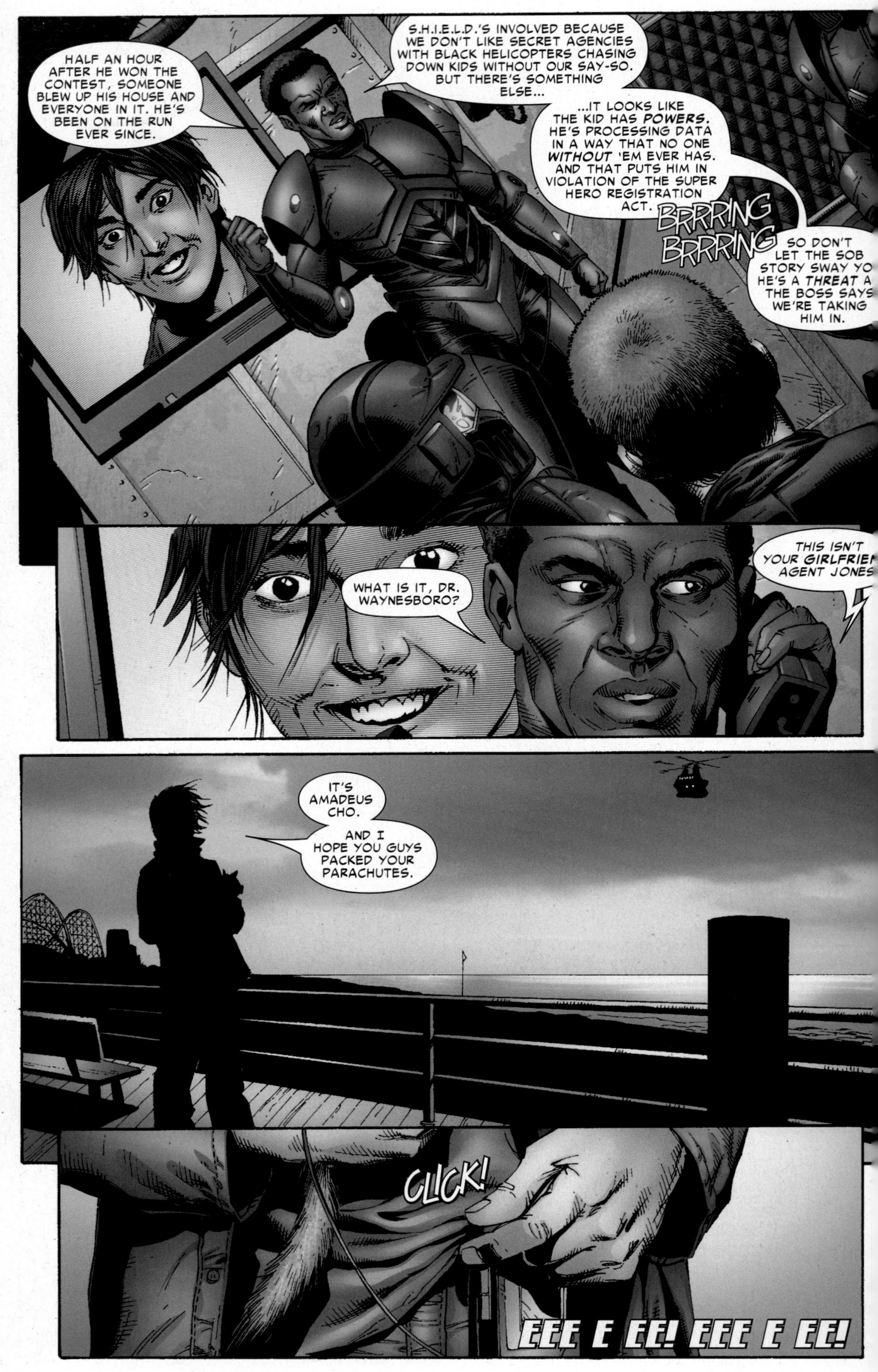
HALF AN HOUR AFTER HE WON THE CONTEST, SOMEONE BLEW UP HIS HOUSE AND EVERYONE IN IT. HE'S BEEN ON THE RUN EVER SINCE.
S.H.I.E.L.D.'S INVOLVED BECAUSE WE DON'T LIKE SECRET AGENCIES WITH BLACK HELICOPTERS CHASING DOWN KIDS WITHOUT OUR SAY-SO. BUT THERE'S SOMETHING ELSE...
...IT LOOKS LIKE THE KID HAS POWERS. HE'S PROCESSING DATA IN A WAY THAT NO ONE WITHOUT 'EM EVER HAS. AND THAT PUTS HIM IN VIOLATION OF THE SUPER HERO REGISTRATION ACT.
BRRRING BRRRING
SO DON'T LET THE SOB STORY SWAY YO HE'S A THREAT A THE BOSS SAYS WE'RE TAKING HIM IN.
WHAT IS IT, DR. WAYNESBORO?
THIS ISN'T YOUR GIRLFRIE AGENT JONES
IT'S AMADEUS CHO.
AND I HOPE YOU GUYS PACKED YOUR PARACHUTES.
CLICK!
EEE E EE! EEE E EE!

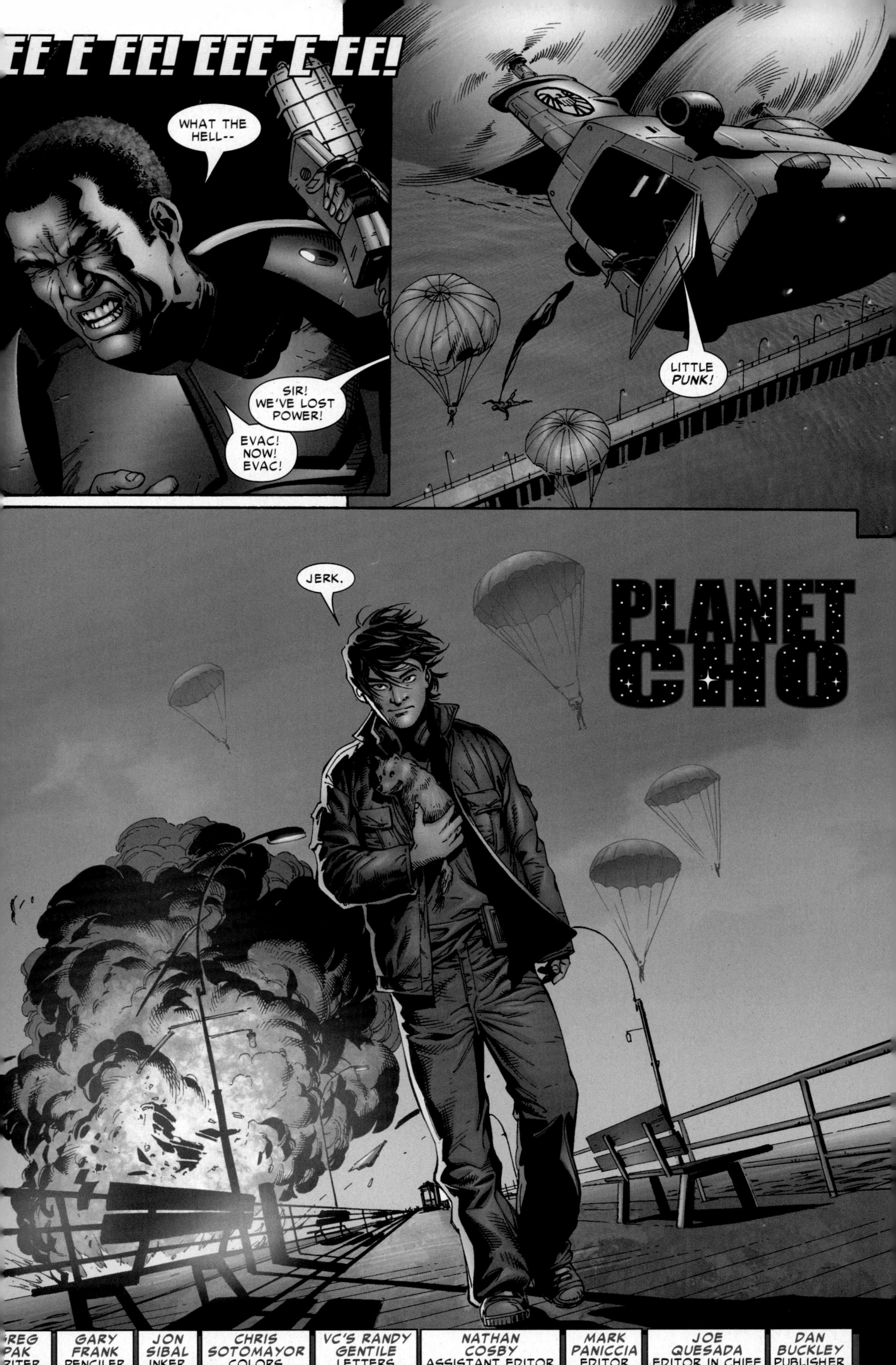
EE E EE! EEE E EE!
WHAT THE HELL--
SIR! WE'VE LOST POWER!
EVAC! NOW! EVAC!
LITTLE PUNK!
JERK.
PLANET CHO

GREG PAK WRITER | GARY FRANK PENCILER | JON SIBAL INKER | CHRIS SOTOMAYOR COLORS | VC'S RANDY GENTILE LETTERS | NATHAN COSBY ASSISTANT EDITOR | MARK PANICCIA EDITOR | JOE QUESADA EDITOR IN CHIEF | DAN BUCKLEY PUBLISHER

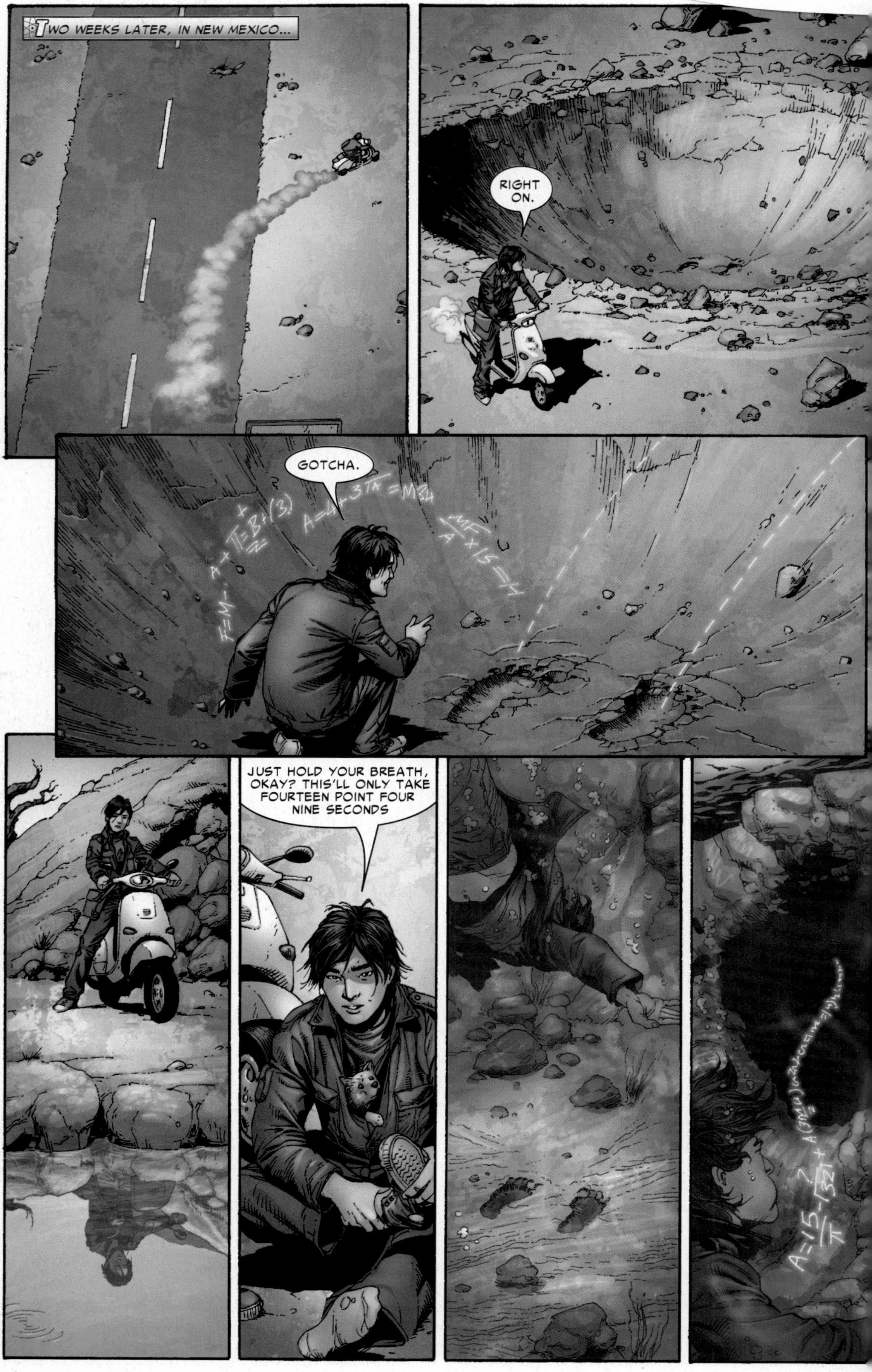
TWO WEEKS LATER, IN NEW MEXICO...
RIGHT ON.
GOTCHA.
JUST HOLD YOUR BREATH, OKAY? THIS'LL ONLY TAKE FOURTEEN POINT FOUR NINE SECONDS

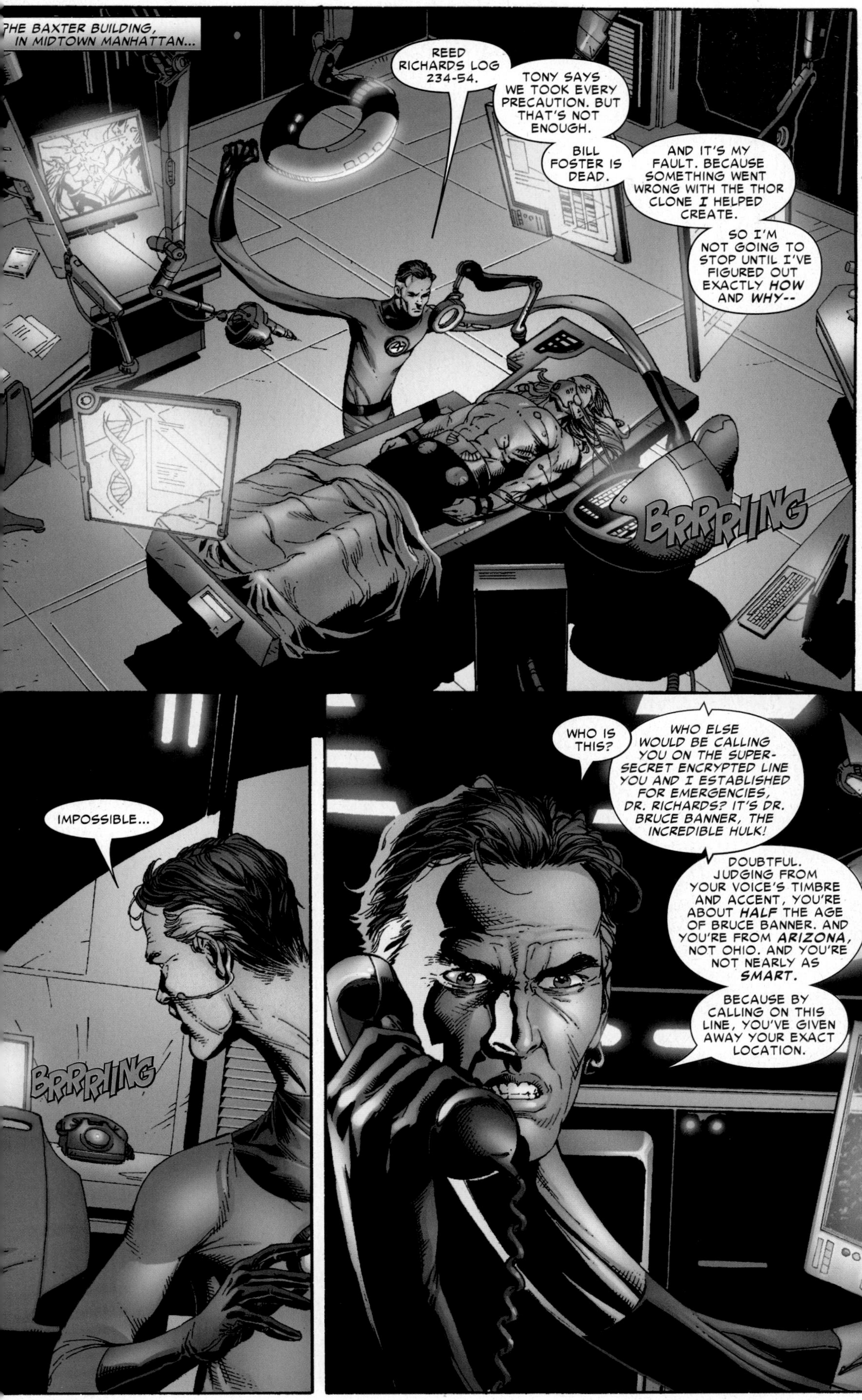
THE BAXTER BUILDING, IN MIDTOWN MANHATTAN...
REED RICHARDS LOG 234-54.
TONY SAYS WE TOOK EVERY PRECAUTION. BUT THAT'S NOT ENOUGH.
BILL FOSTER IS DEAD.
AND IT'S MY FAULT. BECAUSE SOMETHING WENT WRONG WITH THE THOR CLONE *I* HELPED CREATE.
SO I'M NOT GOING TO STOP UNTIL I'VE FIGURED OUT EXACTLY *HOW* AND *WHY*--
BRRRRING
IMPOSSIBLE...
BRRRRING
WHO IS THIS?
WHO ELSE WOULD BE CALLING YOU ON THE SUPER-SECRET ENCRYPTED LINE YOU AND I ESTABLISHED FOR EMERGENCIES, DR. RICHARDS? IT'S DR. BRUCE BANNER, THE INCREDIBLE HULK!
DOUBTFUL. JUDGING FROM YOUR VOICE'S TIMBRE AND ACCENT, YOU'RE ABOUT *HALF* THE AGE OF BRUCE BANNER. AND YOU'RE FROM *ARIZONA*, NOT OHIO. AND YOU'RE NOT NEARLY AS *SMART*.
BECAUSE BY CALLING ON THIS LINE, YOU'VE GIVEN AWAY YOUR EXACT LOCATION.

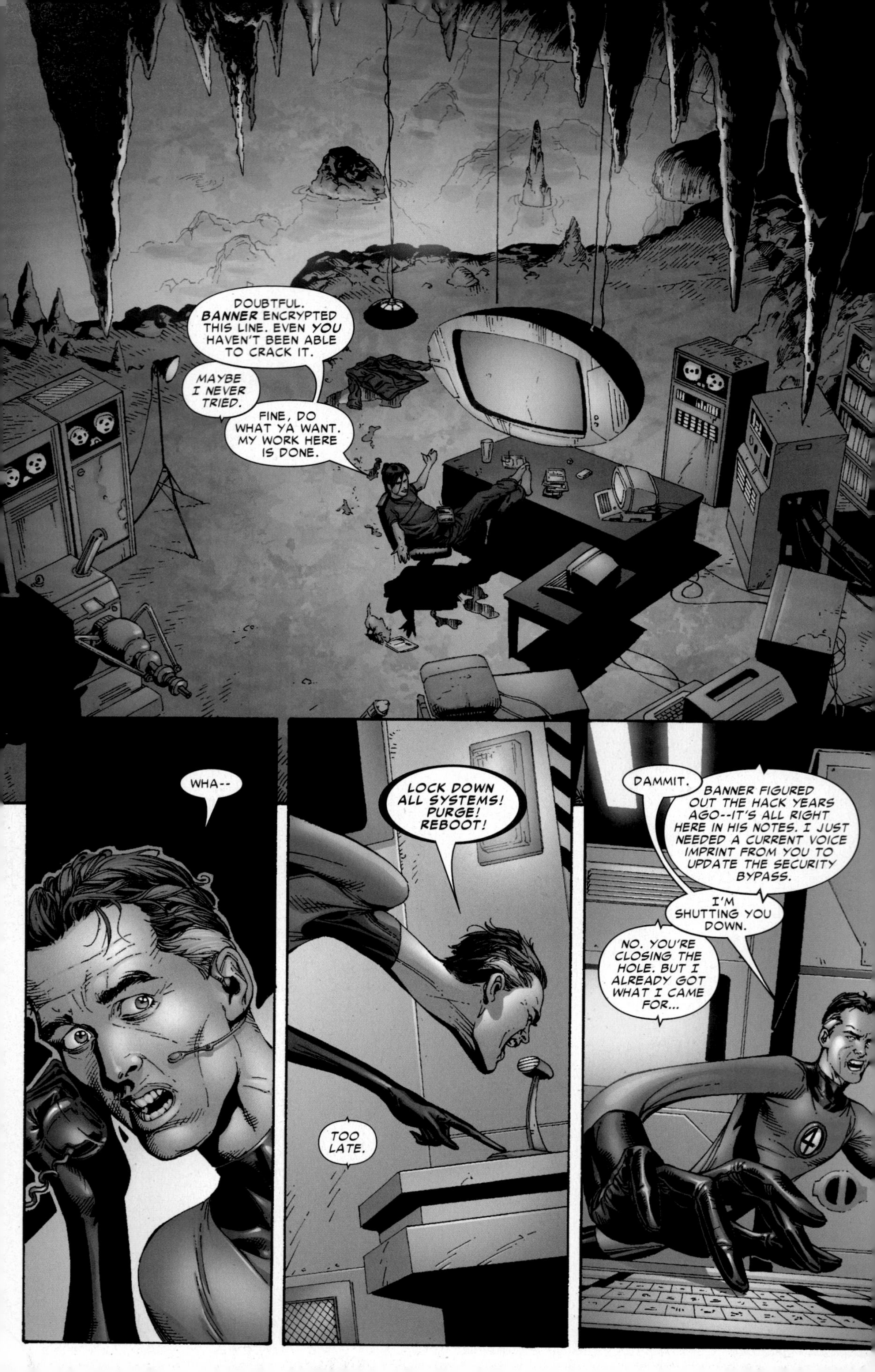
DOUBTFUL. BANNER ENCRYPTED THIS LINE. EVEN YOU HAVEN'T BEEN ABLE TO CRACK IT.
MAYBE I NEVER TRIED.
FINE, DO WHAT YA WANT. MY WORK HERE IS DONE.
WHA--
LOCK DOWN ALL SYSTEMS! PURGE! REBOOT!
TOO LATE.
DAMMIT.
BANNER FIGURED OUT THE HACK YEARS AGO--IT'S ALL RIGHT HERE IN HIS NOTES. I JUST NEEDED A CURRENT VOICE IMPRINT FROM YOU TO UPDATE THE SECURITY BYPASS.
I'M SHUTTING YOU DOWN.
NO. YOU'RE CLOSING THE HOLE. BUT I ALREADY GOT WHAT I CAME FOR...

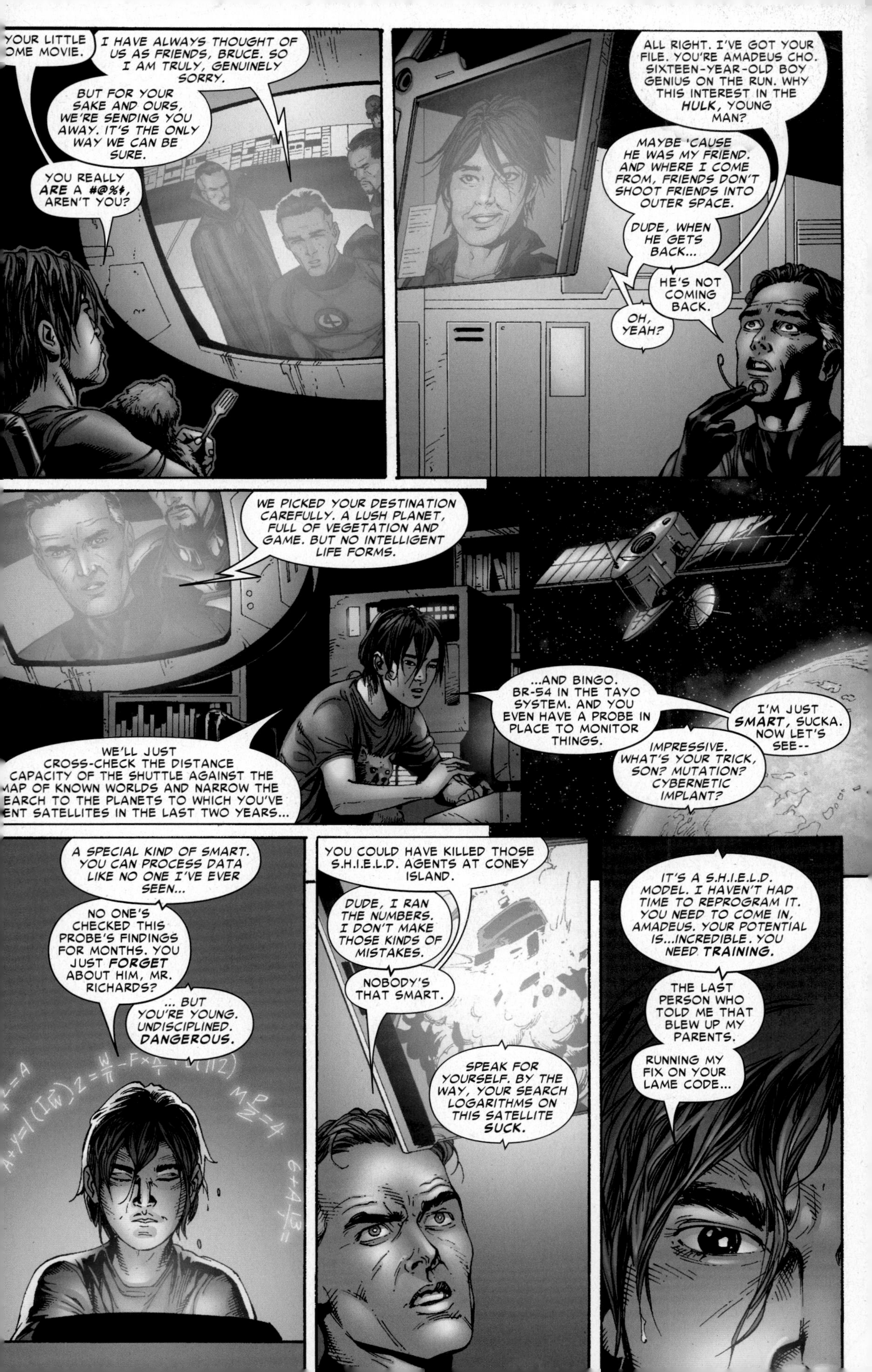
YOUR LITTLE OME MOVIE.
I HAVE ALWAYS THOUGHT OF US AS FRIENDS, BRUCE. SO I AM TRULY, GENUINELY SORRY.
BUT FOR YOUR SAKE AND OURS, WE'RE SENDING YOU AWAY. IT'S THE ONLY WAY WE CAN BE SURE.
YOU REALLY ARE A #@%$, AREN'T YOU?
ALL RIGHT. I'VE GOT YOUR FILE. YOU'RE AMADEUS CHO. SIXTEEN-YEAR-OLD BOY GENIUS ON THE RUN. WHY THIS INTEREST IN THE HULK, YOUNG MAN?
MAYBE 'CAUSE HE WAS MY FRIEND. AND WHERE I COME FROM, FRIENDS DON'T SHOOT FRIENDS INTO OUTER SPACE.
DUDE, WHEN HE GETS BACK...
HE'S NOT COMING BACK.
OH, YEAH?
WE PICKED YOUR DESTINATION CAREFULLY. A LUSH PLANET, FULL OF VEGETATION AND GAME. BUT NO INTELLIGENT LIFE FORMS.
WE'LL JUST CROSS-CHECK THE DISTANCE CAPACITY OF THE SHUTTLE AGAINST THE MAP OF KNOWN WORLDS AND NARROW THE EARCH TO THE PLANETS TO WHICH YOU'VE ENT SATELLITES IN THE LAST TWO YEARS...
...AND BINGO. BR-54 IN THE TAYO SYSTEM. AND YOU EVEN HAVE A PROBE IN PLACE TO MONITOR THINGS.
IMPRESSIVE. WHAT'S YOUR TRICK, SON? MUTATION? CYBERNETIC IMPLANT?
I'M JUST SMART, SUCKA. NOW LET'S SEE--
A SPECIAL KIND OF SMART. YOU CAN PROCESS DATA LIKE NO ONE I'VE EVER SEEN...
NO ONE'S CHECKED THIS PROBE'S FINDINGS FOR MONTHS. YOU JUST FORGET ABOUT HIM, MR. RICHARDS?
... BUT YOU'RE YOUNG. UNDISCIPLINED. DANGEROUS.
YOU COULD HAVE KILLED THOSE S.H.I.E.L.D. AGENTS AT CONEY ISLAND.
DUDE, I RAN THE NUMBERS. I DON'T MAKE THOSE KINDS OF MISTAKES.
NOBODY'S THAT SMART.
SPEAK FOR YOURSELF. BY THE WAY, YOUR SEARCH LOGARITHMS ON THIS SATELLITE SUCK.
IT'S A S.H.I.E.L.D. MODEL. I HAVEN'T HAD TIME TO REPROGRAM IT. YOU NEED TO COME IN, AMADEUS. YOUR POTENTIAL IS...INCREDIBLE. YOU NEED TRAINING.
THE LAST PERSON WHO TOLD ME THAT BLEW UP MY PARENTS.
RUNNING MY FIX ON YOUR LAME CODE...

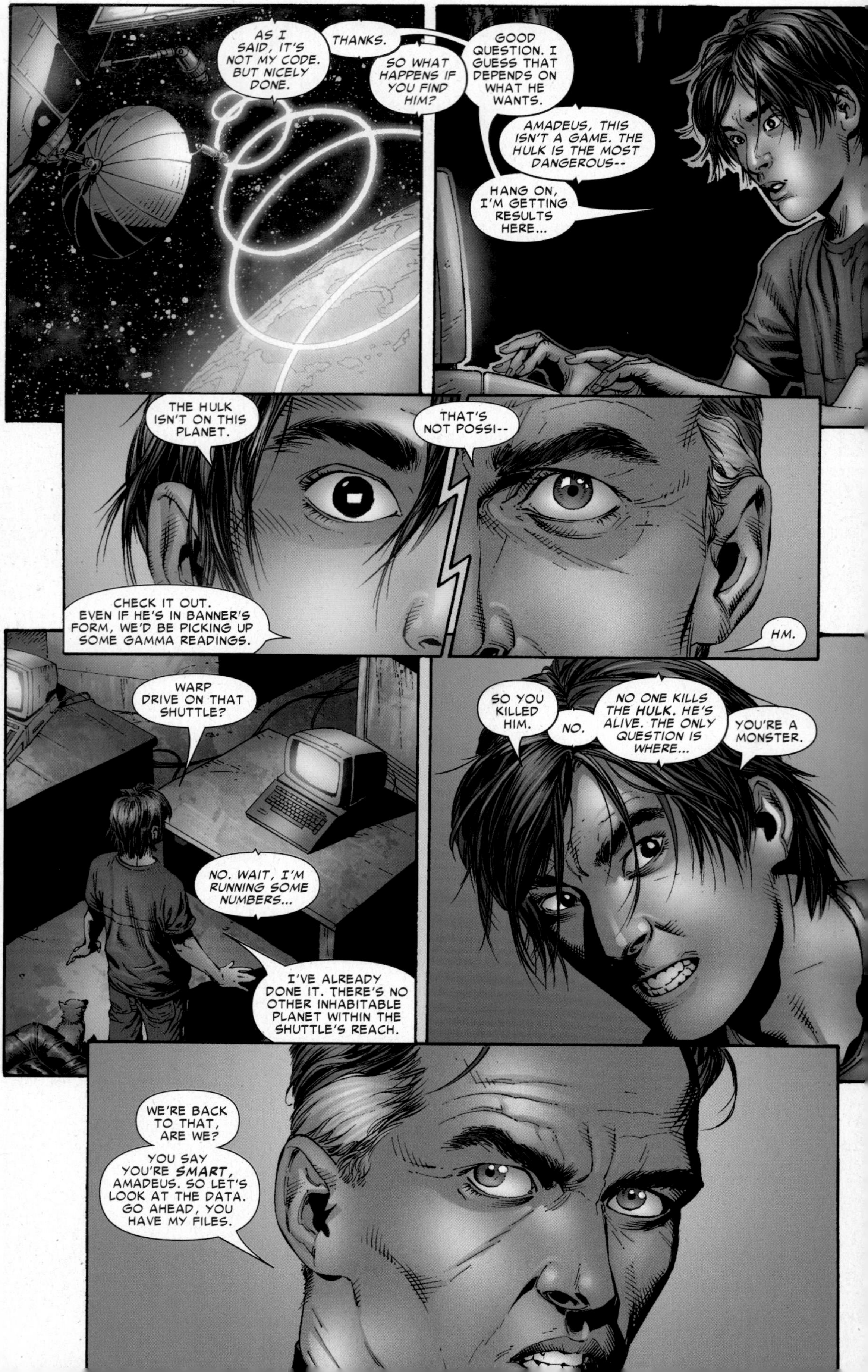
AS I SAID, IT'S NOT MY CODE. BUT NICELY DONE.
THANKS.
SO WHAT HAPPENS IF YOU FIND HIM?
GOOD QUESTION. I GUESS THAT DEPENDS ON WHAT HE WANTS.
AMADEUS, THIS ISN'T A GAME. THE HULK IS THE MOST DANGEROUS--
HANG ON, I'M GETTING RESULTS HERE...
THE HULK ISN'T ON THIS PLANET.
THAT'S NOT POSSI--
CHECK IT OUT. EVEN IF HE'S IN BANNER'S FORM, WE'D BE PICKING UP SOME GAMMA READINGS.
HM.
WARP DRIVE ON THAT SHUTTLE?
NO. WAIT, I'M RUNNING SOME NUMBERS...
I'VE ALREADY DONE IT. THERE'S NO OTHER INHABITABLE PLANET WITHIN THE SHUTTLE'S REACH.
SO YOU KILLED HIM.
NO.
NO ONE KILLS THE HULK. HE'S ALIVE. THE ONLY QUESTION IS WHERE...
YOU'RE A MONSTER.
WE'RE BACK TO THAT, ARE WE?
YOU SAY YOU'RE SMART, AMADEUS. SO LET'S LOOK AT THE DATA. GO AHEAD, YOU HAVE MY FILES.

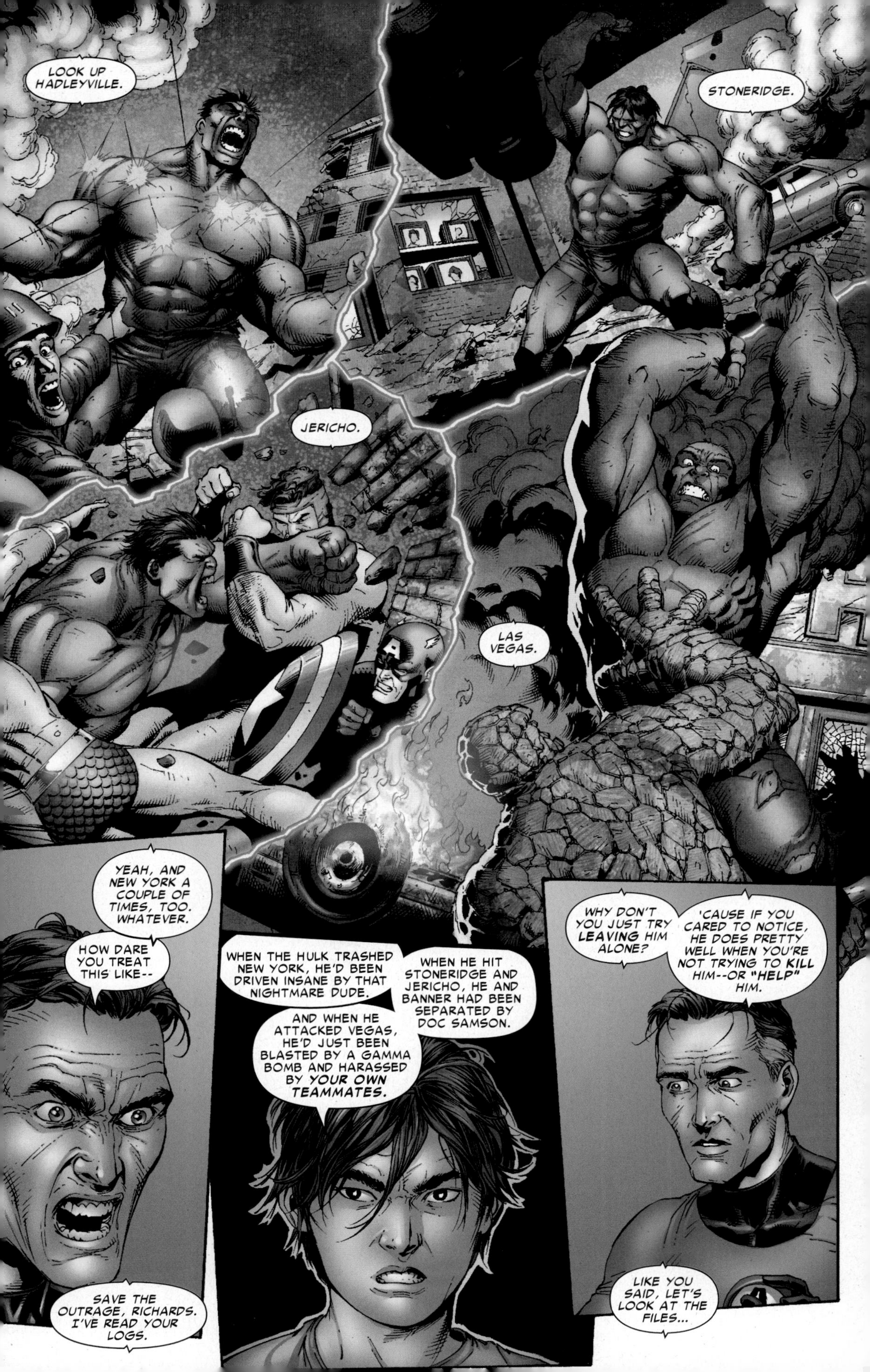
LOOK UP HADLEYVILLE.
STONERIDGE.
JERICHO.
LAS VEGAS.
YEAH, AND NEW YORK A COUPLE OF TIMES, TOO. WHATEVER.
HOW DARE YOU TREAT THIS LIKE--
SAVE THE OUTRAGE, RICHARDS. I'VE READ YOUR LOGS.
WHEN THE HULK TRASHED NEW YORK, HE'D BEEN DRIVEN INSANE BY THAT NIGHTMARE DUDE.
WHEN HE HIT STONERIDGE AND JERICHO, HE AND BANNER HAD BEEN SEPARATED BY DOC SAMSON.
AND WHEN HE ATTACKED VEGAS, HE'D JUST BEEN BLASTED BY A GAMMA BOMB AND HARASSED BY YOUR OWN TEAMMATES.
WHY DON'T YOU JUST TRY LEAVING HIM ALONE?
'CAUSE IF YOU CARED TO NOTICE, HE DOES PRETTY WELL WHEN YOU'RE NOT TRYING TO KILL HIM--OR "HELP" HIM.
LIKE YOU SAID, LET'S LOOK AT THE FILES...

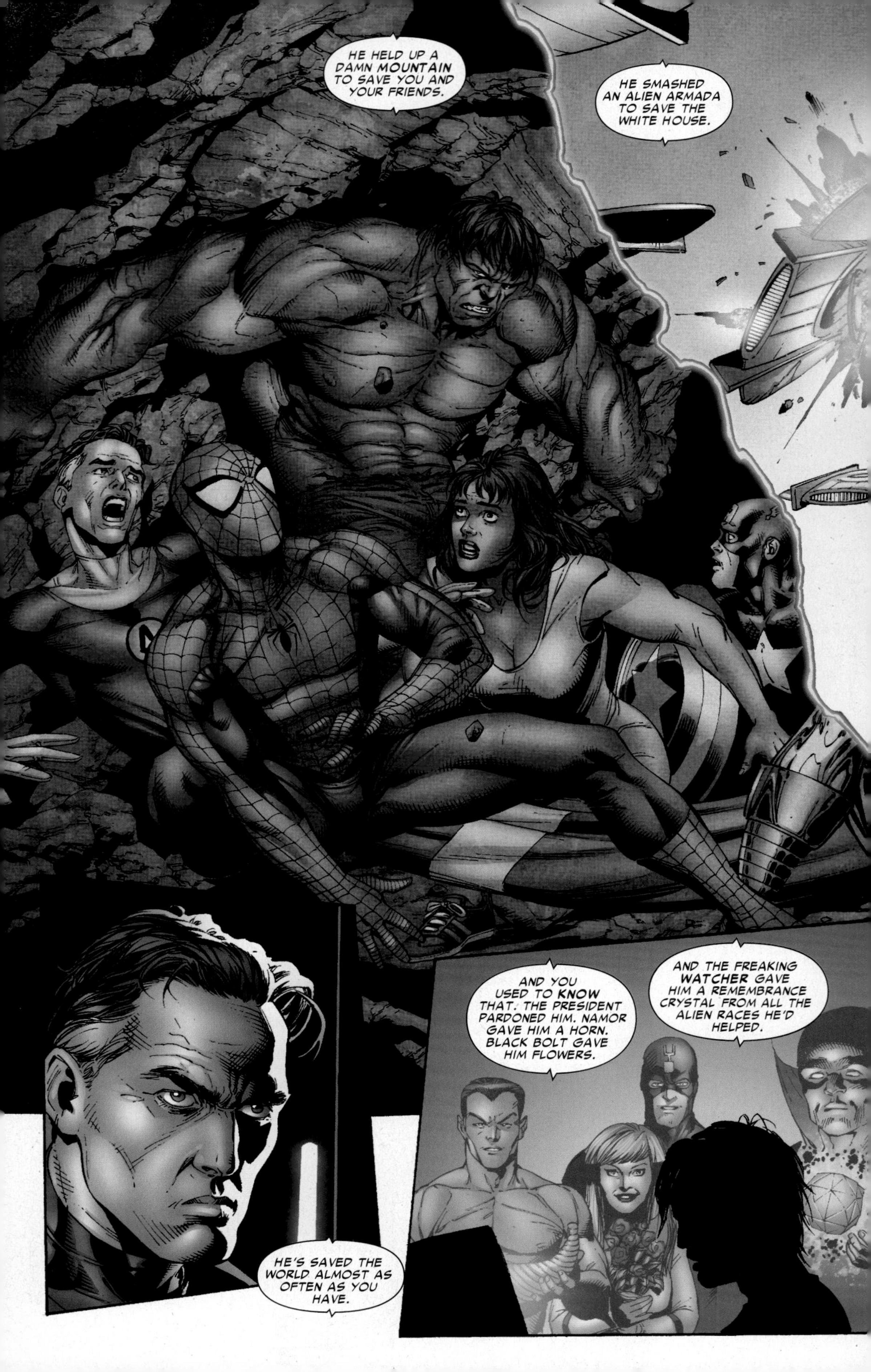
HE HELD UP A DAMN MOUNTAIN TO SAVE YOU AND YOUR FRIENDS.
HE SMASHED AN ALIEN ARMADA TO SAVE THE WHITE HOUSE.
HE'S SAVED THE WORLD ALMOST AS OFTEN AS YOU HAVE.
AND YOU USED TO KNOW THAT. THE PRESIDENT PARDONED HIM. NAMOR GAVE HIM A HORN. BLACK BOLT GAVE HIM FLOWERS.
AND THE FREAKING WATCHER GAVE HIM A REMEMBRANCE CRYSTAL FROM ALL THE ALIEN RACES HE'D HELPED.

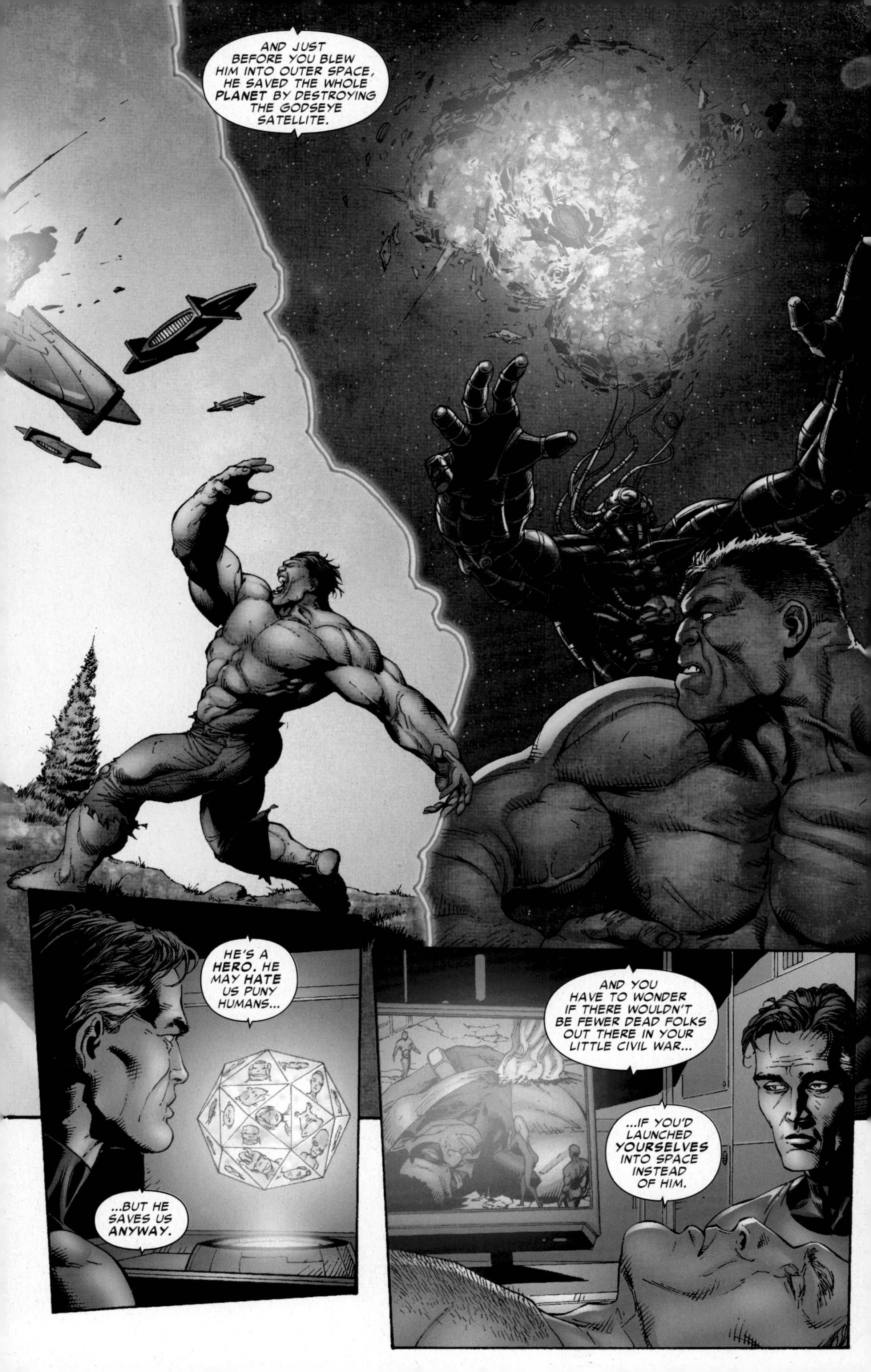
AND JUST BEFORE YOU BLEW HIM INTO OUTER SPACE, HE SAVED THE WHOLE PLANET BY DESTROYING THE GODSEYE SATELLITE.
HE'S A HERO. HE MAY HATE US PUNY HUMANS...
...BUT HE SAVES US ANYWAY.
AND YOU HAVE TO WONDER IF THERE WOULDN'T BE FEWER DEAD FOLKS OUT THERE IN YOUR LITTLE CIVIL WAR...
...IF YOU'D LAUNCHED YOURSELVES INTO SPACE INSTEAD OF HIM.

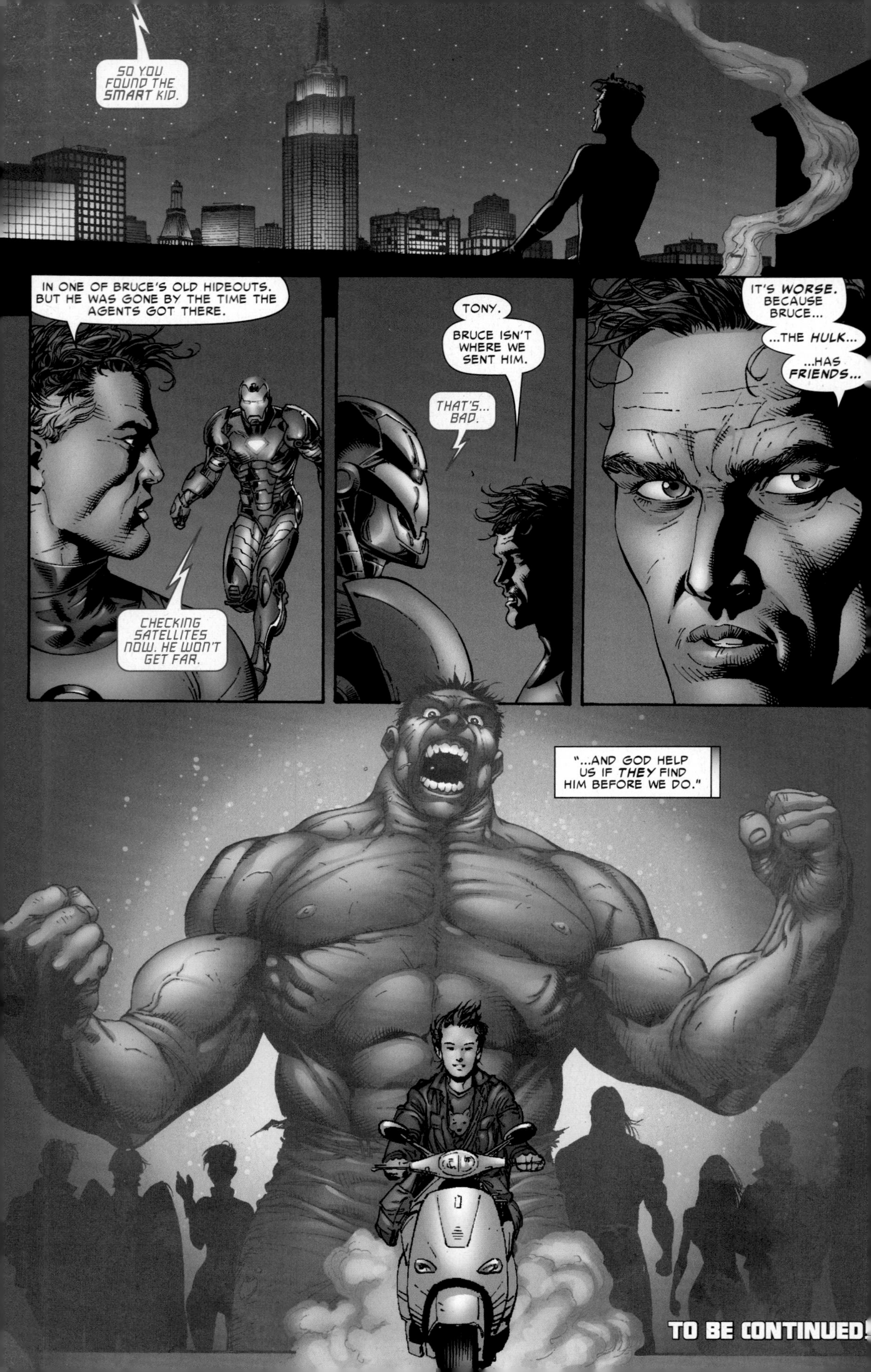

SO YOU FOUND THE SMART KID.
IN ONE OF BRUCE'S OLD HIDEOUTS. BUT HE WAS GONE BY THE TIME THE AGENTS GOT THERE.
CHECKING SATELLITES NOW. HE WON'T GET FAR.
TONY.
BRUCE ISN'T WHERE WE SENT HIM.
THAT'S... BAD.
IT'S WORSE. BECAUSE BRUCE...
...THE HULK...
...HAS FRIENDS...
"...AND GOD HELP US IF THEY FIND HIM BEFORE WE DO."
TO BE CONTINUED!

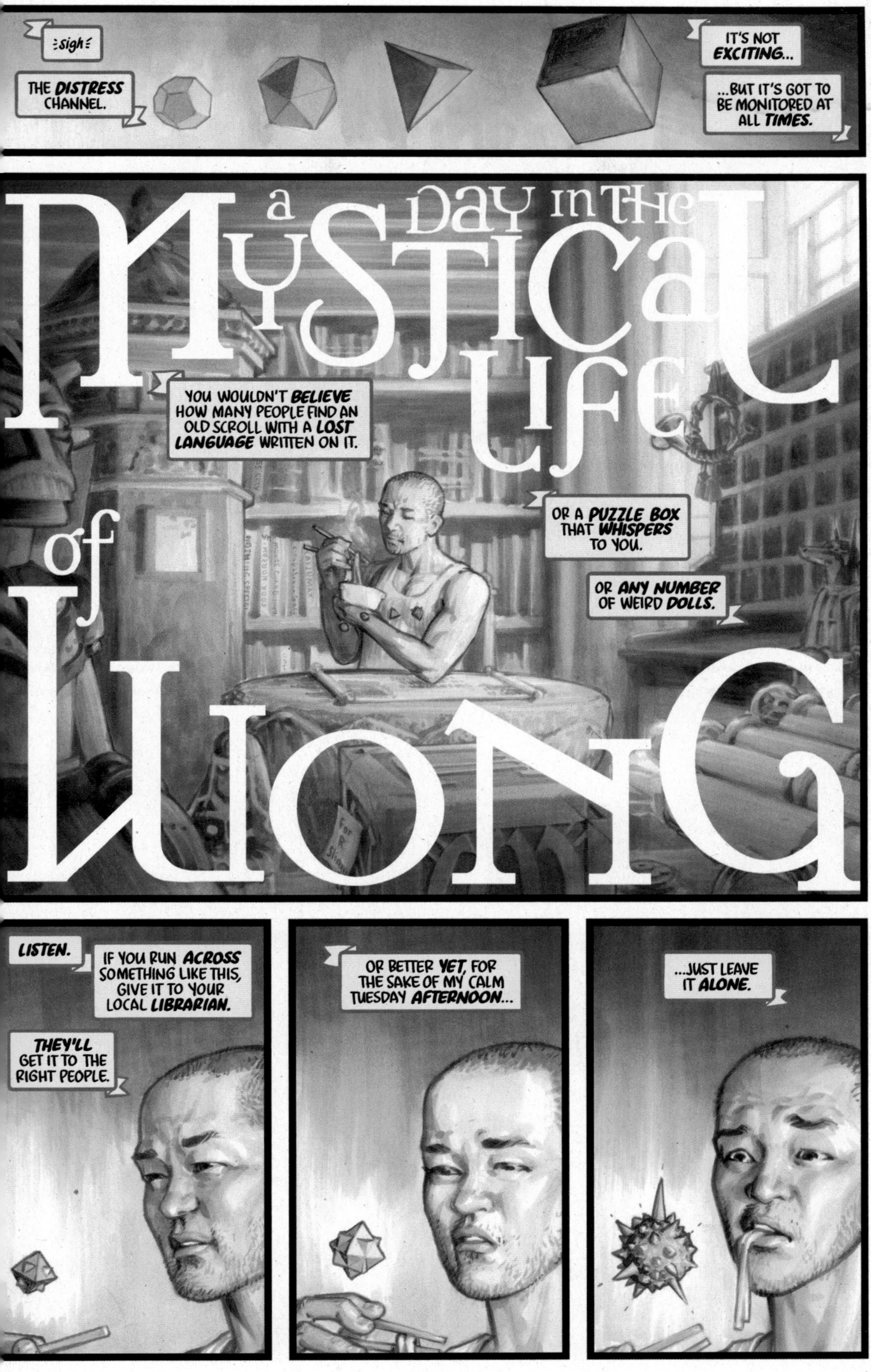
sigh
THE DISTRESS CHANNEL.
IT'S NOT EXCITING...
...BUT IT'S GOT TO BE MONITORED AT ALL TIMES.
a DAY in THE MYSTICAL LIFE of WONG
YOU WOULDN'T BELIEVE HOW MANY PEOPLE FIND AN OLD SCROLL WITH A LOST LANGUAGE WRITTEN ON IT.
OR A PUZZLE BOX THAT WHISPERS TO YOU.
OR ANY NUMBER OF WEIRD DOLLS.
LISTEN.
IF YOU RUN ACROSS SOMETHING LIKE THIS, GIVE IT TO YOUR LOCAL LIBRARIAN.
THEY'LL GET IT TO THE RIGHT PEOPLE.
OR BETTER YET, FOR THE SAKE OF MY CALM TUESDAY AFTERNOON...
...JUST LEAVE IT ALONE.

STRANGE?

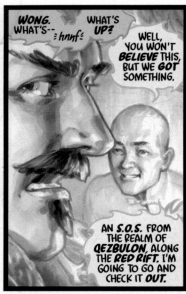

WONG. WHAT'S-- WHAT'S ₹hnnf₹ UP?

WELL, YOU WON'T *BELIEVE* THIS, BUT WE *GOT* SOMETHING.

AN *S.O.S.* FROM THE REALM OF *QEZBULON*, ALONG THE *RED RIFT*. I'M GOING TO GO AND CHECK IT *OUT*.

TO THE *RED RIFT? REALLY?* NO ONE'S BEEN THROUGH *THERE* IN--

I *KNOW*. I'M SURE IT'S SOME *RICH KIDS* FROM THAT *BOARDING SCHOOL*. GOT IN OVER THEIR *HEADS*, TRIED TO SUMMON A *DEMON PET* OR WHATEVER--

I'LL *HANDLE* IT.

WAIT, WHERE *ARE* YOU NOW?

₹hnnf₹ MILWAUKEE.

WONG, I REALLY HAVE TO *GO*.

THERE ARE *TECHNOMAGICAL HUMAN HYBRIDS* COMING THROUGH TIME PORTALS, AND IT'S JUST A LITTLE *CRAZY* AT THE MOMENT--

OH, WOW, *MILWAUKEE*, huh?

LISTEN, THERE'S A *BANH MI SHOP* CALLED *CHU'S* THERE. IF YOU HAVE A *SECOND*, DO YOU THINK YOU COULD PICK SOMETHING *UP?* THE ONE HERE'S A *CHAIN* AND IT'S ALL *FUSION-Y*--

UH, YEAH, *SURE.*

WHEN I *GET* A SECOND.

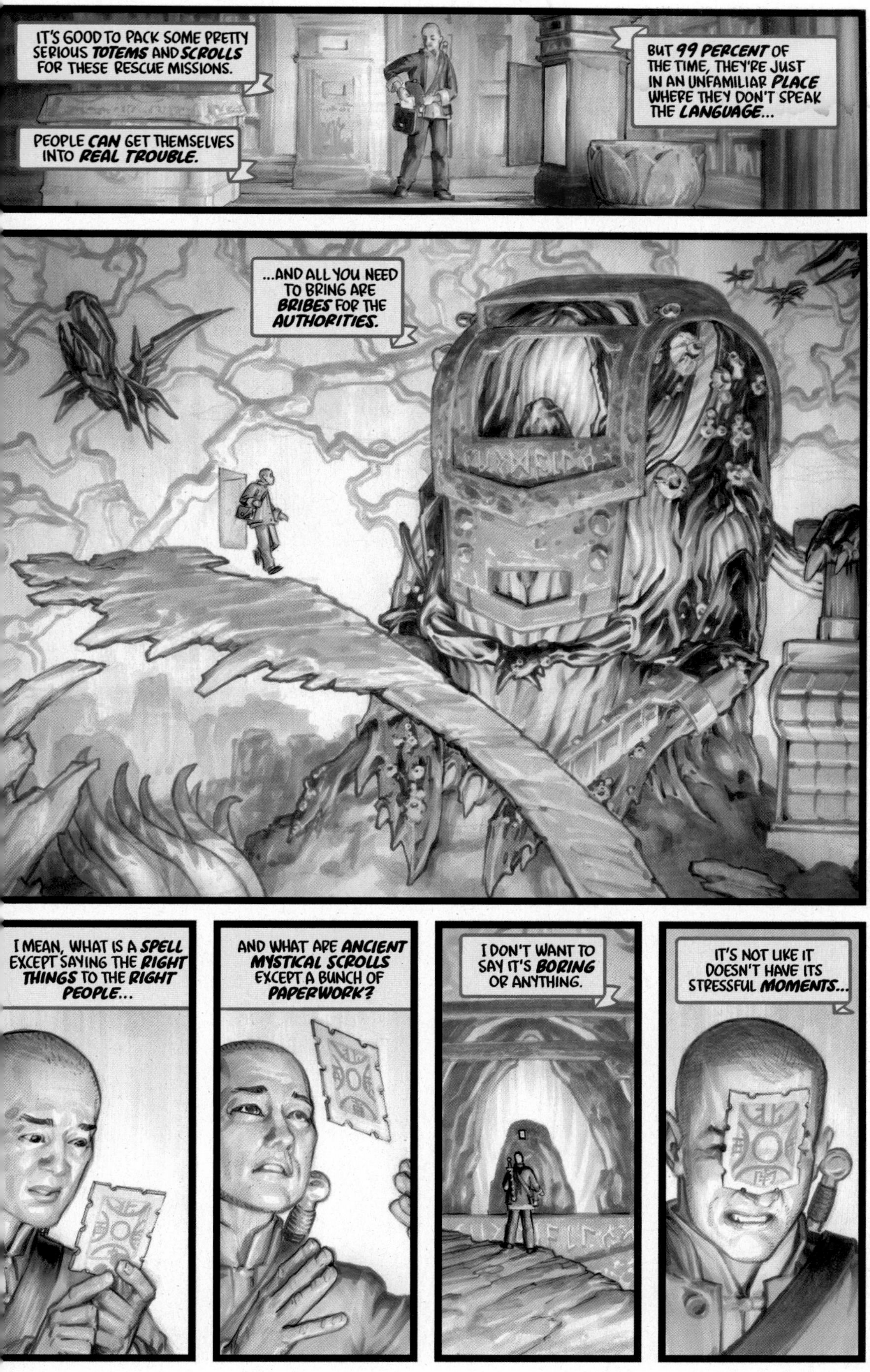
IT'S GOOD TO PACK SOME PRETTY SERIOUS TOTEMS AND SCROLLS FOR THESE RESCUE MISSIONS.
PEOPLE CAN GET THEMSELVES INTO REAL TROUBLE.
BUT 99 PERCENT OF THE TIME, THEY'RE JUST IN AN UNFAMILIAR PLACE WHERE THEY DON'T SPEAK THE LANGUAGE...
...AND ALL YOU NEED TO BRING ARE BRIBES FOR THE AUTHORITIES.
I MEAN, WHAT IS A SPELL EXCEPT SAYING THE RIGHT THINGS TO THE RIGHT PEOPLE...
AND WHAT ARE ANCIENT MYSTICAL SCROLLS EXCEPT A BUNCH OF PAPERWORK?
I DON'T WANT TO SAY IT'S BORING OR ANYTHING.
IT'S NOT LIKE IT DOESN'T HAVE ITS STRESSFUL MOMENTS...

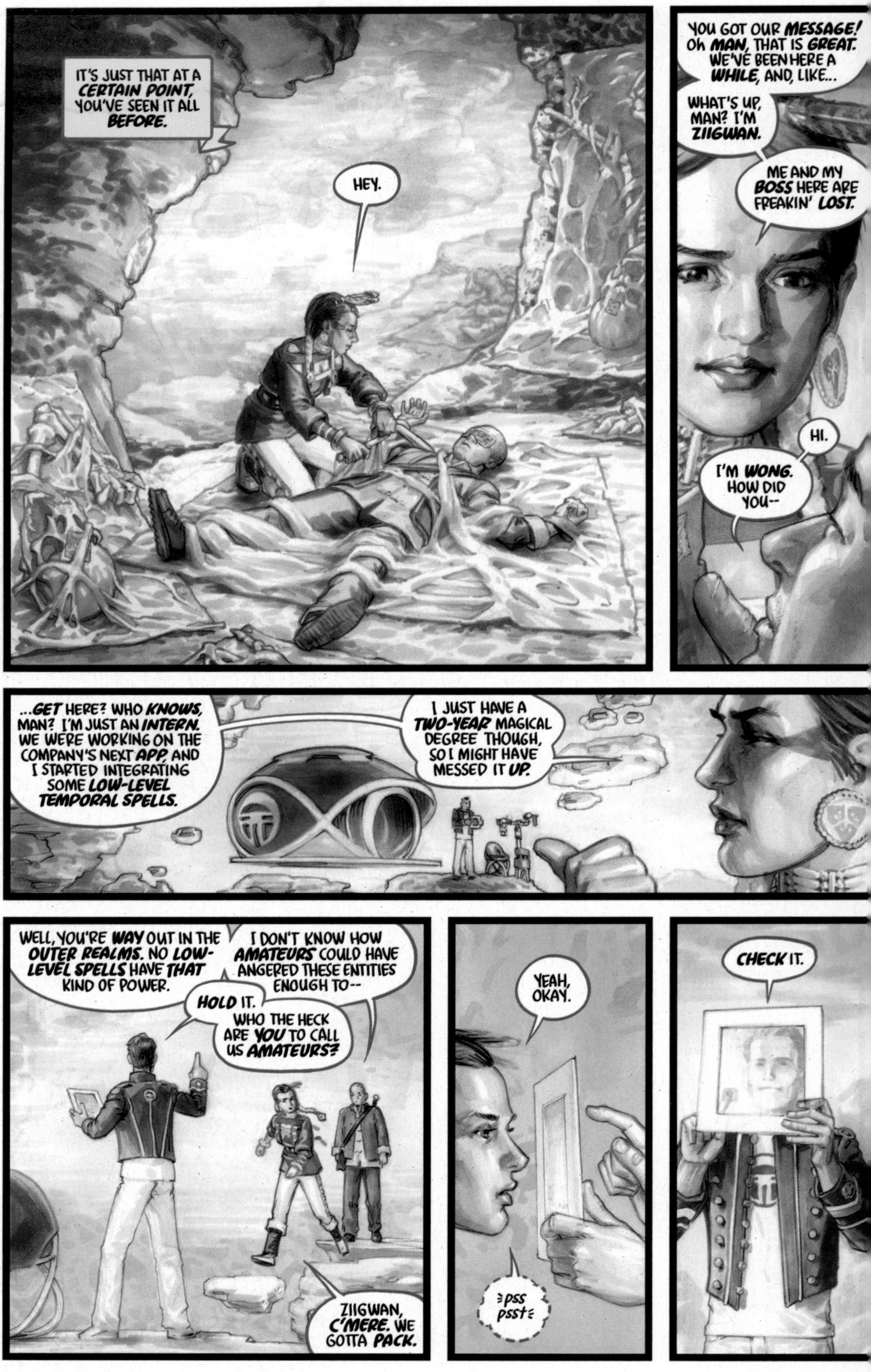
IT'S JUST THAT AT A CERTAIN POINT, YOU'VE SEEN IT ALL BEFORE.
HEY.
YOU GOT OUR MESSAGE! Oh MAN, THAT IS GREAT. WE'VE BEEN HERE A WHILE, AND, LIKE...
WHAT'S UP, MAN? I'M ZIIGWAN.
ME AND MY BOSS HERE ARE FREAKIN' LOST.
HI.
I'M WONG. HOW DID YOU--
...GET HERE? WHO KNOWS, MAN? I'M JUST AN INTERN. WE WERE WORKING ON THE COMPANY'S NEXT APP, AND I STARTED INTEGRATING SOME LOW-LEVEL TEMPORAL SPELLS.
I JUST HAVE A TWO-YEAR MAGICAL DEGREE THOUGH, SO I MIGHT HAVE MESSED IT UP.
WELL, YOU'RE WAY OUT IN THE OUTER REALMS. NO LOW-LEVEL SPELLS HAVE THAT KIND OF POWER.
I DON'T KNOW HOW AMATEURS COULD HAVE ANGERED THESE ENTITIES ENOUGH TO--
HOLD IT.
WHO THE HECK ARE YOU TO CALL US AMATEURS?
ZIIGWAN, C'MERE. WE GOTTA PACK.
YEAH, OKAY.
pss psst
CHECK IT.

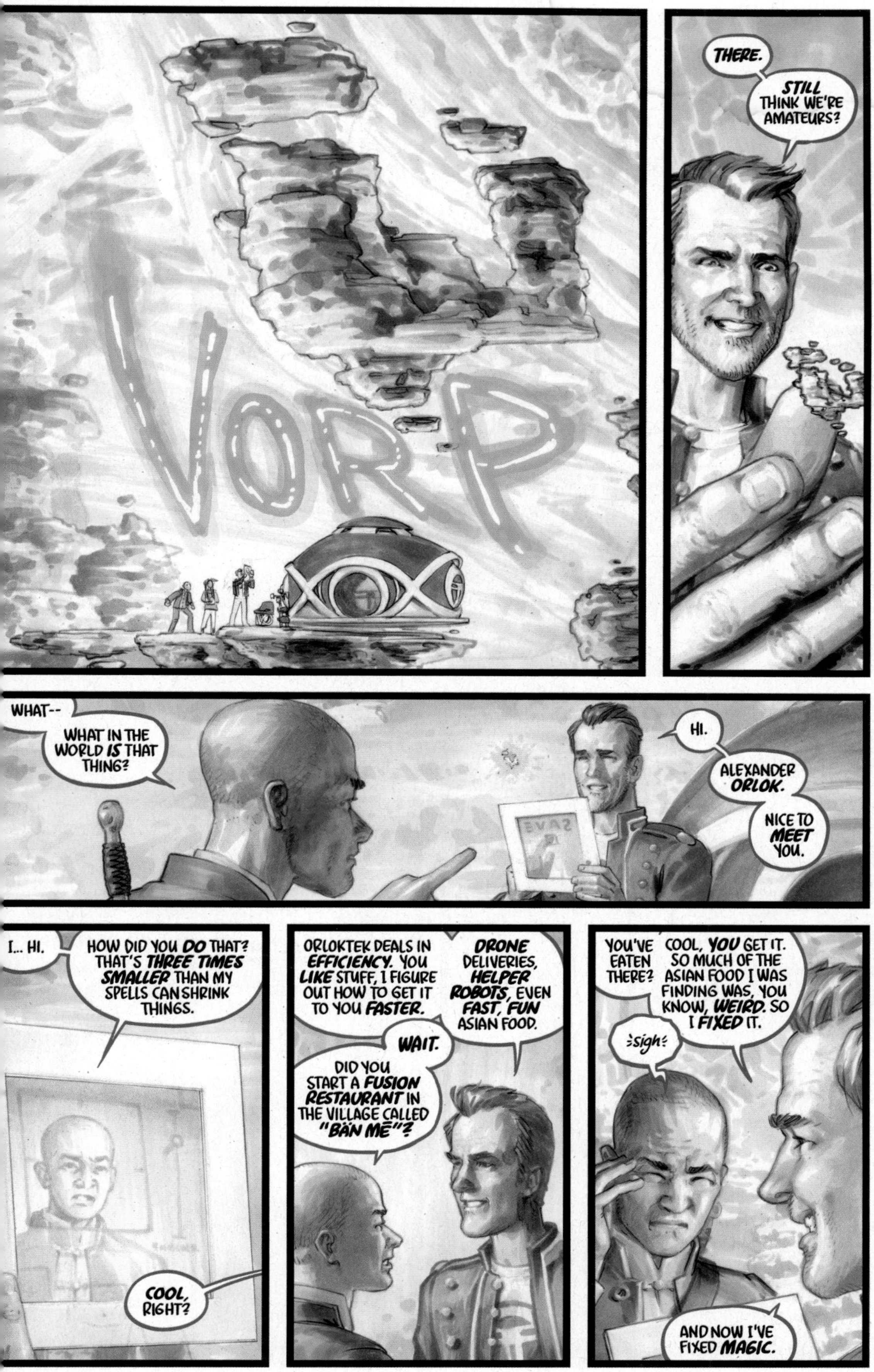
VORP
THERE.
STILL THINK WE'RE AMATEURS?
WHAT--
WHAT IN THE WORLD IS THAT THING?
HI.
ALEXANDER ORLOK.
NICE TO MEET YOU.
I... HI.
HOW DID YOU DO THAT? THAT'S THREE TIMES SMALLER THAN MY SPELLS CAN SHRINK THINGS.
COOL, RIGHT?
ORLOKTEK DEALS IN EFFICIENCY. YOU LIKE STUFF, I FIGURE OUT HOW TO GET IT TO YOU FASTER.
DRONE DELIVERIES, HELPER ROBOTS, EVEN FAST, FUN ASIAN FOOD.
WAIT.
DID YOU START A FUSION RESTAURANT IN THE VILLAGE CALLED "BÄN MĒ"?
YOU'VE EATEN THERE?
COOL, YOU GET IT. SO MUCH OF THE ASIAN FOOD I WAS FINDING WAS, YOU KNOW, WEIRD. SO I FIXED IT.
sigh
AND NOW I'VE FIXED MAGIC.

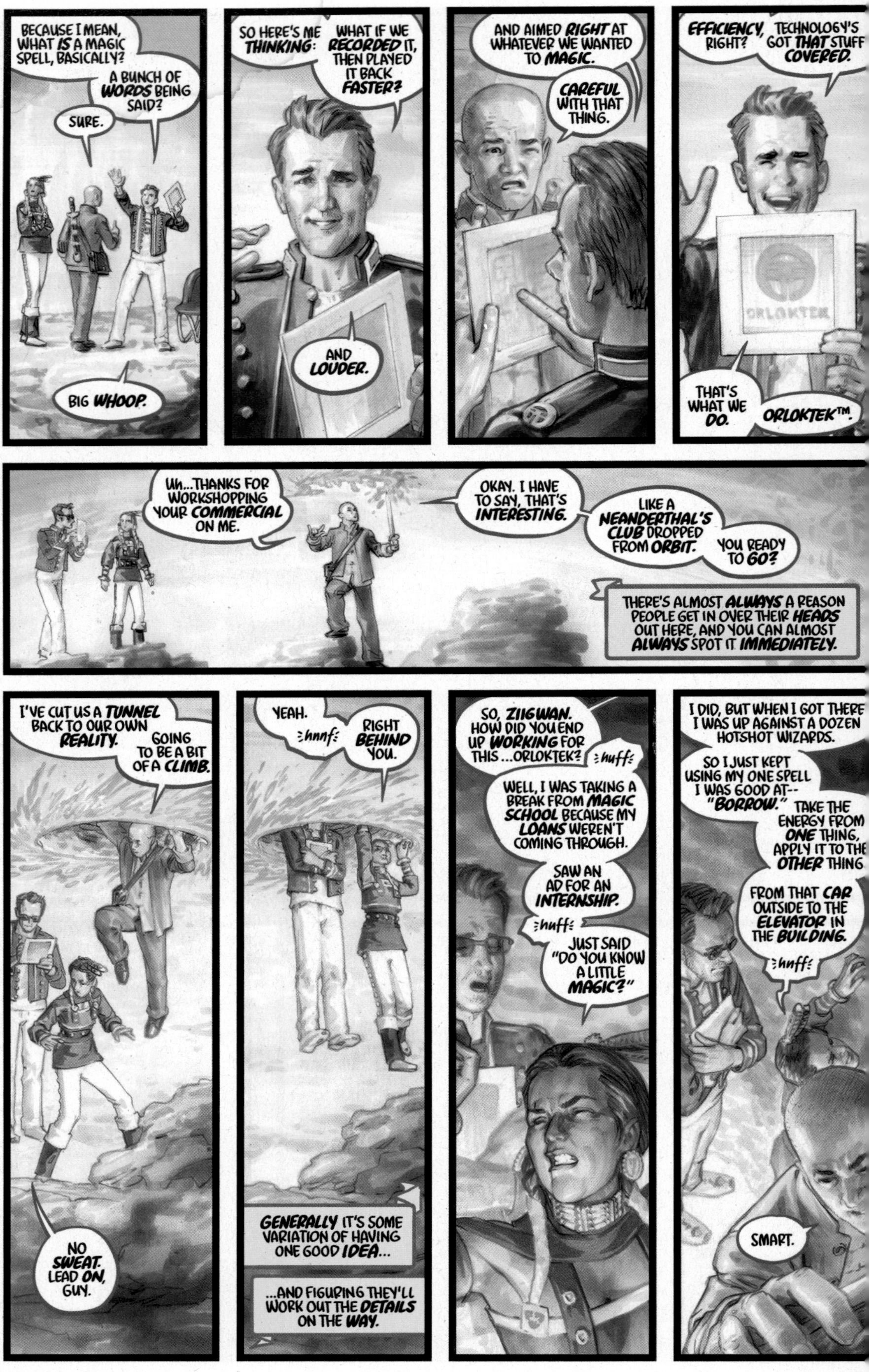

BECAUSE I MEAN, WHAT IS A MAGIC SPELL, BASICALLY?
A BUNCH OF WORDS BEING SAID?
SURE.
BIG WHOOP.
SO HERE'S ME THINKING:
WHAT IF WE RECORDED IT, THEN PLAYED IT BACK FASTER?
AND LOUDER.
AND AIMED RIGHT AT WHATEVER WE WANTED TO MAGIC.
CAREFUL WITH THAT THING.
EFFICIENCY, RIGHT?
TECHNOLOGY'S GOT THAT STUFF COVERED.
ORLOKTEK
THAT'S WHAT WE DO.
ORLOKTEK™.
Uh...THANKS FOR WORKSHOPPING YOUR COMMERCIAL ON ME.
OKAY. I HAVE TO SAY, THAT'S INTERESTING.
LIKE A NEANDERTHAL'S CLUB DROPPED FROM ORBIT.
YOU READY TO GO?
THERE'S ALMOST ALWAYS A REASON PEOPLE GET IN OVER THEIR HEADS OUT HERE, AND YOU CAN ALMOST ALWAYS SPOT IT IMMEDIATELY.
I'VE CUT US A TUNNEL BACK TO OUR OWN REALITY.
GOING TO BE A BIT OF A CLIMB.
NO SWEAT. LEAD ON, GUY.
YEAH.
hnnf
RIGHT BEHIND YOU.
GENERALLY IT'S SOME VARIATION OF HAVING ONE GOOD IDEA...
...AND FIGURING THEY'LL WORK OUT THE DETAILS ON THE WAY.
SO, ZIGWAN. HOW DID YOU END UP WORKING FOR THIS ...ORLOKTEK?
huff
WELL, I WAS TAKING A BREAK FROM MAGIC SCHOOL BECAUSE MY LOANS WEREN'T COMING THROUGH.
SAW AN AD FOR AN INTERNSHIP.
huff
JUST SAID "DO YOU KNOW A LITTLE MAGIC?"
I DID, BUT WHEN I GOT THERE I WAS UP AGAINST A DOZEN HOTSHOT WIZARDS.
SO I JUST KEPT USING MY ONE SPELL I WAS GOOD AT-- "BORROW."
TAKE THE ENERGY FROM ONE THING, APPLY IT TO THE OTHER THING.
FROM THAT CAR OUTSIDE TO THE ELEVATOR IN THE BUILDING.
hnff
SMART.

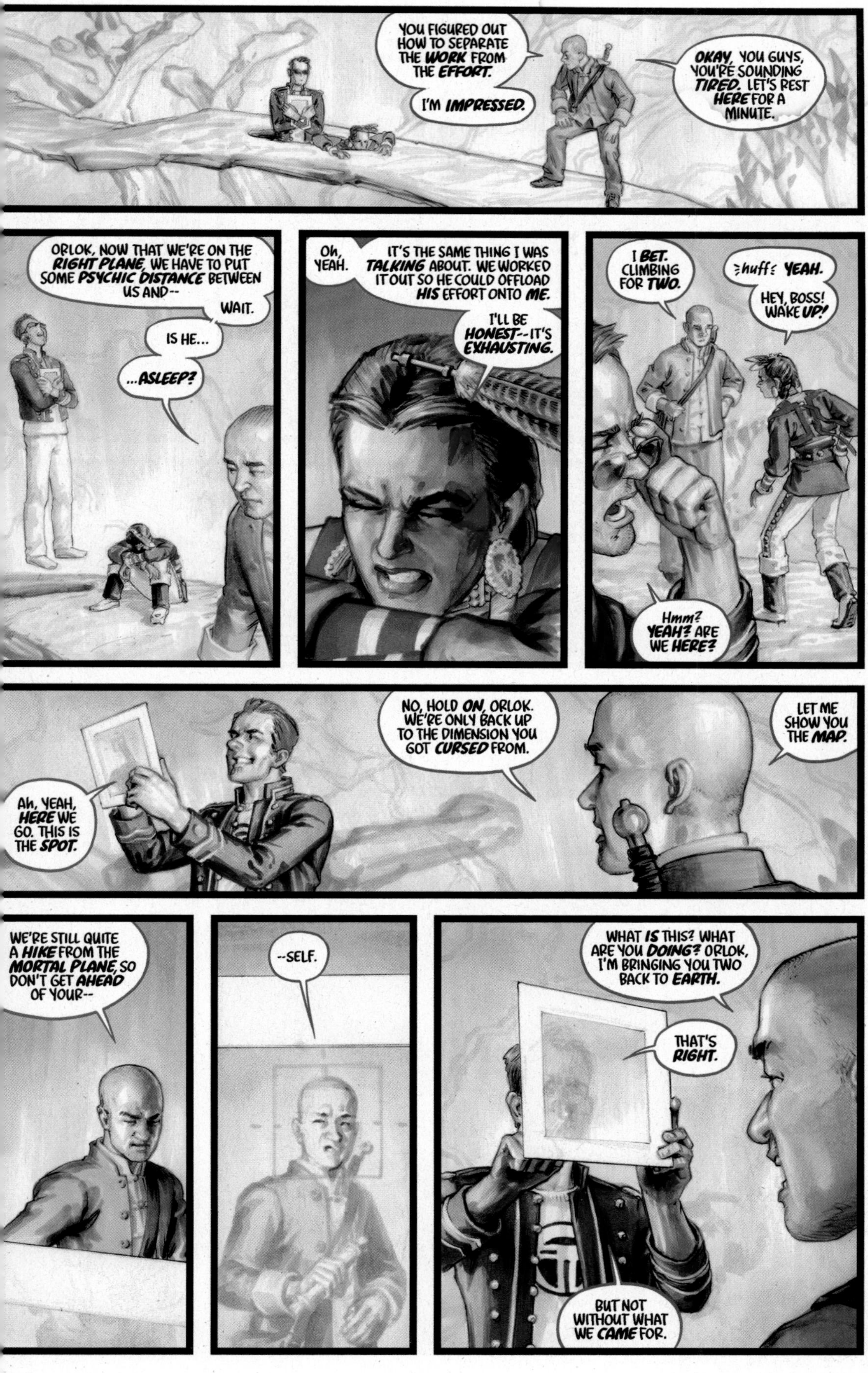
YOU FIGURED OUT HOW TO SEPARATE THE WORK FROM THE EFFORT.
I'M IMPRESSED.
OKAY, YOU GUYS, YOU'RE SOUNDING TIRED. LET'S REST HERE FOR A MINUTE.
ORLOK, NOW THAT WE'RE ON THE RIGHT PLANE, WE HAVE TO PUT SOME PSYCHIC DISTANCE BETWEEN US AND--
WAIT.
IS HE...
...ASLEEP?
Oh, YEAH.
IT'S THE SAME THING I WAS TALKING ABOUT. WE WORKED IT OUT SO HE COULD OFFLOAD HIS EFFORT ONTO ME.
I'LL BE HONEST--IT'S EXHAUSTING.
I BET. CLIMBING FOR TWO.
huff YEAH.
HEY, BOSS! WAKE UP!
Hmm? YEAH? ARE WE HERE?
Ah, YEAH, HERE WE GO. THIS IS THE SPOT.
NO, HOLD ON, ORLOK. WE'RE ONLY BACK UP TO THE DIMENSION YOU GOT CURSED FROM.
LET ME SHOW YOU THE MAP.
WE'RE STILL QUITE A HIKE FROM THE MORTAL PLANE, SO DON'T GET AHEAD OF YOUR--
--SELF.
WHAT IS THIS? WHAT ARE YOU DOING? ORLOK, I'M BRINGING YOU TWO BACK TO EARTH.
THAT'S RIGHT.
BUT NOT WITHOUT WHAT WE CAME FOR.

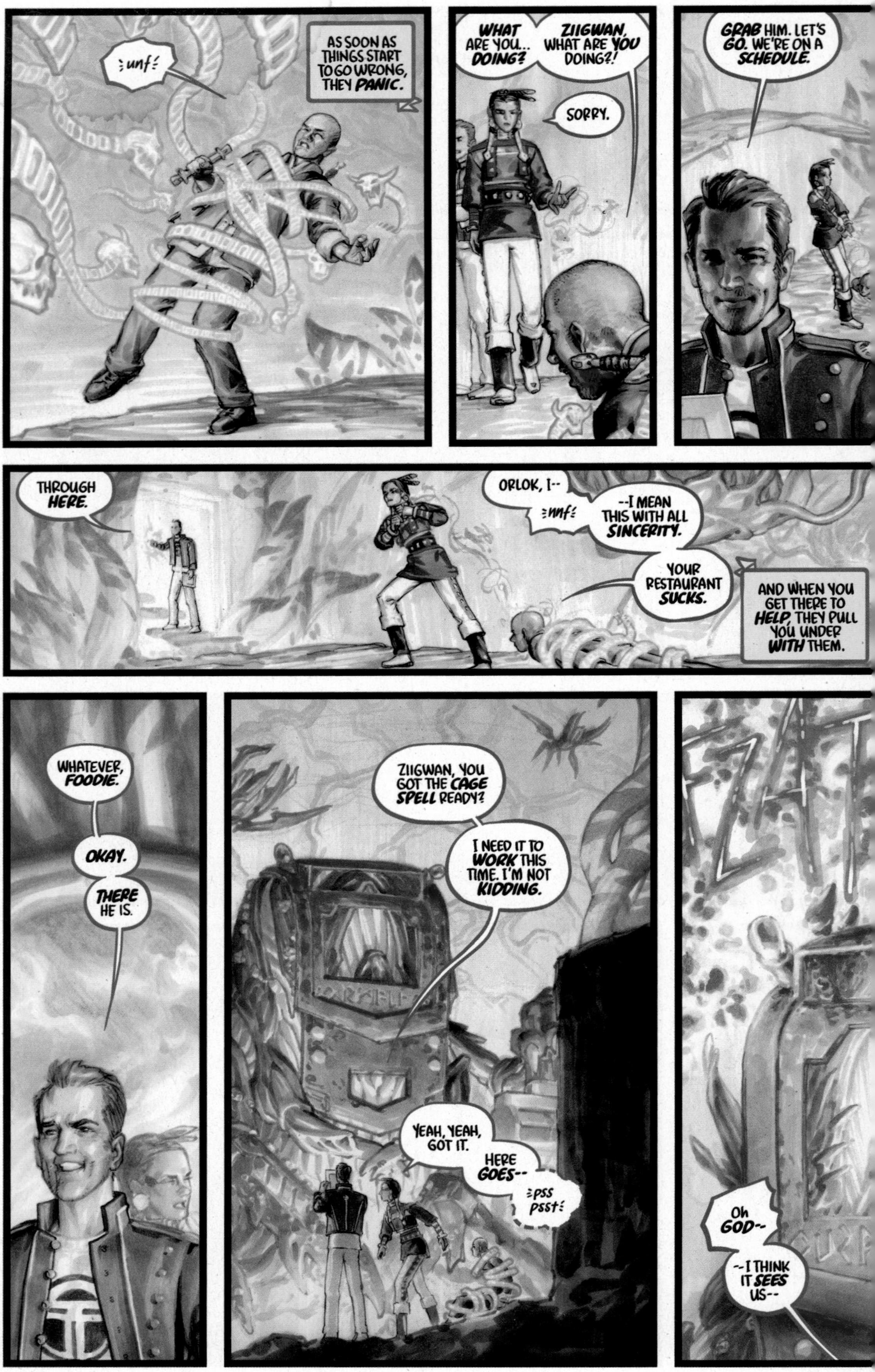

AS SOON AS THINGS START TO GO WRONG, THEY PANIC.
unf
WHAT ARE YOU... DOING?
ZIIGWAN, WHAT ARE YOU DOING?!
SORRY.
GRAB HIM. LET'S GO. WE'RE ON A SCHEDULE.
THROUGH HERE.
ORLOK, I--
unf
--I MEAN THIS WITH ALL SINCERITY.
YOUR RESTAURANT SUCKS.
AND WHEN YOU GET THERE TO HELP, THEY PULL YOU UNDER WITH THEM.
WHATEVER, FOODIE.
OKAY.
THERE HE IS.
ZIIGWAN, YOU GOT THE CAGE SPELL READY?
I NEED IT TO WORK THIS TIME. I'M NOT KIDDING.
YEAH, YEAH, GOT IT.
HERE GOES--
pss psst
Oh GOD--
--I THINK IT SEES US--

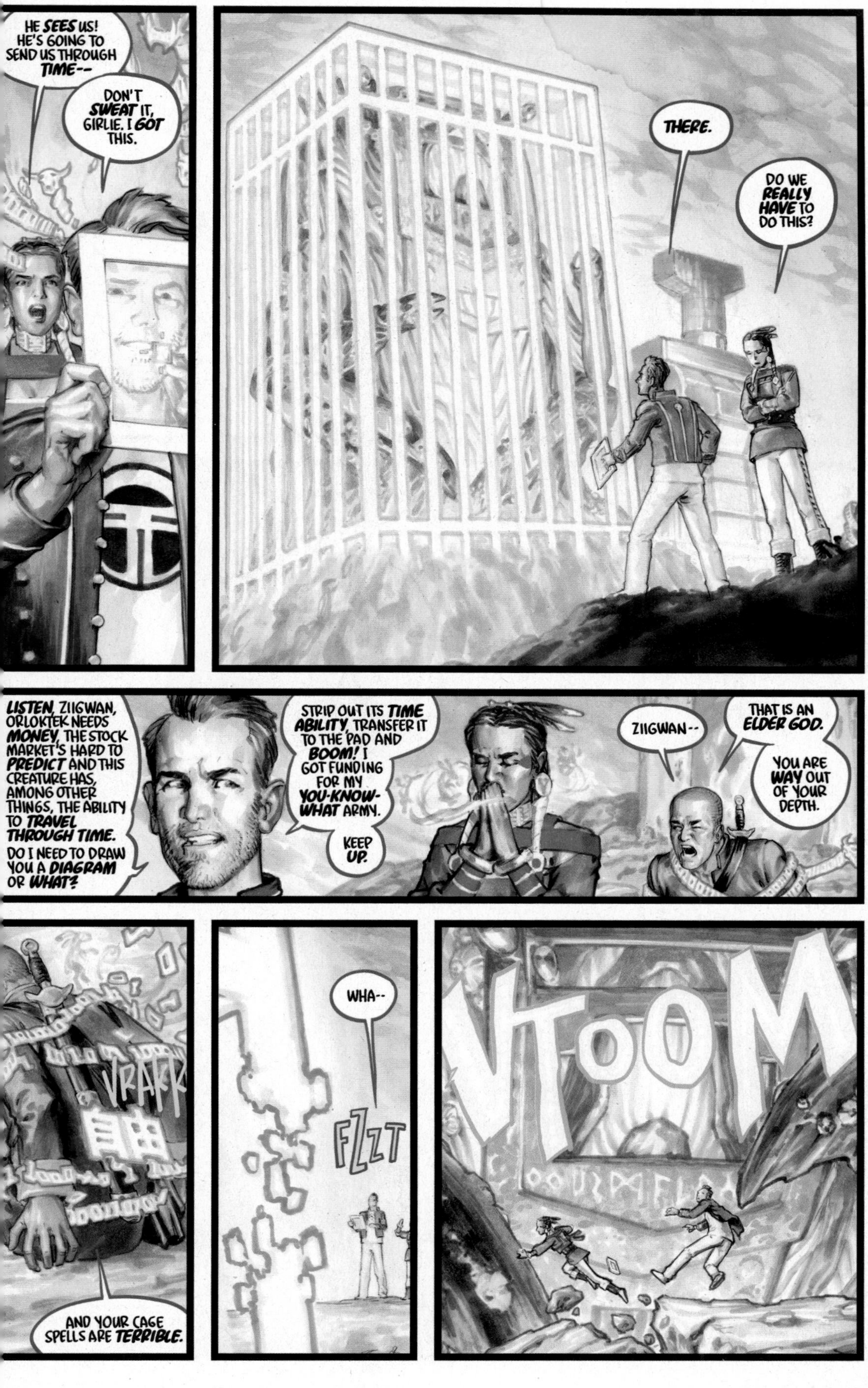

HE SEES US! HE'S GOING TO SEND US THROUGH TIME--
DON'T SWEAT IT, GIRLIE. I GOT THIS.
THERE.
DO WE REALLY HAVE TO DO THIS?
LISTEN, ZIIGWAN, ORLOKTEK NEEDS MONEY, THE STOCK MARKET'S HARD TO PREDICT AND THIS CREATURE HAS, AMONG OTHER THINGS, THE ABILITY TO TRAVEL THROUGH TIME.
DO I NEED TO DRAW YOU A DIAGRAM OR WHAT?
STRIP OUT ITS TIME ABILITY, TRANSFER IT TO THE PAD AND BOOM! I GOT FUNDING FOR MY YOU-KNOW-WHAT ARMY.
KEEP UP.
ZIIGWAN--
THAT IS AN ELDER GOD.
YOU ARE WAY OUT OF YOUR DEPTH.
VRAKK
AND YOUR CAGE SPELLS ARE TERRIBLE.
WHA--
FZZT
VTOOM

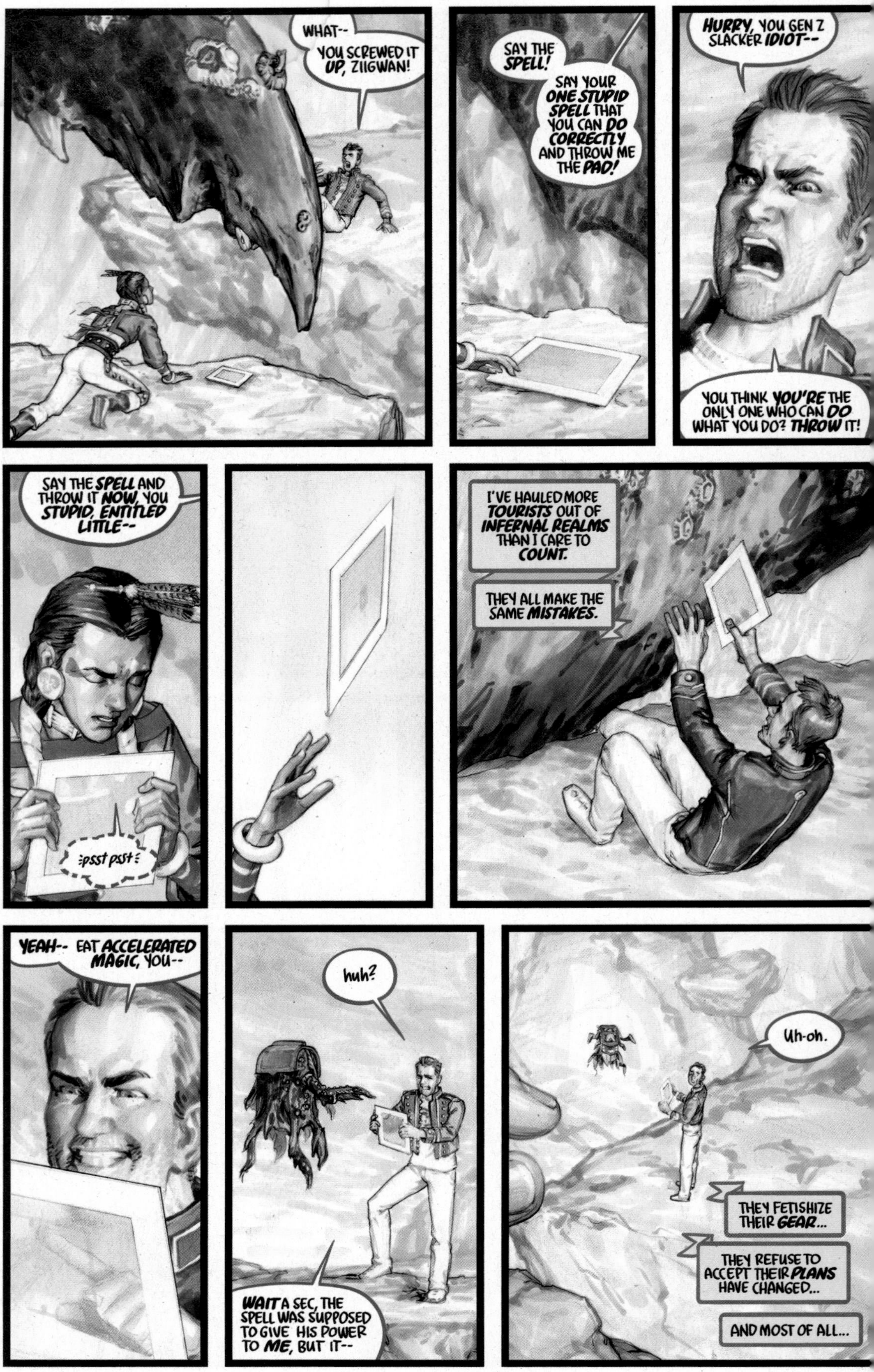
WHAT--
YOU SCREWED IT UP, ZIIGWAN!
SAY THE SPELL!
SAY YOUR ONE STUPID SPELL THAT YOU CAN DO CORRECTLY AND THROW ME THE PAD!
HURRY, YOU GEN Z SLACKER IDIOT--
YOU THINK YOU'RE THE ONLY ONE WHO CAN DO WHAT YOU DO? THROW IT!
SAY THE SPELL AND THROW IT NOW, YOU STUPID, ENTITLED LITTLE--
psst psst
I'VE HAULED MORE TOURISTS OUT OF INFERNAL REALMS THAN I CARE TO COUNT.
THEY ALL MAKE THE SAME MISTAKES.
YEAH-- EAT ACCELERATED MAGIC, YOU--
huh?
WAIT A SEC, THE SPELL WAS SUPPOSED TO GIVE HIS POWER TO ME, BUT IT--
Uh-oh.
THEY FETISHIZE THEIR GEAR...
THEY REFUSE TO ACCEPT THEIR PLANS HAVE CHANGED...
AND MOST OF ALL...

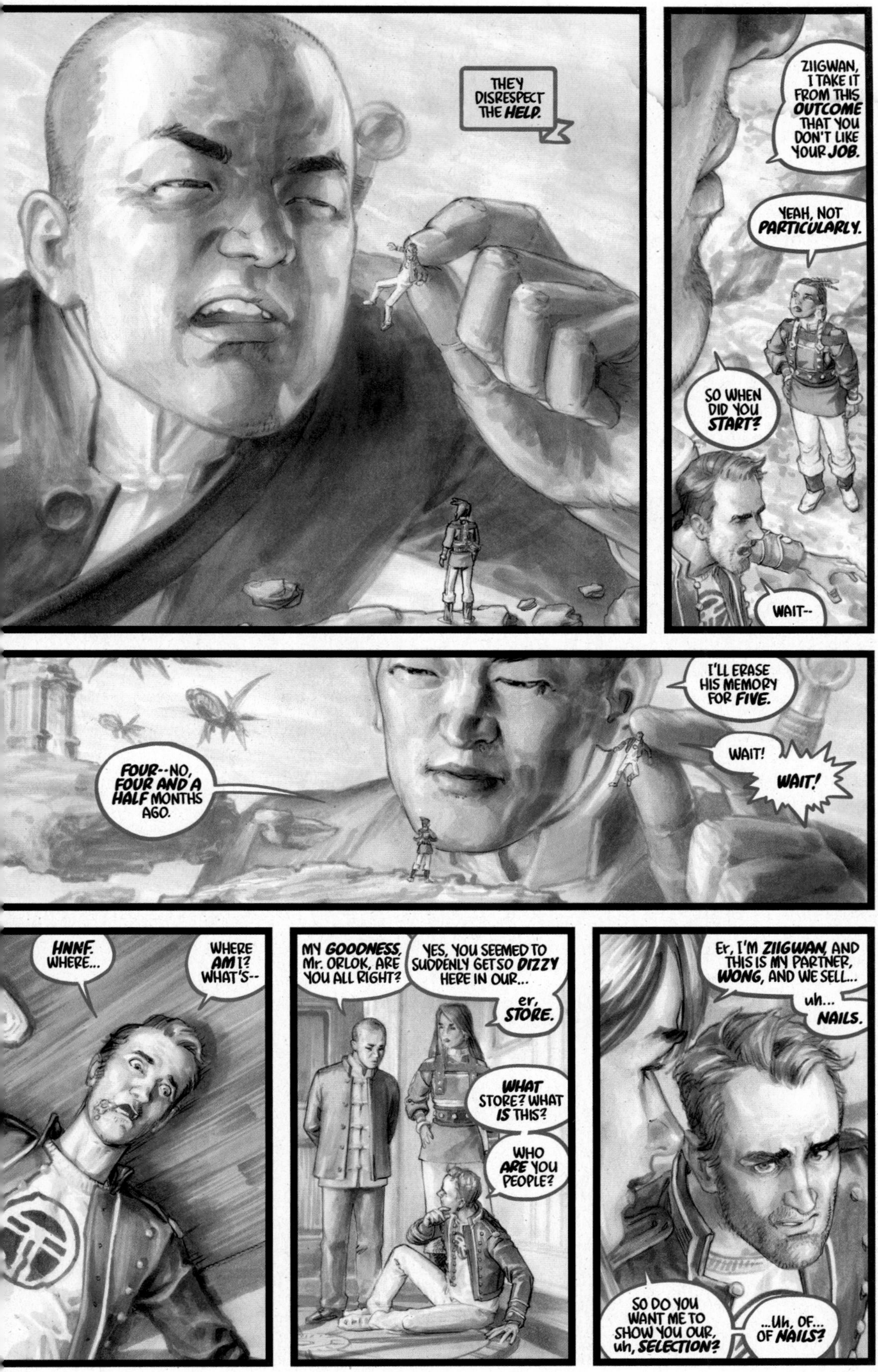
THEY DISRESPECT THE HELP.
ZIIGWAN, I TAKE IT FROM THIS OUTCOME THAT YOU DON'T LIKE YOUR JOB.
YEAH, NOT PARTICULARLY.
SO WHEN DID YOU START?
WAIT--
FOUR--NO, FOUR AND A HALF MONTHS AGO.
I'LL ERASE HIS MEMORY FOR FIVE.
WAIT!
WAIT!
HNNF. WHERE...
WHERE AM I? WHAT'S--
MY GOODNESS, Mr. ORLOK, ARE YOU ALL RIGHT?
YES, YOU SEEMED TO SUDDENLY GET SO DIZZY HERE IN OUR...
er, STORE.
WHAT STORE? WHAT IS THIS?
WHO ARE YOU PEOPLE?
Er, I'M ZIIGWAN, AND THIS IS MY PARTNER, WONG, AND WE SELL...
uh... NAILS.
SO DO YOU WANT ME TO SHOW YOU OUR, uh, SELECTION?
...Uh, OF... OF NAILS?

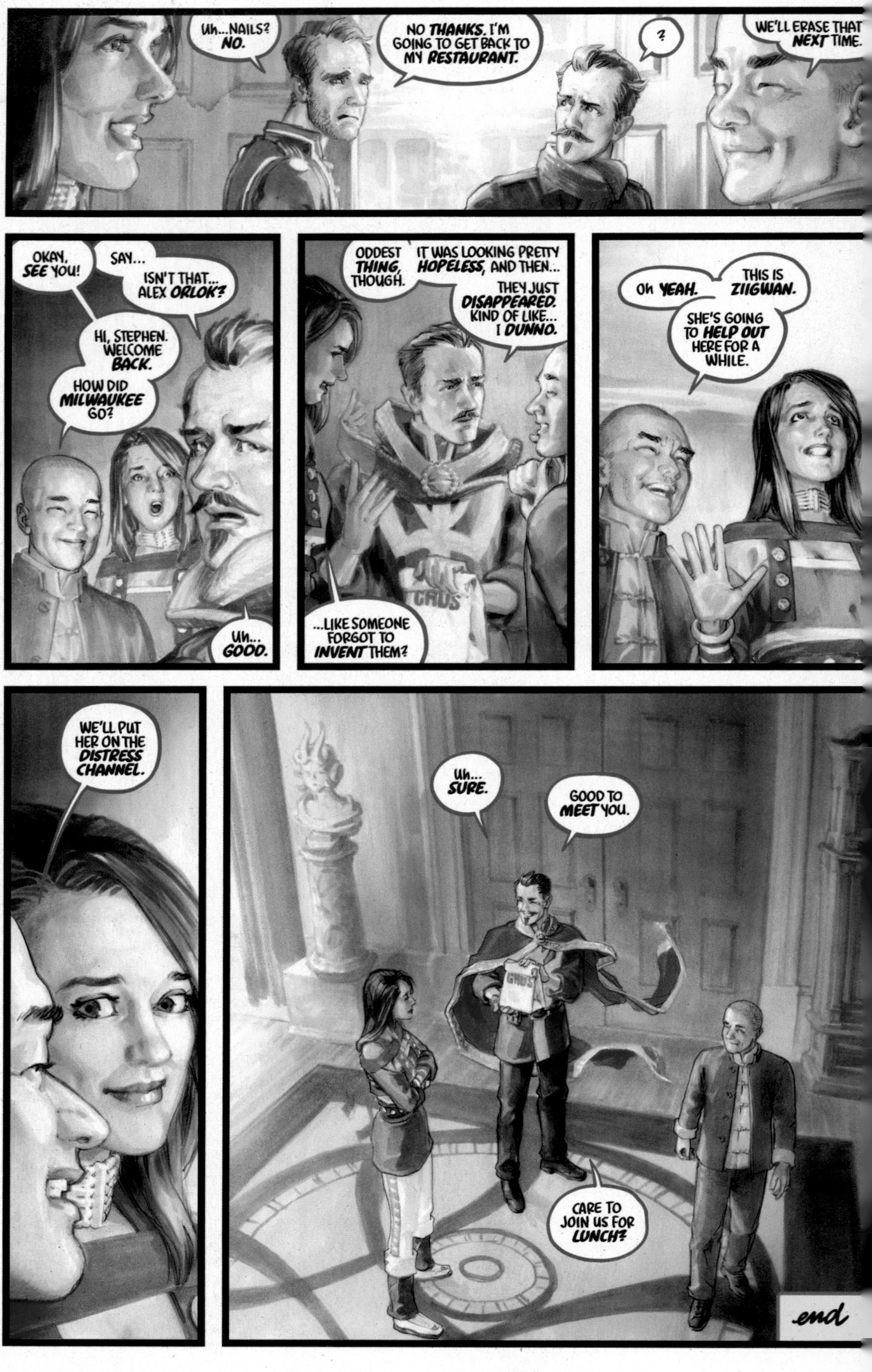
Uh...NAILS? NO.
NO THANKS. I'M GOING TO GET BACK TO MY RESTAURANT.
?
WE'LL ERASE THAT NEXT TIME.
OKAY, SEE YOU!
SAY... ISN'T THAT... ALEX ORLOK?
HI, STEPHEN. WELCOME BACK.
HOW DID MILWAUKEE GO?
Uh... GOOD.
ODDEST THING, THOUGH.
IT WAS LOOKING PRETTY HOPELESS, AND THEN...
THEY JUST DISAPPEARED. KIND OF LIKE... I DUNNO.
...LIKE SOMEONE FORGOT TO INVENT THEM?
Oh YEAH.
THIS IS ZIIGWAN.
SHE'S GOING TO HELP OUT HERE FOR A WHILE.
WE'LL PUT HER ON THE DISTRESS CHANNEL.
Uh... SURE.
GOOD TO MEET YOU.
CARE TO JOIN US FOR LUNCH?
end

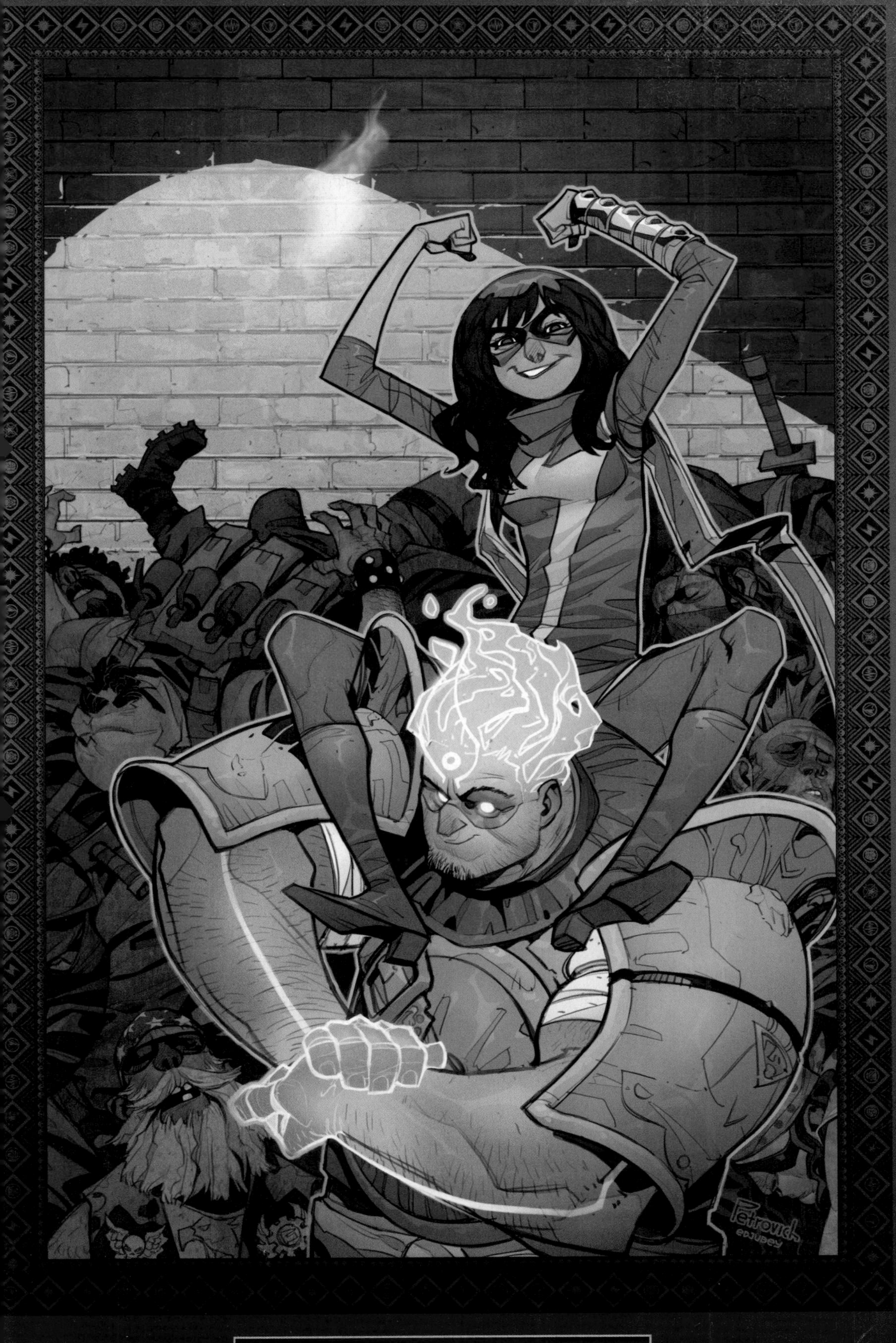
Petrovich
edjubey

MAGNIFICENT MS. MARVEL #13

WHEN A STRANGE TERRIGEN MIST DESCENDED UPON JERSEY CITY, KAMAL
KHAN WAS IMBUED WITH POLYMORPH POWERS. USING HER NEW ABILITIES T
FIGHT EVIL AND PROTECT JERSEY CITY, SHE BECAME...

THE MAGNIFICENT MS. MARVEL

RECENTLY, KAMALA'S FATHER FEL
ILL WITH A SEEMINGLY INCURABL
DISEASE, BUT NOT ALL HOPE WAS LOS
DOCTOR STRANGE AGREED TO OPERAT
AFTER THEORIZING THAT MR. KHAN
ILLNESS STEMMED FROM LATEN
INHUMAN DNA

DOCTOR STRANGE DETERMINED THA
ABU COULD RECOVER WITH THE AID C
A BLOOD TRANSFUSION FROM KAMALA
BUT KAMALA TOOK TOO LONG TRYING TO STOP HE
NANOTECH COSTUME FROM KILLING HER CLASSMAT
TURNED NEMESIS, DISCORD, AND DIDN'T RETURN T
THE HOSPITAL IN TIME FOR THE TRANSFUSIO
TO HAVE ITS FULL IMPAC

FOR NOW, ABU CAN COME HOME. BUT HAV
KAMALA'S ACTIONS CAUSE
PERMANENT HARM

WRITER • **SALADIN AHMEI**

ARTIST • **JOEY VAZQUE**

INKER • **JUAN VLASC**

COLOR ARTIST • **IAN HERRIN**

LETTERER • **VC'S JOE CARAMAGNA**

COVER • **EDUARD PETROVICH**

GRAPHIC DESIGNER • **CARLOS LA**

ASST. EDITOR • **SHANNON ANDREWS BALLESTEROS**

EDITOR • **ALANNA SMITH**

CONSULTING EDITOR • **SANA AMANA**

EDITOR IN CHIE
C.B. CEBULSK

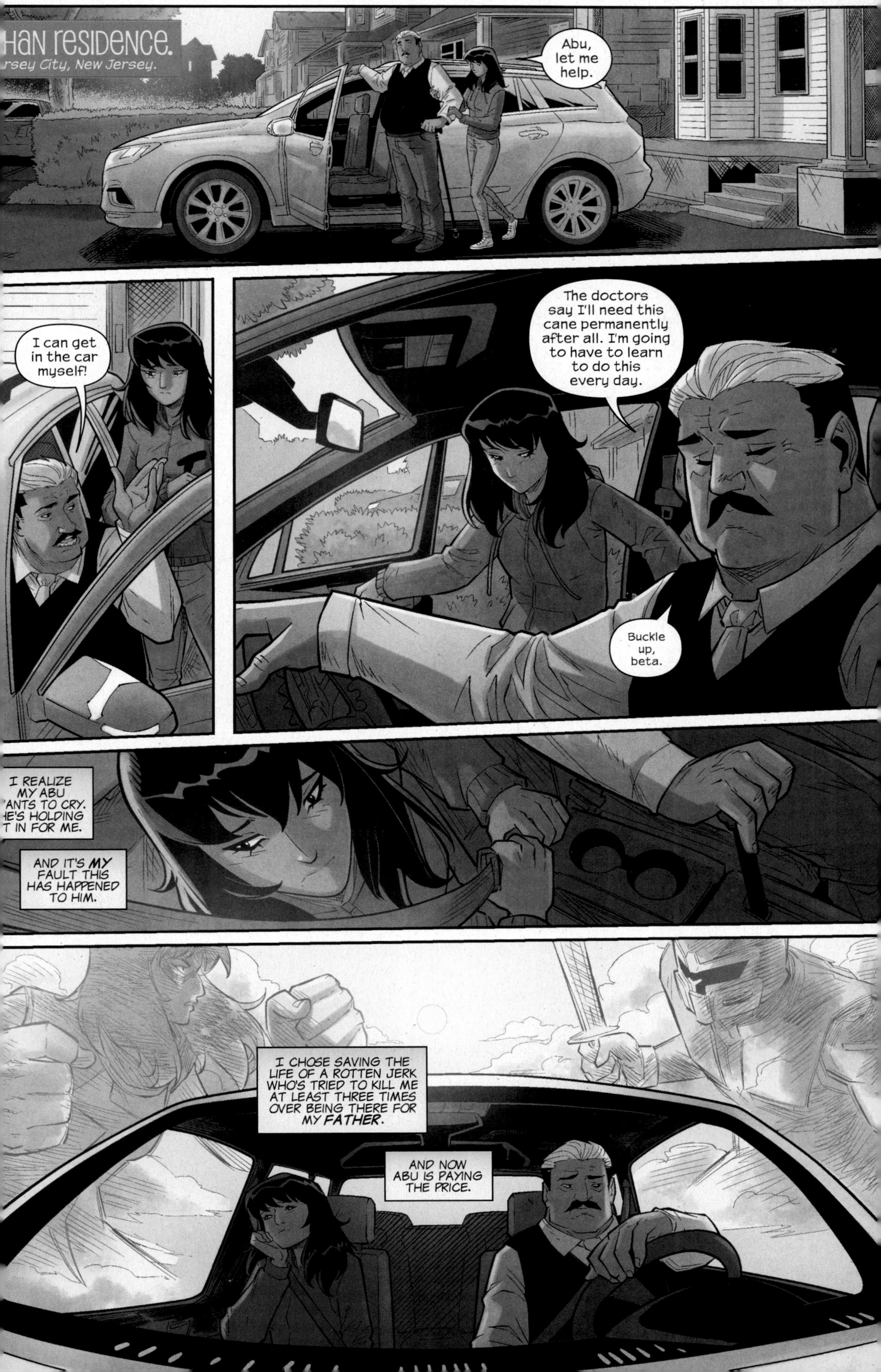

HAN RESIDENCE.
rsey City, New Jersey.
Abu, let me help.
I can get in the car myself!
The doctors say I'll need this cane permanently after all. I'm going to have to learn to do this every day.
Buckle up, beta.
I REALIZE MY ABU ANTS TO CRY. HE'S HOLDING T IN FOR ME.
AND IT'S MY FAULT THIS HAS HAPPENED TO HIM.
I CHOSE SAVING THE LIFE OF A ROTTEN JERK WHO'S TRIED TO KILL ME AT LEAST THREE TIMES OVER BEING THERE FOR MY FATHER.
AND NOW ABU IS PAYING THE PRICE.

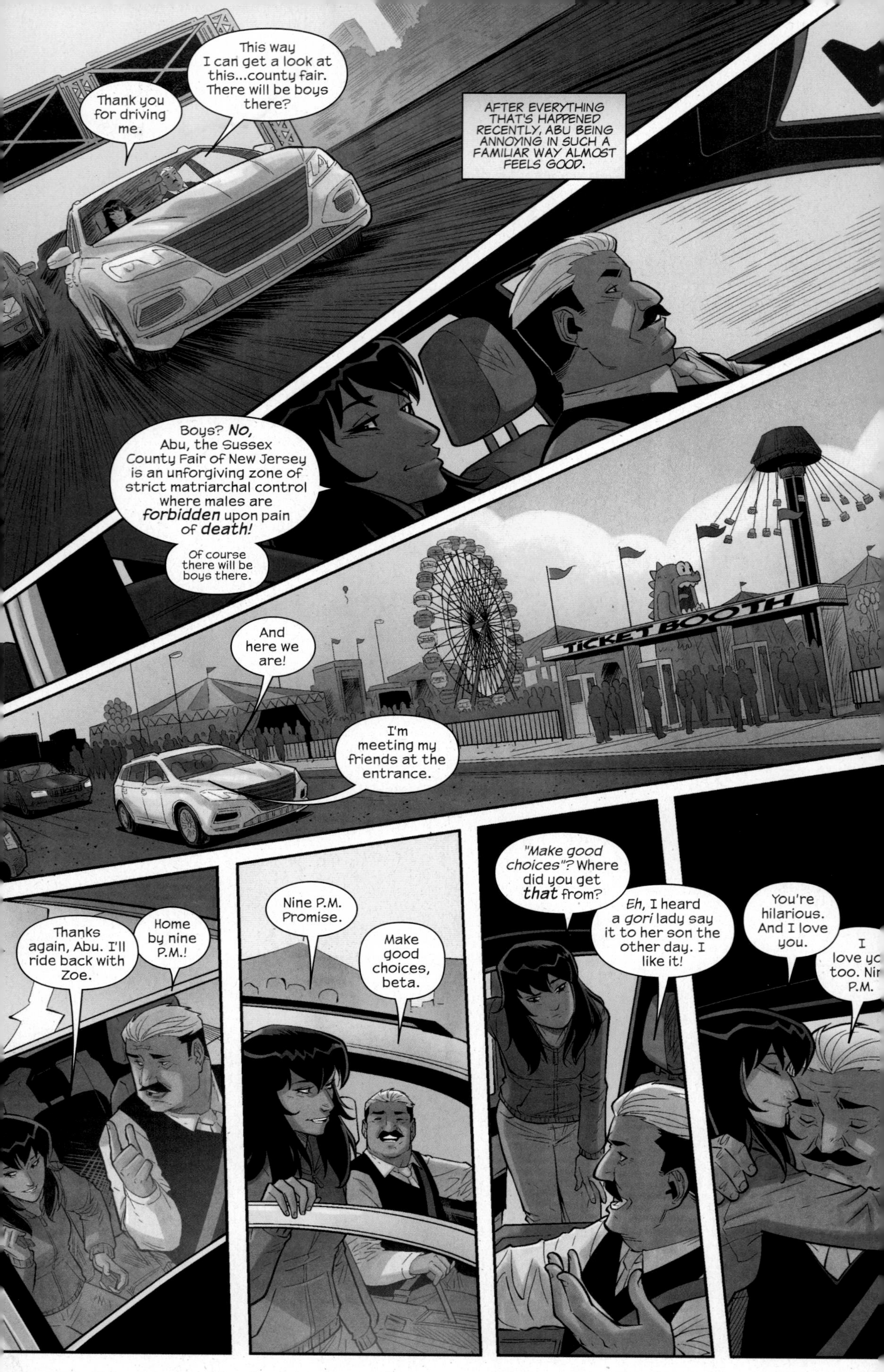

Thank you for driving me.
This way I can get a look at this...county fair. There will be boys there?
AFTER EVERYTHING THAT'S HAPPENED RECENTLY, ABU BEING ANNOYING IN SUCH A FAMILIAR WAY ALMOST FEELS GOOD.
Boys? **No,** Abu, the Sussex County Fair of New Jersey is an unforgiving zone of strict matriarchal control where males are ***forbidden*** upon pain of ***death!***
Of course there will be boys there.
TICKET BOOTH
And here we are!
I'm meeting my friends at the entrance.
Thanks again, Abu. I'll ride back with Zoe.
Home by nine P.M.!
Nine P.M. Promise.
Make good choices, beta.
"Make good choices"? Where did you get ***that*** from?
Eh, I heard a *gori* lady say it to her son the other day. I like it!
You're hilarious. And I love you.

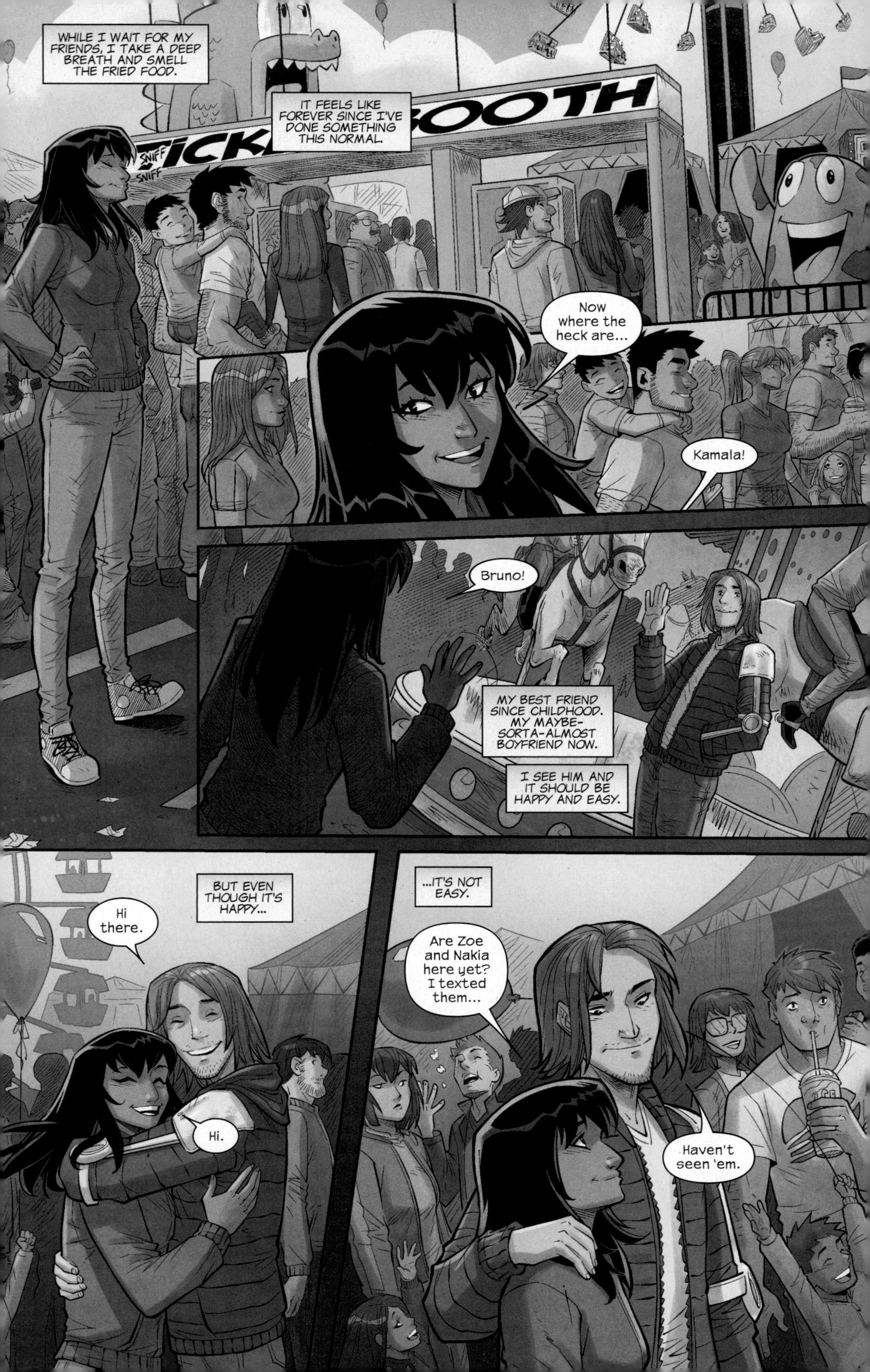
WHILE I WAIT FOR MY FRIENDS, I TAKE A DEEP BREATH AND SMELL THE FRIED FOOD.
IT FEELS LIKE FOREVER SINCE I'VE DONE SOMETHING THIS NORMAL.
TICK BOOTH
SNIFF
SNIFF
Now where the heck are...
Kamala!
Bruno!
MY BEST FRIEND SINCE CHILDHOOD. MY MAYBE-SORTA-ALMOST BOYFRIEND NOW.
I SEE HIM AND IT SHOULD BE HAPPY AND EASY.
BUT EVEN THOUGH IT'S HAPPY...
Hi there.
Hi.
...IT'S NOT EASY.
Are Zoe and Nakia here yet? I texted them...
Haven't seen 'em.

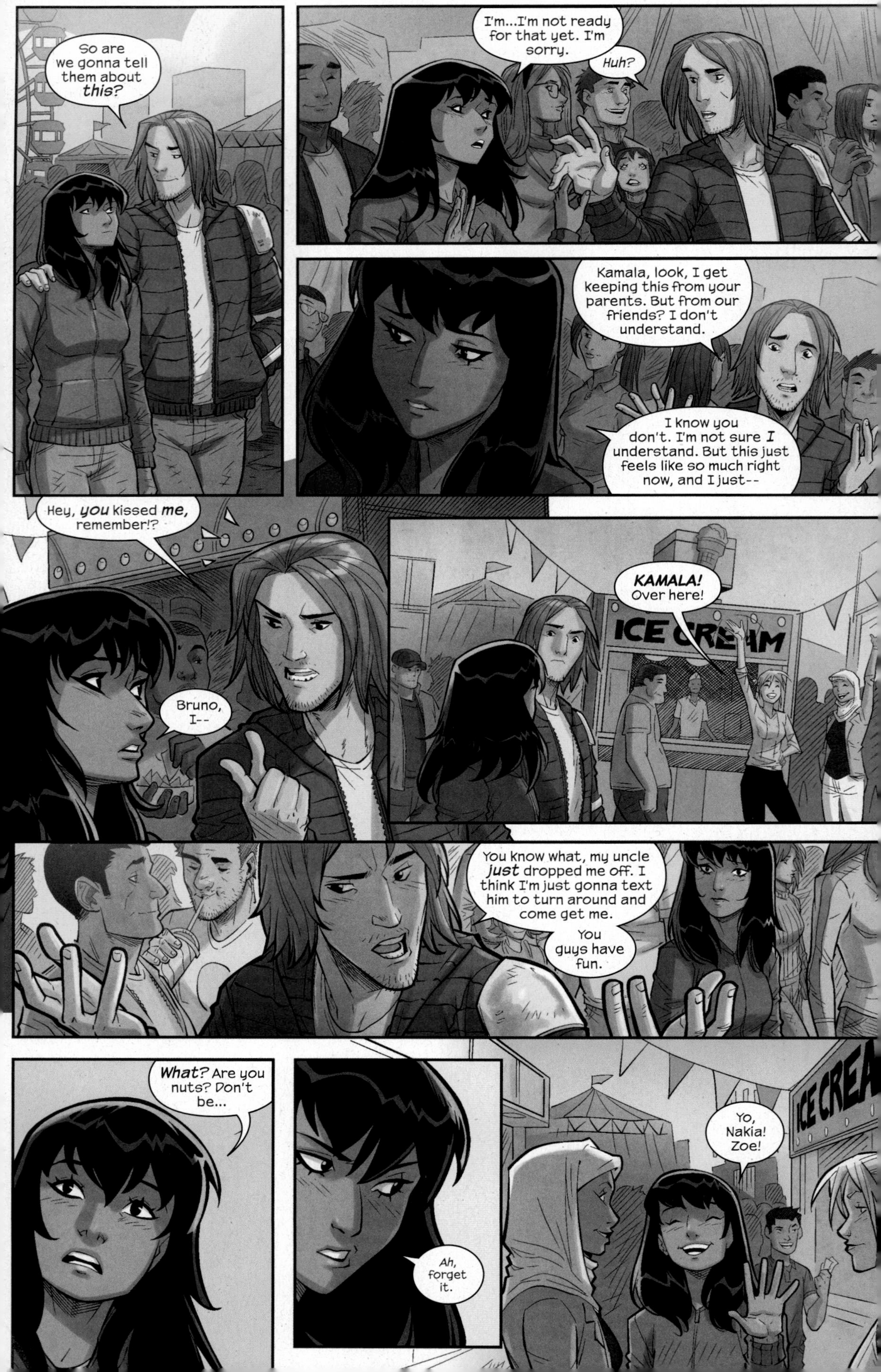

So are we gonna tell them about *this?*
I'm...I'm not ready for that yet. I'm sorry.
Huh?
Kamala, look, I get keeping this from your parents. But from our friends? I don't understand.
I know you don't. I'm not sure *I* understand. But this just feels like so much right now, and I just--
Hey, *you* kissed *me,* remember!?
Bruno, I--
KAMALA! Over here!
ICE CREAM
You know what, my uncle *just* dropped me off. I think I'm just gonna text him to turn around and come get me.
You guys have fun.
What? Are you nuts? Don't be...
Ah, forget it.
Yo, Nakia! Zoe!

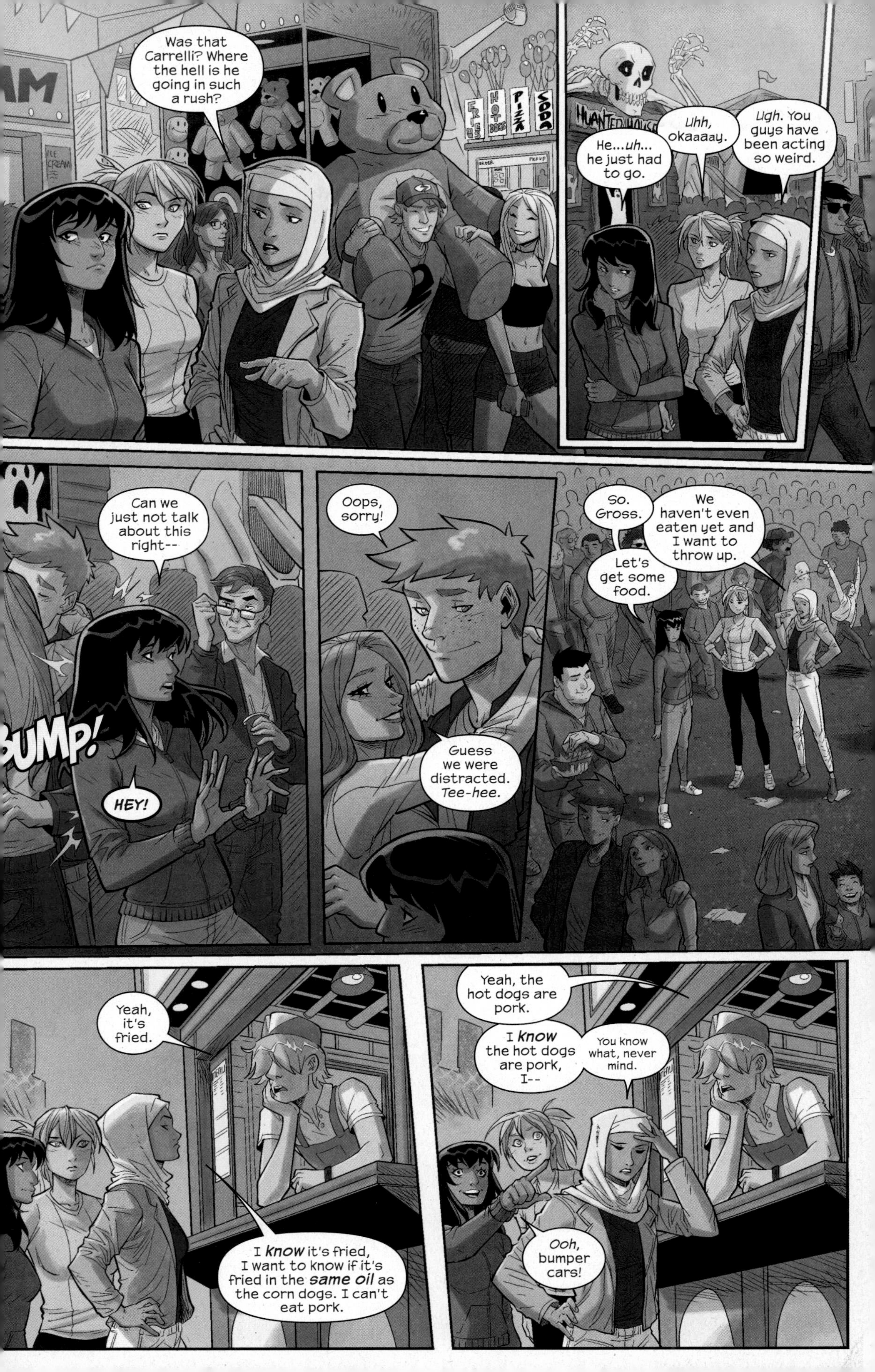

Was that Carrelli? Where the hell is he going in such a rush?
FRIES
HOT DOGS
PIZZA
SODA
HUANTED HOUSE
He...uh... he just had to go.
Uhh, okaaaay.
Ugh. You guys have been acting so weird.
Can we just not talk about this right--
BUMP!
HEY!
Oops, sorry!
Guess we were distracted. Tee-hee.
So. Gross.
We haven't even eaten yet and I want to throw up.
Let's get some food.
Yeah, it's fried.
I KNOW it's fried, I want to know if it's fried in the same oil as the corn dogs. I can't eat pork.
Yeah, the hot dogs are pork.
I KNOW the hot dogs are pork, I--
You know what, never mind.
Ooh, bumper cars!

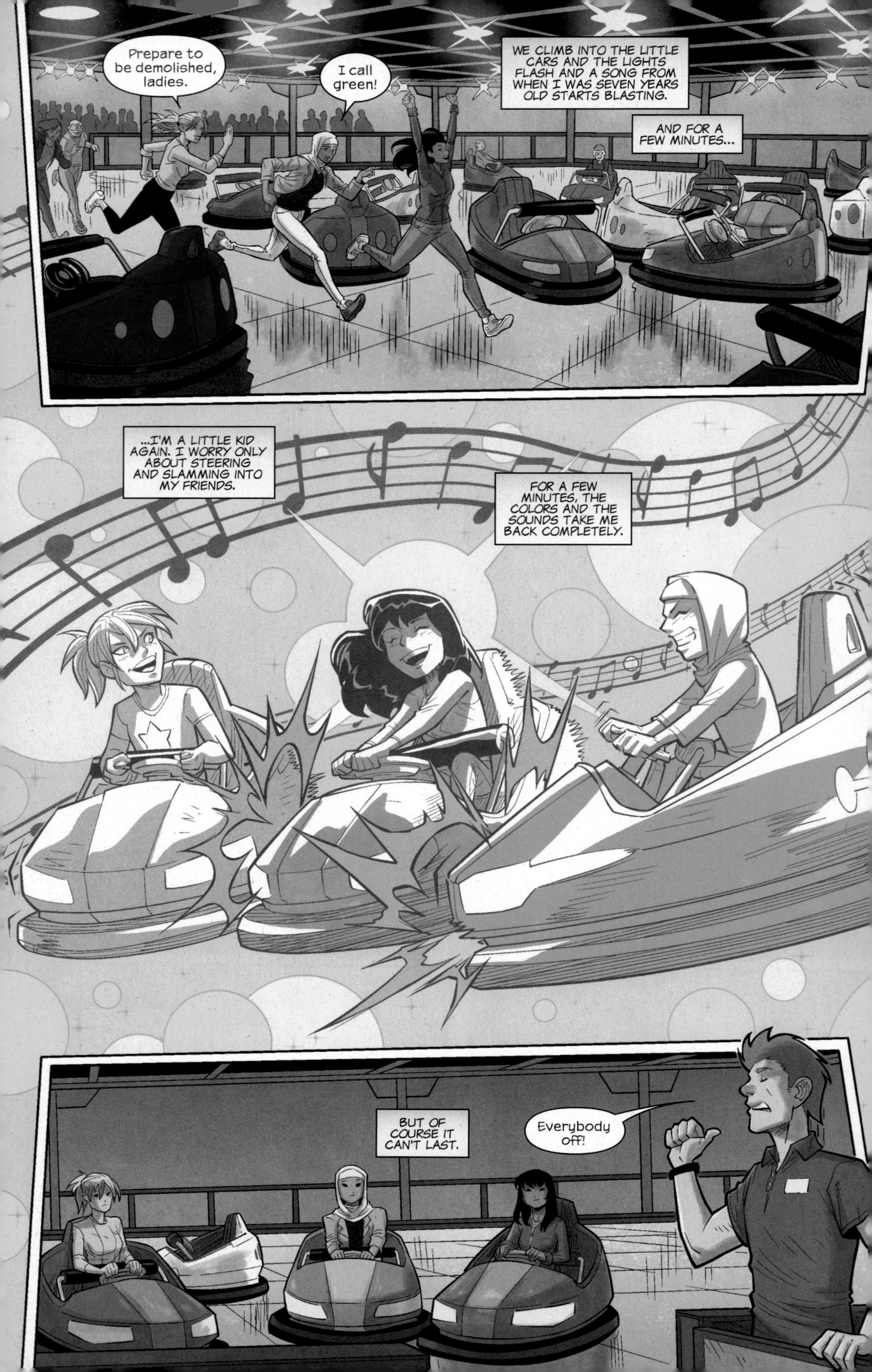
Prepare to be demolished, ladies.
I call green!
WE CLIMB INTO THE LITTLE CARS AND THE LIGHTS FLASH AND A SONG FROM WHEN I WAS SEVEN YEARS OLD STARTS BLASTING.
AND FOR A FEW MINUTES...
...I'M A LITTLE KID AGAIN. I WORRY ONLY ABOUT STEERING AND SLAMMING INTO MY FRIENDS.
FOR A FEW MINUTES, THE COLORS AND THE SOUNDS TAKE ME BACK COMPLETELY.
BUT OF COURSE IT CAN'T LAST.
Everybody off!

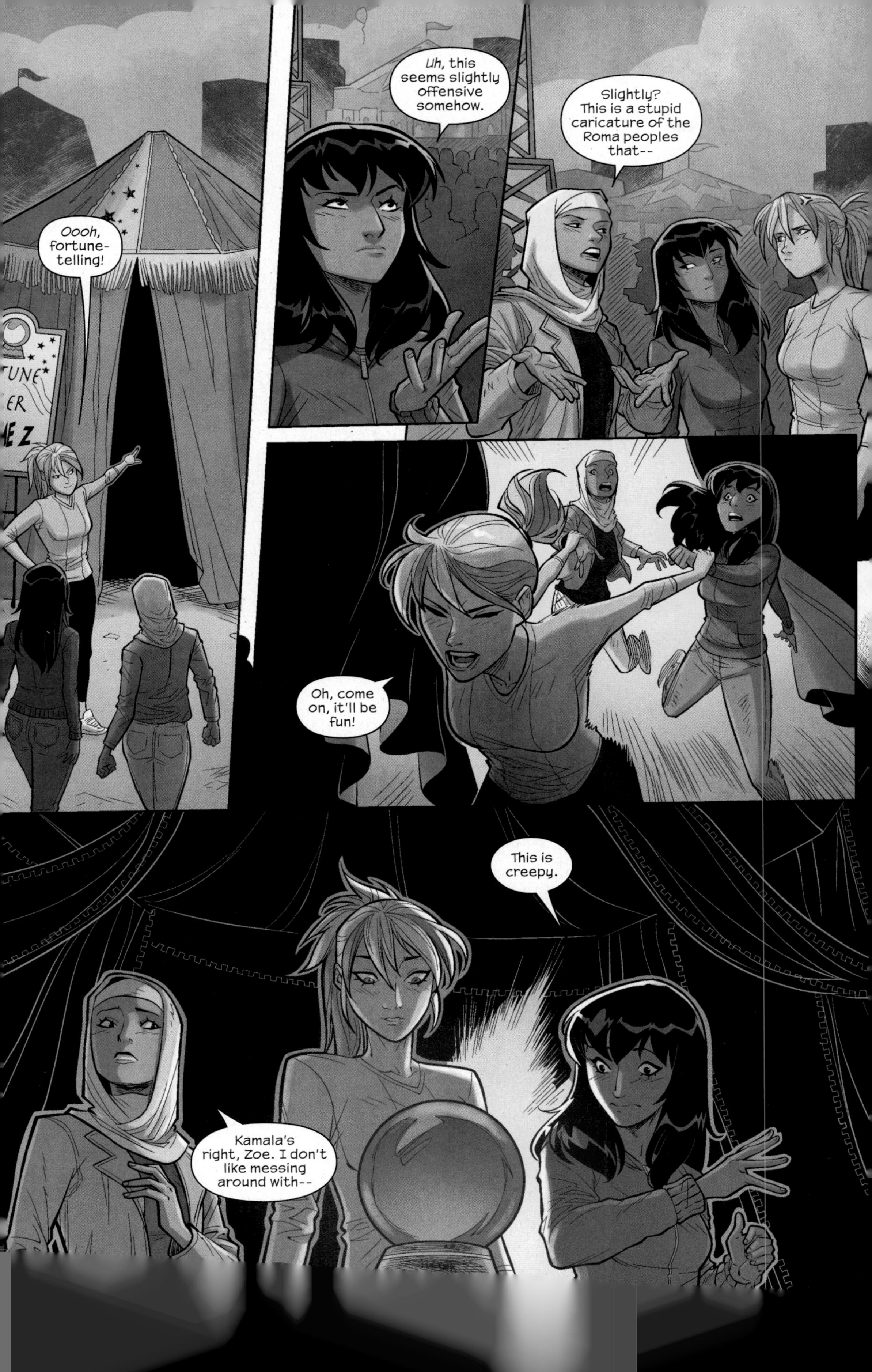
Oooh, fortune-telling!
Uh, this seems slightly offensive somehow.
Slightly? This is a stupid caricature of the Roma peoples that--
Oh, come on, it'll be fun!
This is creepy.
Kamala's right, Zoe. I don't like messing around with--

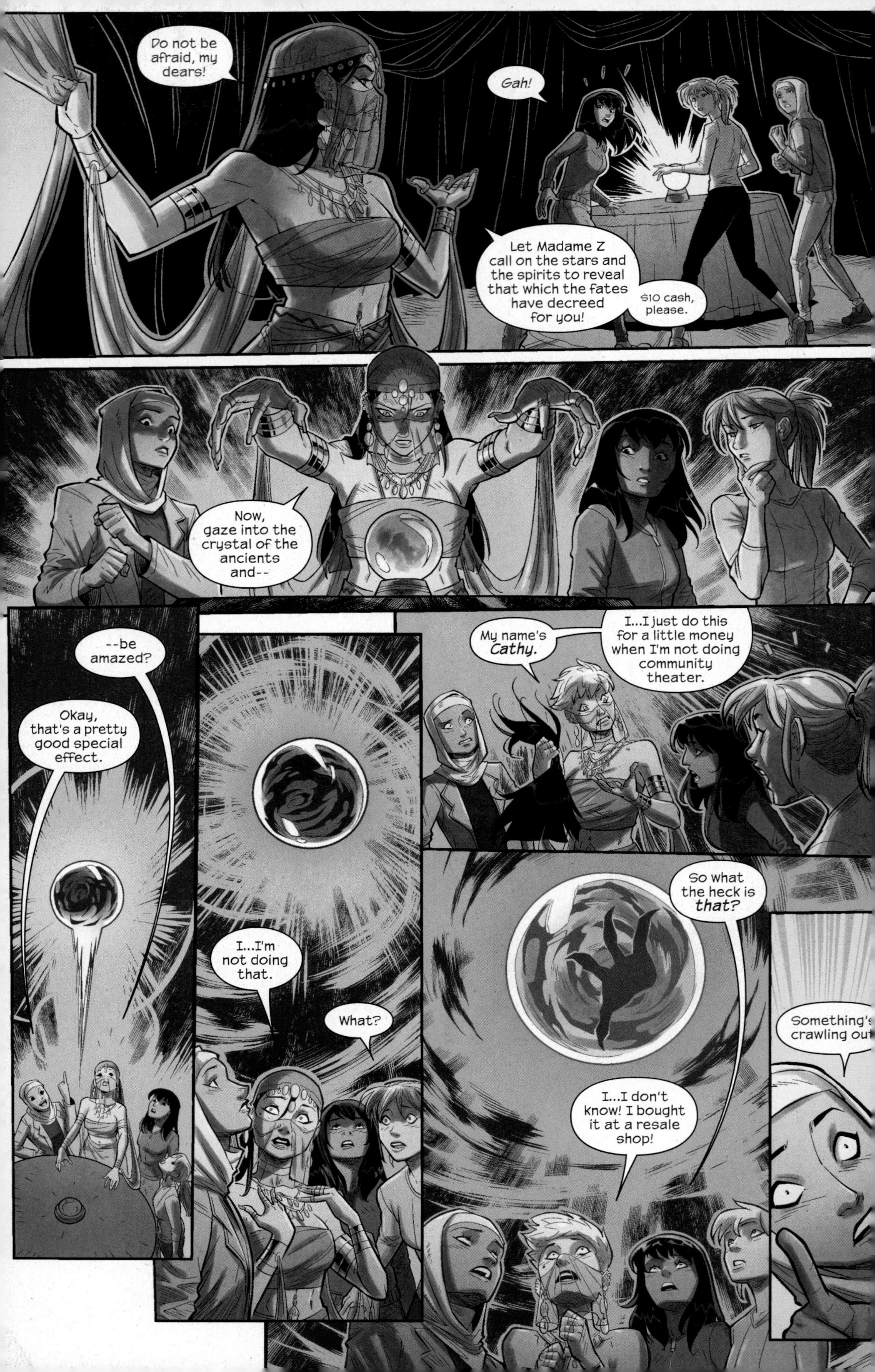
Do not be afraid, my dears!
Gah!
Let Madame Z call on the stars and the spirits to reveal that which the fates have decreed for you!
$10 cash, please.
Now, gaze into the crystal of the ancients and--
--be amazed?
Okay, that's a pretty good special effect.
I...I'm not doing that.
What?
My name's *Cathy.*
I...I just do this for a little money when I'm not doing community theater.
So what the heck is *that?*
I...I don't know! I bought it at a resale shop!
Something's crawling ou

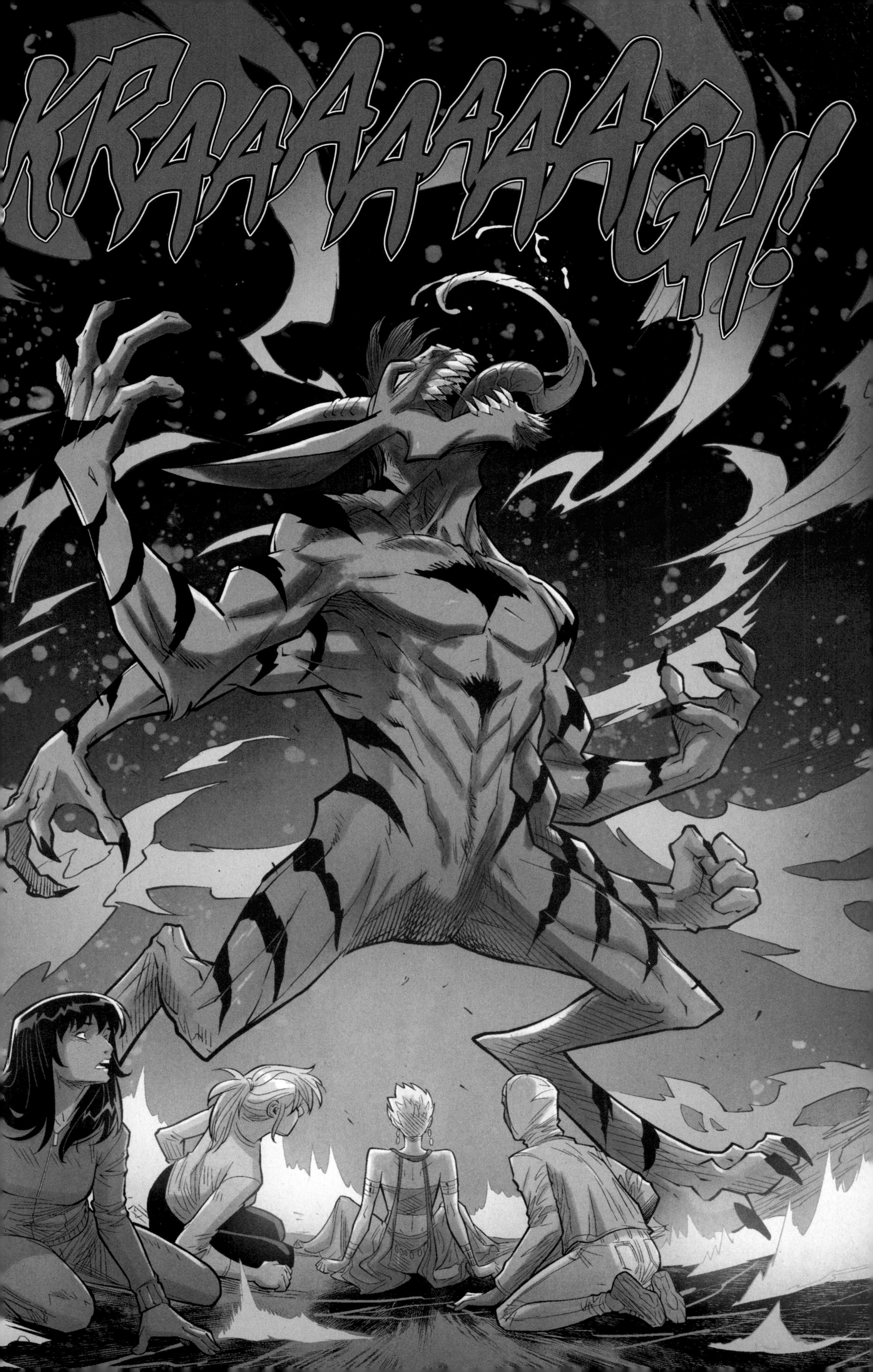
KRAAAAAAAGH!

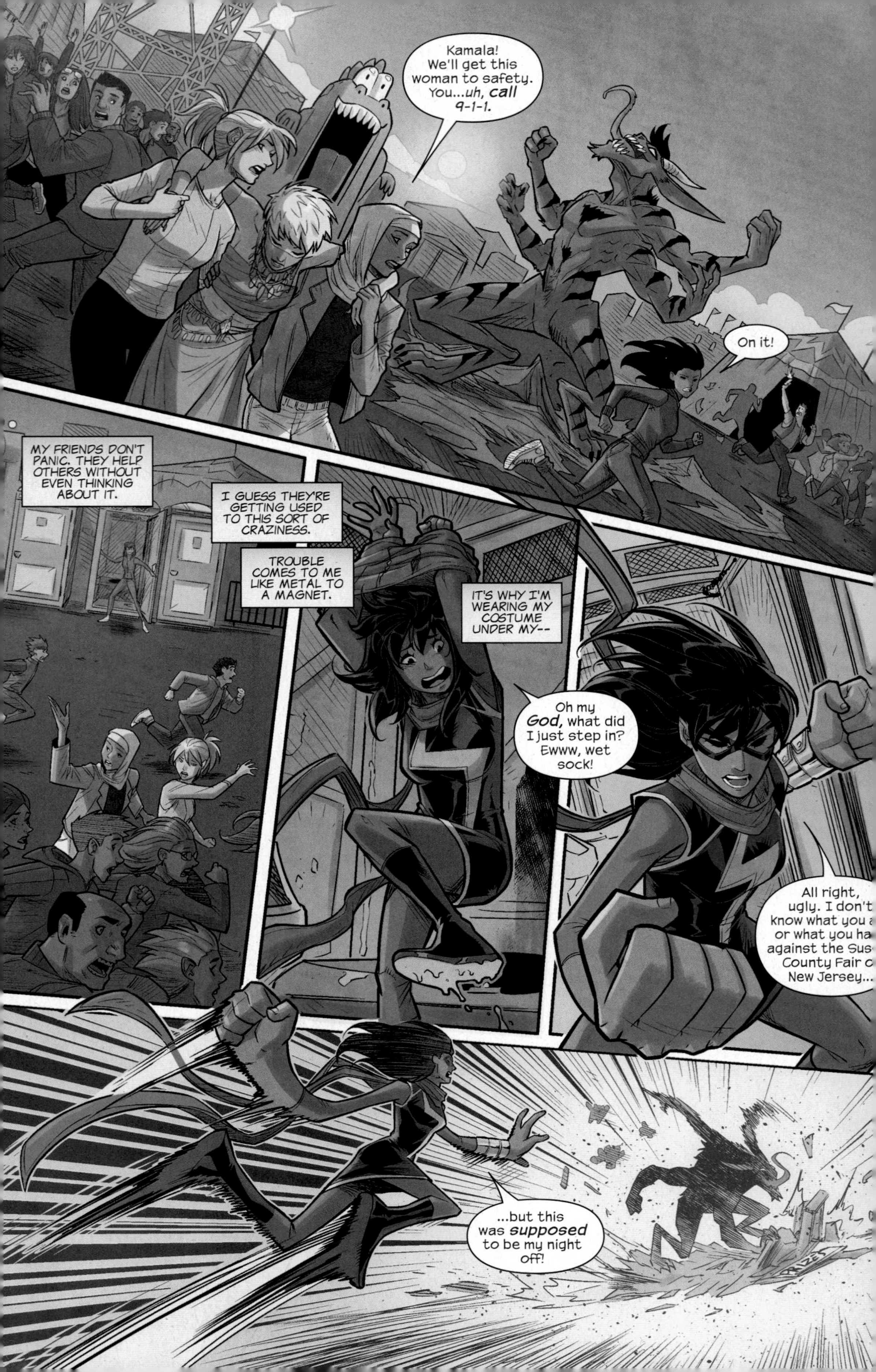

Kamala! We'll get this woman to safety. You...uh, call 9-1-1.
On it!
MY FRIENDS DON'T PANIC. THEY HELP OTHERS WITHOUT EVEN THINKING ABOUT IT.
I GUESS THEY'RE GETTING USED TO THIS SORT OF CRAZINESS.
TROUBLE COMES TO ME LIKE METAL TO A MAGNET.
IT'S WHY I'M WEARING MY COSTUME UNDER MY--
Oh my God, what did I just step in? Ewww, wet sock!
...but this was supposed to be my night off!

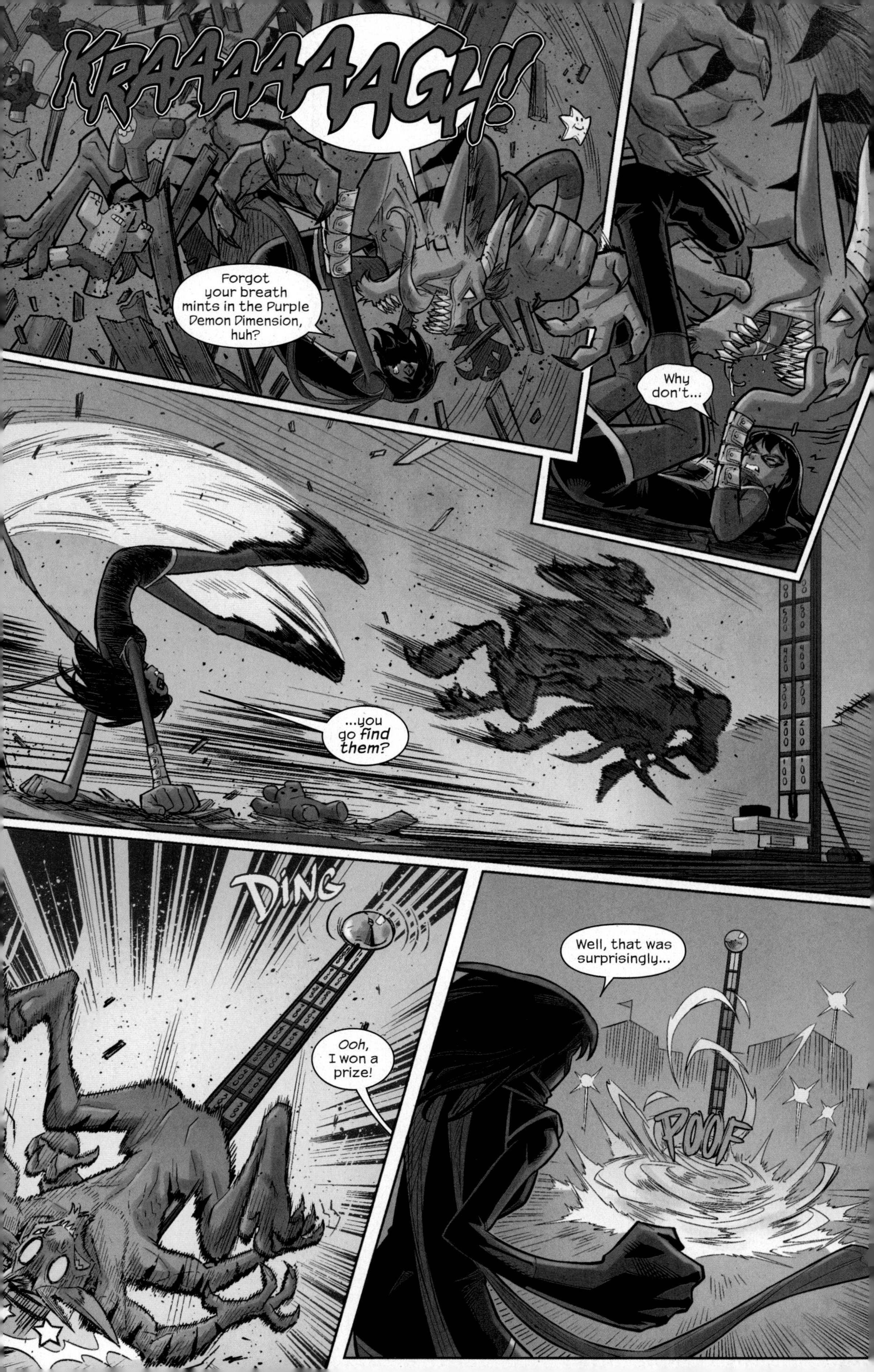
KRAAAAAAAGH!
Forgot your breath mints in the Purple Demon Dimension, huh?
Why don't...
...you go find them?
DING
Ooh, I won a prize!
Well, that was surprisingly...
POOF

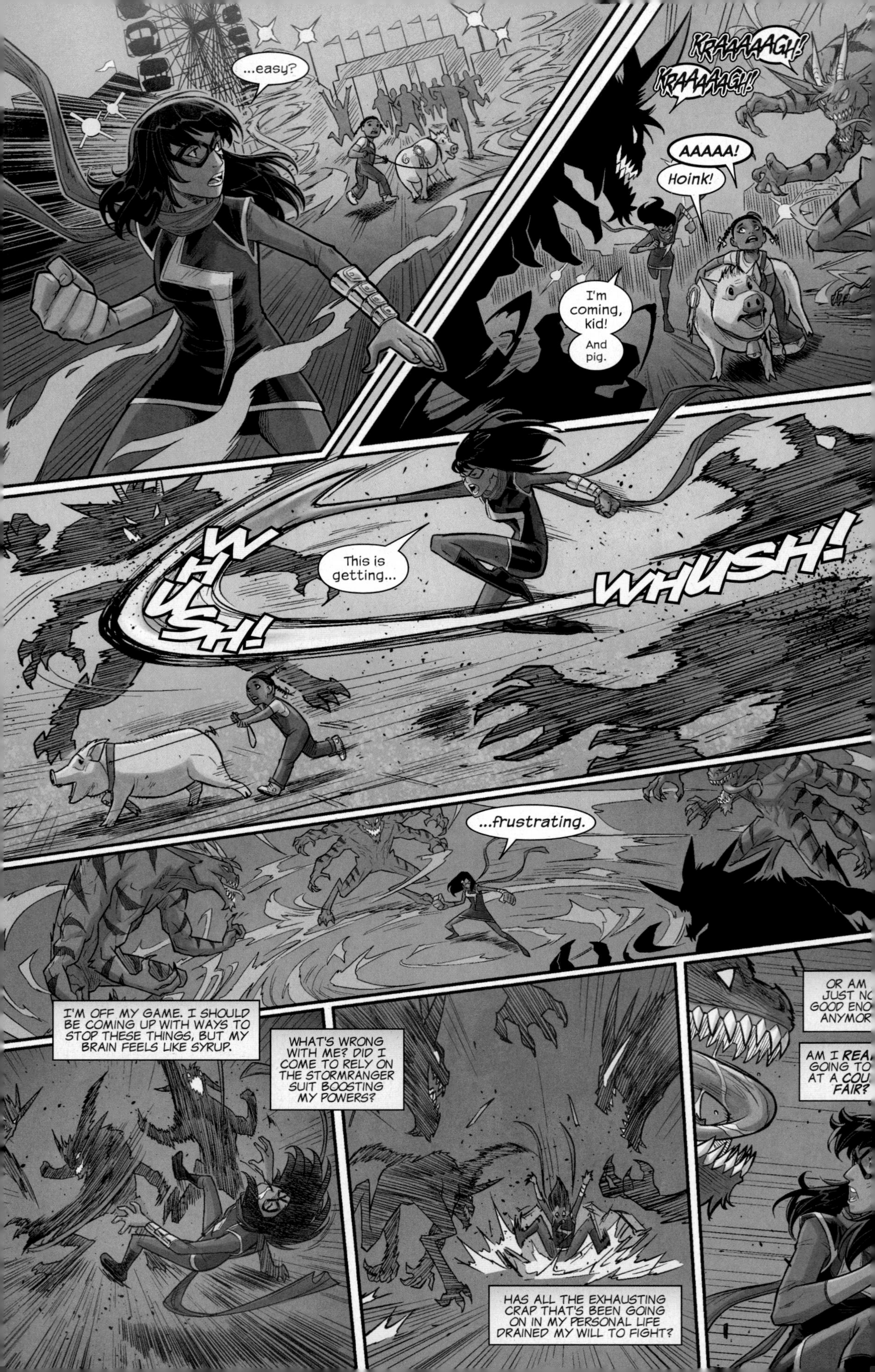
...easy?
KRAAAAAGH!
KRAAAAAGH!
AAAAA!
Hoink!
I'm coming, kid!
And pig.
WHUSH!
This is getting...
WHUSH!
...frustrating.
I'M OFF MY GAME. I SHOULD BE COMING UP WITH WAYS TO STOP THESE THINGS, BUT MY BRAIN FEELS LIKE SYRUP.
WHAT'S WRONG WITH ME? DID I COME TO RELY ON THE STORMRANGER SUIT BOOSTING MY POWERS?
HAS ALL THE EXHAUSTING CRAP THAT'S BEEN GOING ON IN MY PERSONAL LIFE DRAINED MY WILL TO FIGHT?

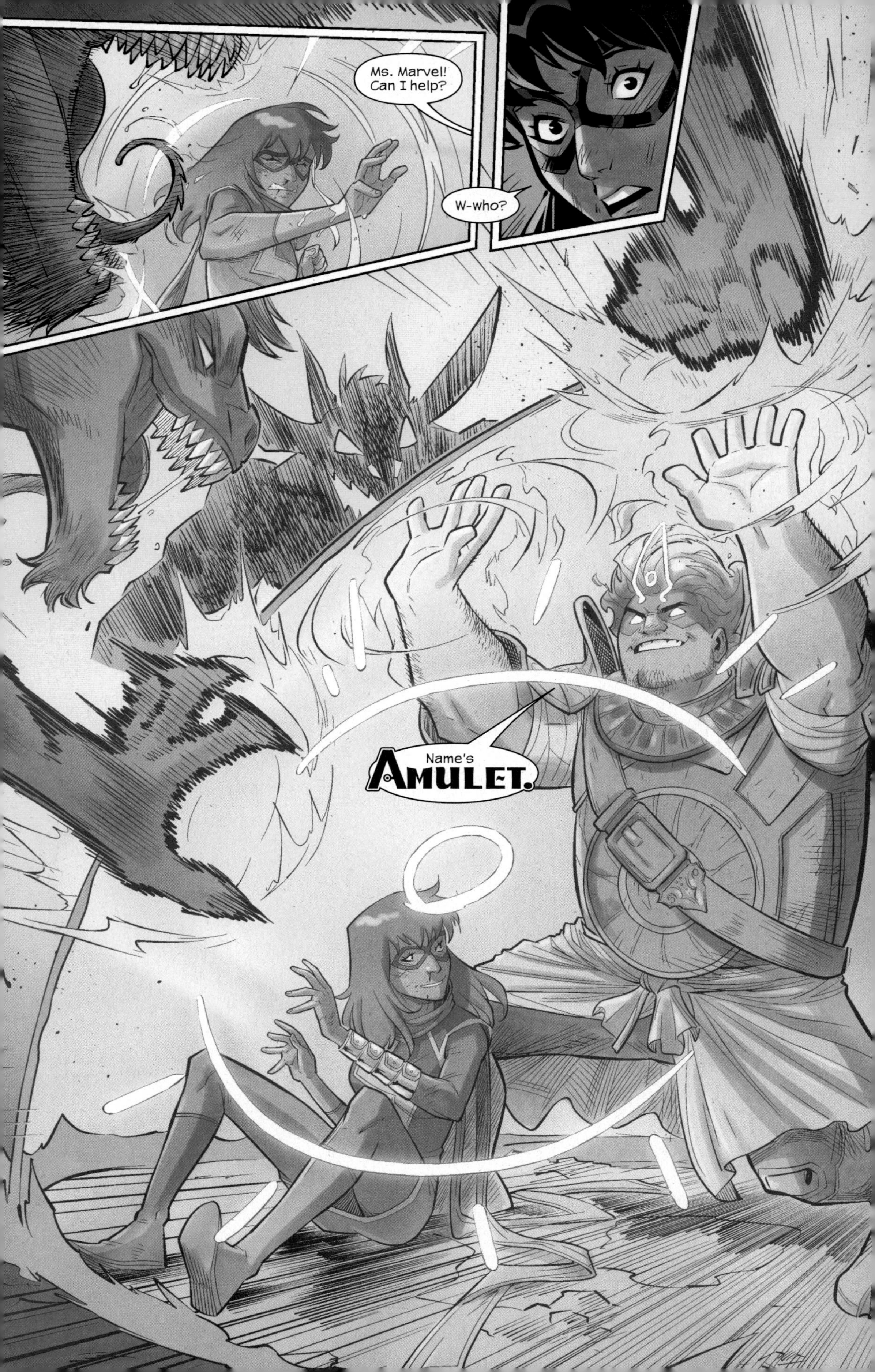
Ms. Marvel! Can I help?
W-who?
Name's AMULET.

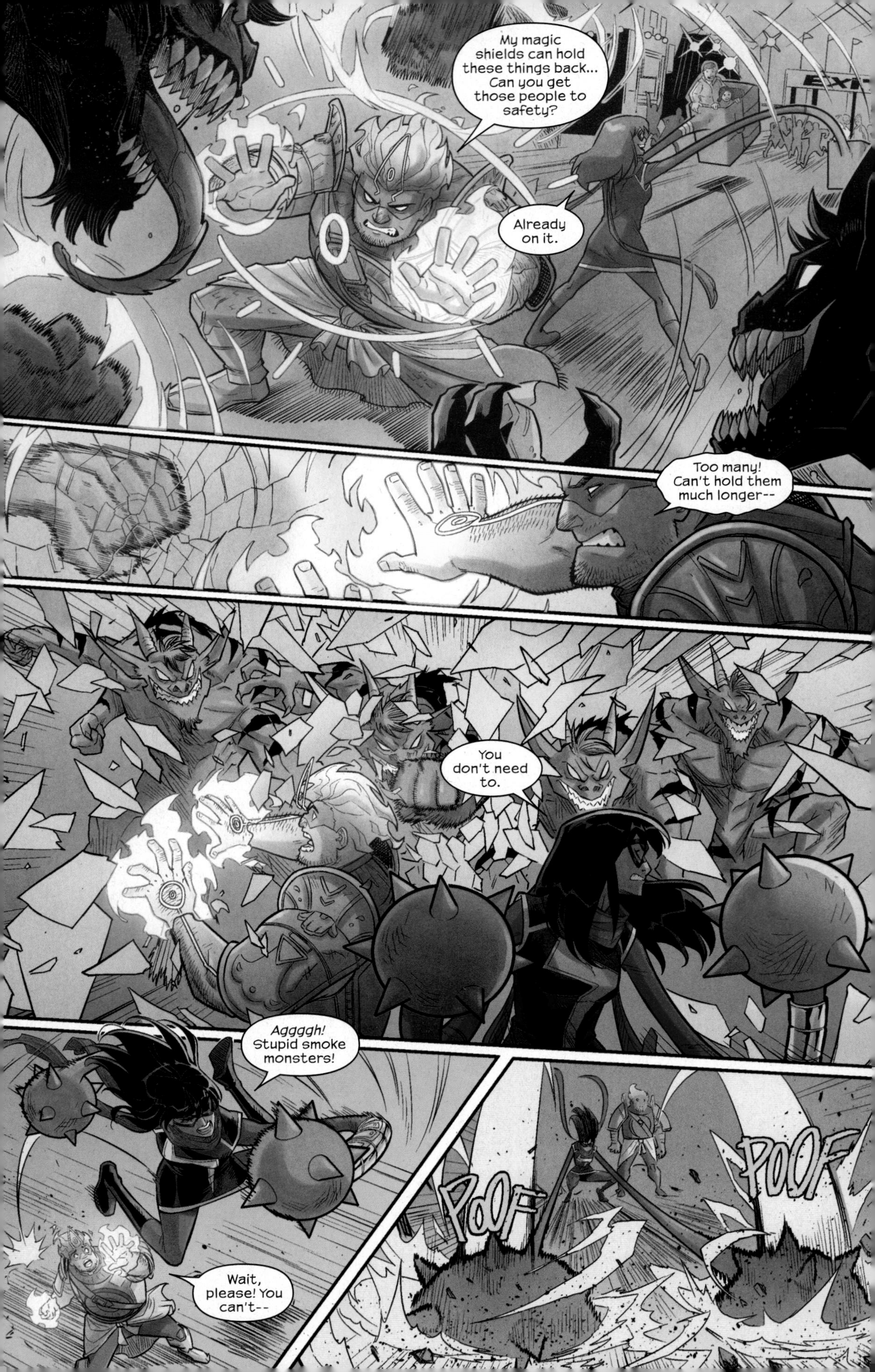
My magic shields can hold these things back... Can you get those people to safety?
Already on it.
Too many! Can't hold them much longer--
You don't need to.
Aggggh! Stupid smoke monsters!
Wait, please! You can't--
POOF
POOF

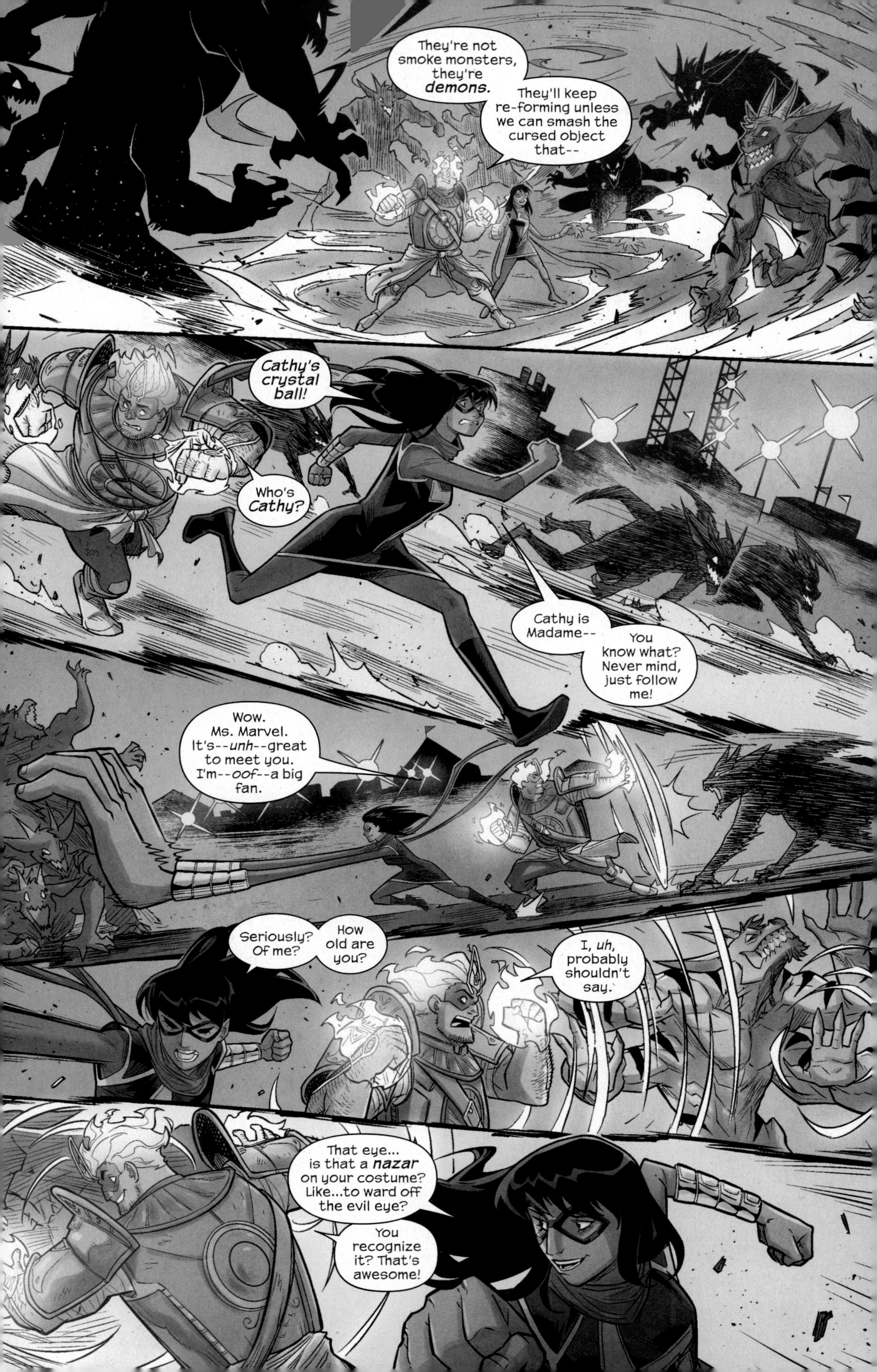
They're not smoke monsters, they're *demons.*
They'll keep re-forming unless we can smash the cursed object that--
Cathy's crystal ball!
Who's *Cathy?*
Cathy is Madame--
You know what? Never mind, just follow me!
Wow. Ms. Marvel. It's--*unh*--great to meet you. I'm--*oof*--a big fan.
Seriously? Of me?
How old are you?
I, *uh,* probably shouldn't say.
That eye... is that a ***nazar*** on your costume? Like...to ward off the evil eye?
You recognize it? That's awesome!

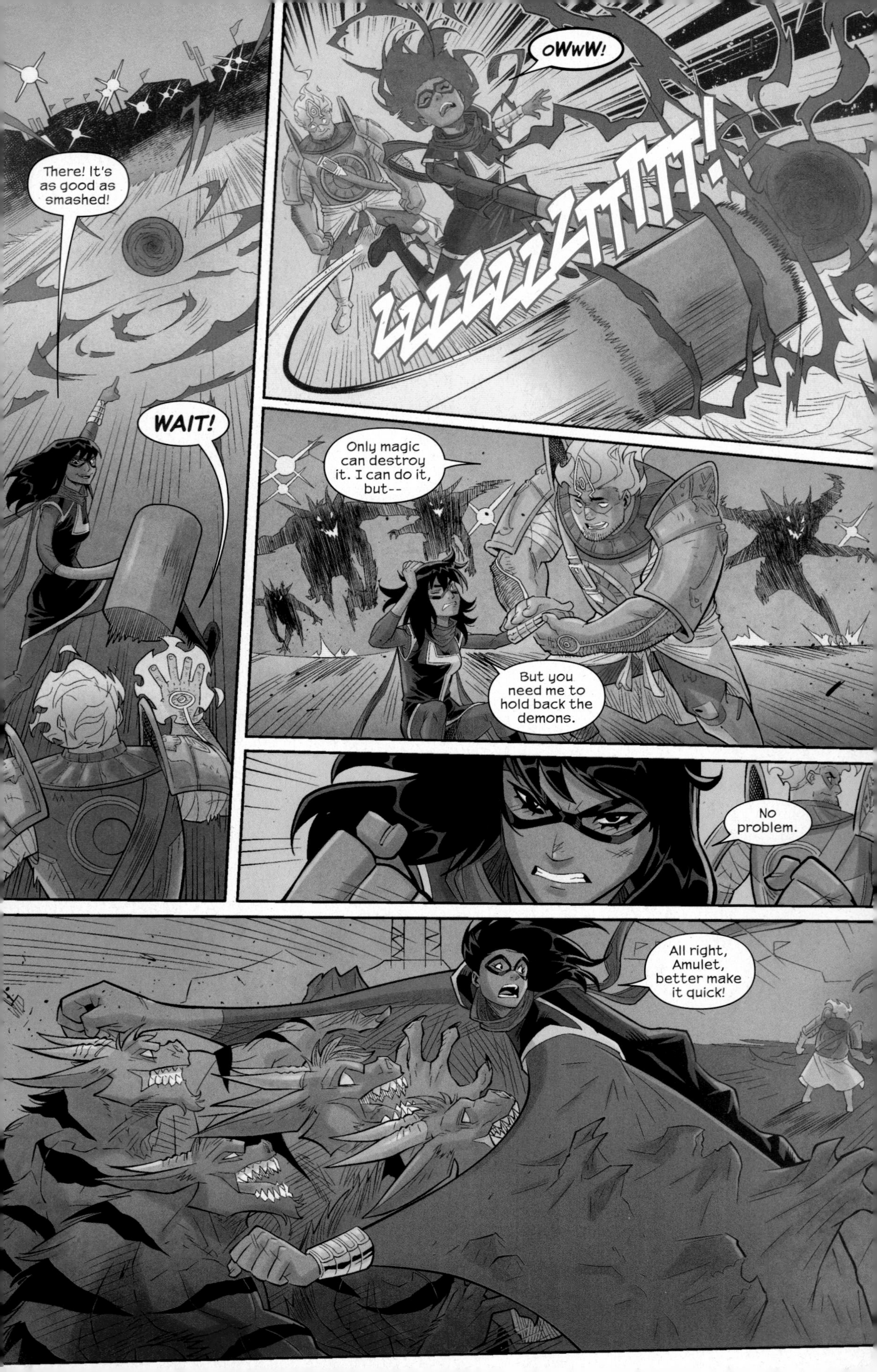
There! It's as good as smashed!
OWWW!
ZZZZZZZZTTTTT!
WAIT!
Only magic can destroy it. I can do it, but--
But you need me to hold back the demons.
No problem.
All right, Amulet, better make it quick!

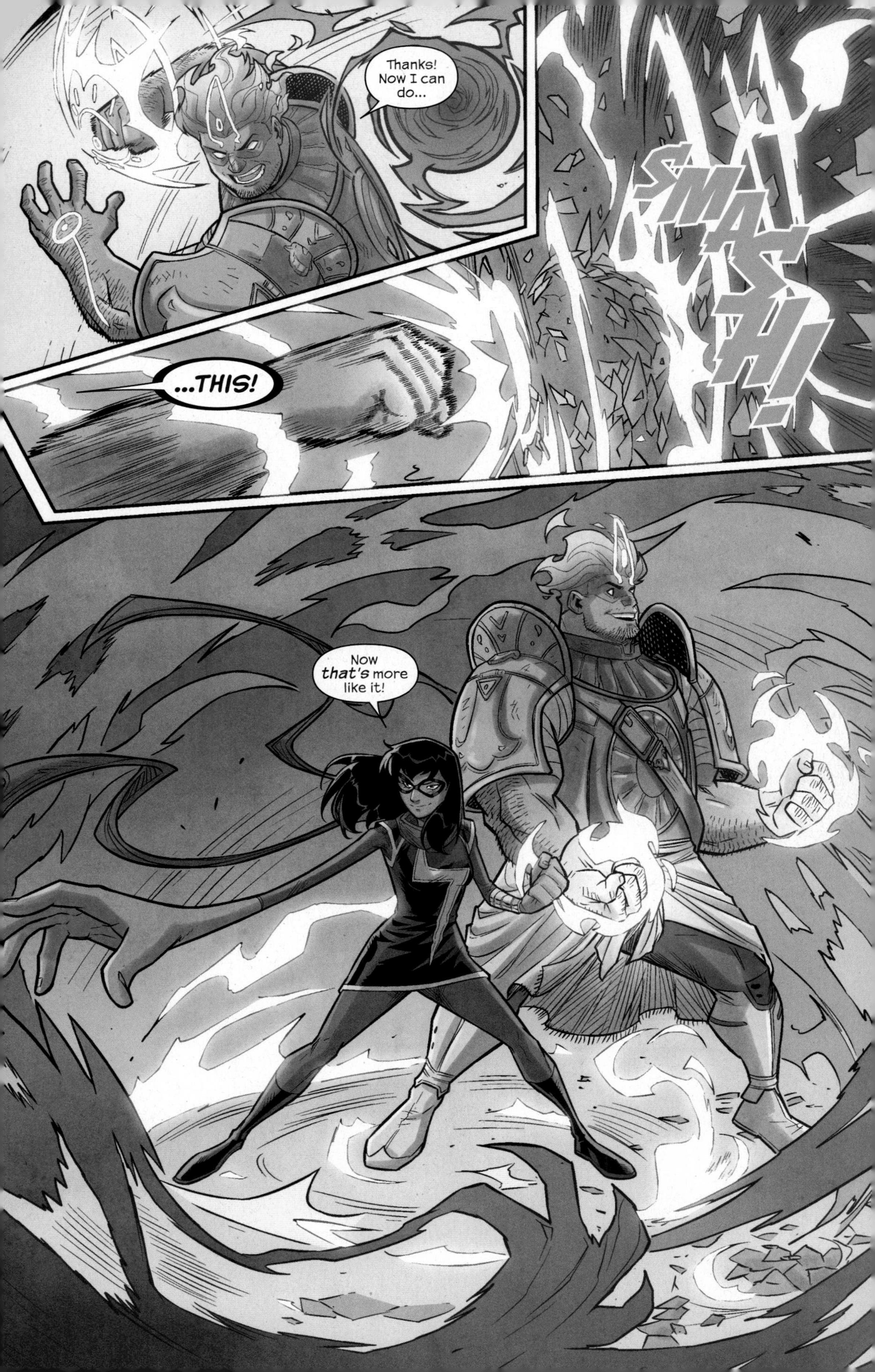
Thanks! Now I can do...
...THIS!
SMASH!
Now *that's* more like it!

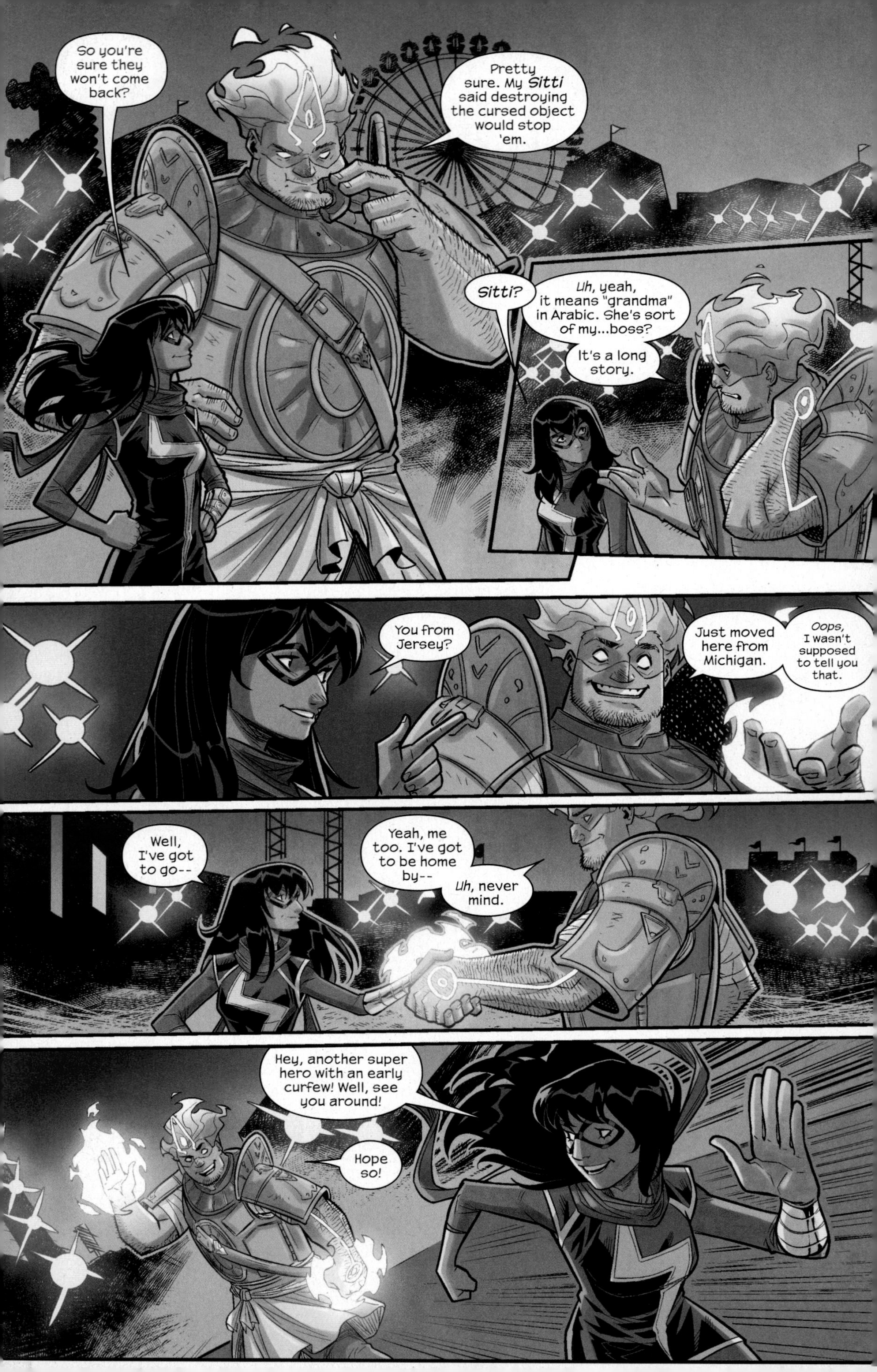
So you're sure they won't come back?
Pretty sure. My *Sitti* said destroying the cursed object would stop 'em.
Sitti?
Uh, yeah, it means "grandma" in Arabic. She's sort of my...boss?
It's a long story.
You from Jersey?
Just moved here from Michigan.
Oops, I wasn't supposed to tell you that.
Well, I've got to go--
Yeah, me too. I've got to be home by--
Uh, never mind.
Hey, another super hero with an early curfew! Well, see you around!
Hope so!

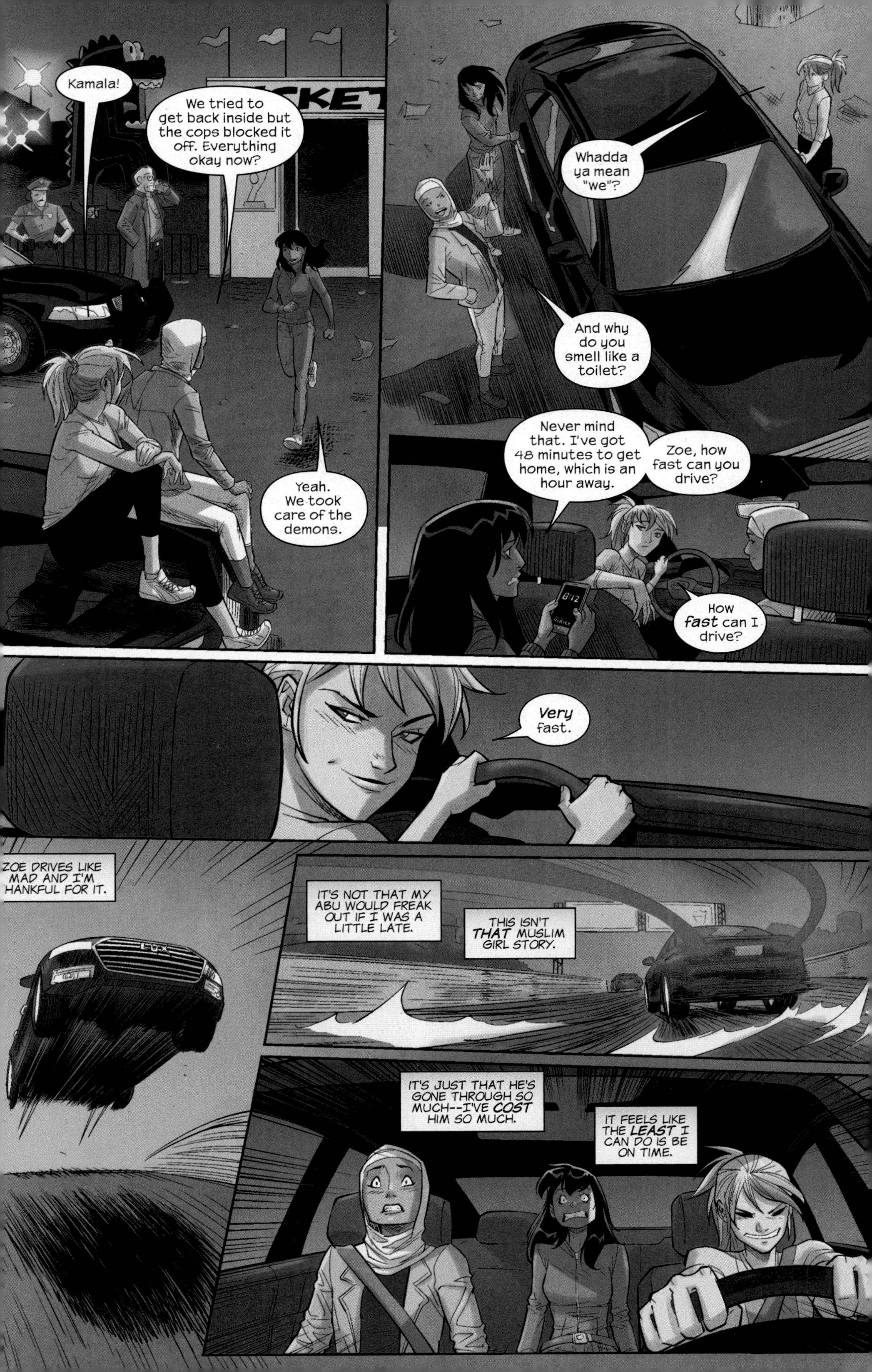
Kamala!
We tried to get back inside but the cops blocked it off. Everything okay now?
Yeah. We took care of the demons.
Whadda ya mean "we"?
And why do you smell like a toilet?
Never mind that. I've got 48 minutes to get home, which is an hour away.
Zoe, how fast can you drive?
How *fast* can I drive?
Very fast.
ZOE DRIVES LIKE MAD AND I'M HANKFUL FOR IT.
IT'S NOT THAT MY ABU WOULD FREAK OUT IF I WAS A LITTLE LATE.
THIS ISN'T *THAT* MUSLIM GIRL STORY.
IT'S JUST THAT HE'S GONE THROUGH SO MUCH--I'VE *COST* HIM SO MUCH.
IT FEELS LIKE THE *LEAST* I CAN DO IS BE ON TIME.

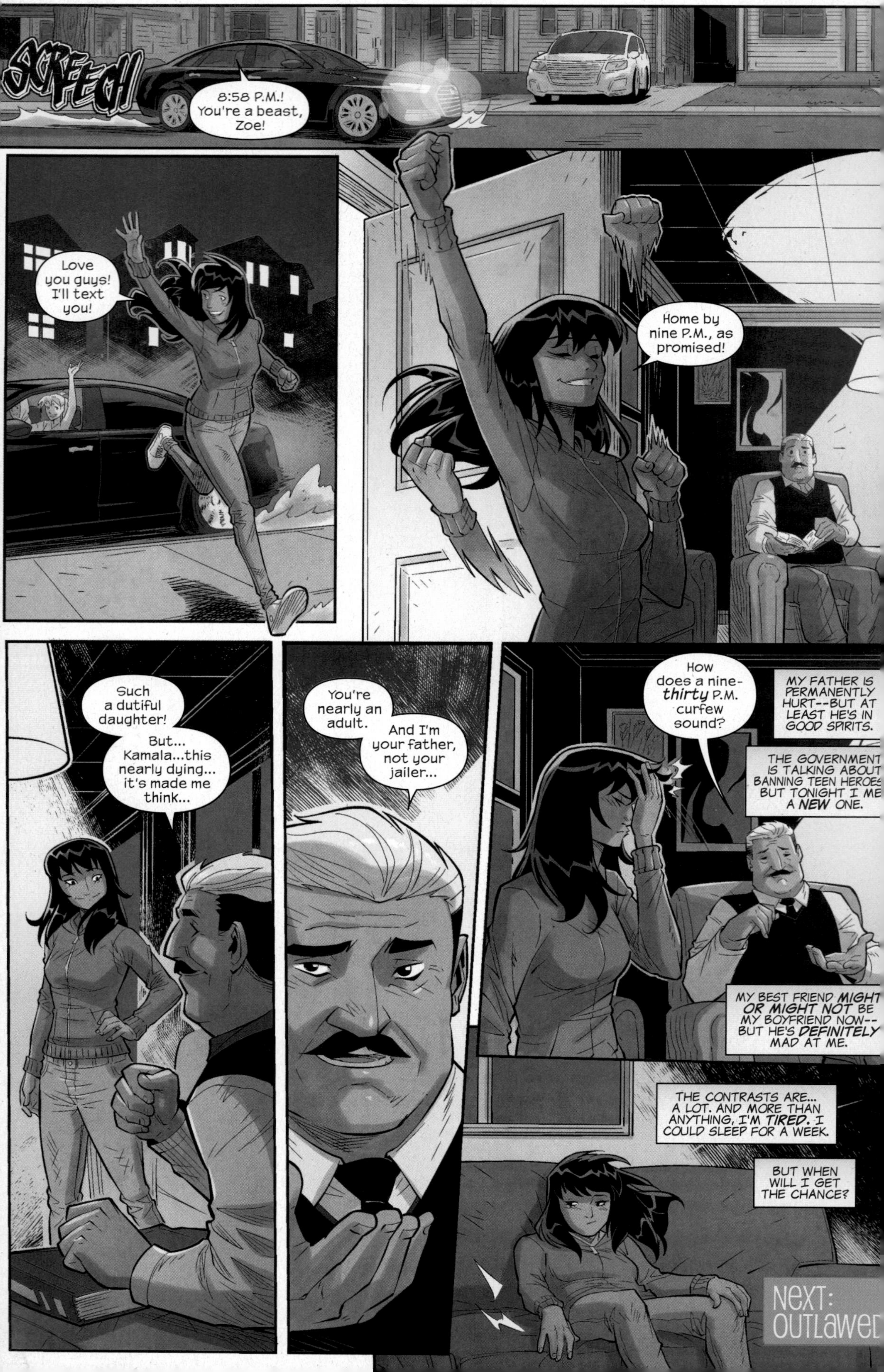

SCREECH
8:58 P.M.! You're a beast, Zoe!
Love you guys! I'll text you!
Home by nine P.M., as promised!
Such a dutiful daughter!
But... Kamala...this nearly dying... it's made me think...
You're nearly an adult.
And I'm your father, not your jailer...
How does a nine-thirty P.M. curfew sound?
MY FATHER IS PERMANENTLY HURT--BUT AT LEAST HE'S IN GOOD SPIRITS.
THE GOVERNMENT IS TALKING ABOUT BANNING TEEN HEROES BUT TONIGHT I ME A NEW ONE.
MY BEST FRIEND MIGHT OR MIGHT NOT BE MY BOYFRIEND NOW--BUT HE'S DEFINITELY MAD AT ME.
THE CONTRASTS ARE... A LOT. AND MORE THAN ANYTHING, I'M TIRED. I COULD SLEEP FOR A WEEK.
BUT WHEN WILL I GET THE CHANCE?
NEXT: OUTLAWED

HOLLA @ KAMALA

Hey there, True Believers! We're so excited to introduce you to AMULET! Amulet, A.K.A. Fadi Adlalah, is a new supporting character in MAGNIFICENT MS. MARVEL, co-created by our wonderful writer, Saladin Ahmed and incredible illustrator Sara Alfageeh!

Amulet's costume is based on the nazar, a talisman traditionally thought by many Middle Eastern cultures to ward off evil intentions. To learn more about the mysterious new fella in Kamala's life, pick up the next arc of MAGNIFICENT MS. MARVEL, where Kamala and her teen super hero allies find themselves…OUTLAWED!

3 pieces so he can raise his arms

Family heirloom
leather strap worn around neck, tucked under shirt

size comparison to kamala

casual wear

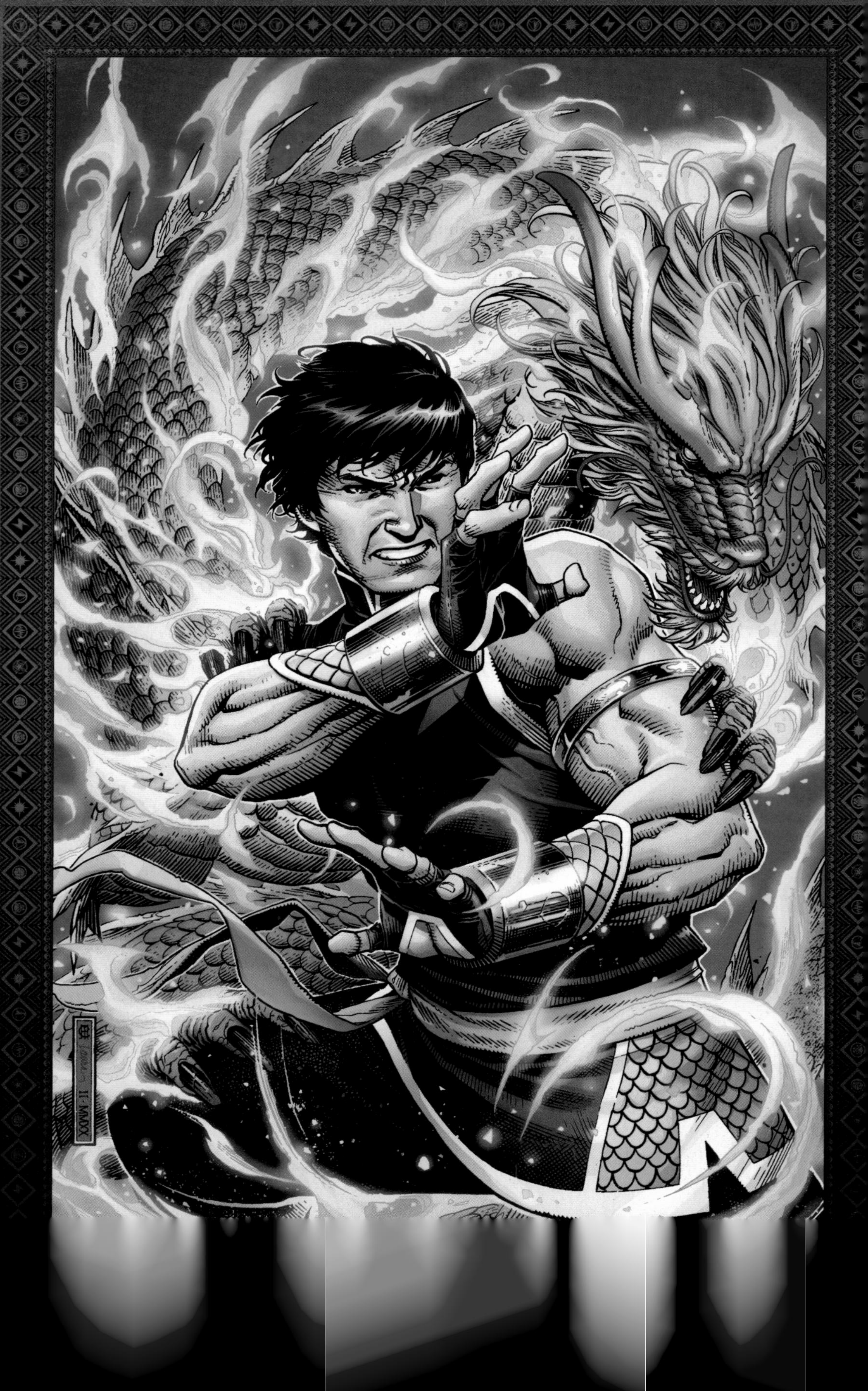

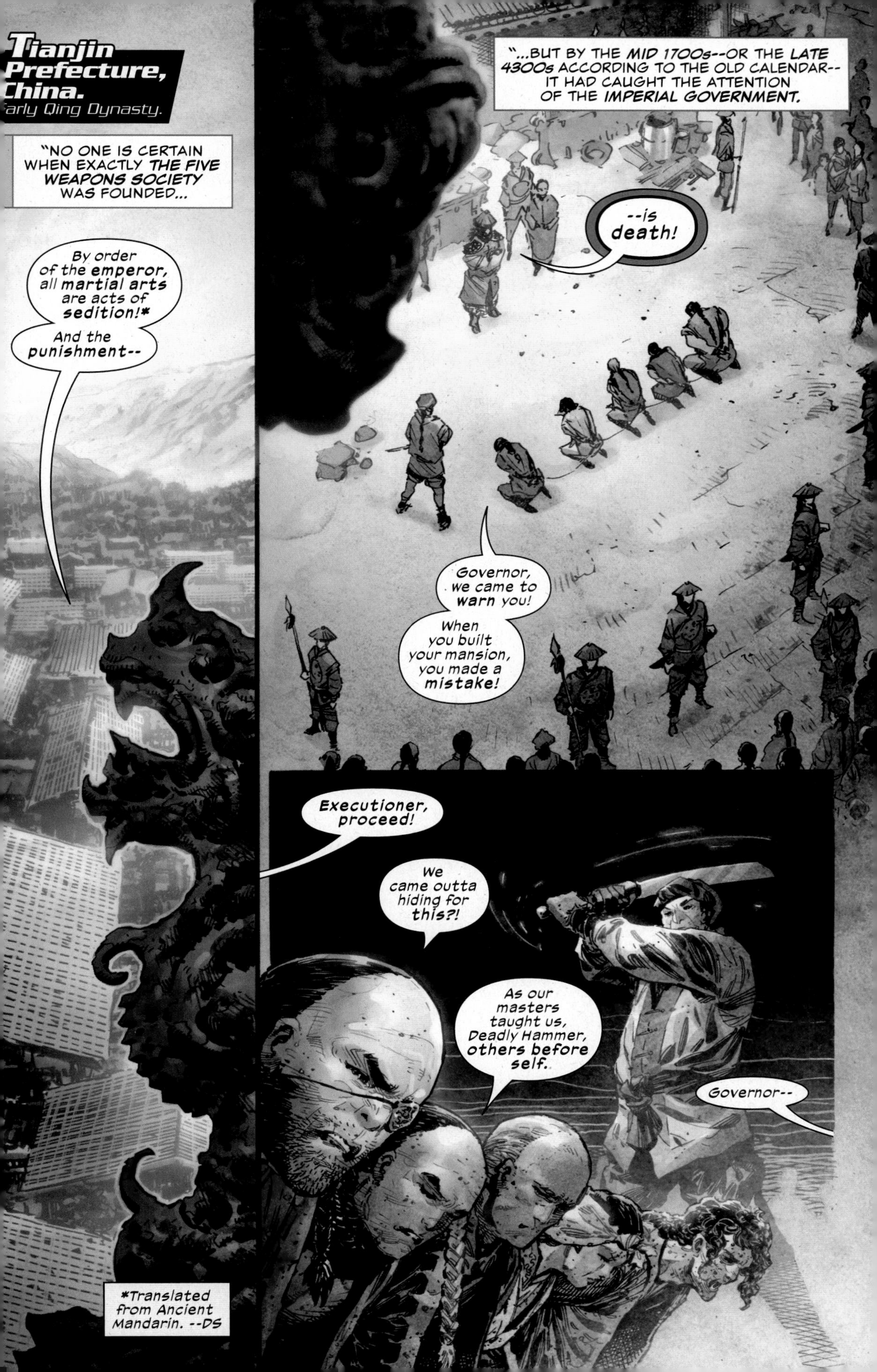
Tianjin Prefecture, China.
Early Qing Dynasty.
"NO ONE IS CERTAIN WHEN EXACTLY THE FIVE WEAPONS SOCIETY WAS FOUNDED...
"...BUT BY THE MID 1700s--OR THE LATE 4300s ACCORDING TO THE OLD CALENDAR--IT HAD CAUGHT THE ATTENTION OF THE IMPERIAL GOVERNMENT.
By order of the emperor, all martial arts are acts of sedition!*
And the punishment--
--is death!
Governor, we came to warn you!
When you built your mansion, you made a mistake!
Executioner, proceed!
We came outta hiding for this?!
As our masters taught us, Deadly Hammer, others before self.
Governor--
*Translated from Ancient Mandarin. --DS

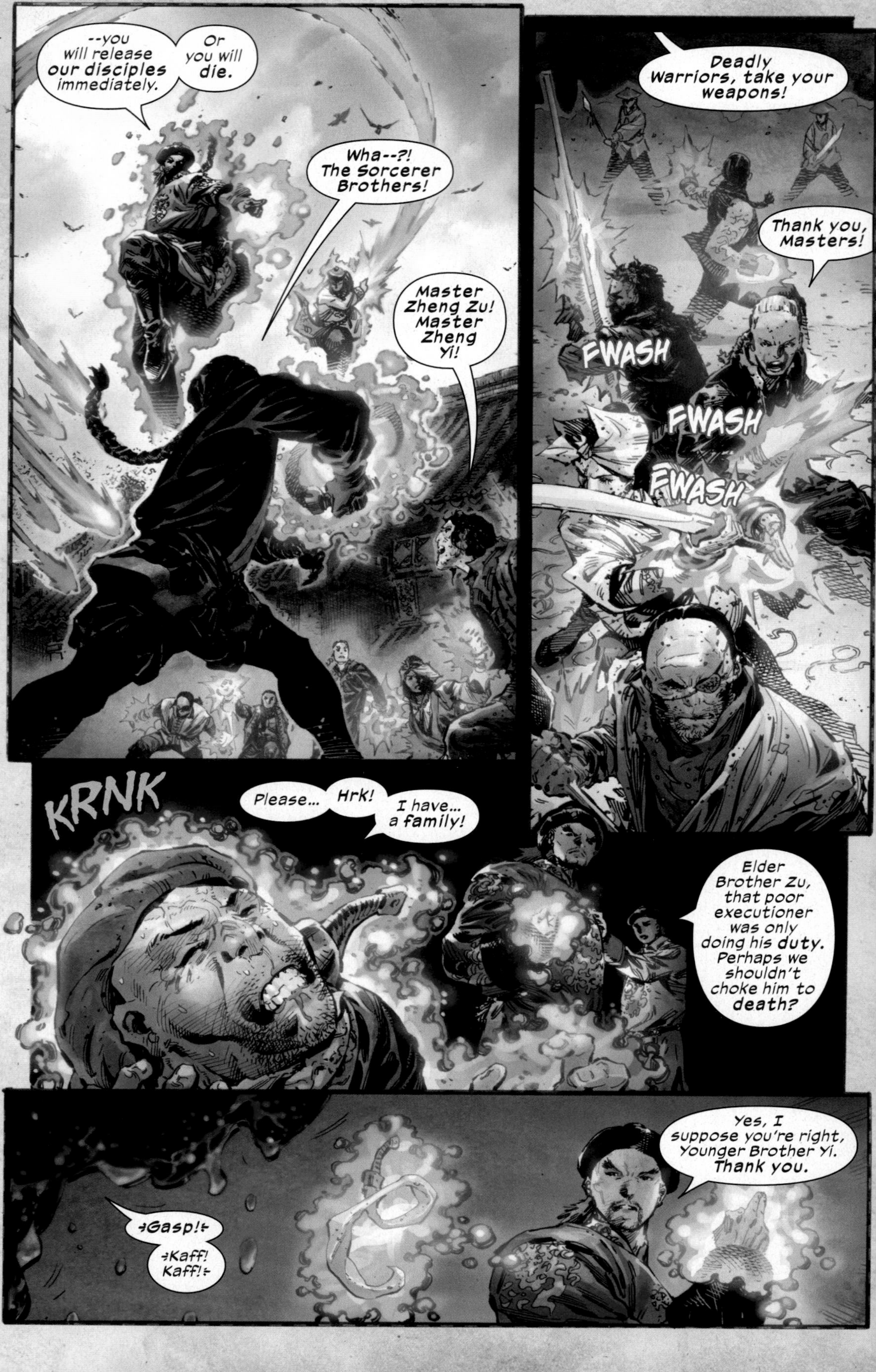
--you will release our disciples immediately.
Or you will die.
Wha--?! The Sorcerer Brothers!
Master Zheng Zu! Master Zheng Yi!
Deadly Warriors, take your weapons!
Thank you, Masters!
FWASH
FWASH
FWASH
KRNK
Please...
Hrk!
I have... a family!
Elder Brother Zu, that poor executioner was only doing his duty. Perhaps we shouldn't choke him to death?
Yes, I suppose you're right, Younger Brother Yi. Thank you.
Gasp!
Kaff! Kaff!

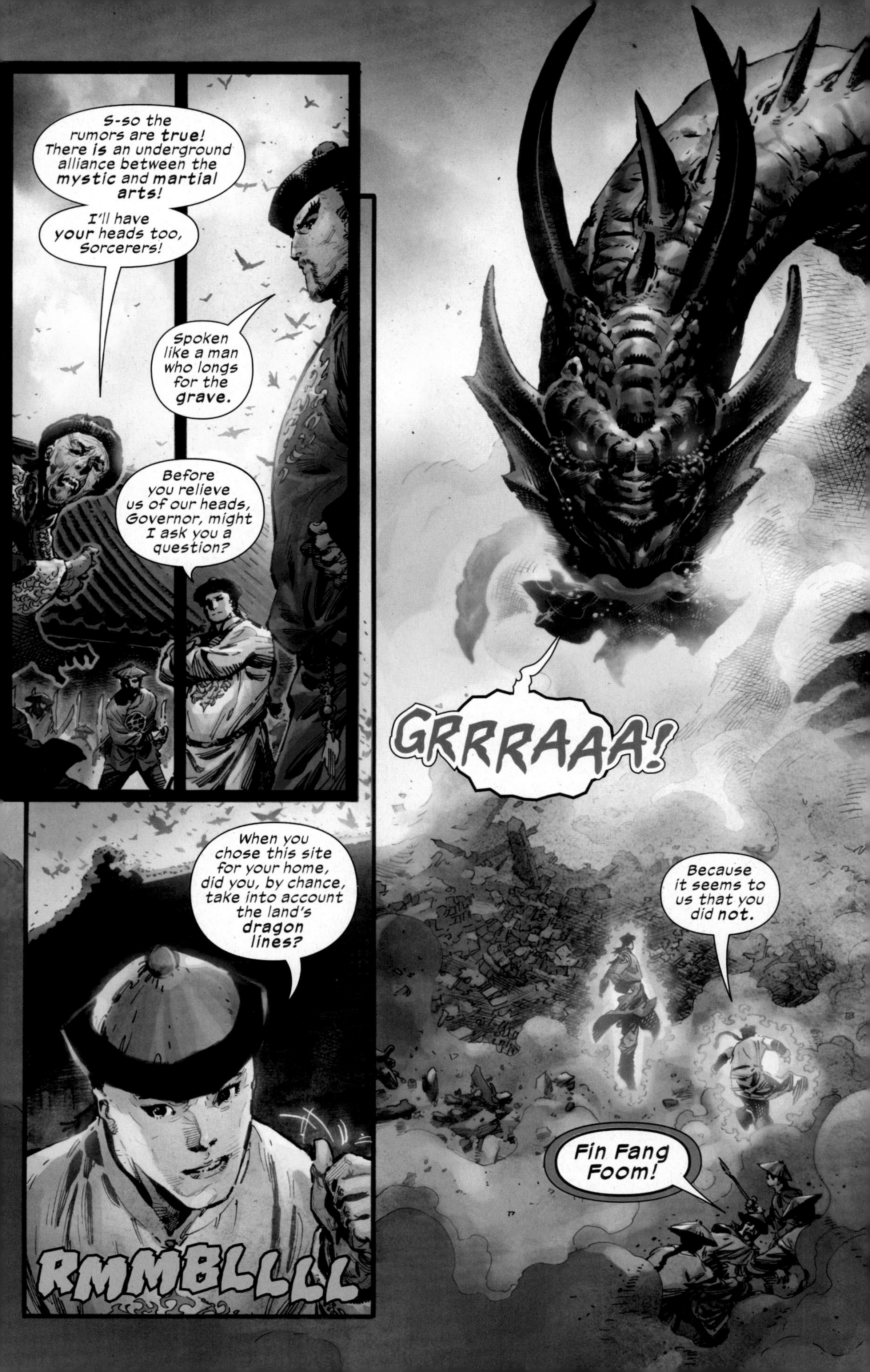
S-so the rumors are true! There is an underground alliance between the mystic and martial arts!
I'll have your heads too, Sorcerers!
Spoken like a man who longs for the grave.
Before you relieve us of our heads, Governor, might I ask you a question?
When you chose this site for your home, did you, by chance, take into account the land's dragon lines?
RMMBLLLL
GRRRAAA!
Because it seems to us that you did not.
Fin Fang Foom!

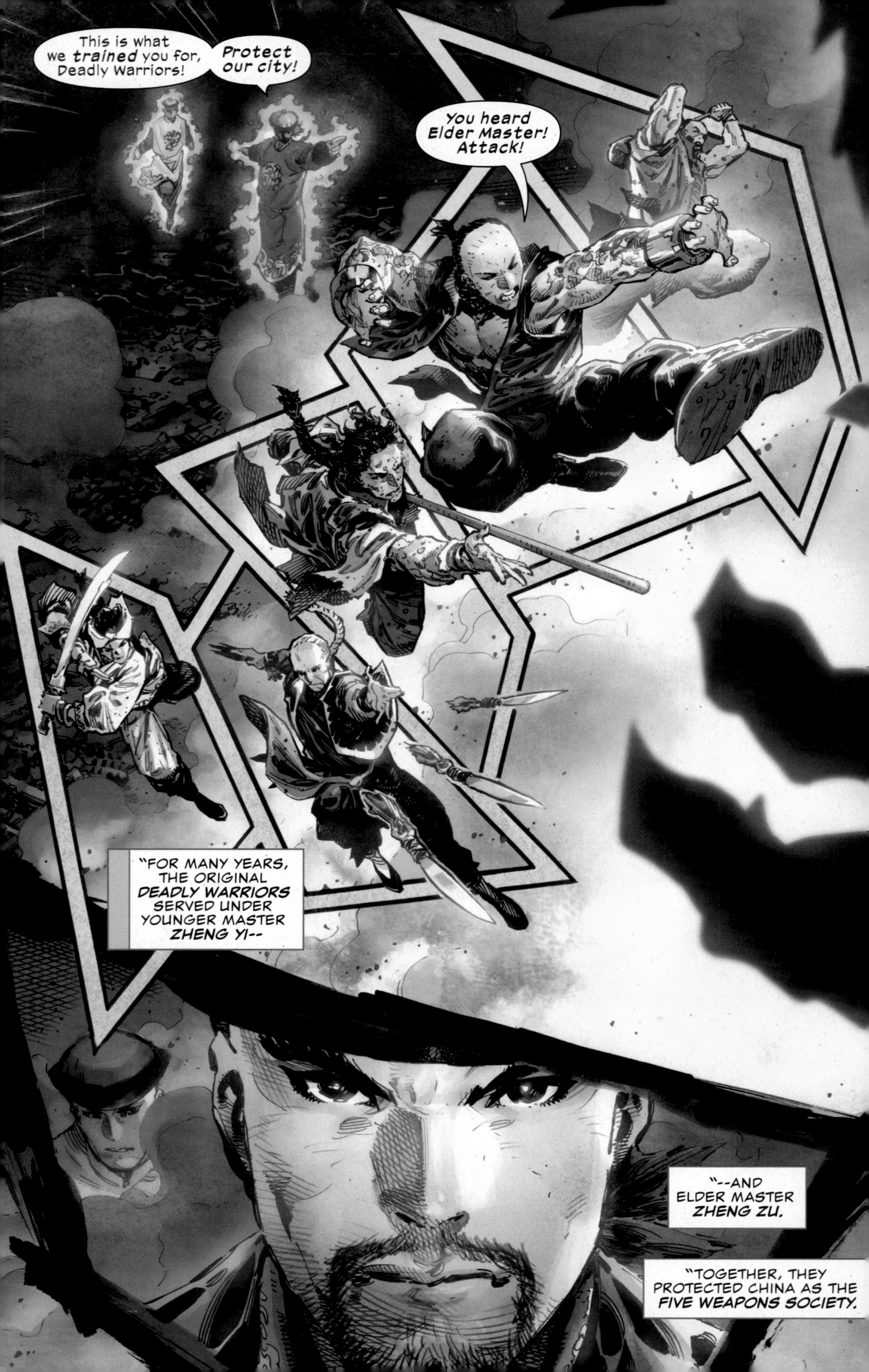

This is what we *trained* you for, Deadly Warriors!
Protect our city!
You heard Elder Master! Attack!
"FOR MANY YEARS, THE ORIGINAL *DEADLY WARRIORS* SERVED UNDER YOUNGER MASTER *ZHENG YI--*
"--AND ELDER MASTER *ZHENG ZU.*
"TOGETHER, THEY PROTECTED CHINA AS THE *FIVE WEAPONS SOCIETY.*

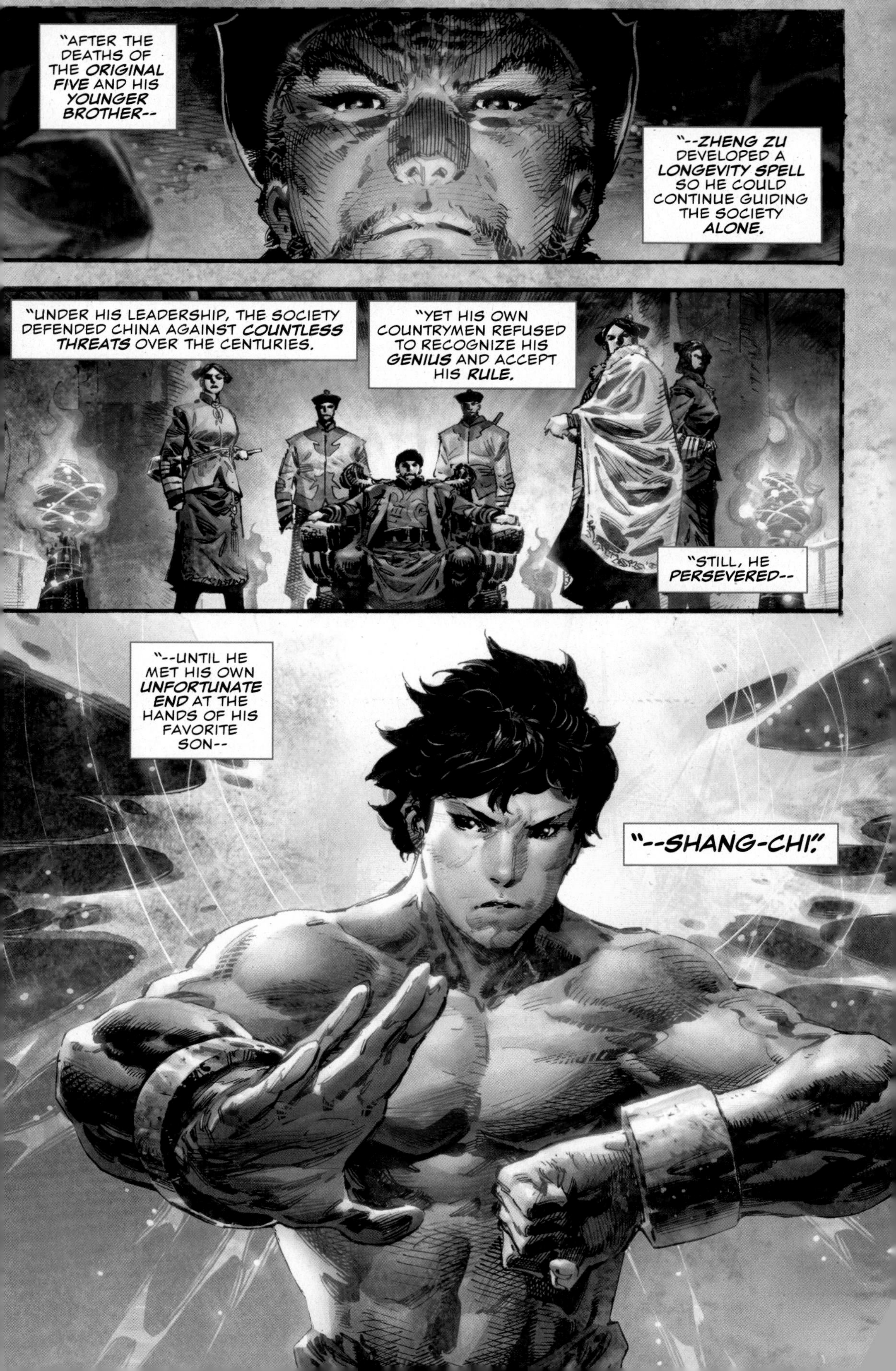
"AFTER THE DEATHS OF THE ORIGINAL FIVE AND HIS YOUNGER BROTHER--
"--ZHENG ZU DEVELOPED A LONGEVITY SPELL SO HE COULD CONTINUE GUIDING THE SOCIETY ALONE.
"UNDER HIS LEADERSHIP, THE SOCIETY DEFENDED CHINA AGAINST COUNTLESS THREATS OVER THE CENTURIES.
"YET HIS OWN COUNTRYMEN REFUSED TO RECOGNIZE HIS GENIUS AND ACCEPT HIS RULE.
"STILL, HE PERSEVERED--
"--UNTIL HE MET HIS OWN UNFORTUNATE END AT THE HANDS OF HIS FAVORITE SON--
"--SHANG-CHI!"

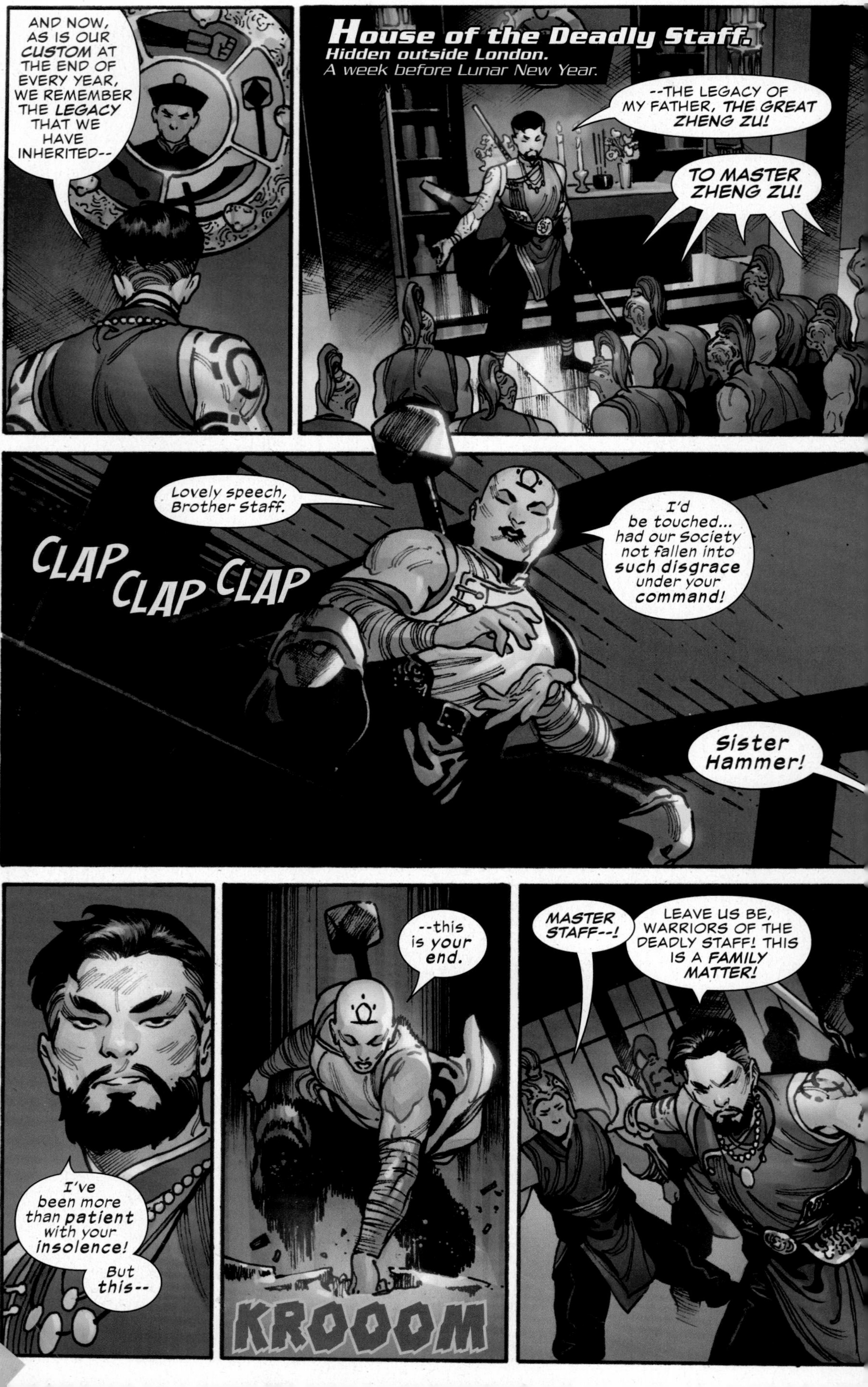
AND NOW, AS IS OUR CUSTOM AT THE END OF EVERY YEAR, WE REMEMBER THE LEGACY THAT WE HAVE INHERITED--
House of the Deadly Staff.
Hidden outside London.
A week before Lunar New Year.
--THE LEGACY OF MY FATHER, THE GREAT ZHENG ZU!
TO MASTER ZHENG ZU!
Lovely speech, Brother Staff.
CLAP CLAP CLAP
I'd be touched... had our Society not fallen into such disgrace under your command!
Sister Hammer!
I've been more than patient with your insolence!
But this--
--this is your end.
KROOOM
MASTER STAFF--!
LEAVE US BE, WARRIORS OF THE DEADLY STAFF! THIS IS A FAMILY MATTER!

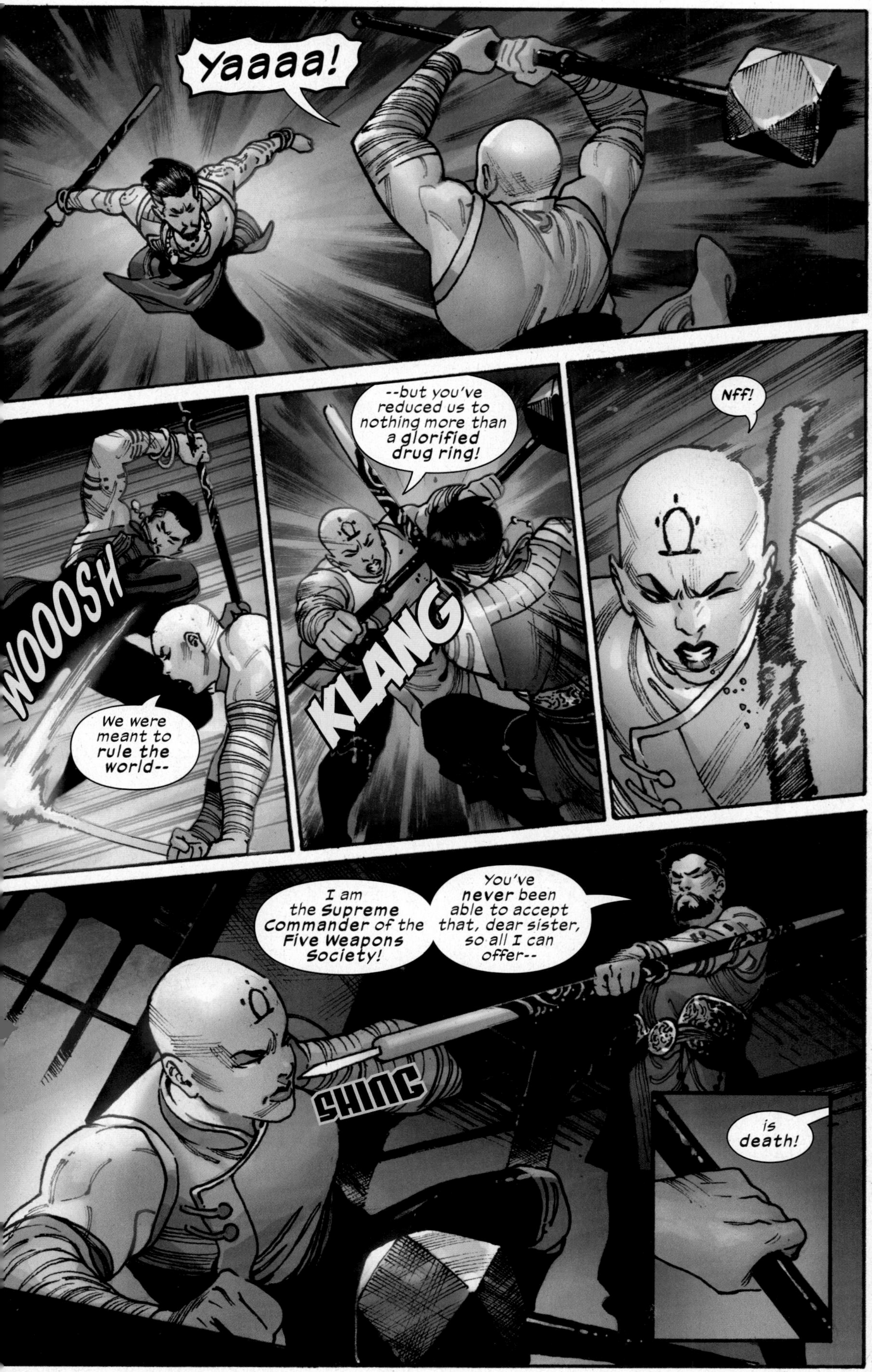
Yaaaa!
WOOOSH
We were meant to rule the world--
--but you've reduced us to nothing more than a glorified drug ring!
KLANG
Nff!
I am the Supreme Commander of the Five Weapons Society!
You've never been able to accept that, dear sister, so all I can offer--
SHING
is death!

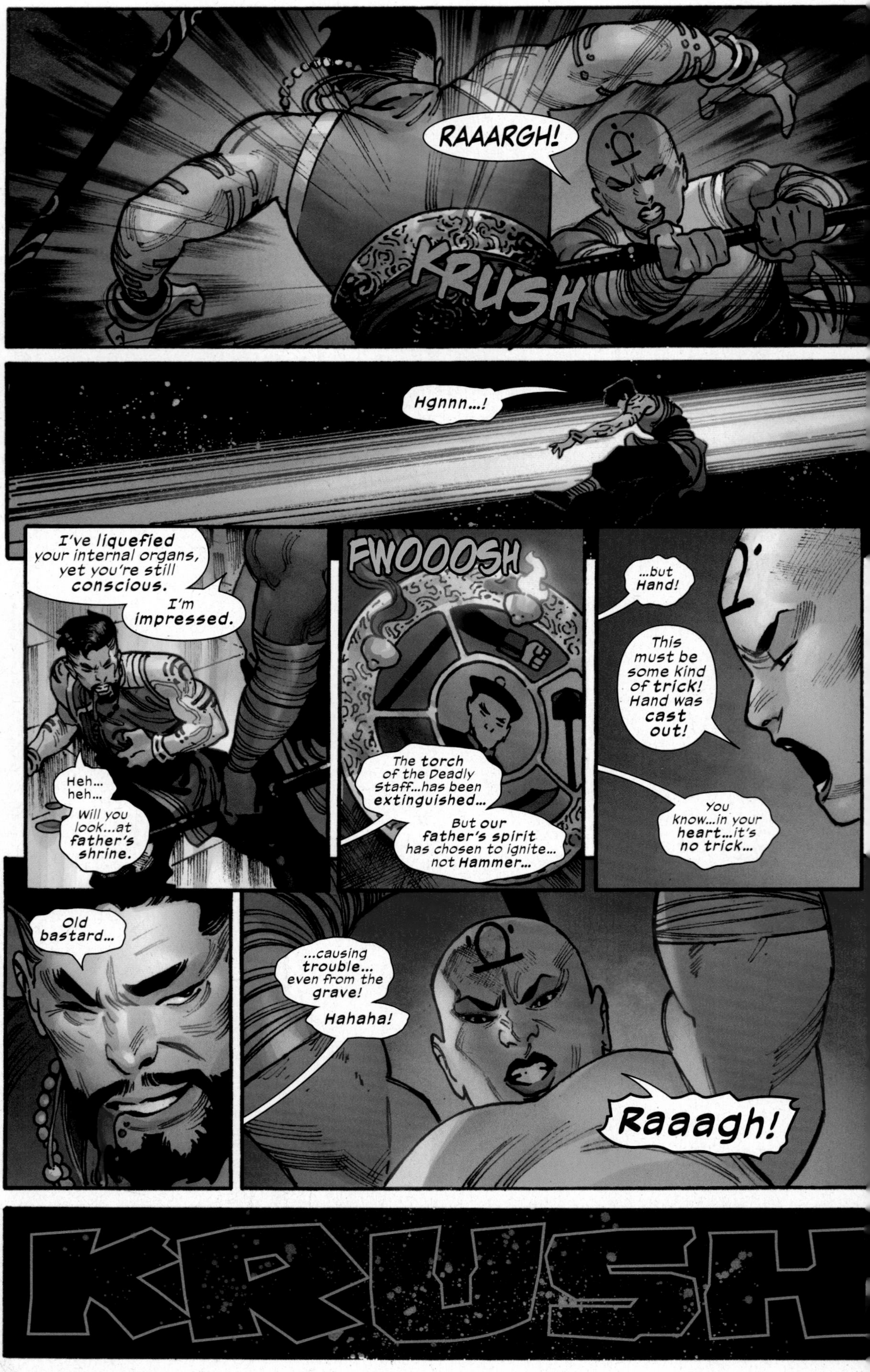
RAAARGH!
KRUSH
Hgnnn...!
I've liquefied your internal organs, yet you're still conscious.
I'm impressed.
Heh... heh...
Will you look...at father's shrine.
FWOOOSH
The torch of the Deadly Staff...has been extinguished...
But our father's spirit has chosen to ignite... not Hammer...
...but Hand!
This must be some kind of trick! Hand was cast out!
You know...in your heart...it's no trick...
Old bastard...
...causing trouble... even from the grave!
Hahaha!
Raaagh!
KRUSH

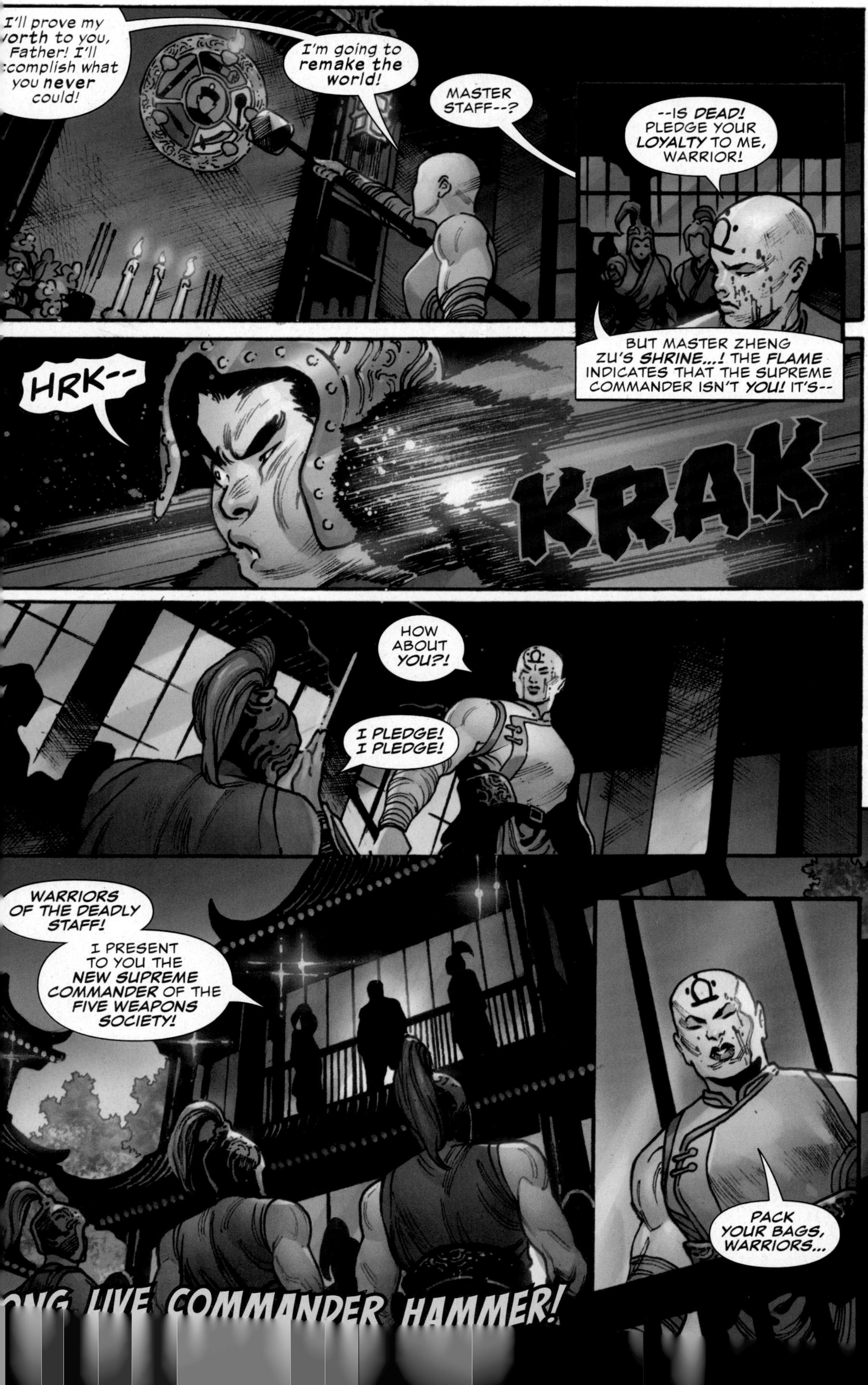
I'll prove my worth to you, Father! I'll accomplish what you never could!
I'm going to remake the world!
MASTER STAFF--?
--IS DEAD! PLEDGE YOUR LOYALTY TO ME, WARRIOR!
BUT MASTER ZHENG ZU'S SHRINE...! THE FLAME INDICATES THAT THE SUPREME COMMANDER ISN'T YOU! IT'S--
HRK--
KRAK
HOW ABOUT YOU?!
I PLEDGE! I PLEDGE!
WARRIORS OF THE DEADLY STAFF!
I PRESENT TO YOU THE NEW SUPREME COMMANDER OF THE FIVE WEAPONS SOCIETY!
PACK YOUR BAGS, WARRIORS...
ONG LIVE COMMANDER HAMMER!

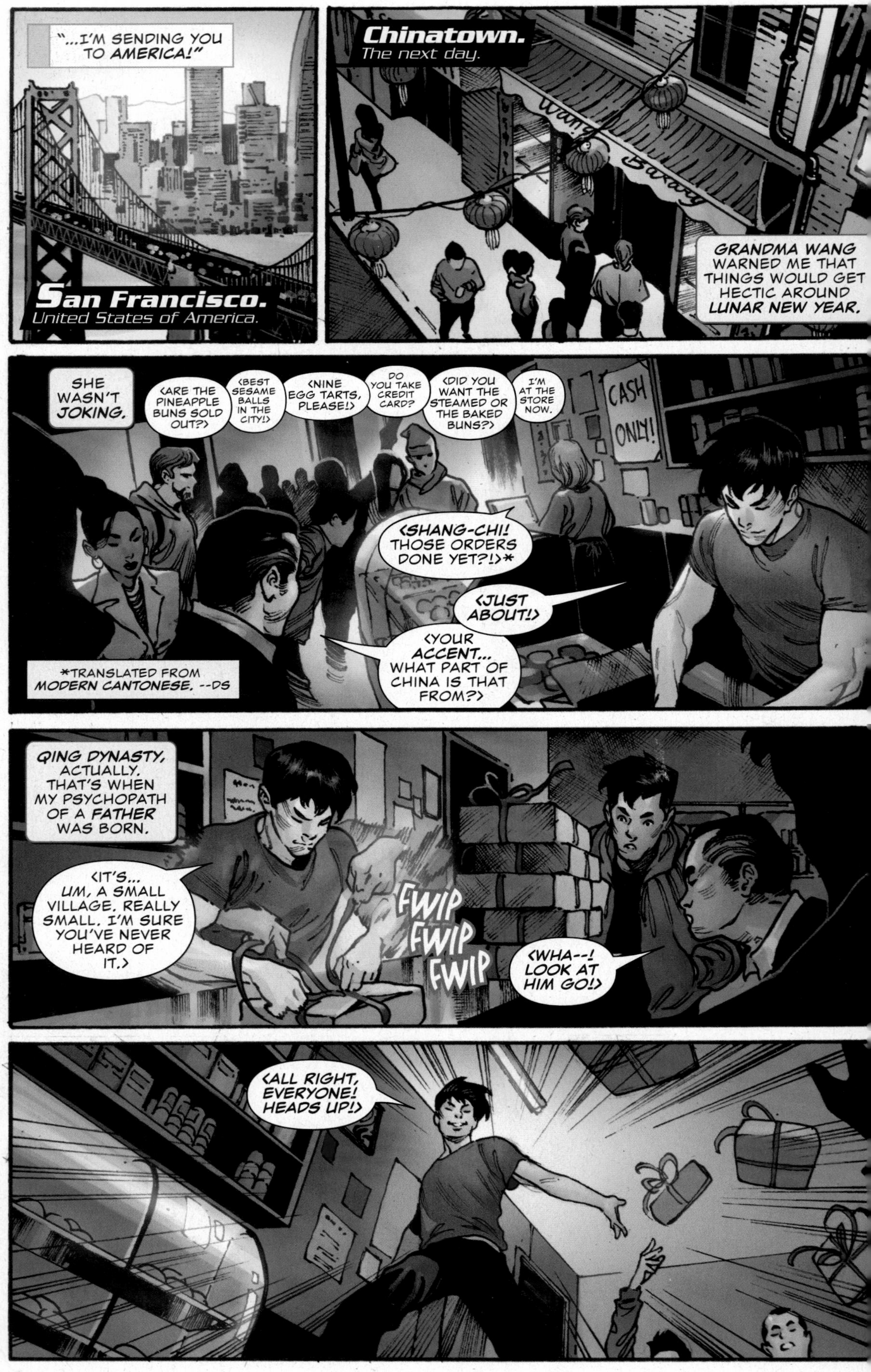
"...I'M SENDING YOU TO AMERICA!"
San Francisco. United States of America.
Chinatown. The next day.
GRANDMA WANG WARNED ME THAT THINGS WOULD GET HECTIC AROUND LUNAR NEW YEAR.
SHE WASN'T JOKING.
<ARE THE PINEAPPLE BUNS SOLD OUT?>
<BEST SESAME BALLS IN THE CITY!>
<NINE EGG TARTS, PLEASE!>
DO YOU TAKE CREDIT CARD?
<DID YOU WANT THE STEAMED OR THE BAKED BUNS?>
I'M AT THE STORE NOW.
CASH ONLY!
<SHANG-CHI! THOSE ORDERS DONE YET?!>*
<JUST ABOUT!>
<YOUR ACCENT... WHAT PART OF CHINA IS THAT FROM?>
*TRANSLATED FROM MODERN CANTONESE. --DS
QING DYNASTY, ACTUALLY. THAT'S WHEN MY PSYCHOPATH OF A FATHER WAS BORN.
<IT'S... UM, A SMALL VILLAGE. REALLY SMALL. I'M SURE YOU'VE NEVER HEARD OF IT.>
FWIP FWIP FWIP
<WHA--! LOOK AT HIM GO!>
<ALL RIGHT, EVERYONE! HEADS UP!>

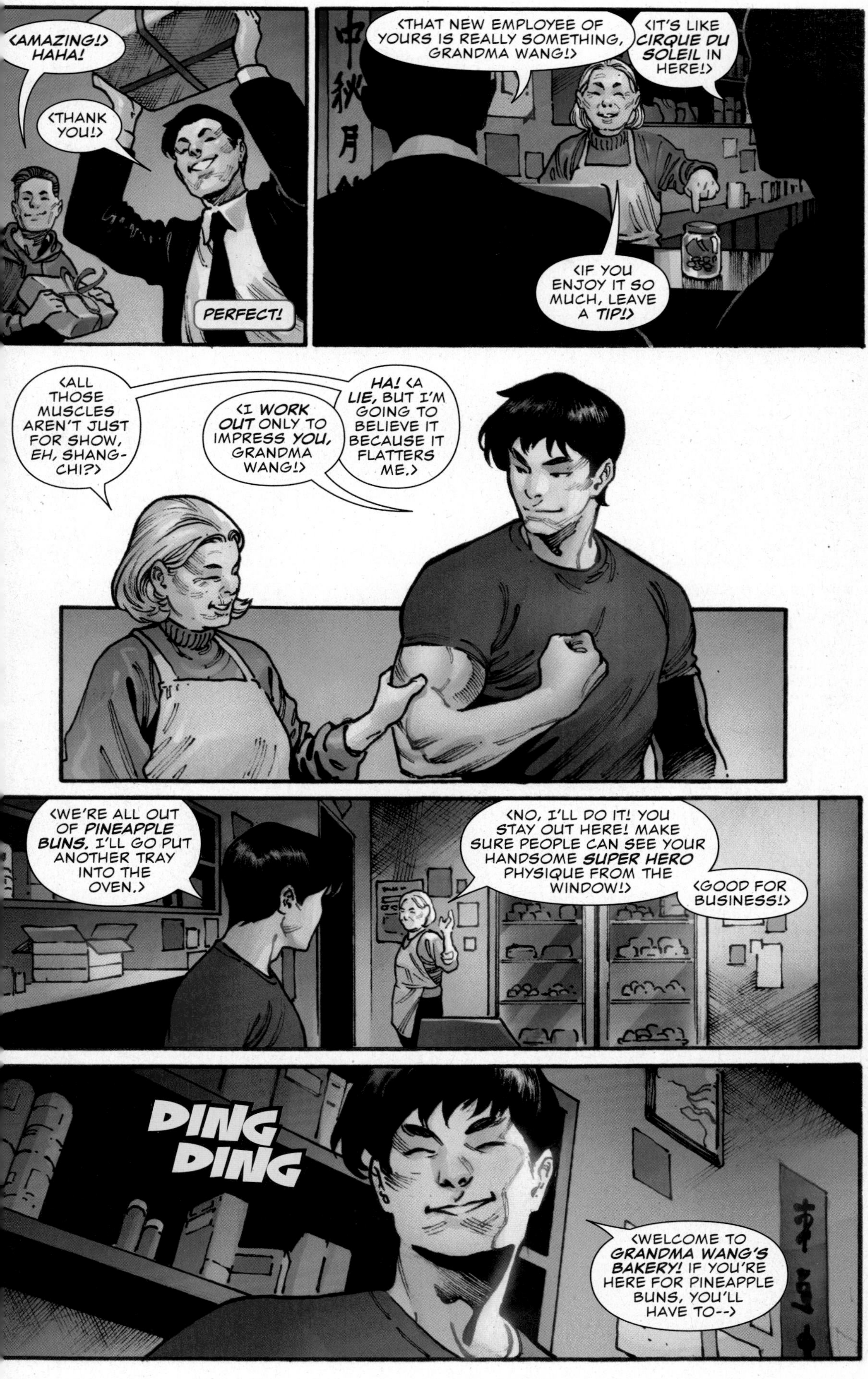
<AMAZING!> HAHA!
<THANK YOU!>
PERFECT!
<THAT NEW EMPLOYEE OF YOURS IS REALLY SOMETHING, GRANDMA WANG!>
<IT'S LIKE CIRQUE DU SOLEIL IN HERE!>
<IF YOU ENJOY IT SO MUCH, LEAVE A TIP!>
<ALL THOSE MUSCLES AREN'T JUST FOR SHOW, EH, SHANG-CHI?>
<I WORK OUT ONLY TO IMPRESS YOU, GRANDMA WANG!>
HA! <A LIE, BUT I'M GOING TO BELIEVE IT BECAUSE IT FLATTERS ME.>
<WE'RE ALL OUT OF PINEAPPLE BUNS. I'LL GO PUT ANOTHER TRAY INTO THE OVEN.>
<NO, I'LL DO IT! YOU STAY OUT HERE! MAKE SURE PEOPLE CAN SEE YOUR HANDSOME SUPER HERO PHYSIQUE FROM THE WINDOW!>
<GOOD FOR BUSINESS!>
DING DING
<WELCOME TO GRANDMA WANG'S BAKERY! IF YOU'RE HERE FOR PINEAPPLE BUNS, YOU'LL HAVE TO-->

HELLO.

<OH.> UM. HELLO.

USUALLY WHEN I MEET A WOMAN THIS *STUNNING*, SHE'S POINTING SOME SORT OF *WEAPON* AT MY FACE.

YOU MUST BE *SHANG-CHI!* I'VE HEARD SO MUCH ABOUT YOU! I'M *DELILAH*, GRANDMA WANG'S NIECE.

DELILAH. HELLO.

THE CALLOUSES ON HER HAND ARE FROM HOLDING A *PEN.*

NOT A GUN. NOT A KNIFE. NOT A *TWELFTH CENTURY KATANA.*

A PEN.

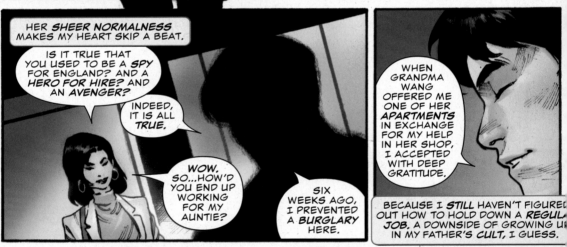

HER *SHEER NORMALNESS* MAKES MY HEART SKIP A BEAT.

IS IT TRUE THAT YOU USED TO BE A *SPY* FOR ENGLAND? AND A *HERO FOR HIRE?* AND AN *AVENGER?*

INDEED, IT IS ALL *TRUE.*

WOW. SO...HOW'D YOU END UP WORKING FOR MY AUNTIE?

SIX WEEKS AGO, I PREVENTED A *BURGLARY* HERE.

WHEN GRANDMA WANG OFFERED ME ONE OF HER *APARTMENTS* IN EXCHANGE FOR MY HELP IN HER SHOP, I ACCEPTED WITH DEEP GRATITUDE.

BECAUSE I *STILL* HAVEN'T FIGURED OUT HOW TO HOLD DOWN A *REGUL[AR]* JOB, A DOWNSIDE OF GROWING U[P] IN MY FATHER'S *CULT*, I GUESS.

DELILAH! <HOW *GENEROUS* OF YOU TO FIT ME INTO YOUR SCHEDULE!>

AUNTIE, I--

<NO NEED TO FEEL GUILTY! YOU'RE A *BIG-TIME* LAWYER! HOW COULD YOU POSSIBLY FIND TIME TO VISIT THE *AUNTIE* WHO SCRIMPED AND SAVED TO PUT YOU THROUGH *LAW SCHOOL?*>

IT'S NICE TO FINALLY MEET YOU, SHANG-CHI.

THE HONOR IS *MINE*, DELILAH.

<COME, DELILAH! LET ME FEED YOU A BOWL OF SOUP! GOOD FOR YOUR SKIN!>

<BECAUSE YOUR SKIN LOOKS LIKE *TREE BARK!*>

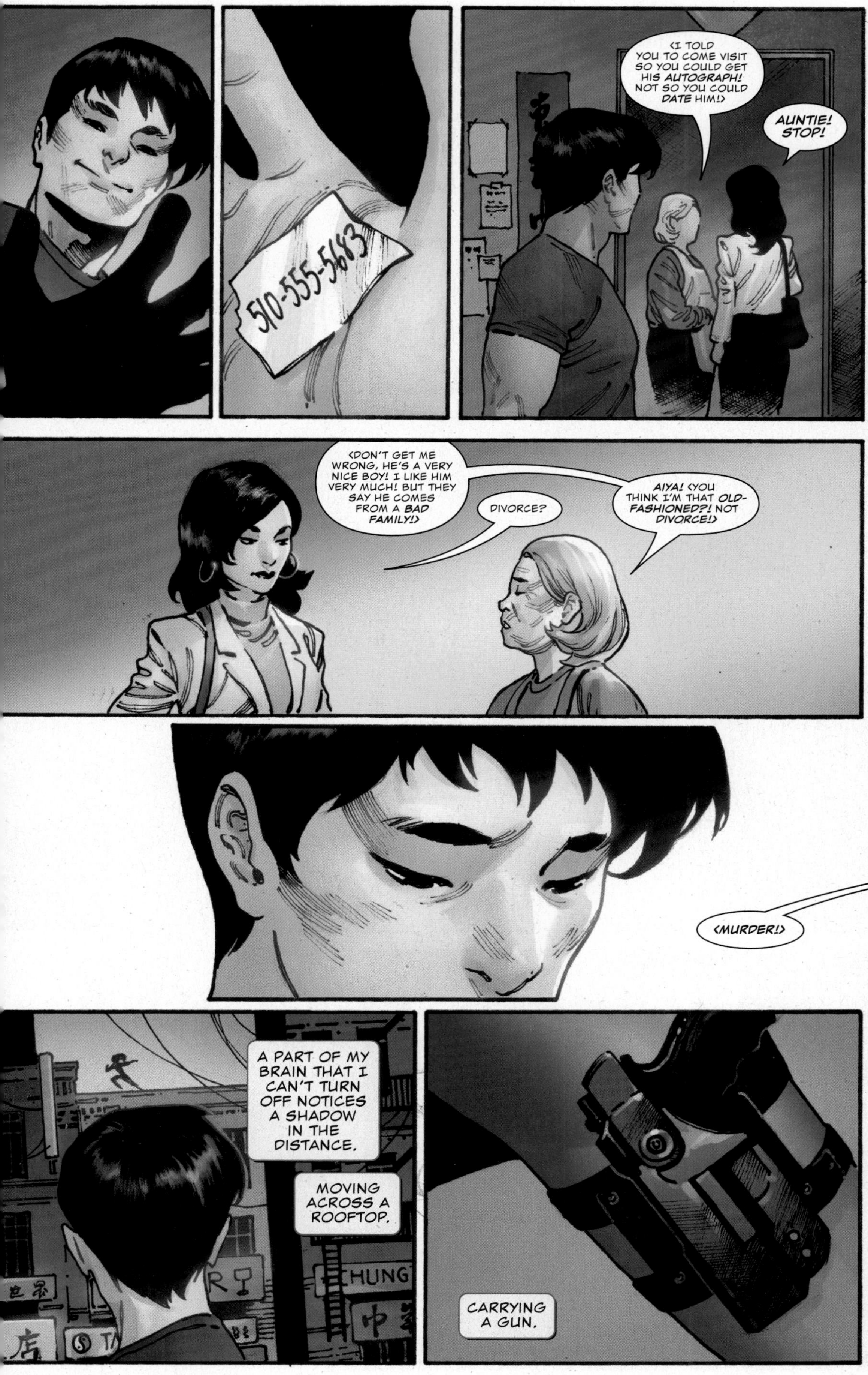
510-555-5683
<I TOLD YOU TO COME VISIT SO YOU COULD GET HIS AUTOGRAPH! NOT SO YOU COULD DATE HIM!>
AUNTIE! STOP!
<DON'T GET ME WRONG, HE'S A VERY NICE BOY! I LIKE HIM VERY MUCH! BUT THEY SAY HE COMES FROM A BAD FAMILY!>
DIVORCE?
AIYA! <YOU THINK I'M THAT OLD-FASHIONED?! NOT DIVORCE!>
<MURDER!>
A PART OF MY BRAIN THAT I CAN'T TURN OFF NOTICES A SHADOW IN THE DISTANCE.
MOVING ACROSS A ROOFTOP.
CHUNG
CARRYING A GUN.

I PRAY TO THE *HEAVENS* THAT MY PRESENCE DOESN'T ENDANGER GRANDMA WANG OR ANY OF HER CUSTOMERS.

OR DELILAH.

WHO AM I KIDDING, THINKING THAT I COULD EVER DATE SOMEONE *NORMAL?*

CLIK

IMPOSSIBLE THAT I GOT THE DROP ON YOU SO EASILY UNLESS YOU WERE *DISTRACTED.*

WHAT'S ON YOUR MIND, LOVE?

LEIKO WU.

BEAUTIFUL BRITISH SECRET AGENT.

GUN IN MY FACE.

THIS IS MY LIFE.

WHAP

AH! THERE HE IS!

FOR WHAT REASON HAVE YOU COME, LEIKO WU?

TO KEEP YOU *ALIVE*, LOVE.

WE NEED TO TALK. PRIVATEL

KNOW PLACE

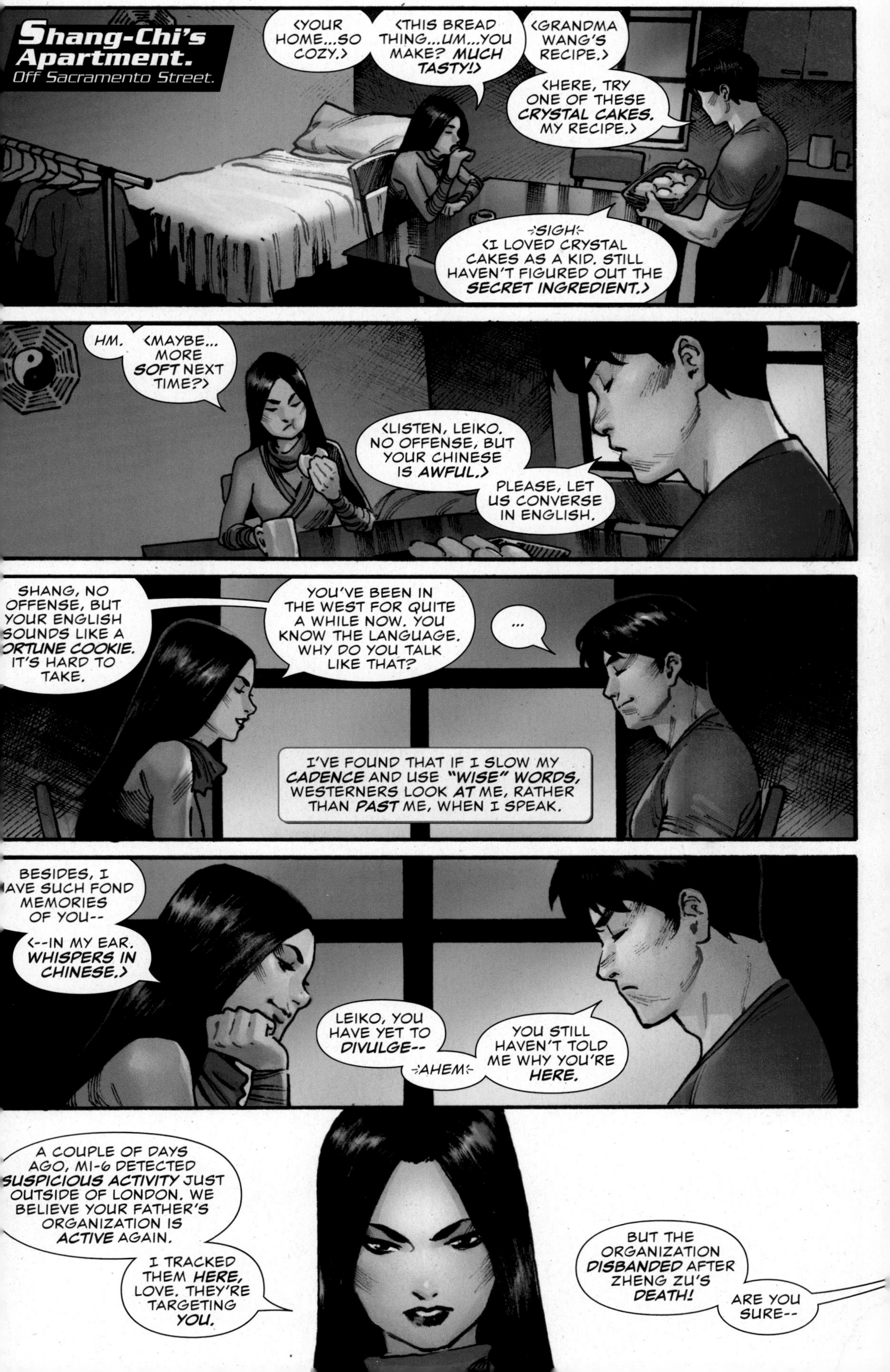
Shang-Chi's Apartment. Off Sacramento Street.
<YOUR HOME...SO COZY.>
<THIS BREAD THING...UM...YOU MAKE? MUCH TASTY!>
<GRANDMA WANG'S RECIPE.>
<HERE, TRY ONE OF THESE CRYSTAL CAKES. MY RECIPE.>
SIGH <I LOVED CRYSTAL CAKES AS A KID. STILL HAVEN'T FIGURED OUT THE SECRET INGREDIENT.>
HM.
<MAYBE... MORE SOFT NEXT TIME?>
<LISTEN, LEIKO. NO OFFENSE, BUT YOUR CHINESE IS AWFUL.>
PLEASE, LET US CONVERSE IN ENGLISH.
SHANG, NO OFFENSE, BUT YOUR ENGLISH SOUNDS LIKE A ORTUNE COOKIE. IT'S HARD TO TAKE.
YOU'VE BEEN IN THE WEST FOR QUITE A WHILE NOW. YOU KNOW THE LANGUAGE. WHY DO YOU TALK LIKE THAT?
...
I'VE FOUND THAT IF I SLOW MY CADENCE AND USE "WISE" WORDS, WESTERNERS LOOK AT ME, RATHER THAN PAST ME, WHEN I SPEAK.
BESIDES, I AVE SUCH FOND MEMORIES OF YOU--
<--IN MY EAR. WHISPERS IN CHINESE.>
LEIKO, YOU HAVE YET TO DIVULGE--
AHEM
YOU STILL HAVEN'T TOLD ME WHY YOU'RE HERE.
A COUPLE OF DAYS AGO, MI-6 DETECTED SUSPICIOUS ACTIVITY JUST OUTSIDE OF LONDON. WE BELIEVE YOUR FATHER'S ORGANIZATION IS ACTIVE AGAIN.
I TRACKED THEM HERE, LOVE. THEY'RE TARGETING YOU.
BUT THE ORGANIZATION DISBANDED AFTER ZHENG ZU'S DEATH!
ARE YOU SURE--

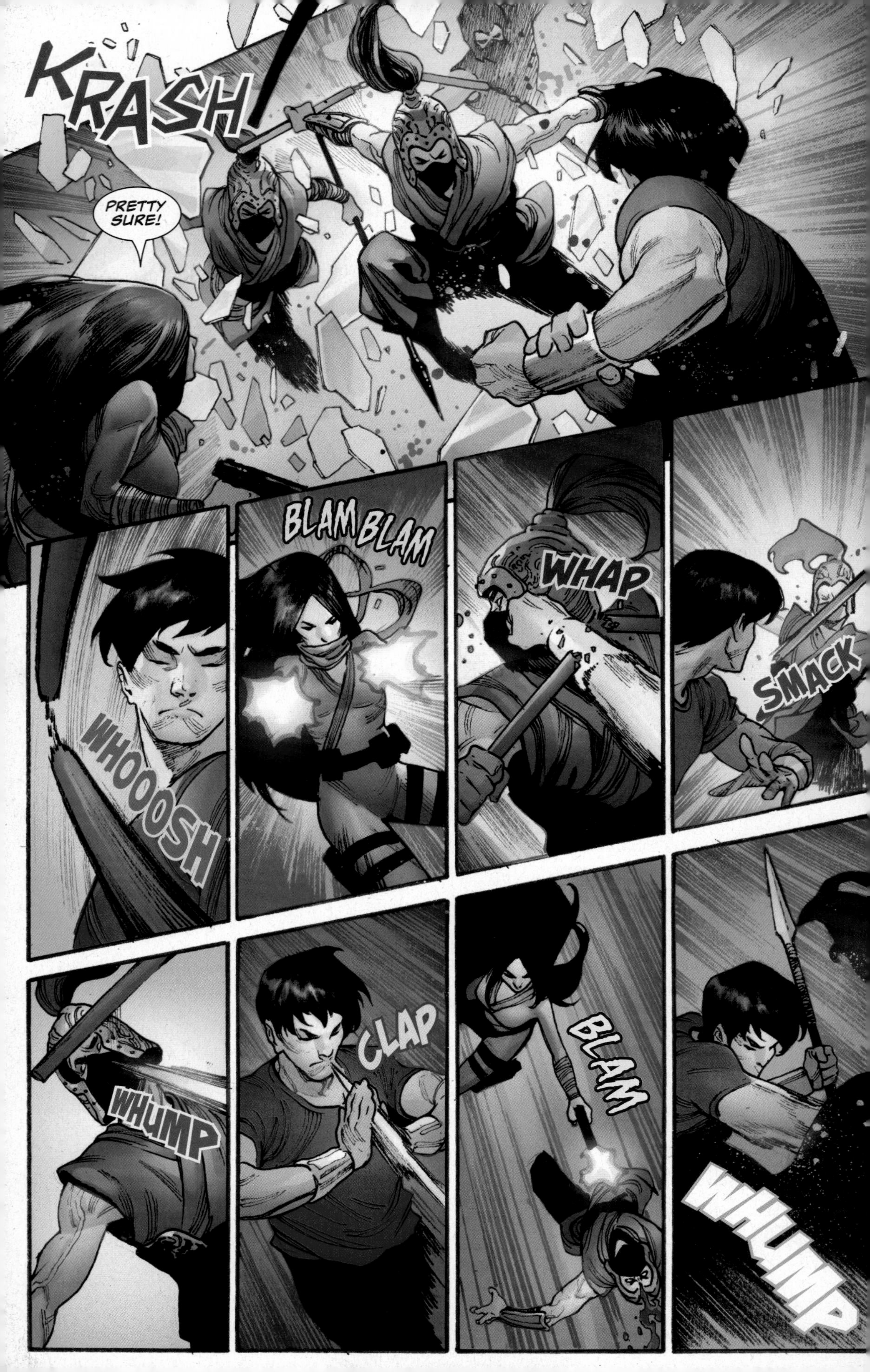
KRASH
PRETTY SURE!
WHOOOSH
BLAM BLAM
WHAP
SMACK
WHUMP
CLAP
BLAM
WHUMP

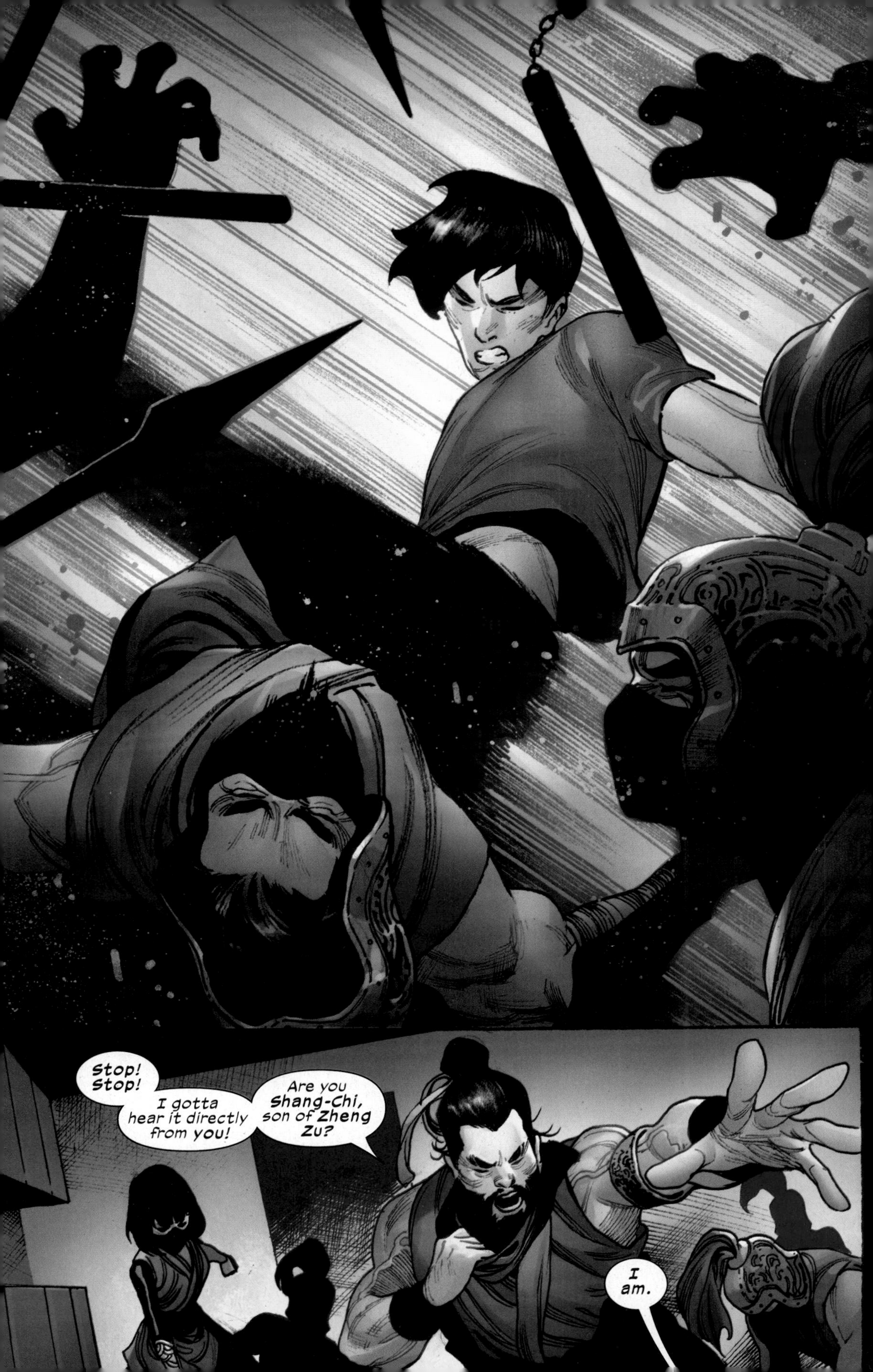

Stop! Stop!
I gotta hear it directly from you!
Are you Shang-Chi, son of Zheng Zu?
I am.

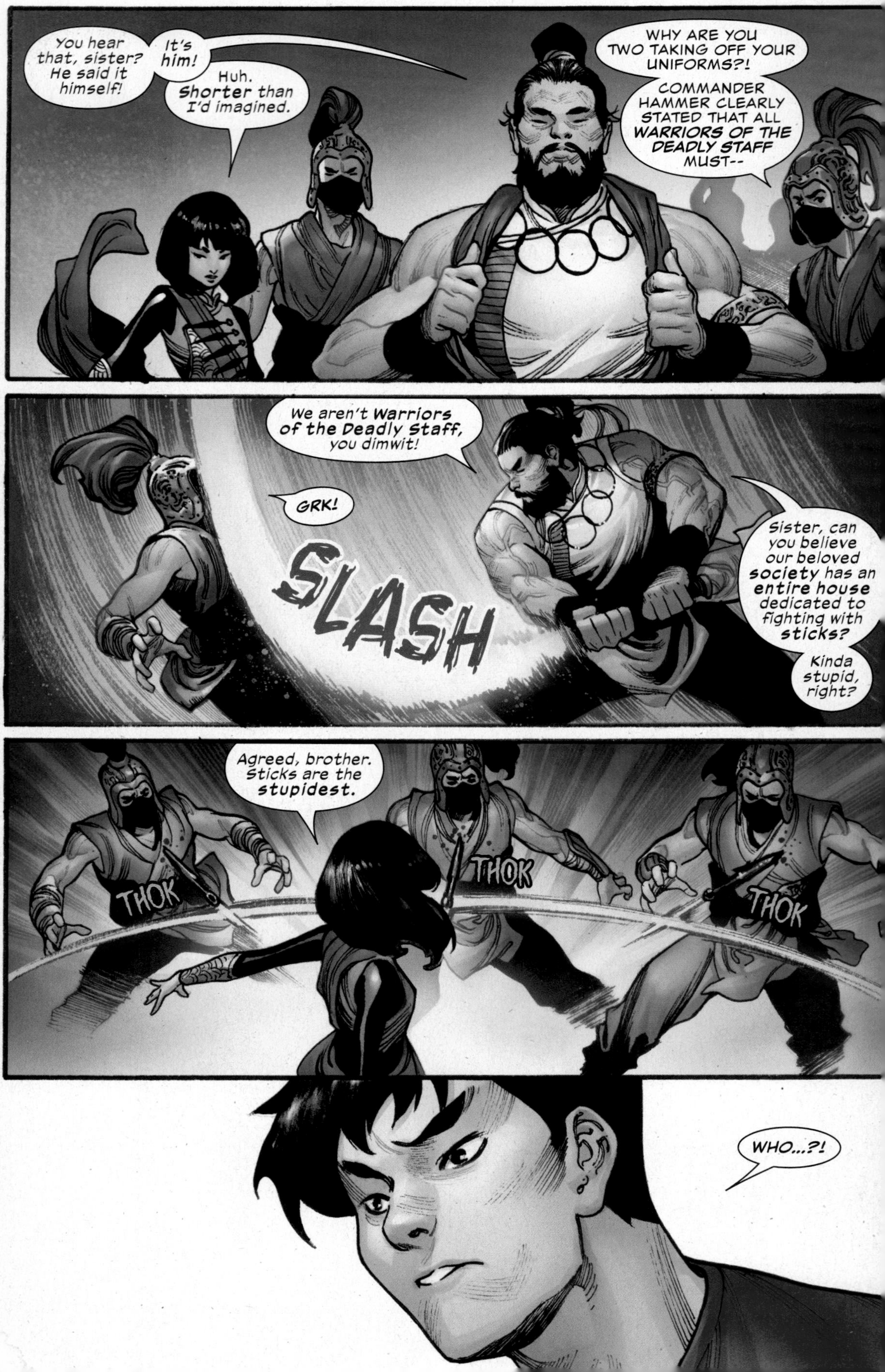

You hear that, sister? He said it himself!
It's him!
Huh. Shorter than I'd imagined.
WHY ARE YOU TWO TAKING OFF YOUR UNIFORMS?!
COMMANDER HAMMER CLEARLY STATED THAT ALL WARRIORS OF THE DEADLY STAFF MUST--
We aren't Warriors of the Deadly Staff, you dimwit!
GRK!
SLASH
Sister, can you believe our beloved society has an entire house dedicated to fighting with sticks?
Kinda stupid, right?
Agreed, brother. Sticks are the stupidest.
THOK
THOK
THOK
WHO...?!

Brother Hand! ...ever since your torch--

Haha! I'm getting ahead of myself! I am **Brother Sabre,** Champion of the House of the Deadly Sabre!

And I'm **Sister Dagger,** Champion of...Bah, you can figure it out.

Why did you call me "Brother Hand"?

Aren't you from the House of the Deadly Hand?

Not that it's any of your business, but I was raised in Zheng Zu's Hunan Retreat!

Same thing. Duh.

We bring you exciting news, brother!

The spirit of our father, the ever-victorious Master Zheng Zu, has selected you to be the next Supreme Commander of the Five Weapons Society!

Unexpected, considering you murdered him.

I didn't murder my father! He--

But that's the beauty of family, right? **Family forgives!**

Even patricide, apparently.

Return to your family, Brother Hand! Assume your rightful place!

Together, we'll depose the illegitimate Supreme Commander before she enacts her terrible plan for the world!

What he's saying is, come back or everyone's gonna die.

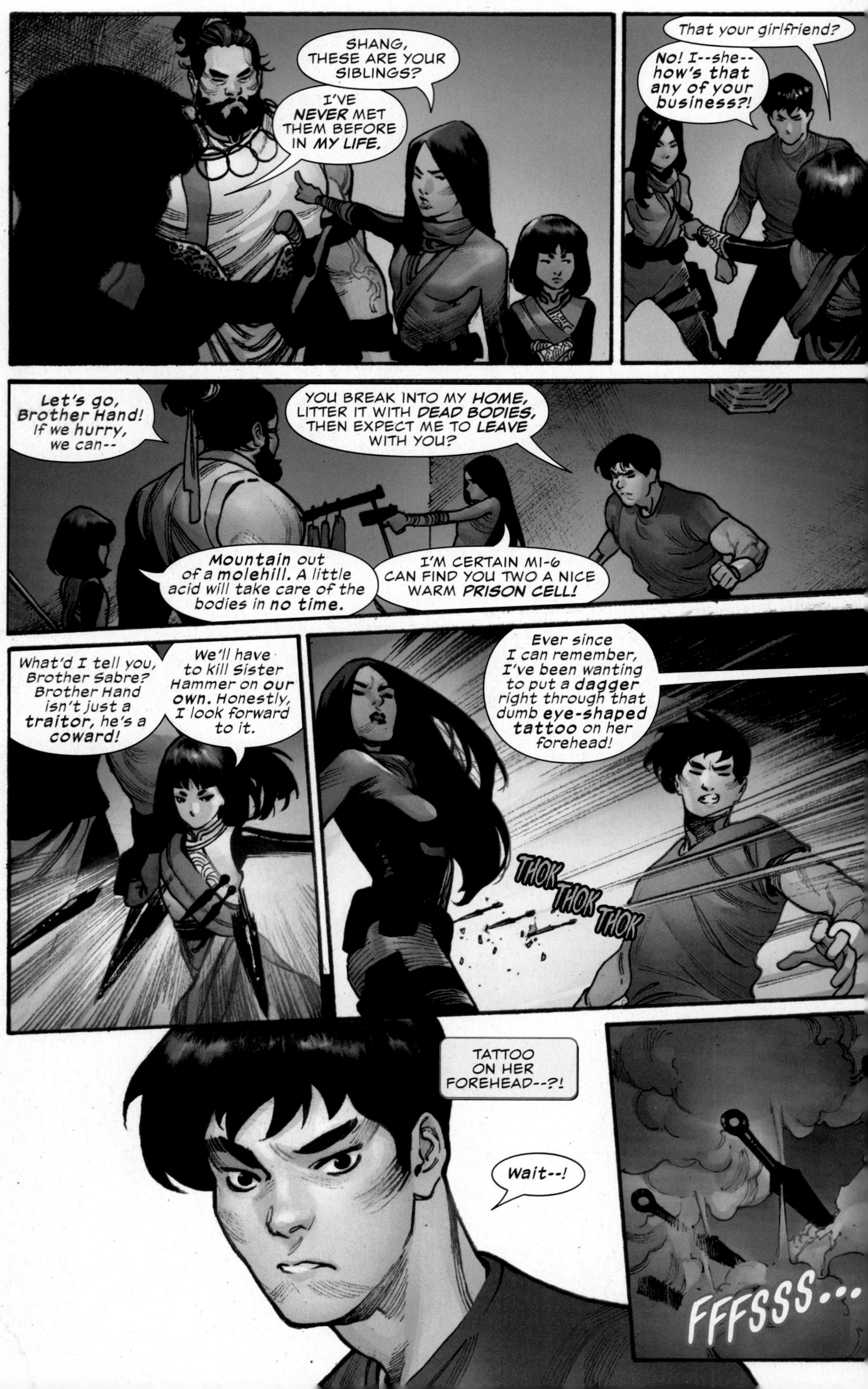
SHANG, THESE ARE YOUR SIBLINGS?
I'VE NEVER MET THEM BEFORE IN MY LIFE.
That your girlfriend?
No! I--she-- how's that any of your business?!
Let's go, Brother Hand! If we hurry, we can--
YOU BREAK INTO MY HOME, LITTER IT WITH DEAD BODIES, THEN EXPECT ME TO LEAVE WITH YOU?
Mountain out of a molehill. A little acid will take care of the bodies in no time.
I'M CERTAIN MI-6 CAN FIND YOU TWO A NICE WARM PRISON CELL!
What'd I tell you, Brother Sabre? Brother Hand isn't just a traitor, he's a coward!
We'll have to kill Sister Hammer on our own. Honestly, I look forward to it.
Ever since I can remember, I've been wanting to put a dagger right through that dumb eye-shaped tattoo on her forehead!
THOK THOK THOK
TATTOO ON HER FOREHEAD--?!
Wait--!
FFFSSS...

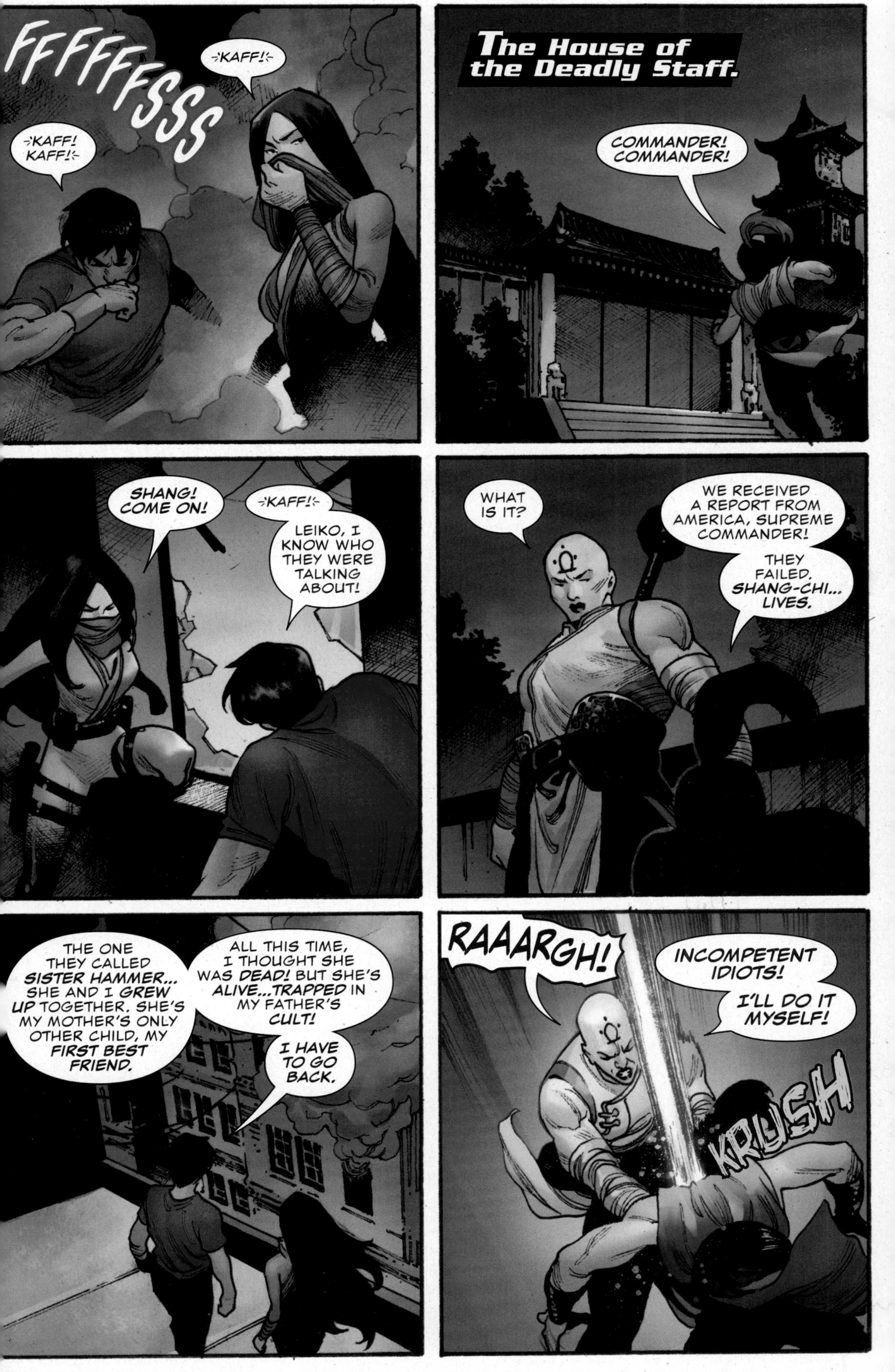
FFFFFFSSS
-KAFF!-
-KAFF! KAFF!-
The House of the Deadly Staff.
COMMANDER! COMMANDER!
SHANG! COME ON!
-KAFF!-
LEIKO, I KNOW WHO THEY WERE TALKING ABOUT!
WHAT IS IT?
WE RECEIVED A REPORT FROM AMERICA, SUPREME COMMANDER!
THEY FAILED. SHANG-CHI... LIVES.
THE ONE THEY CALLED SISTER HAMMER... SHE AND I GREW UP TOGETHER. SHE'S MY MOTHER'S ONLY OTHER CHILD, MY FIRST BEST FRIEND.
ALL THIS TIME, I THOUGHT SHE WAS DEAD! BUT SHE'S ALIVE...TRAPPED IN MY FATHER'S CULT!
I HAVE TO GO BACK.
RAAARGH!
INCOMPETENT IDIOTS!
I'LL DO IT MYSELF!
KRUSH

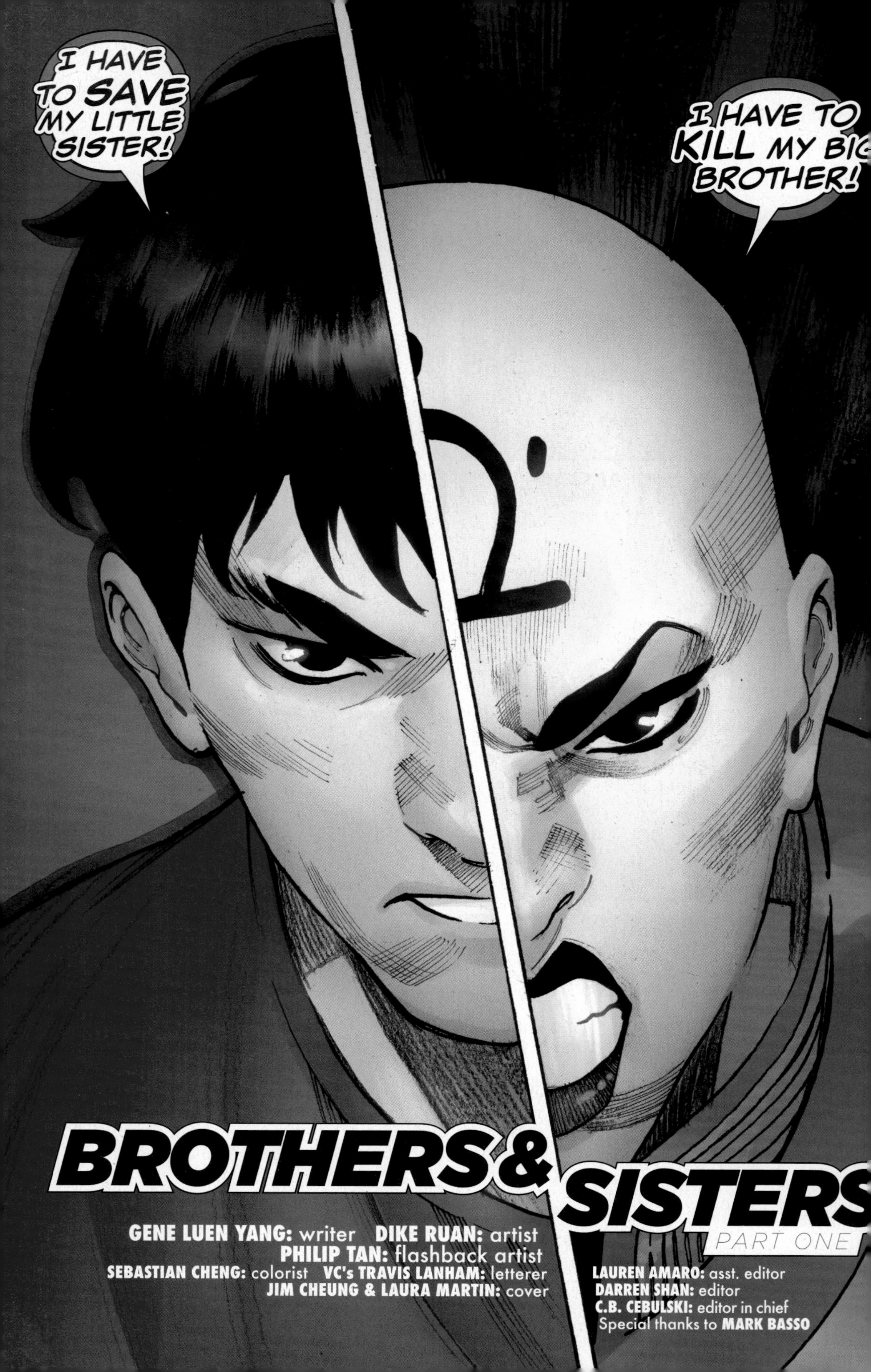

I HAVE TO SAVE MY LITTLE SISTER!
I HAVE TO KILL MY BIG BROTHER!
BROTHERS & SISTERS
PART ONE
GENE LUEN YANG: writer DIKE RUAN: artist
PHILIP TAN: flashback artist
SEBASTIAN CHENG: colorist VC's TRAVIS LANHAM: letterer
JIM CHEUNG & LAURA MARTIN: cover
LAUREN AMARO: asst. editor
DARREN SHAN: editor
C.B. CEBULSKI: editor in chief
Special thanks to MARK BASSO

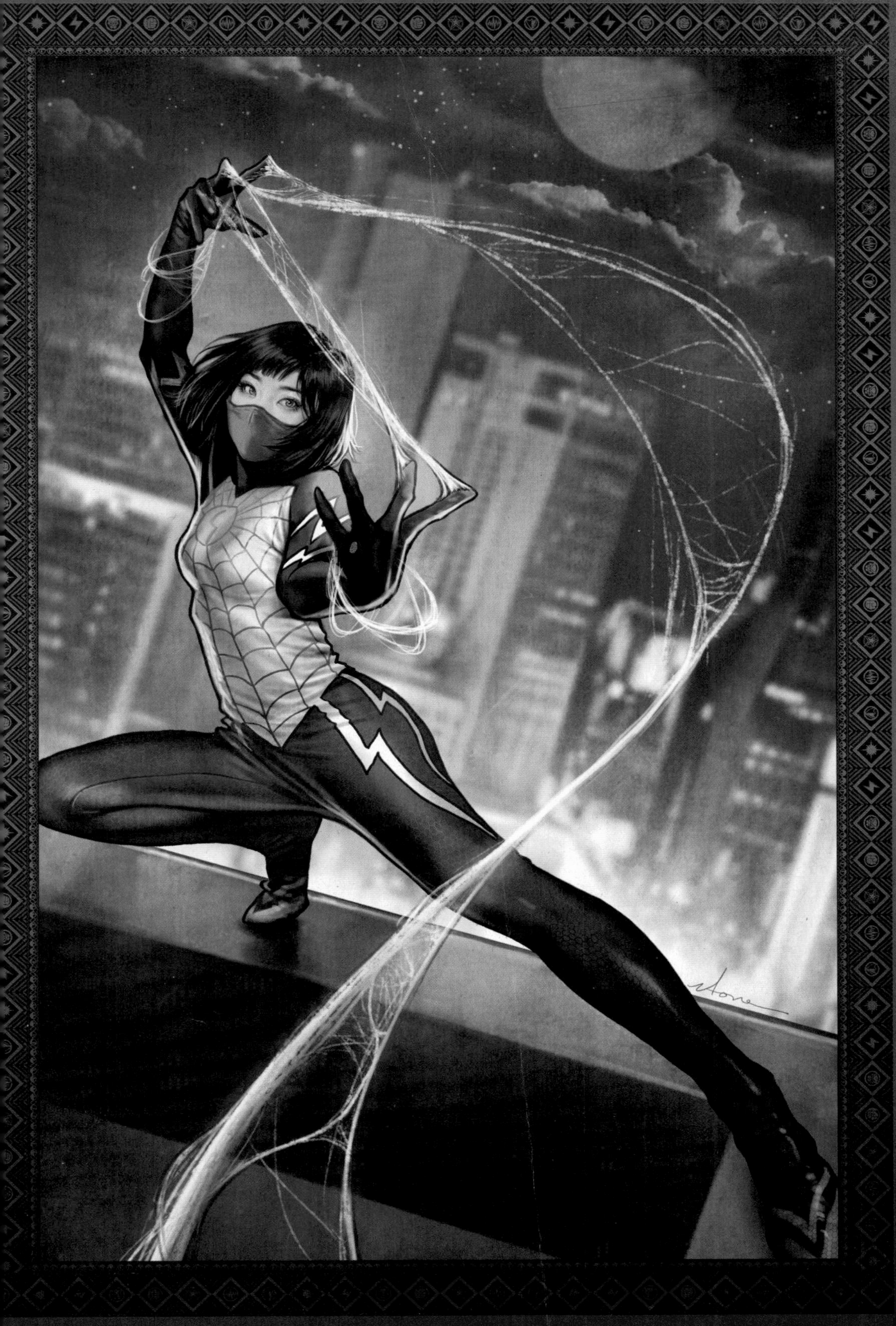

SILK #1

Recap Art by **Jeehyung Lee**

As a teenager, **Cindy Moon** was bitten by the same spider that bit **Peter Parker,** giving her powers similar to those of the **Amazing Spider-Man: adhesion** and a **precognitive awareness** of danger. Unlike Spidey, she shoots versatile webs out of her **fingertips!** Targeted by dangerous people for her powers, she was locked in a bunker for over a decade.

Since rejoining the world, she found her **missing parents,** rescued her **little brother,** and saved **the Multiverse.** She's been a **double agent,** a **new Agent of Atlas,** and a cofounder of the **Order of the Web.** But most just know her as the web-spinning **super hero...**

MAURENE GOO
Writer
TAKESHI MIYAZAWA
Artist
IAN HERRING
Colorist
VC's ARIANA MAHER
Letterer

STONEHOUSE
Cover Artist

**JEEHYUNG LEE;
WOOH NAYOUNG;
SKOTTIE YOUNG;
BENGAL;
JEN BARTEL**
Variant Cover Artists

NICK RUSSELL
Production Design
LINDSEY COHICK
Assistant Editor
JAKE THOMAS
Editor
NICK LOWE
Executive Editor
C.B. CEBULSKI
Editor in Chief

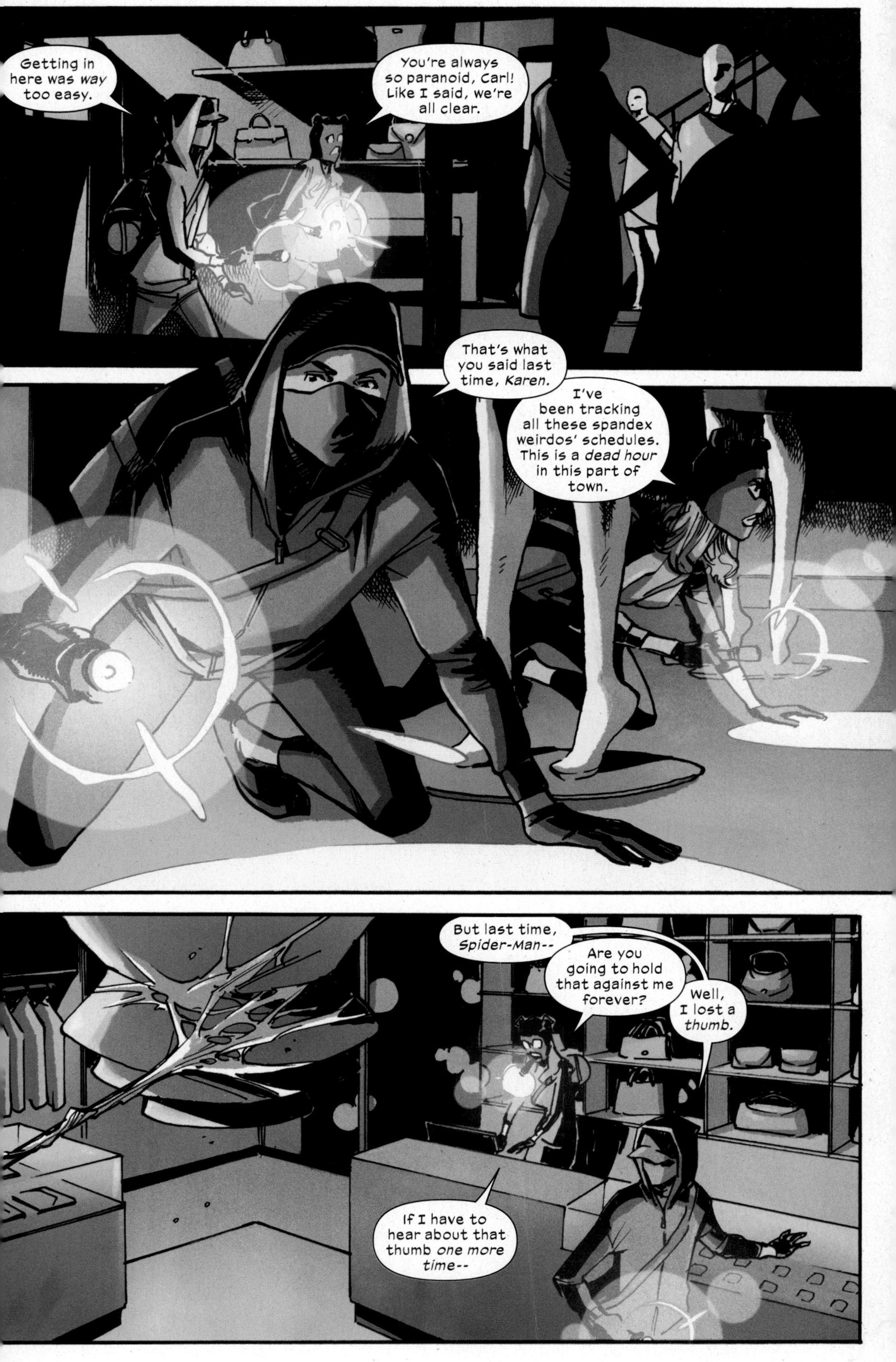
Getting in here was *way* too easy.
You're always so paranoid, Carl! Like I said, we're all clear.
That's what you said last time, *Karen.*
I've been tracking all these spandex weirdos' schedules. This is a *dead hour* in this part of town.
But last time, *Spider-Man--*
Are you going to hold that against me forever?
Well, I lost a *thumb.*
If I have to hear about that thumb *one more time--*

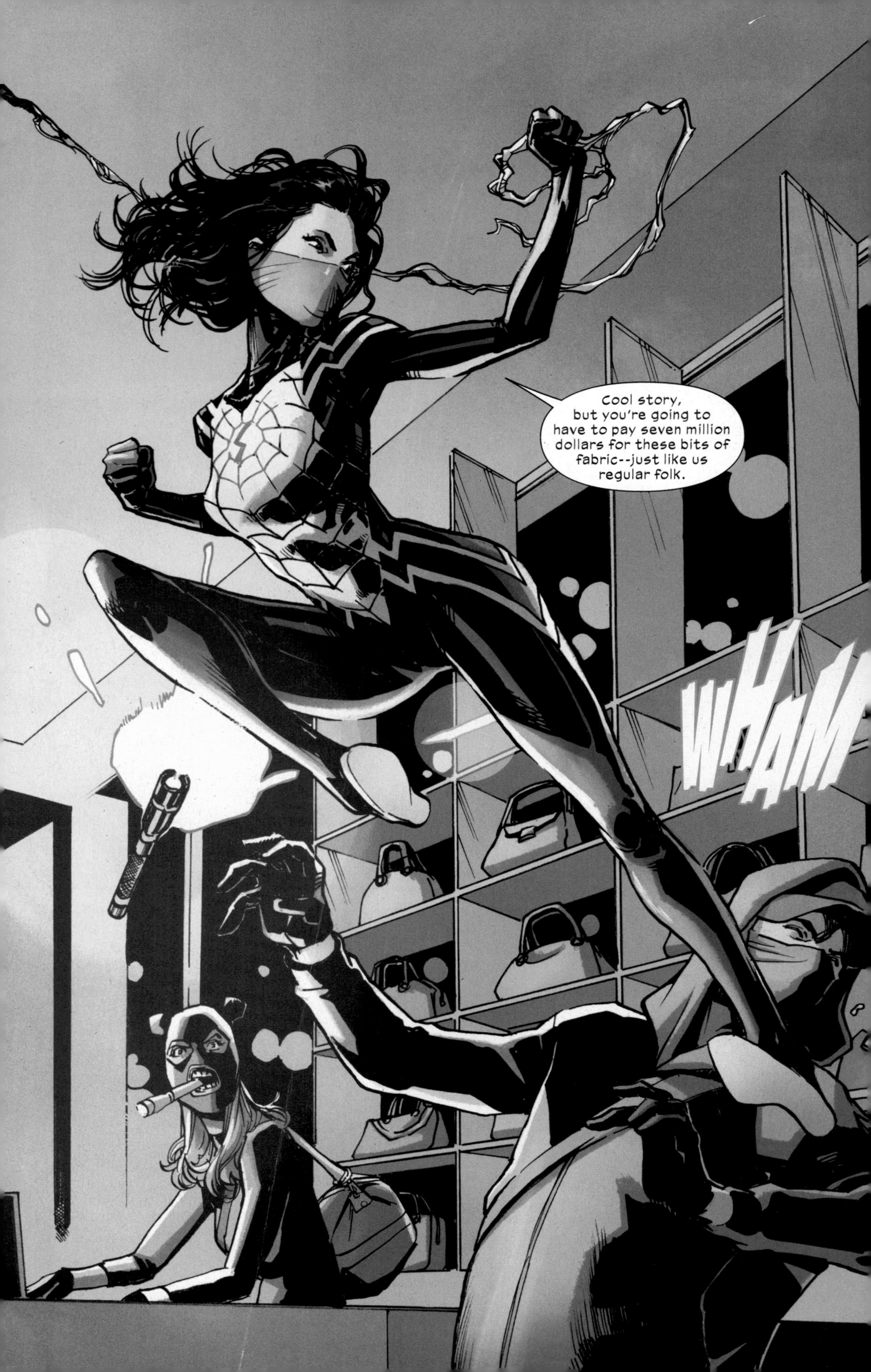
Cool story, but you're going to have to pay seven million dollars for these bits of fabric--just like us regular folk.
WHAM

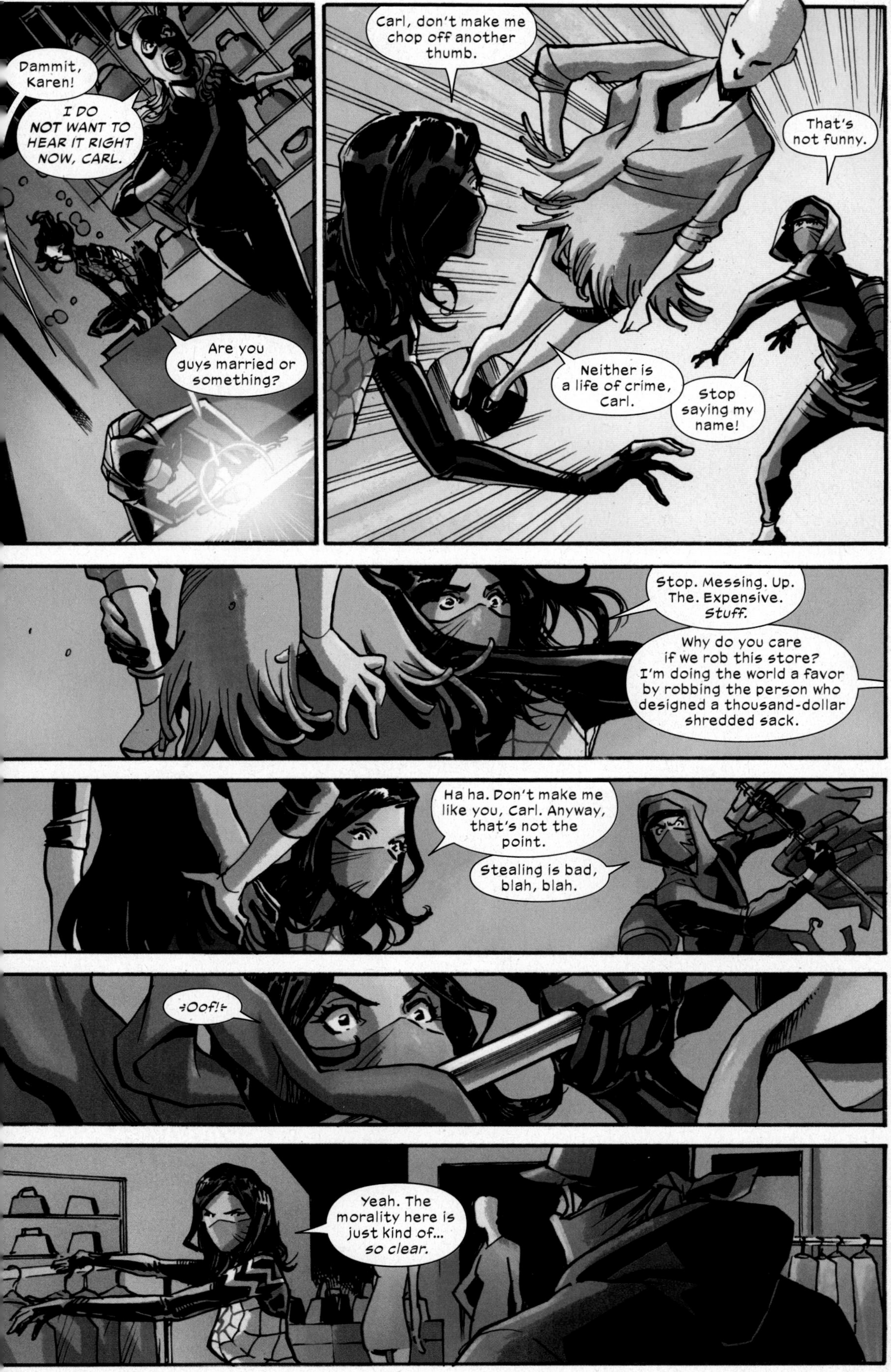

Dammit, Karen!
I DO NOT WANT TO HEAR IT RIGHT NOW, CARL.
Are you guys married or something?
Carl, don't make me chop off another thumb.
That's not funny.
Neither is a life of crime, Carl.
Stop saying my name!
Stop. Messing. Up. The. Expensive. Stuff.
Why do you care if we rob this store? I'm doing the world a favor by robbing the person who designed a thousand-dollar shredded sack.
Ha ha. Don't make me like you, Carl. Anyway, that's not the point.
Stealing is bad, blah, blah.
Oof!
Yeah. The morality here is just kind of... so clear.

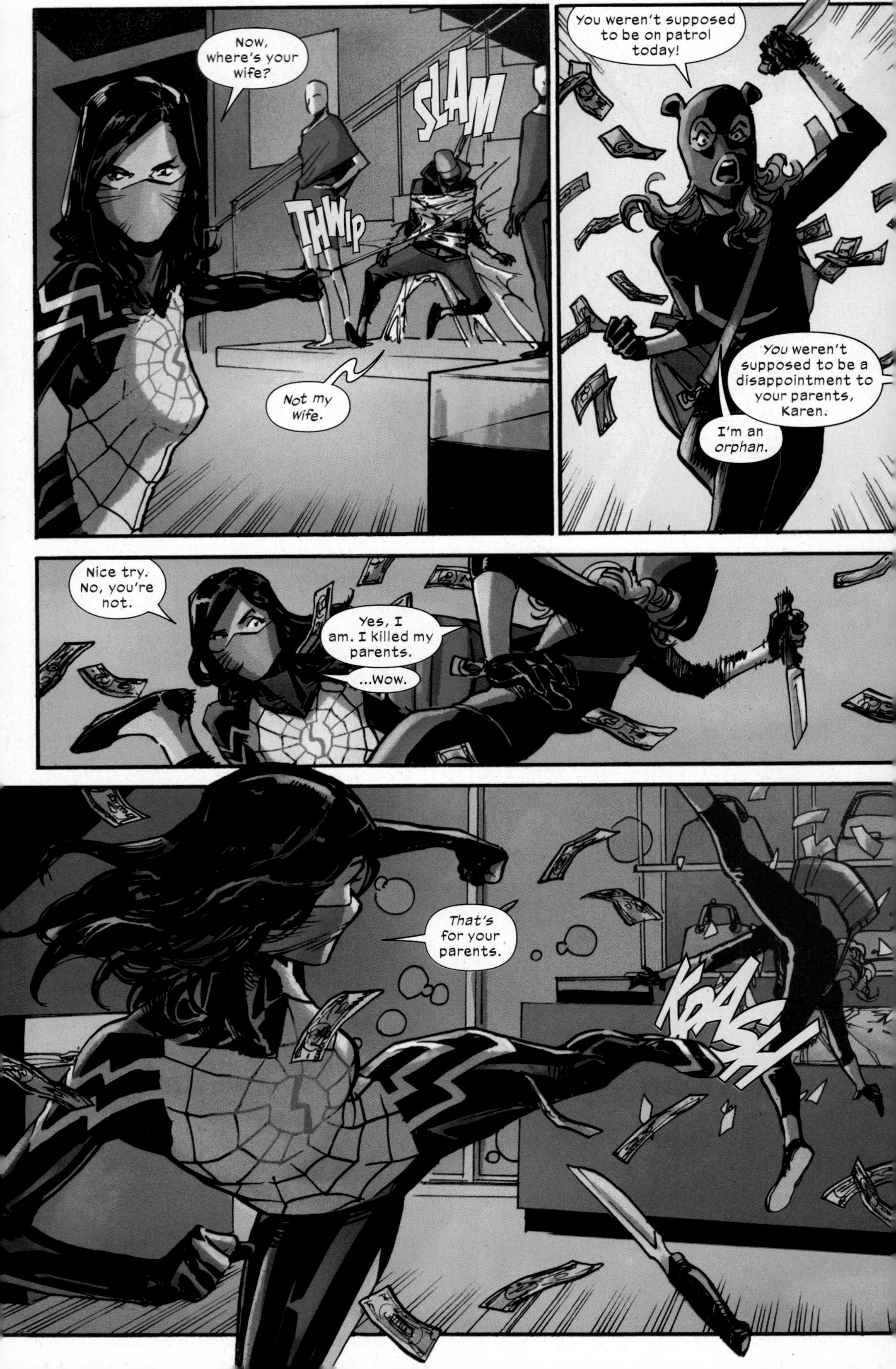
Now, where's your wife?
SLAM
THWIP
Not my wife.
You weren't supposed to be on patrol today!
You weren't supposed to be a disappointment to your parents, Karen.
I'm an orphan.
Nice try. No, you're not.
Yes, I am. I killed my parents.
...Wow.
That's for your parents.
KRASH

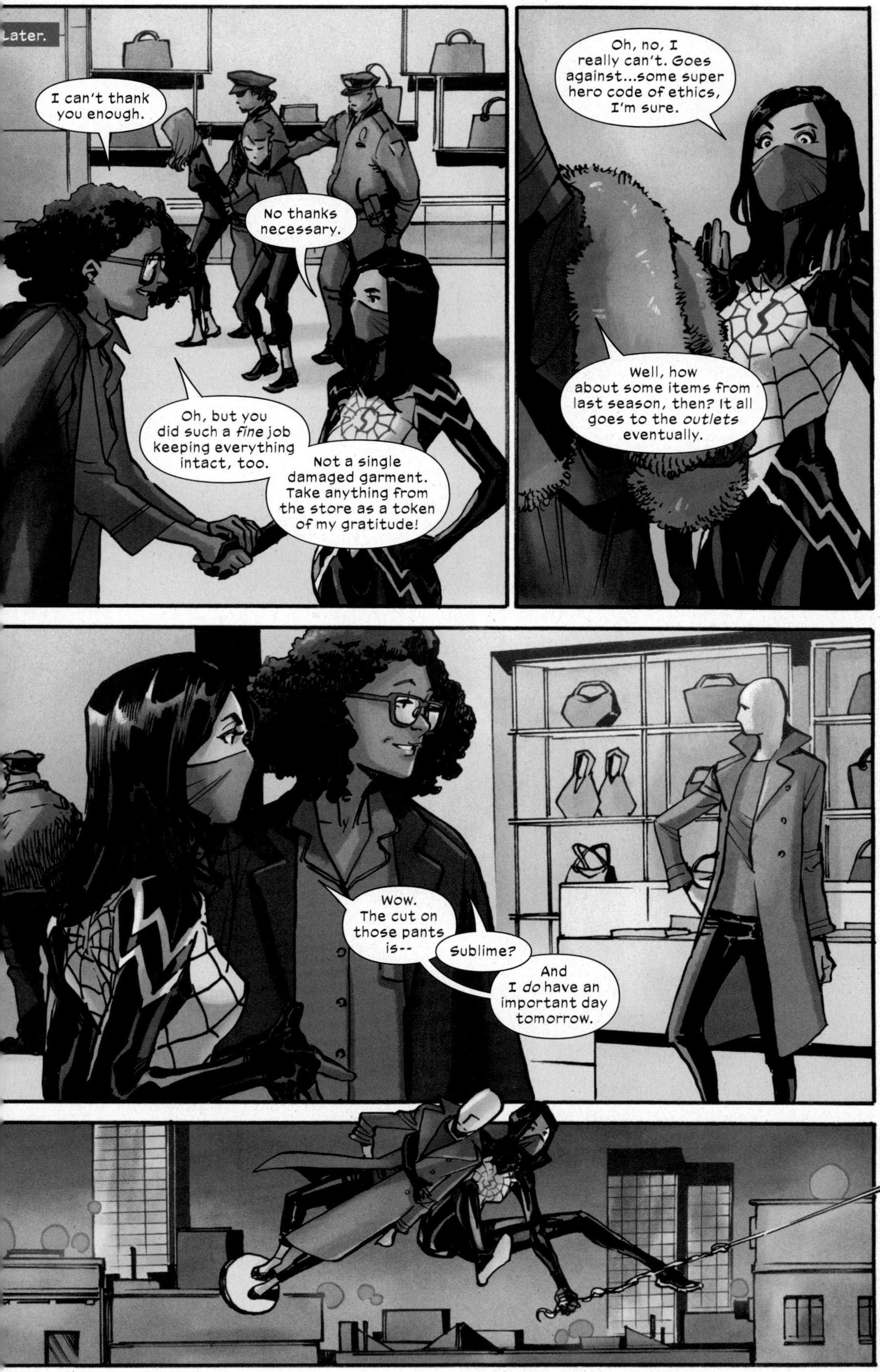
Later.
I can't thank you enough.
No thanks necessary.
Oh, but you did such a *fine* job keeping everything intact, too.
Not a single damaged garment. Take anything from the store as a token of my gratitude!
Oh, no, I really can't. Goes against...some super hero code of ethics, I'm sure.
Well, how about some items from last season, then? It all goes to the *outlets* eventually.
Wow. The cut on those pants is--
Sublime?
And I *do* have an important day tomorrow.

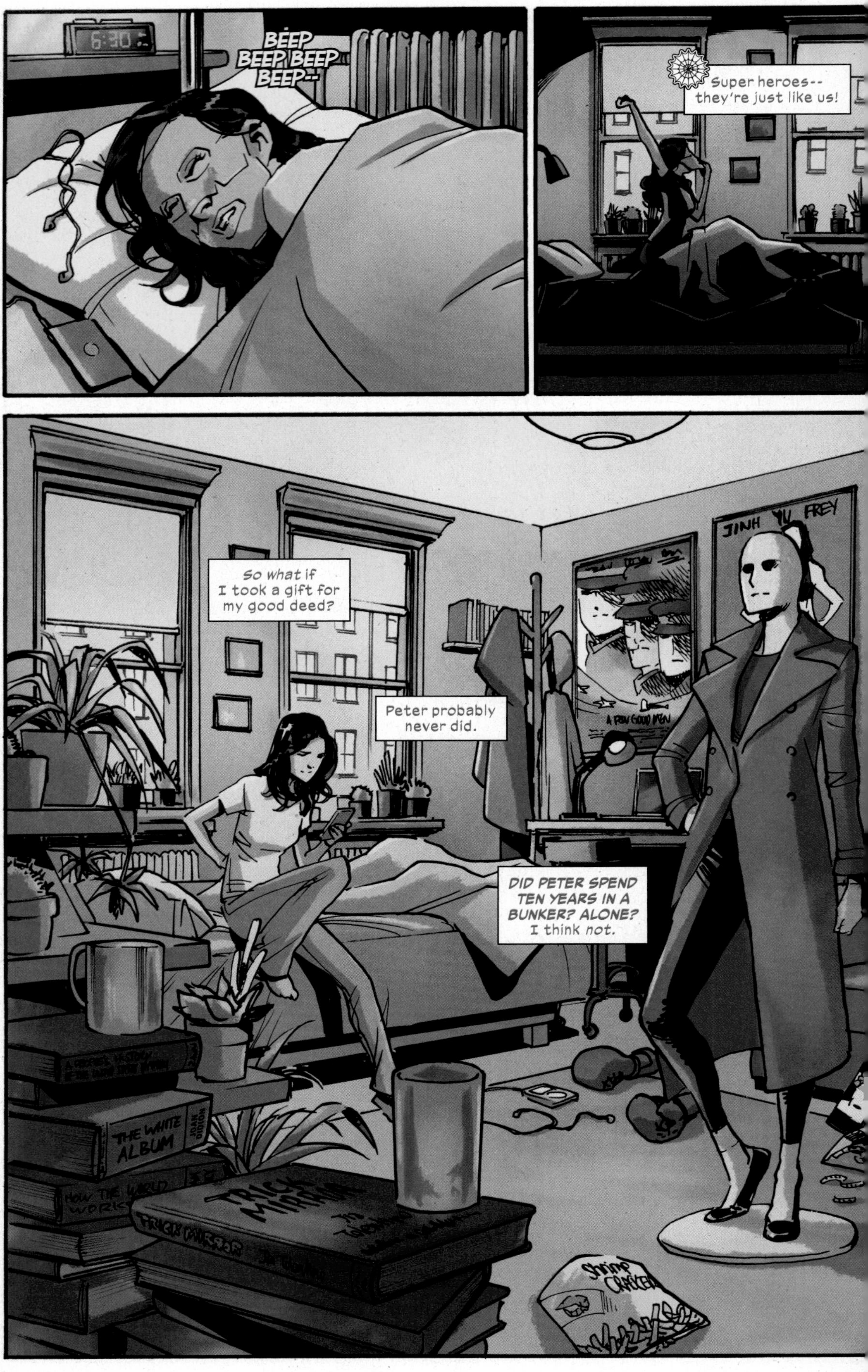

6:30
BEEP BEEP BEEP BEEP--
Super heroes-- they're just like us!
So what if I took a gift for my good deed?
Peter probably never did.
DID PETER SPEND TEN YEARS IN A BUNKER? ALONE? I think not.
JINH YU FREY
THE WHITE ALBUM
JOAN DIDION

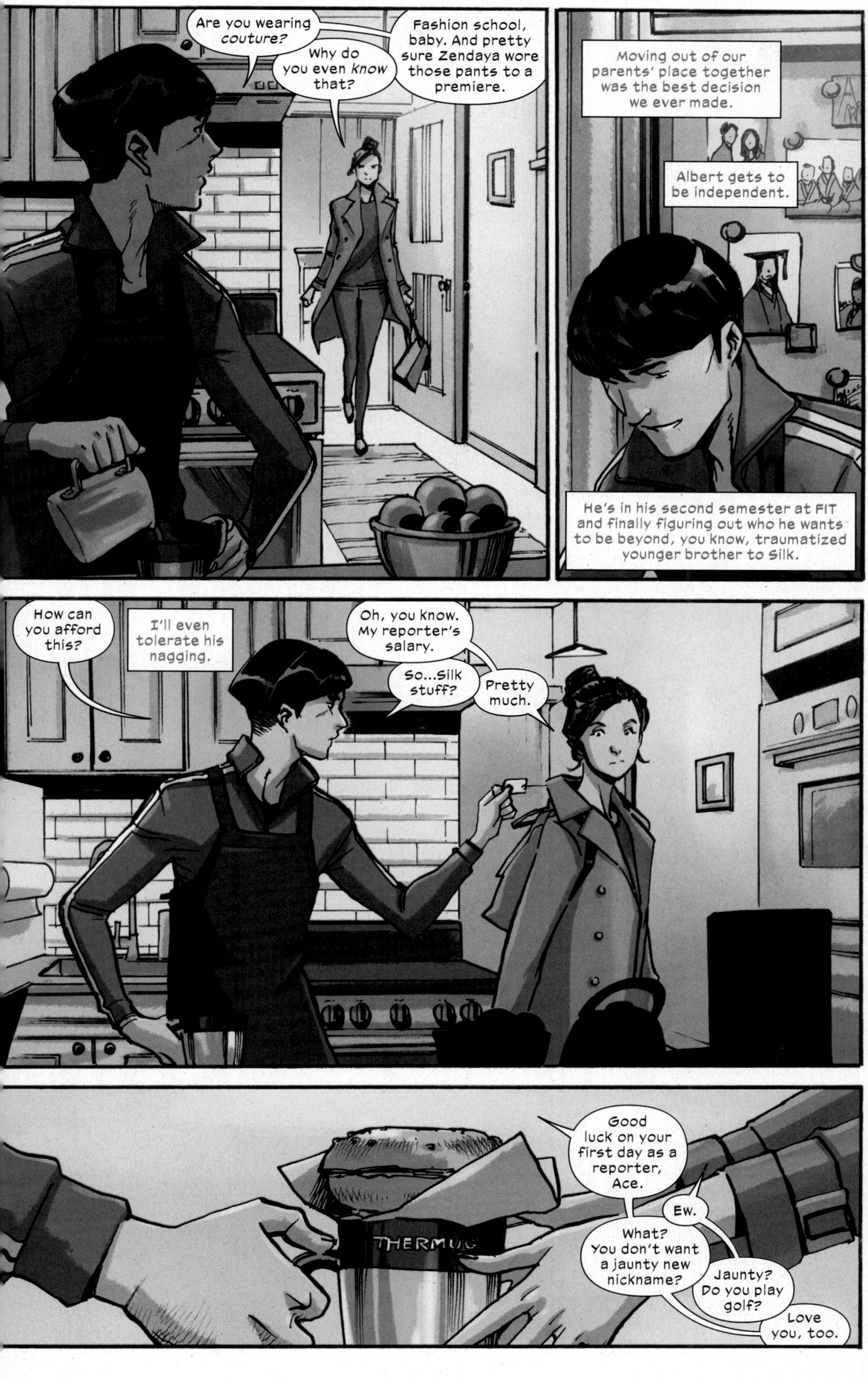
Are you wearing *couture?*
Fashion school, baby. And pretty sure Zendaya wore those pants to a premiere.
Why do you even *know* that?
Moving out of our parents' place together was the best decision we ever made.
Albert gets to be independent.
He's in his second semester at FIT and finally figuring out who he wants to be beyond, you know, traumatized younger brother to Silk.
How can you afford this?
I'll even tolerate his nagging.
Oh, you know. My reporter's salary.
So...Silk stuff?
Pretty much.
Good luck on your first day as a reporter, Ace.
Ew.
What? You don't want a jaunty new nickname?
Jaunty? Do you play golf?
Love you, too.
THERMUG

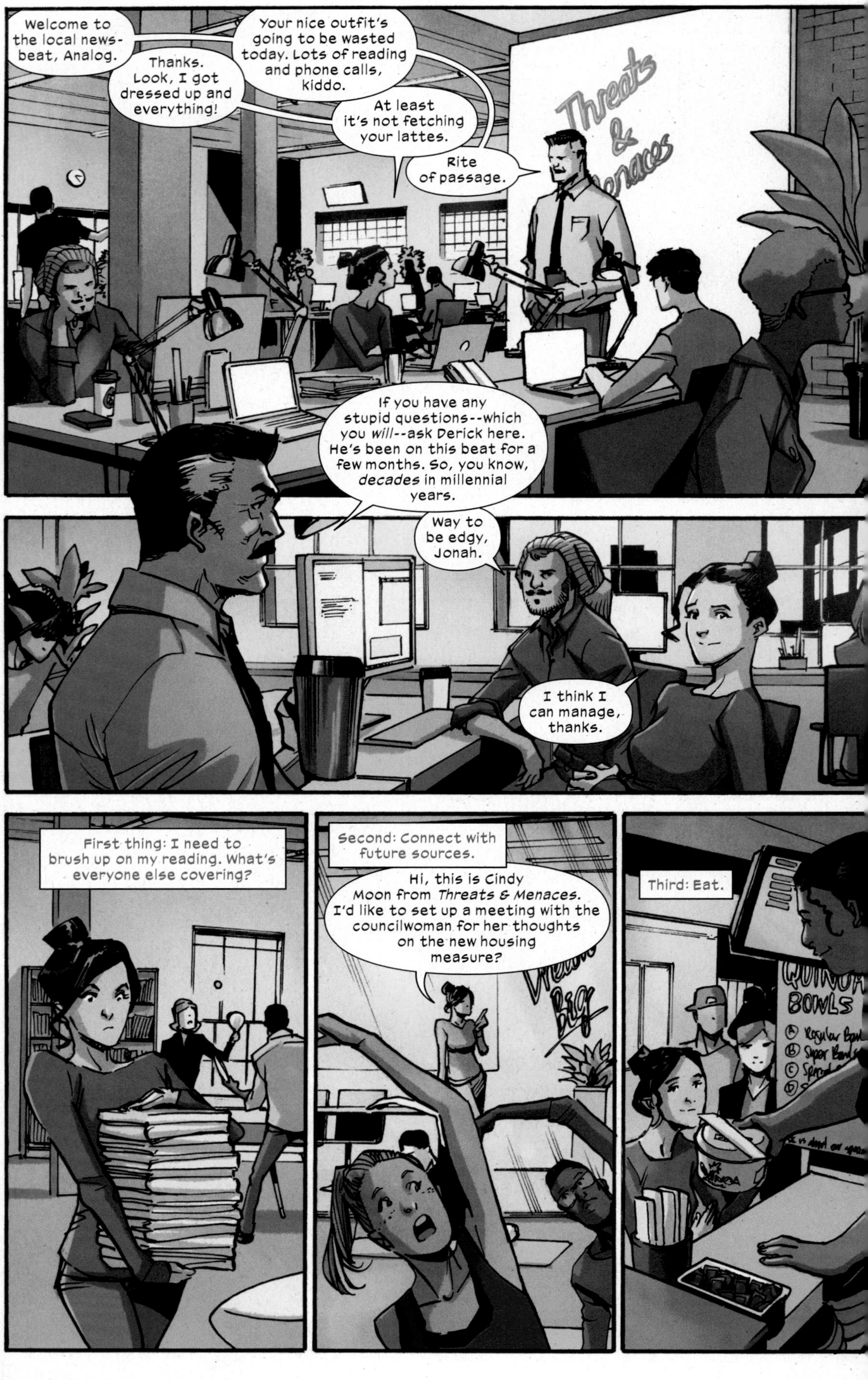
Welcome to the local news-beat, Analog.
Your nice outfit's going to be wasted today. Lots of reading and phone calls, kiddo.
Thanks. Look, I got dressed up and everything!
At least it's not fetching your lattes.
Rite of passage.
Threats & Menaces
If you have any stupid questions--which you *will*--ask Derick here. He's been on this beat for a few months. So, you know, *decades* in millennial years.
Way to be edgy, Jonah.
I think I can manage, thanks.
First thing: I need to brush up on my reading. What's everyone else covering?
Second: Connect with future sources.
Hi, this is Cindy Moon from *Threats & Menaces*. I'd like to set up a meeting with the councilwoman for her thoughts on the new housing measure?
Third: Eat.
QUINOA BOWLS

While most of these guys were playing beer pong in college, I was learning how to strangle men with my legs in a bunker.

I guess you can say that I have something to prove.

Analog. You're Jonah's new pet reporter for local, right?

How am I supposed to respond to that? Yes, I am his pet!

You're funny. I can see why he likes you. But can I give you a tip?

We create digital content. Might want to read more on your phone-- that's our medium.

News is news, last I heard.

Another thing? Don't eat lunch at your desk. Nobody likes a hero.

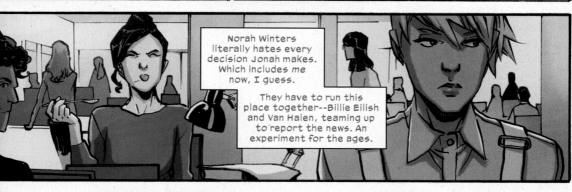

Norah Winters literally hates every decision Jonah makes. Which includes *me* now, I guess.

They have to run this place together--Billie Eilish and Van Halen, teaming up to report the news. An experiment for the ages.

A lot of us eat at our desks--it's fine.

I know it's fine.

It's just Norah's frustration with Jonah's old-school procedures. And, well, she knows he calls you Analog for a reason.

It's not like I *wanted* to be on Jonah's level--but I spent my youth in a bunker. Have I mentioned that I lived in a bunker for ten years?

Interesting.

What?

One of my sources just texted me.

The Mulliganz were shot up behind the edge Pub

All ded

Your source gives you intel via emojis?

I know, total weirdo. But they're reliable. Want to come with? Or keep kissing Jonah's butt?

Shut up. I'm coming!

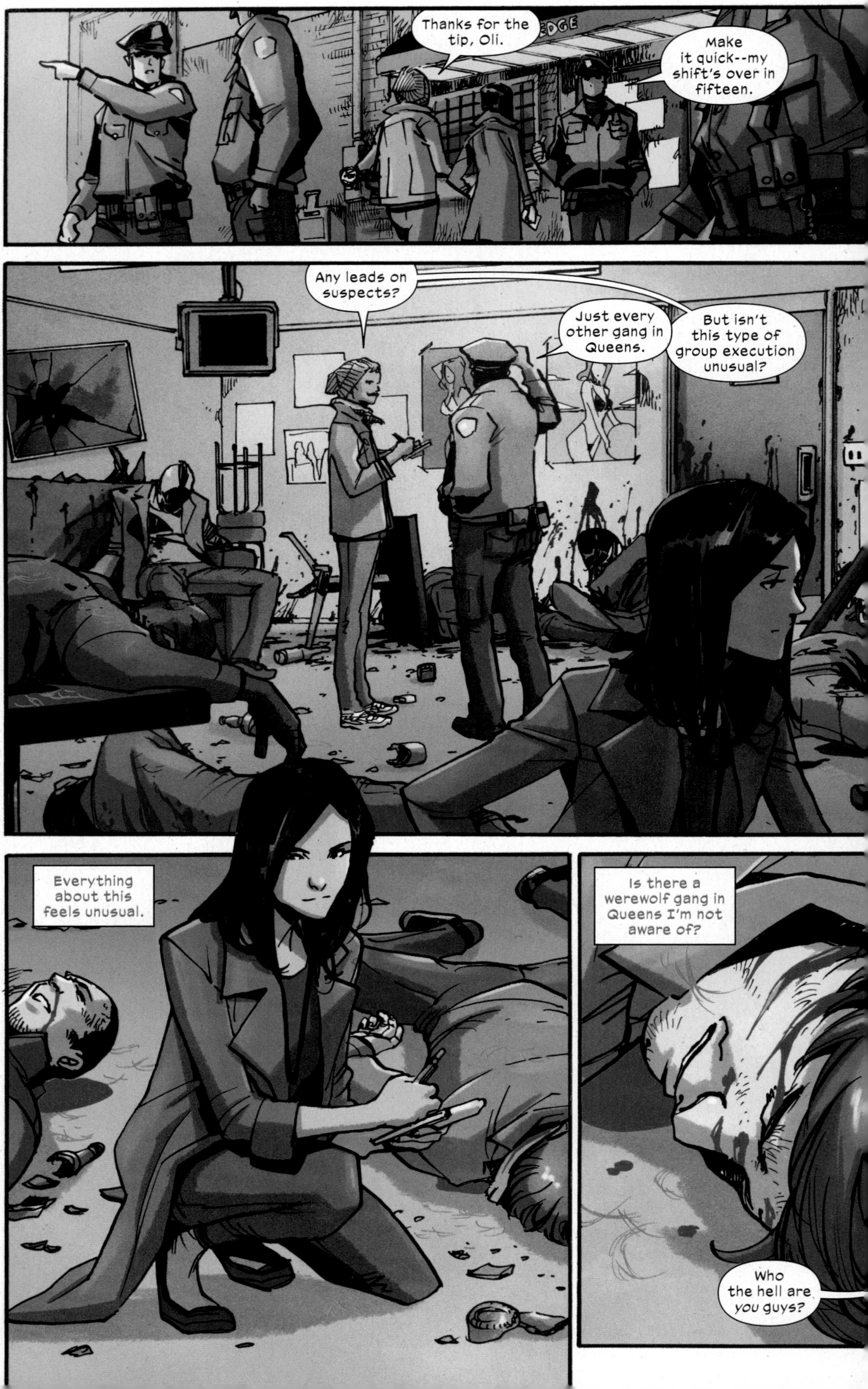
EDGE
Thanks for the tip, Oli.
Make it quick--my shift's over in fifteen.
Any leads on suspects?
Just every other gang in Queens.
But isn't this type of group execution unusual?
Everything about this feels unusual.
Is there a werewolf gang in Queens I'm not aware of?
Who the hell are *you* guys?

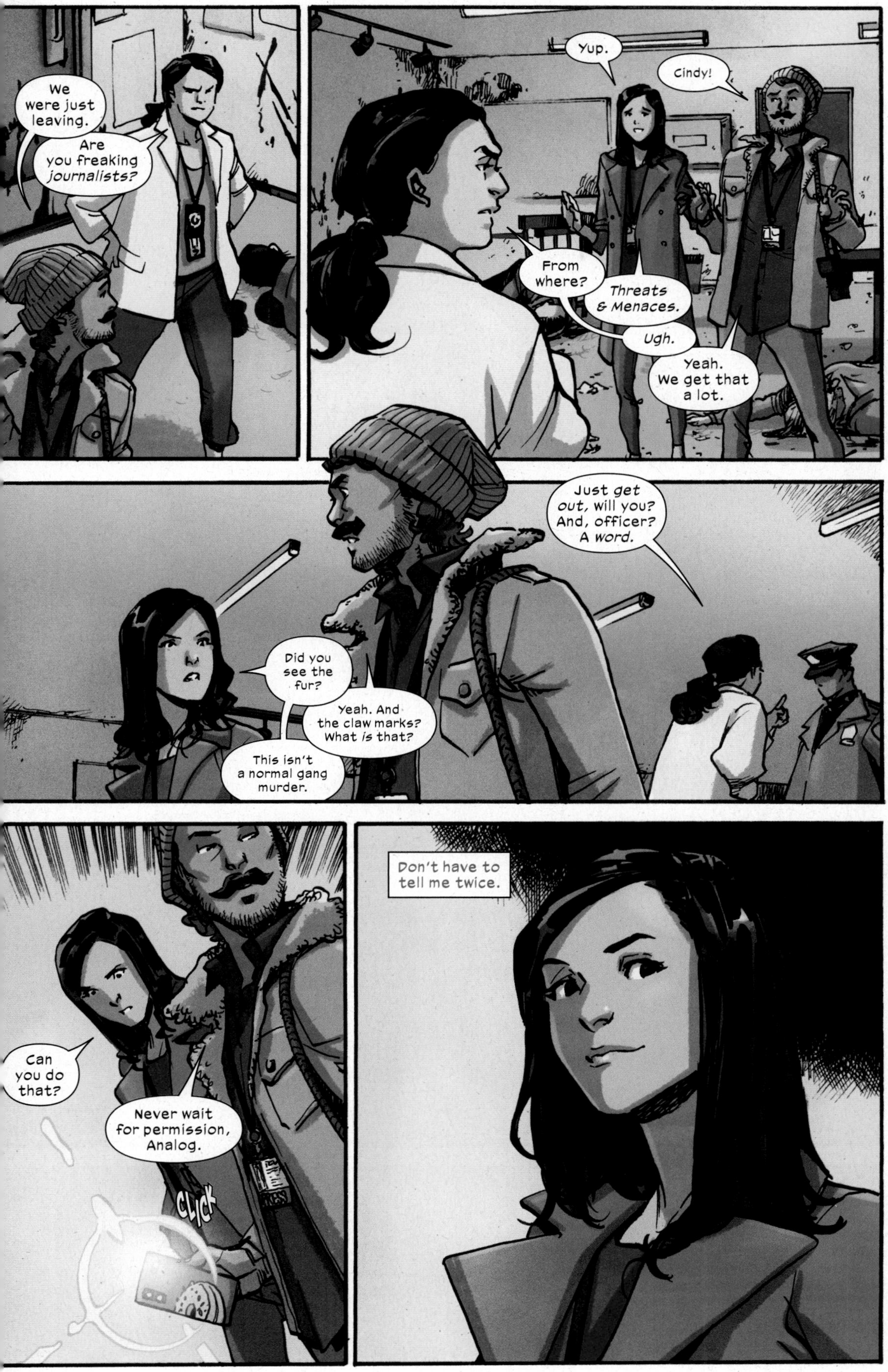

We were just leaving.
Are you freaking *journalists?*
Yup.
Cindy!
From where?
Threats & Menaces.
Ugh.
Yeah. We get that a lot.
Just *get out*, will you? And, officer? A *word.*
Did you see the *fur?*
Yeah. And the claw marks? What *is* that?
This isn't a normal gang murder.
Can you do that?
Never wait for permission, Analog.
CLICK
Don't have to tell me twice.

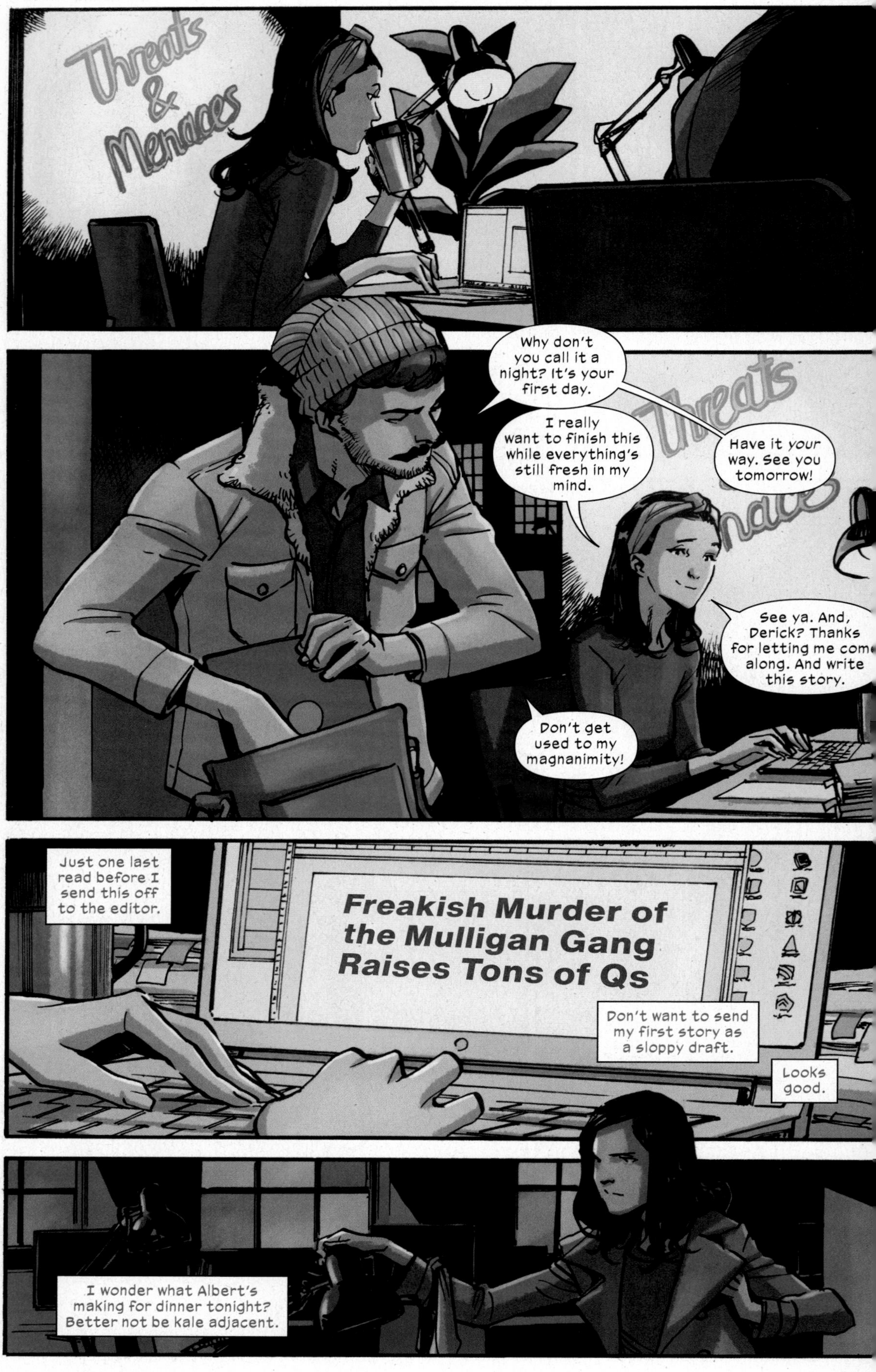

Threats & Menaces
Why don't you call it a night? It's your first day.
I really want to finish this while everything's still fresh in my mind.
Have it *your* way. See you tomorrow!
See ya. And, Derick? Thanks for letting me come along. And write this story.
Don't get used to my magnanimity!
Just one last read before I send this off to the editor.
Freakish Murder of the Mulligan Gang Raises Tons of Qs
Don't want to send my first story as a sloppy draft.
Looks good.
I wonder what Albert's making for dinner tonight? Better not be kale adjacent.

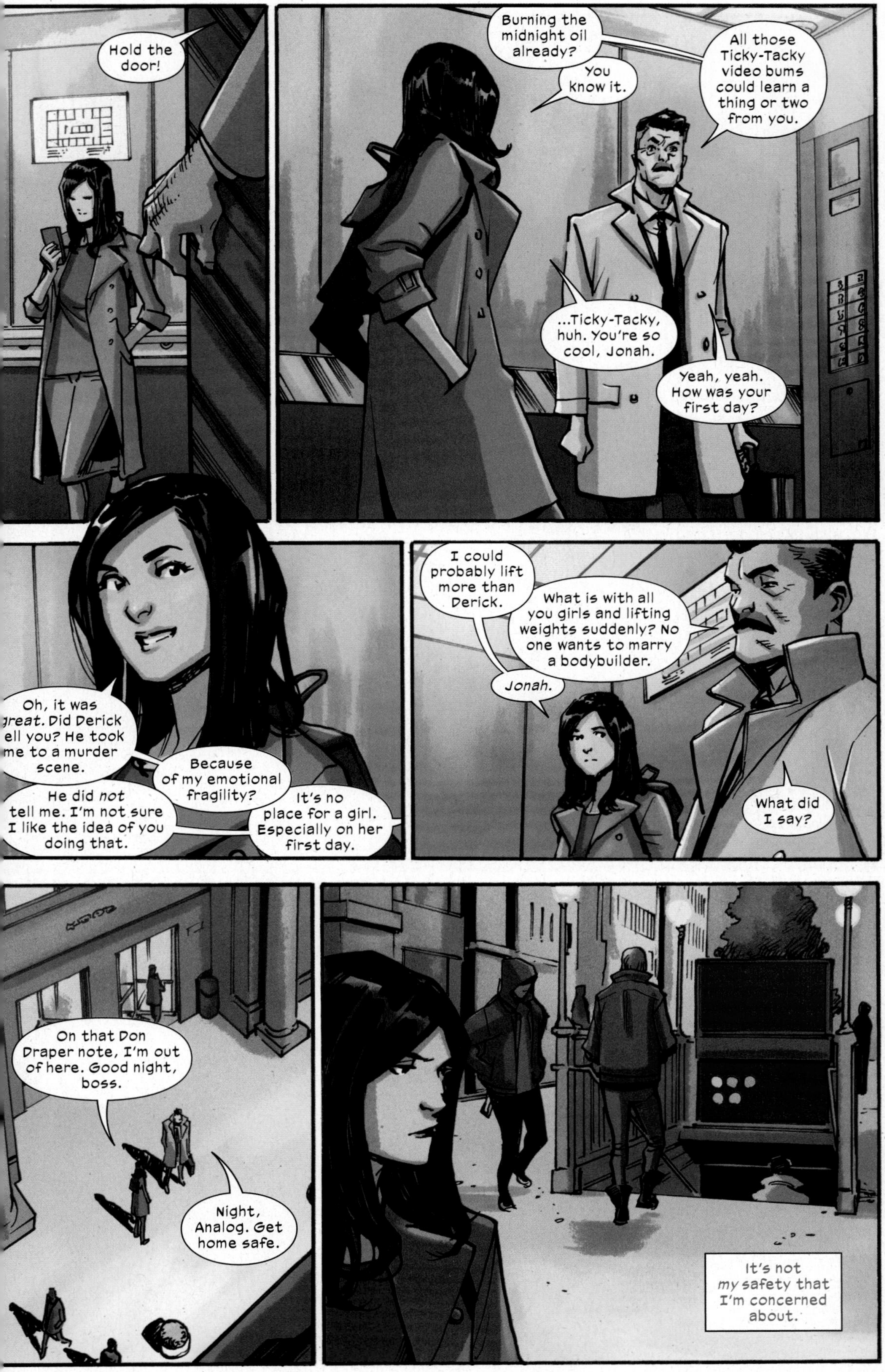

Hold the door!
Burning the midnight oil already?
You know it.
All those Ticky-Tacky video bums could learn a thing or two from you.
...Ticky-Tacky, huh. You're so cool, Jonah.
Yeah, yeah. How was your first day?
Oh, it was great. Did Derick tell you? He took me to a murder scene.
He did not tell me. I'm not sure I like the idea of you doing that.
It's no place for a girl. Especially on her first day.
Because of my emotional fragility?
I could probably lift more than Derick.
What is with all you girls and lifting weights suddenly? No one wants to marry a bodybuilder.
Jonah.
What did I say?
On that Don Draper note, I'm out of here. Good night, boss.
Night, Analog. Get home safe.
It's not my safety that I'm concerned about.

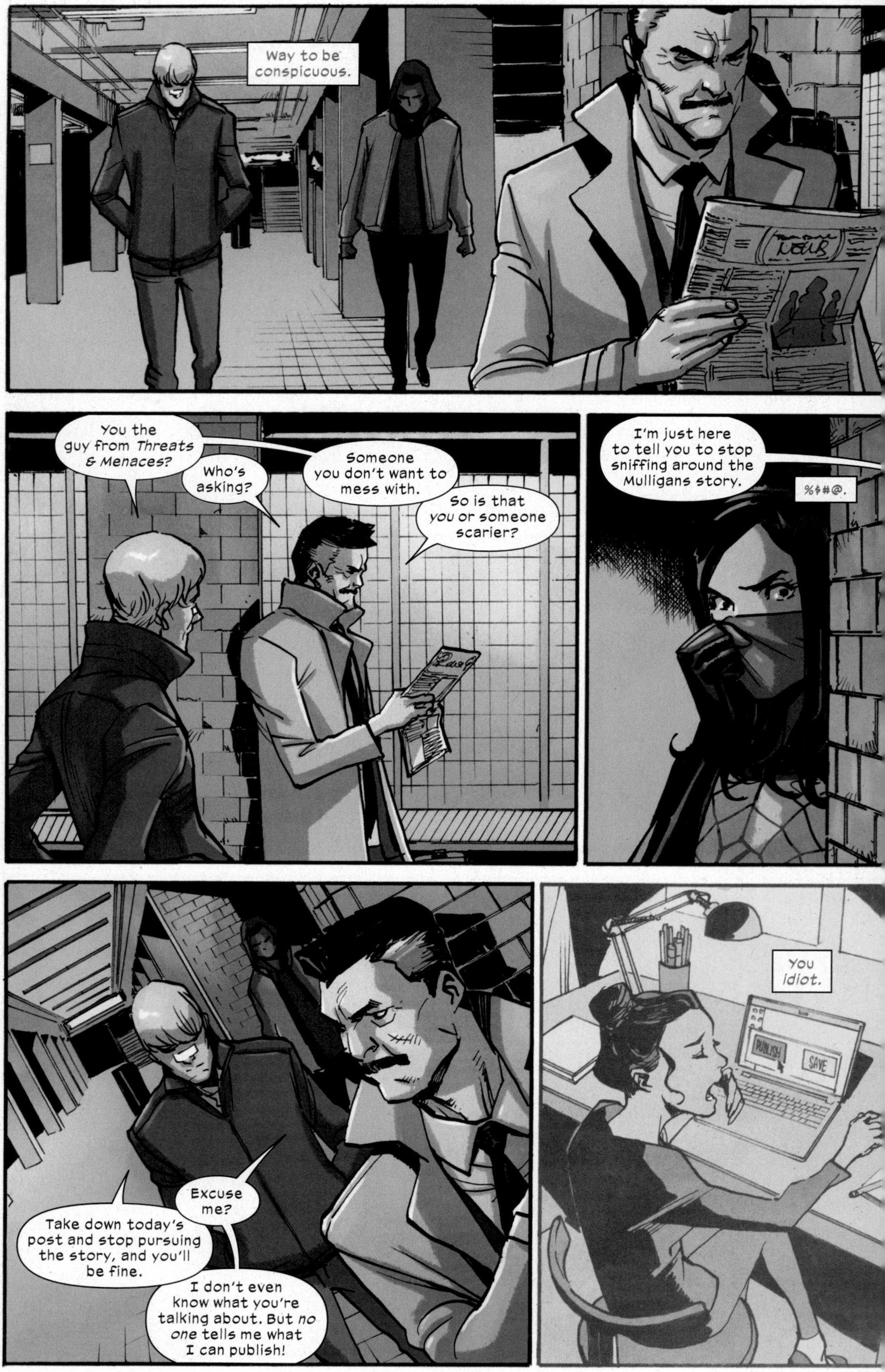

Way to be conspicuous.
You the guy from *Threats & Menaces?*
Who's asking?
Someone you don't want to mess with.
So is that *you* or someone scarier?
I'm just here to tell you to stop sniffing around the Mulligans story.
%$#@.
Take down today's post and stop pursuing the story, and you'll be fine.
Excuse me?
I don't even know what you're talking about. But *no one* tells me what I can publish!
You *idiot.*
PUBLISH
SAVE

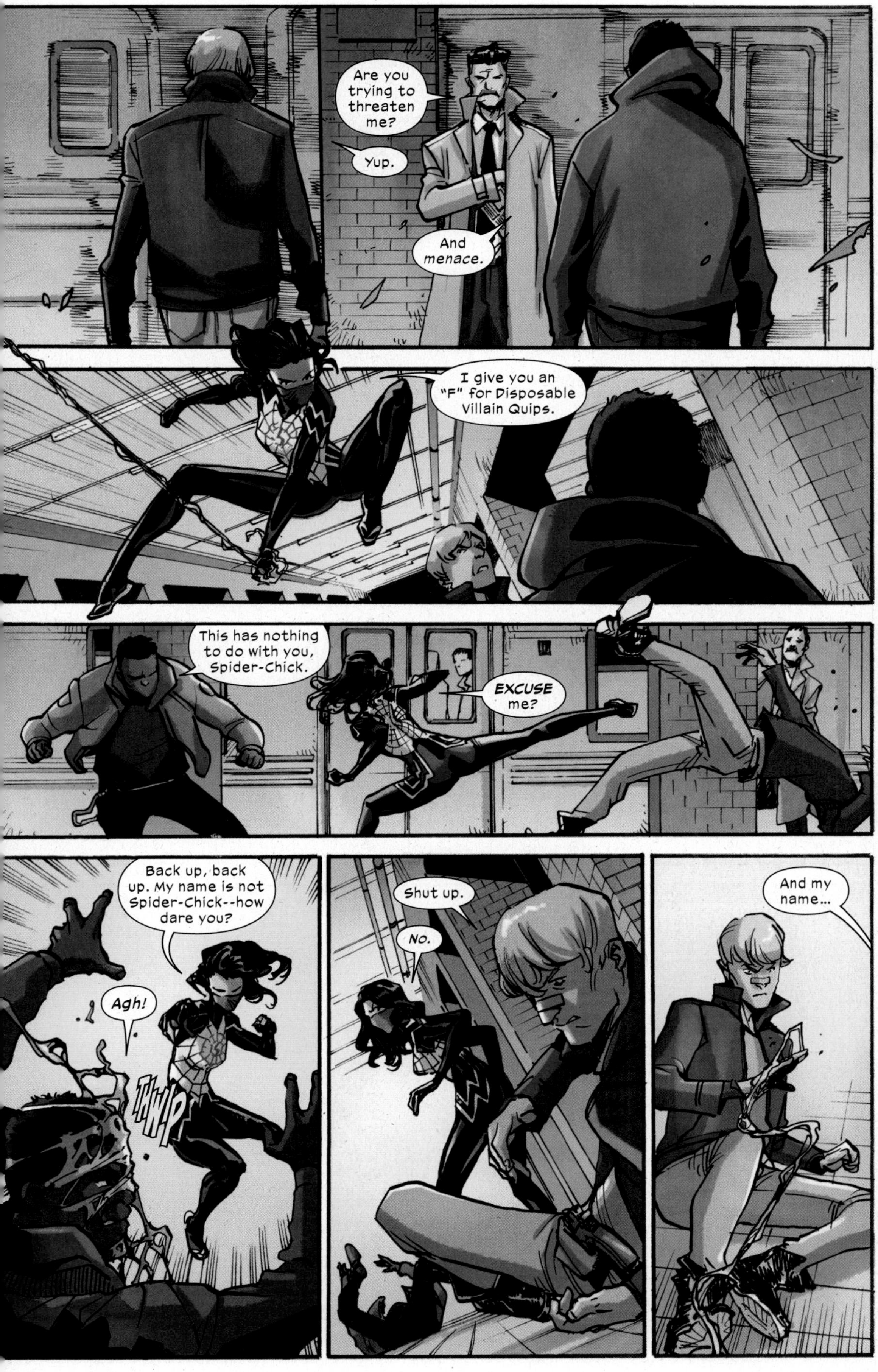
Are you trying to threaten me?
Yup.
And menace.
I give you an "F" for Disposable Villain Quips.
This has nothing to do with you, Spider-Chick.
EXCUSE me?
Back up, back up. My name is not Spider-Chick--how dare you?
Agh!
THWIP
Shut up.
No.
And my name...

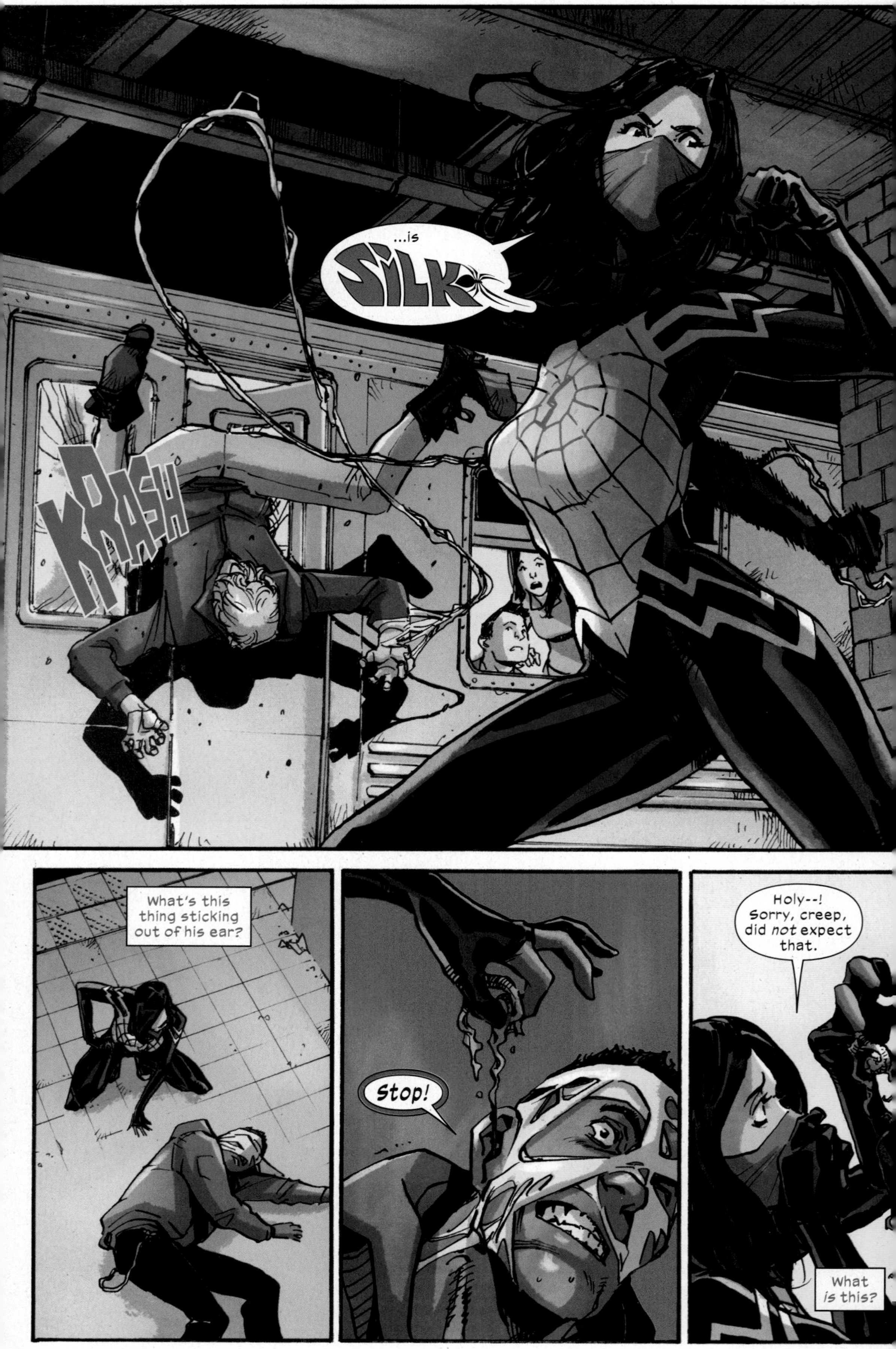

...is
SILK
KRASH
What's this thing sticking out of his ear?
Stop!
Holy--! Sorry, creep, did *not* expect that.
What *is* this?

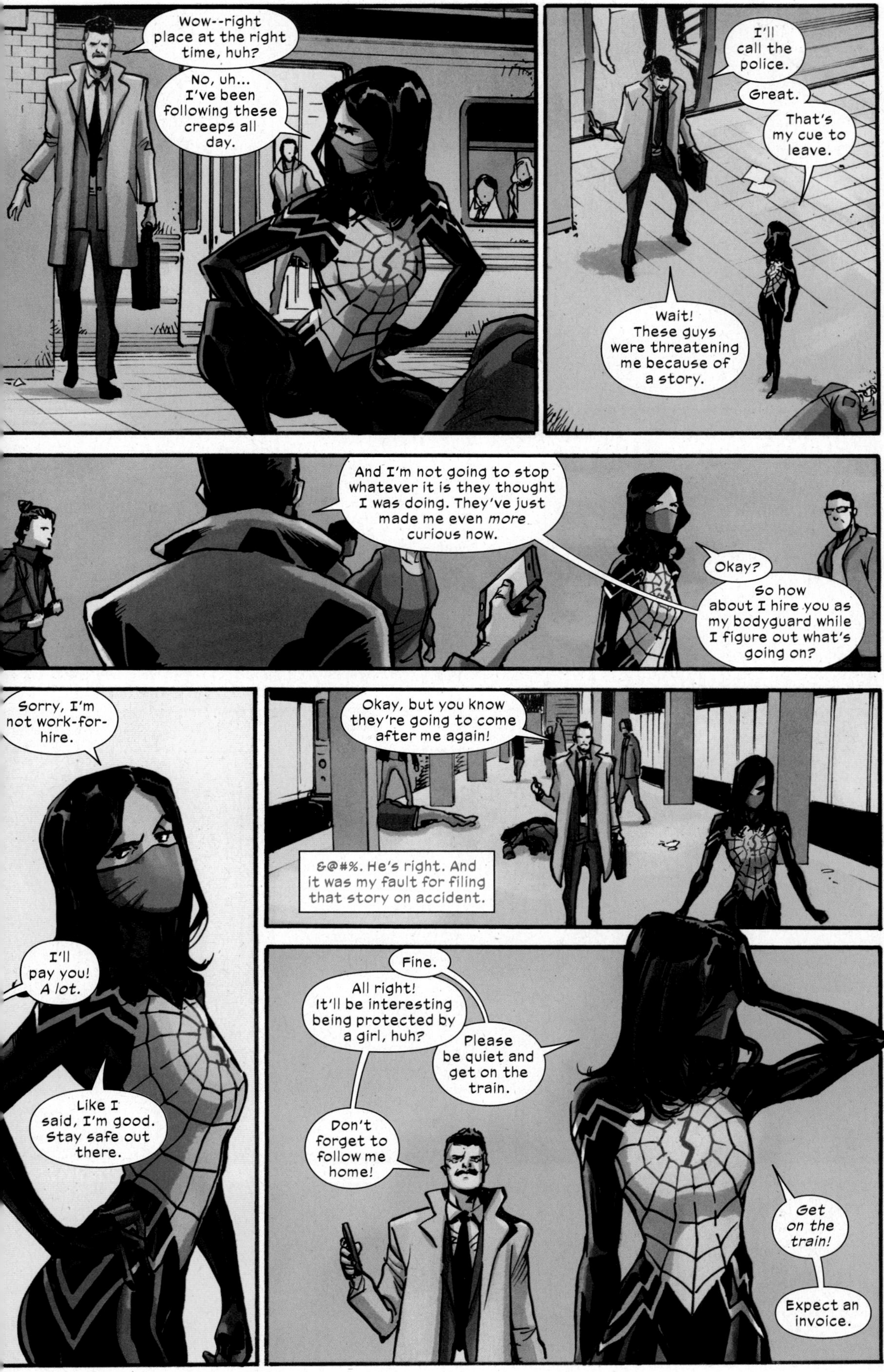

Wow--right place at the right time, huh?
No, uh... I've been following these creeps all day.
I'll call the police.
Great.
That's my cue to leave.
Wait! These guys were threatening me because of a story.
And I'm not going to stop whatever it is they thought I was doing. They've just made me even *more* curious now.
Okay?
So how about I hire you as my bodyguard while I figure out what's going on?
Sorry, I'm not work-for-hire.
Okay, but you know they're going to come after me again!
&@#%. He's right. And it was my fault for filing that story on accident.
I'll pay you! *A lot.*
Like I said, I'm good. Stay safe out there.
Fine.
All right! It'll be interesting being protected by a girl, huh?
Please be quiet and get on the train.
Don't forget to follow me home!
Get on the train!
Expect an invoice.

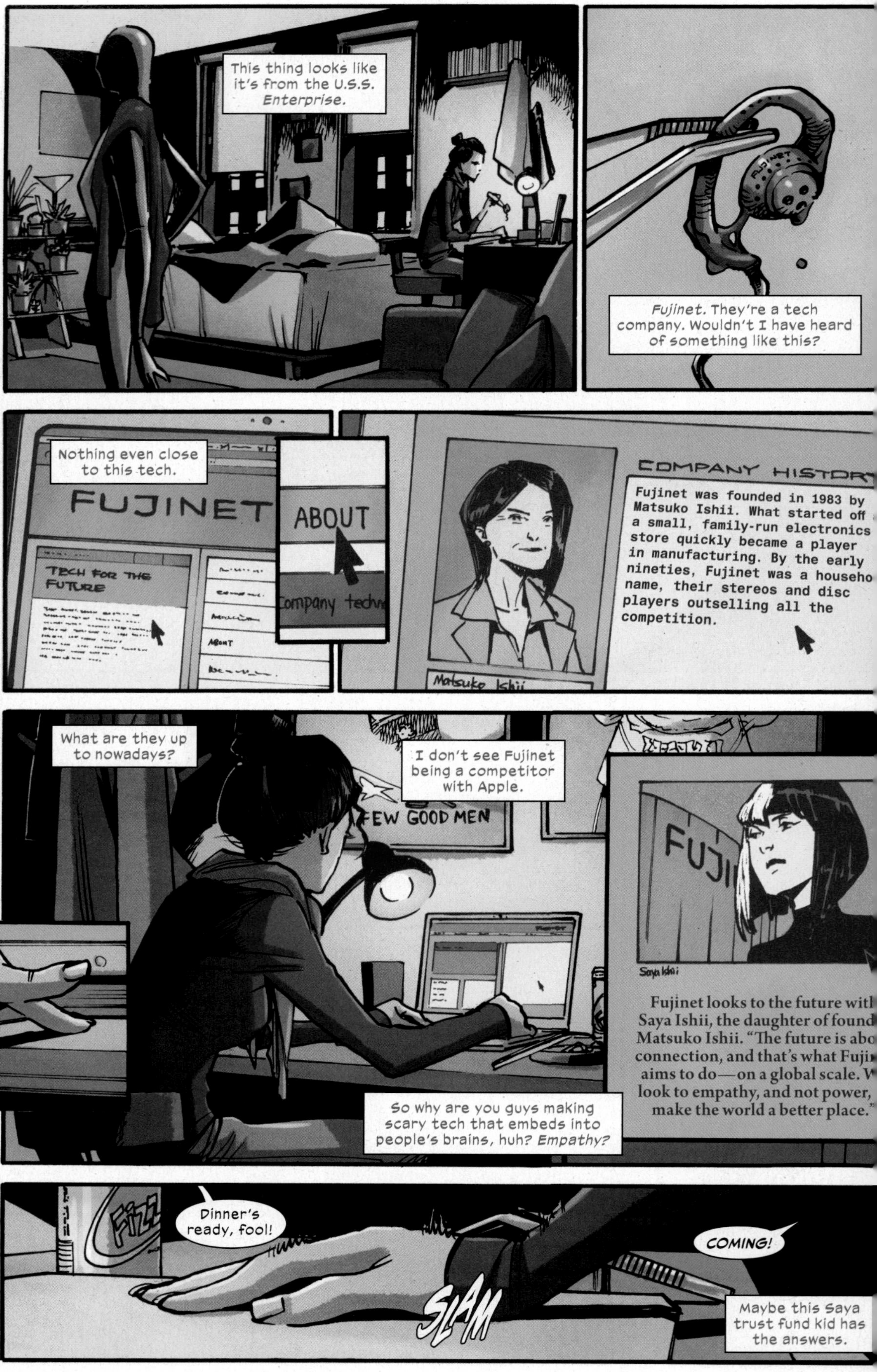
This thing looks like it's from the U.S.S. *Enterprise.*
Fujinet. They're a tech company. Wouldn't I have heard of something like this?
FUJINET
Nothing even close to this tech.
FUJINET
TECH FOR THE FUTURE
ABOUT
ABOUT
Company techn
COMPANY HISTORY
Fujinet was founded in 1983 by Matsuko Ishii. What started off a small, family-run electronics store quickly became a player in manufacturing. By the early nineties, Fujinet was a househo name, their stereos and disc players outselling all the competition.
Matsuko Ishii
What are they up to nowadays?
I don't see Fujinet being a competitor with Apple.
FEW GOOD MEN
FUJI
Saya Ishii
Fujinet looks to the future wit Saya Ishii, the daughter of found Matsuko Ishii. "The future is abo connection, and that's what Fuji aims to do—on a global scale. W look to empathy, and not power, make the world a better place."
So why are you guys making scary tech that embeds into people's brains, huh? *Empathy?*
FIZZ
Dinner's ready, fool!
COMING!
SLAM
Maybe this Saya trust fund kid has the answers.

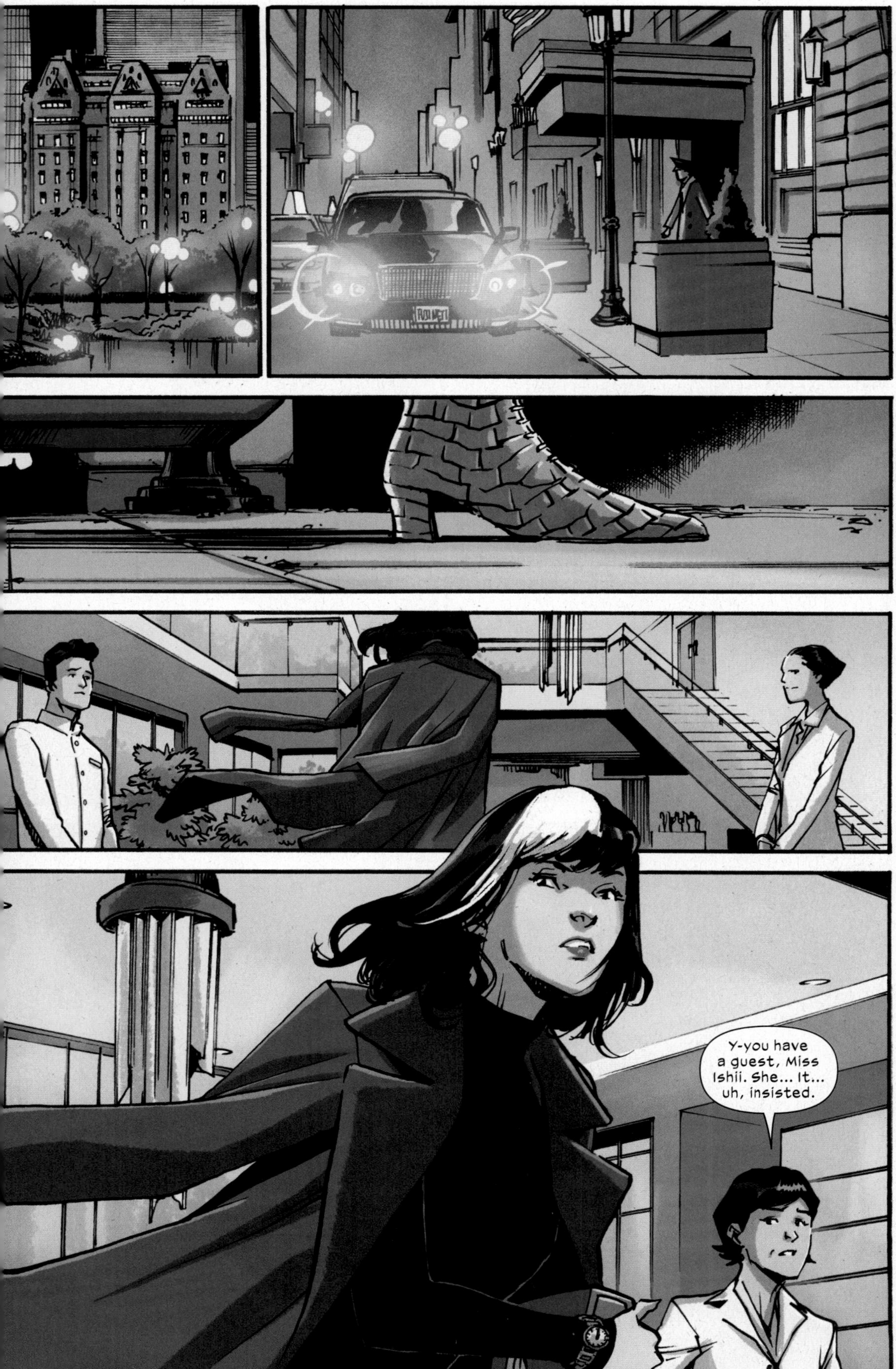
Y-you have a guest, Miss Ishii. She... It... uh, insisted.

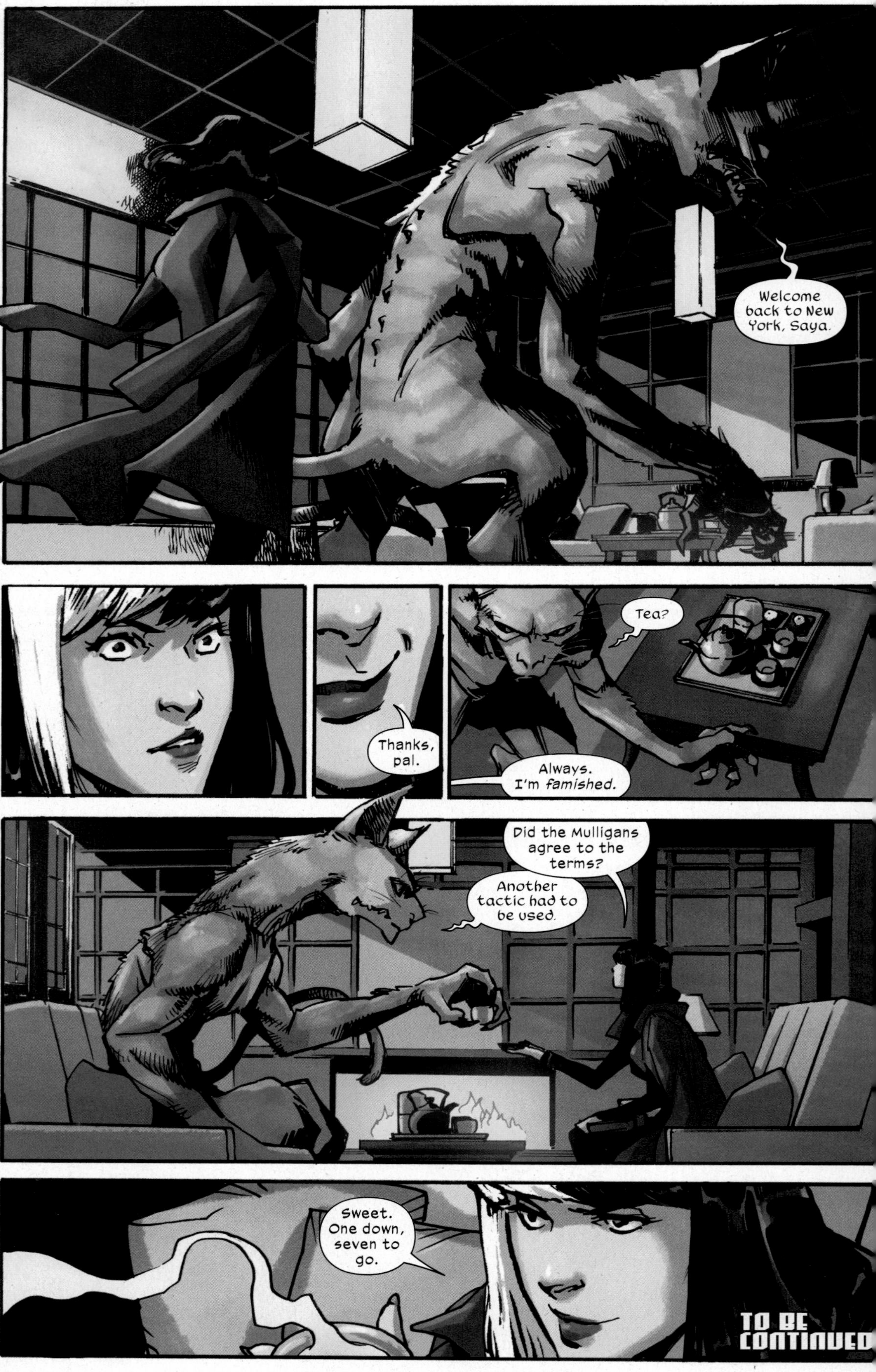
Welcome back to New York, Saya.
Thanks, pal.
Tea?
Always. I'm *famished.*
Did the Mulligans agree to the terms?
Another tactic had to be used.
Sweet. One down, seven to go.
TO BE CONTINUED

--- ***WORDS FROM THE WEB*** ---

How was *that* for a first issue? The Spider-Office is *so* excited to have Cindy Moon, A.K.A. **SILK**, back in action in her very own title! Has this Korean American hero who sees a qualified mental health professional between Spider-villain fights ever felt more relevant? To steal from another Editorial Office: Welcome back, Cindy Moon, we hope you survive the experience!

We knew we needed just the right creative team for a character as special as this. So we reached out to the incredibly talented **MAURENE GOO**, veteran novelist (*I Believe in a Thing Called Love*) and first-time comics writer, and the always amazing **TAKESHI MIYAZAWA**, whom you might know from his work on RUNAWAYS and GHOST-SPIDER. Add to that the gorgeous colors by **IAN HERRING** and creative lettering by **ARIANA MAHER**, and our very own SILK SQUAD was complete!

When we were first putting this book together, we didn't know we were about to tumble headlong into a global health crisis. If we needed Cindy before, we need her even more since the pandemic hit. So despite some setbacks, the team persevered, and the result of all that hard work is the issue #1 you hold in your hands now. Hopefully you enjoyed the ride as much as we did. If so, do *not* miss issue #2! We've got more gangsters, demons, Korean spas, and cool sci-fi tech than you'll know what to do with.

And we want to hear from *you!!!* What did you think? What do you want to see more of? Most importantly, what should we call our letters page?! Write to spideyoffice@marvel.com and mark your message "Okay to print" if you want it to appear in the book!

Catch you next month!

The Silk Editorial Team
Jake, Lindsey, and Nick
3/4/21

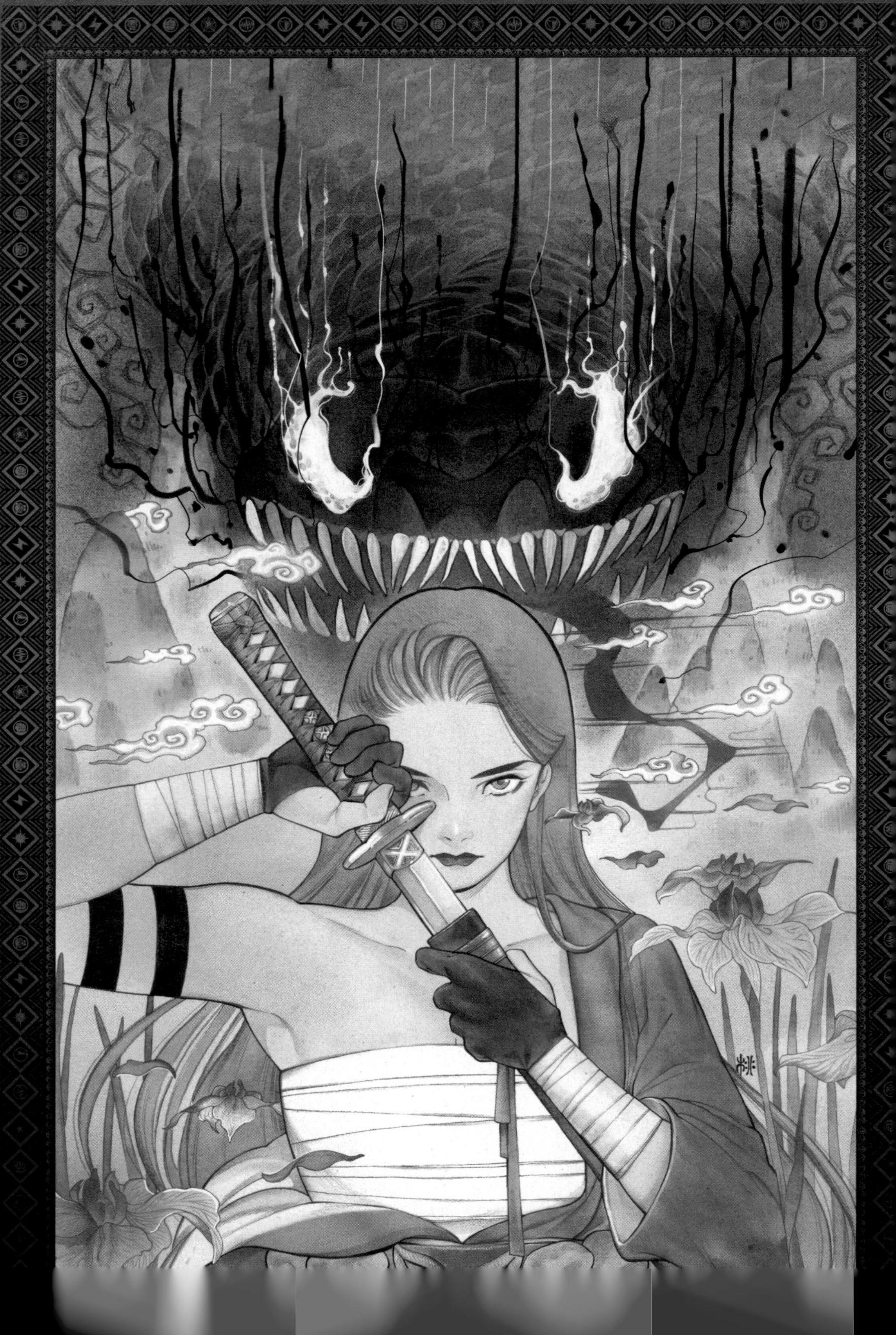

Welcome to a world filled with demons and spirits, monsters and magic.
This is the Marvel Universe like you've never seen it before. This is...

PEACH MOMOKO
STORY & ART

ZACK DAVISSON
ENGLISH ADAPTATION

VC's ARIANA MAHER
LETTERING

PEACH MOMOKO
COVER ARTIST

JAY BOWEN
DESIGNER

LINDSEY COHICK
EDITOR

C.B. CEBULSKI
EDITOR IN CHIEF

X-MEN & HULK created by STAN LEE & JACK KIRBY

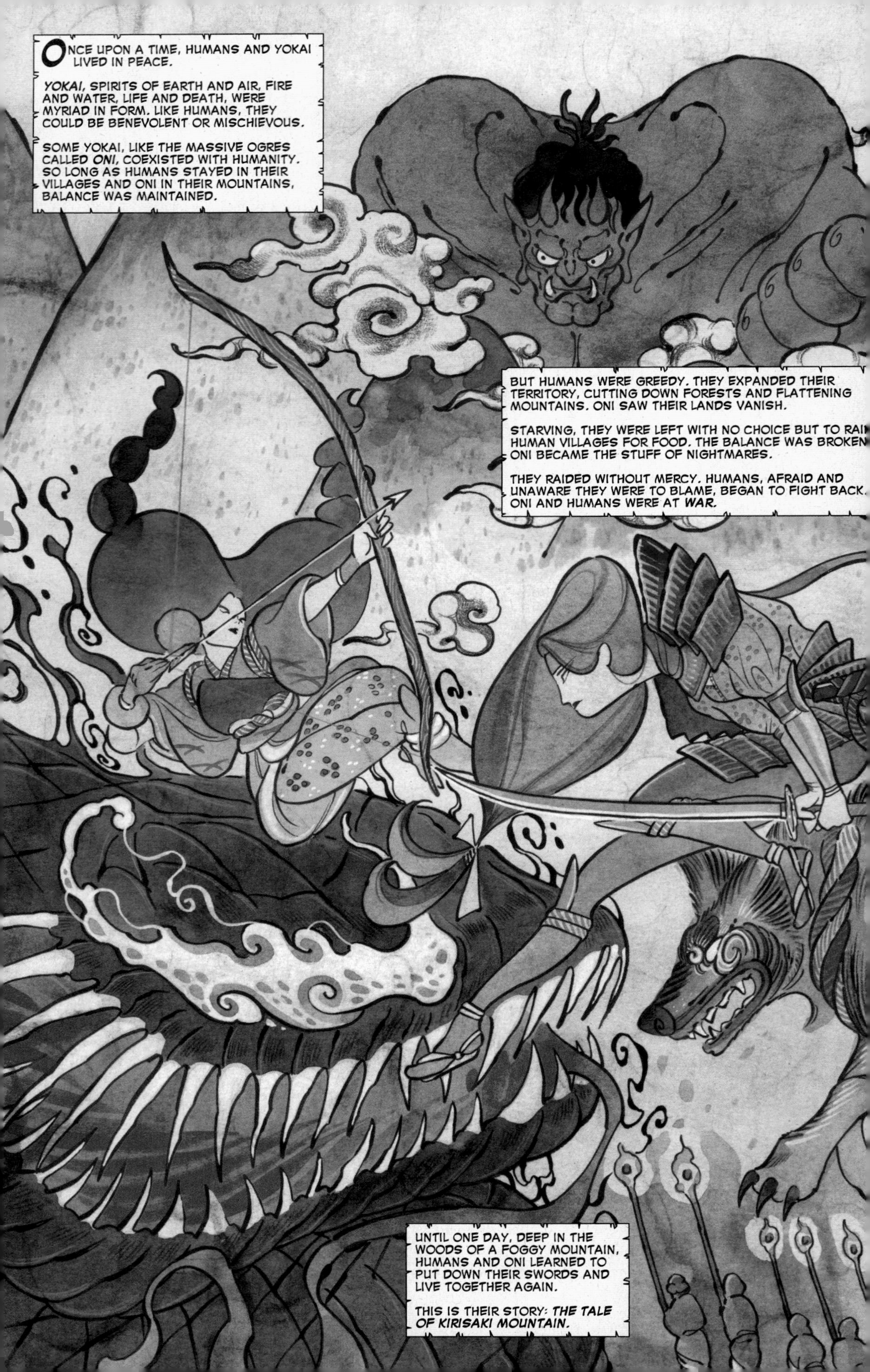
ONCE UPON A TIME, HUMANS AND YOKAI LIVED IN PEACE.
YOKAI, SPIRITS OF EARTH AND AIR, FIRE AND WATER, LIFE AND DEATH, WERE MYRIAD IN FORM. LIKE HUMANS, THEY COULD BE BENEVOLENT OR MISCHIEVOUS.
SOME YOKAI, LIKE THE MASSIVE OGRES CALLED ONI, COEXISTED WITH HUMANITY. SO LONG AS HUMANS STAYED IN THEIR VILLAGES AND ONI IN THEIR MOUNTAINS, BALANCE WAS MAINTAINED.
BUT HUMANS WERE GREEDY. THEY EXPANDED THEIR TERRITORY, CUTTING DOWN FORESTS AND FLATTENING MOUNTAINS. ONI SAW THEIR LANDS VANISH.
STARVING, THEY WERE LEFT WITH NO CHOICE BUT TO RAI HUMAN VILLAGES FOR FOOD. THE BALANCE WAS BROKEN ONI BECAME THE STUFF OF NIGHTMARES.
THEY RAIDED WITHOUT MERCY. HUMANS, AFRAID AND UNAWARE THEY WERE TO BLAME, BEGAN TO FIGHT BACK. ONI AND HUMANS WERE AT WAR.
UNTIL ONE DAY, DEEP IN THE WOODS OF A FOGGY MOUNTAIN, HUMANS AND ONI LEARNED TO PUT DOWN THEIR SWORDS AND LIVE TOGETHER AGAIN.
THIS IS THEIR STORY: THE TALE OF KIRISAKI MOUNTAIN.

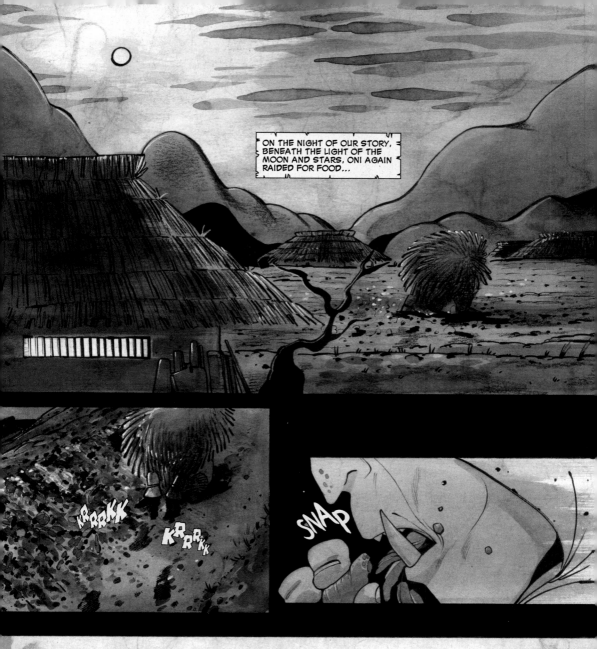

ON THE NIGHT OF OUR STORY, BENEATH THE LIGHT OF THE MOON AND STARS, ONI AGAIN RAIDED FOR FOOD...

KRRRKK

KRRRKK

SNAP

KRNNK KRNNK

TSUKI, CHILD, PLEASE...

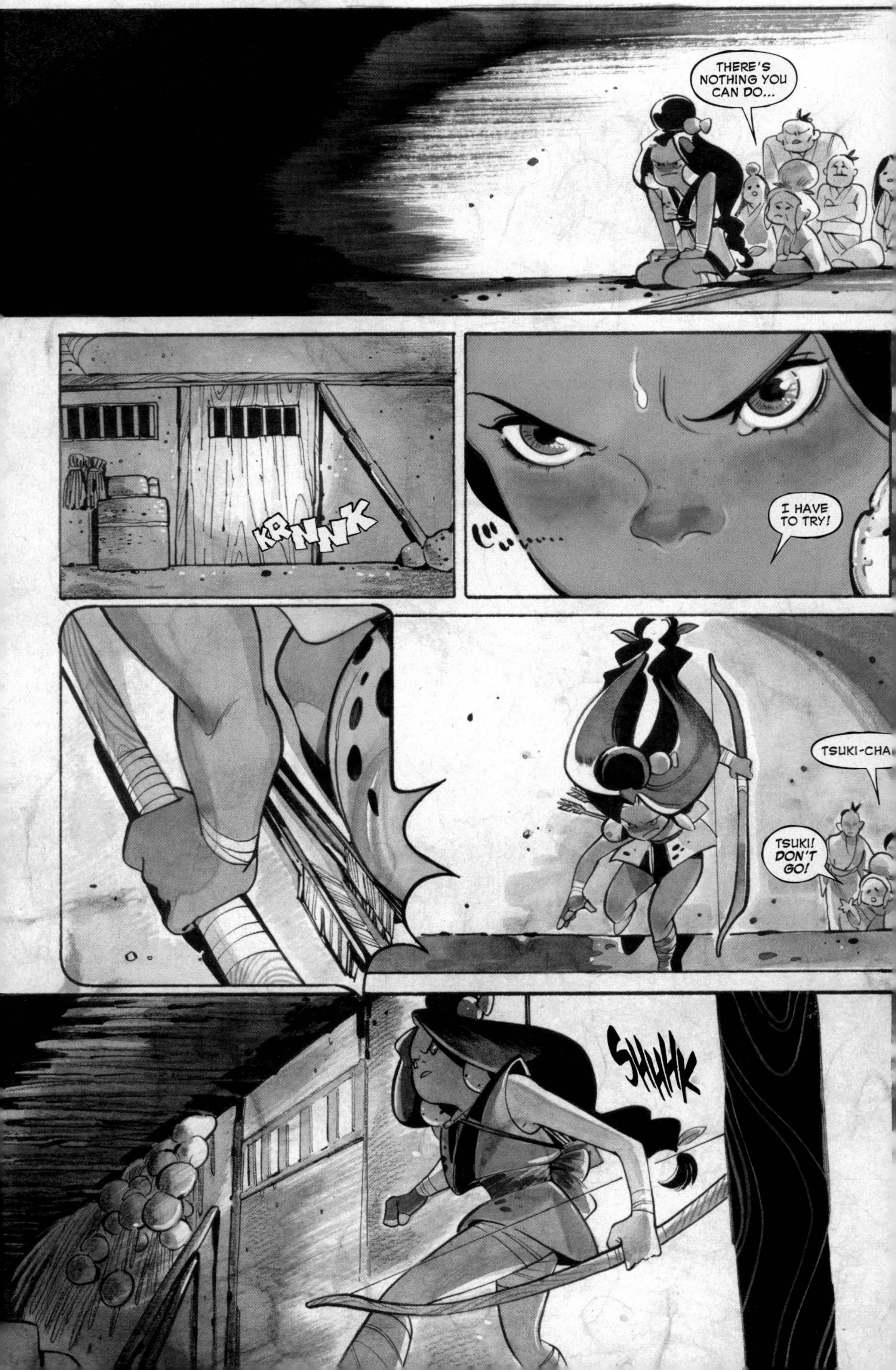

THERE'S NOTHING YOU CAN DO...
KRNNK
I HAVE TO TRY!
TSUKI-CHA
TSUKI! DON'T GO!
SHHHK

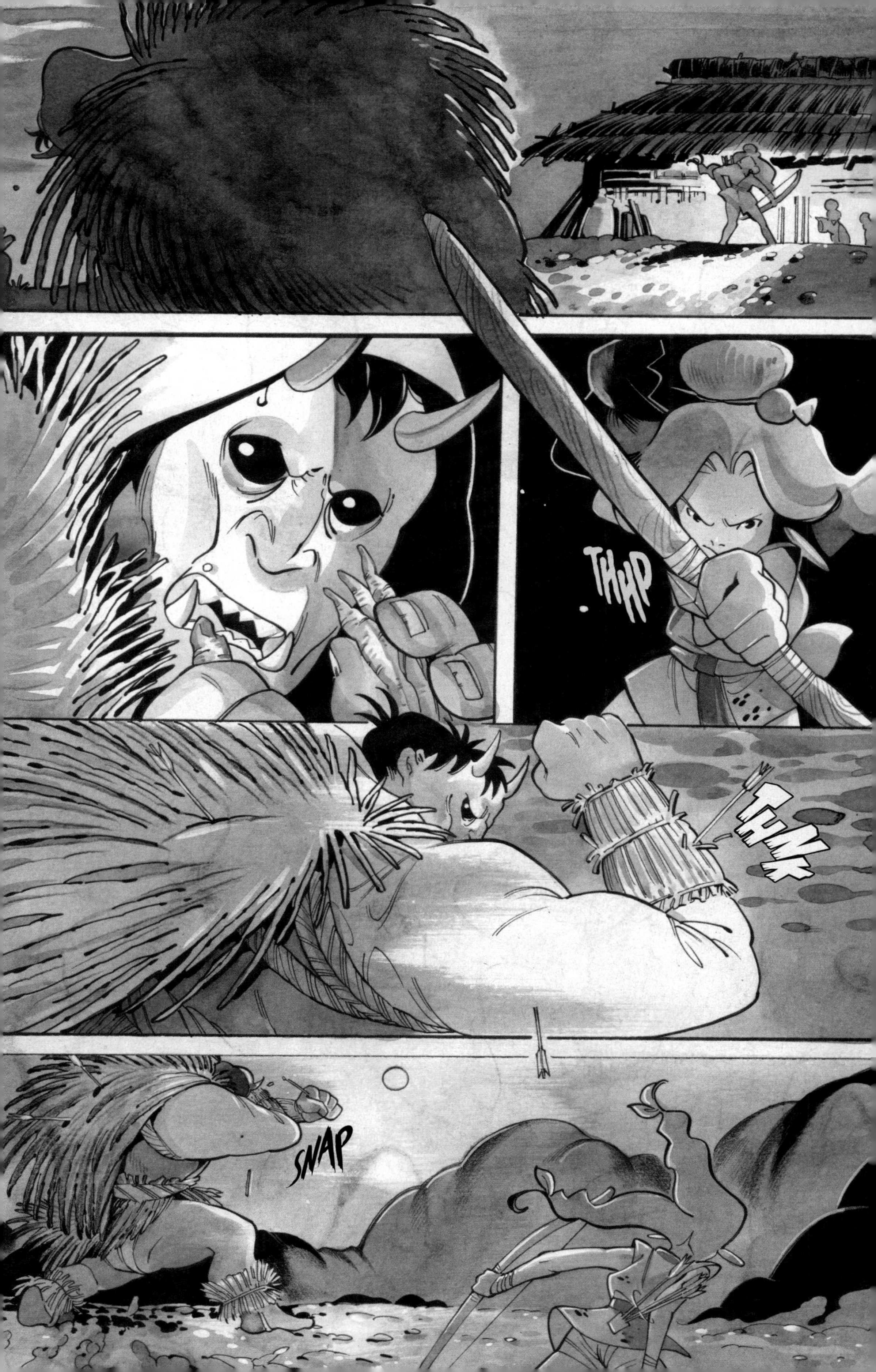
THHP
THNK
SNAP

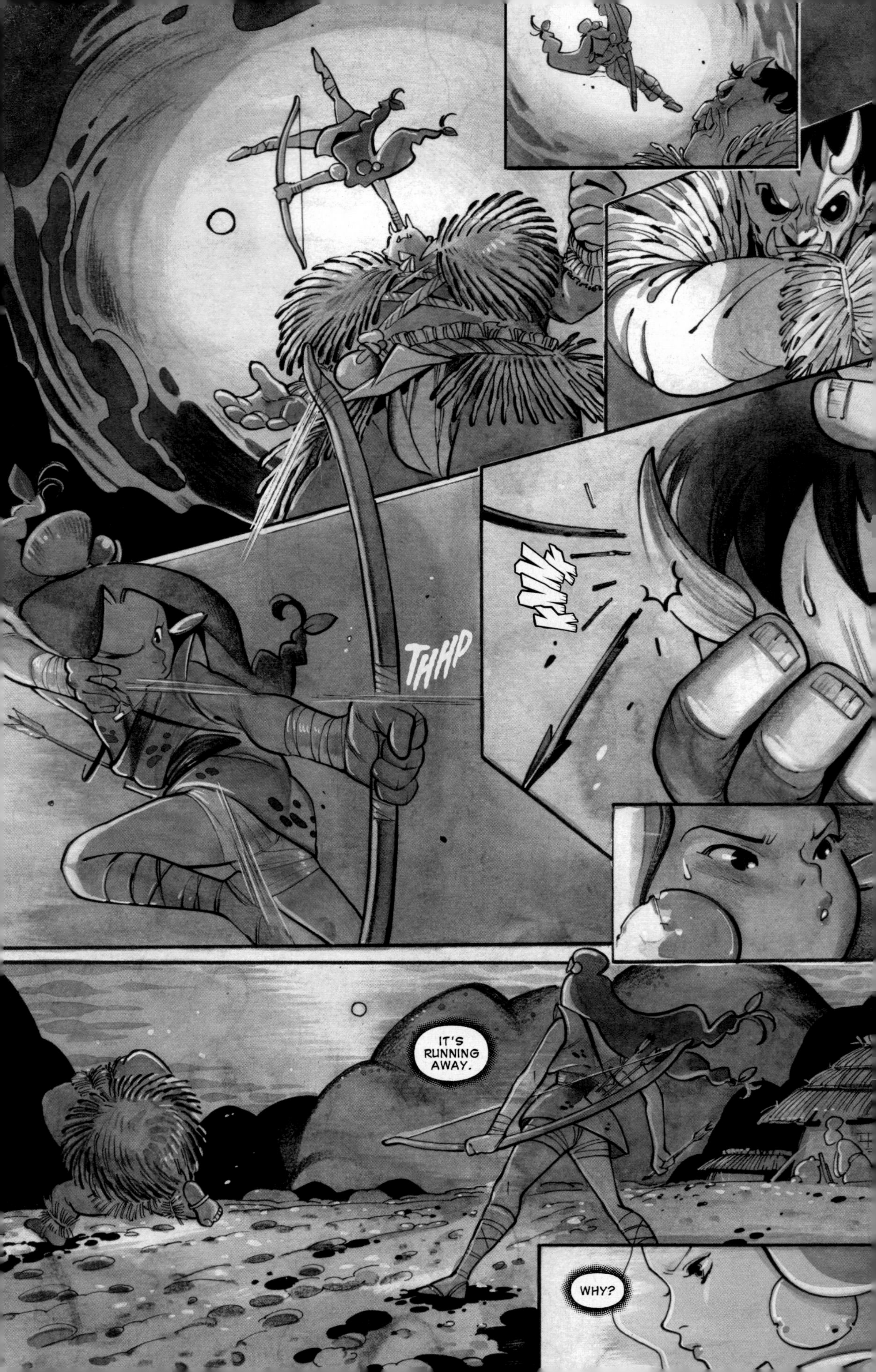
KWIK
THHP
IT'S RUNNING AWAY.
WHY?

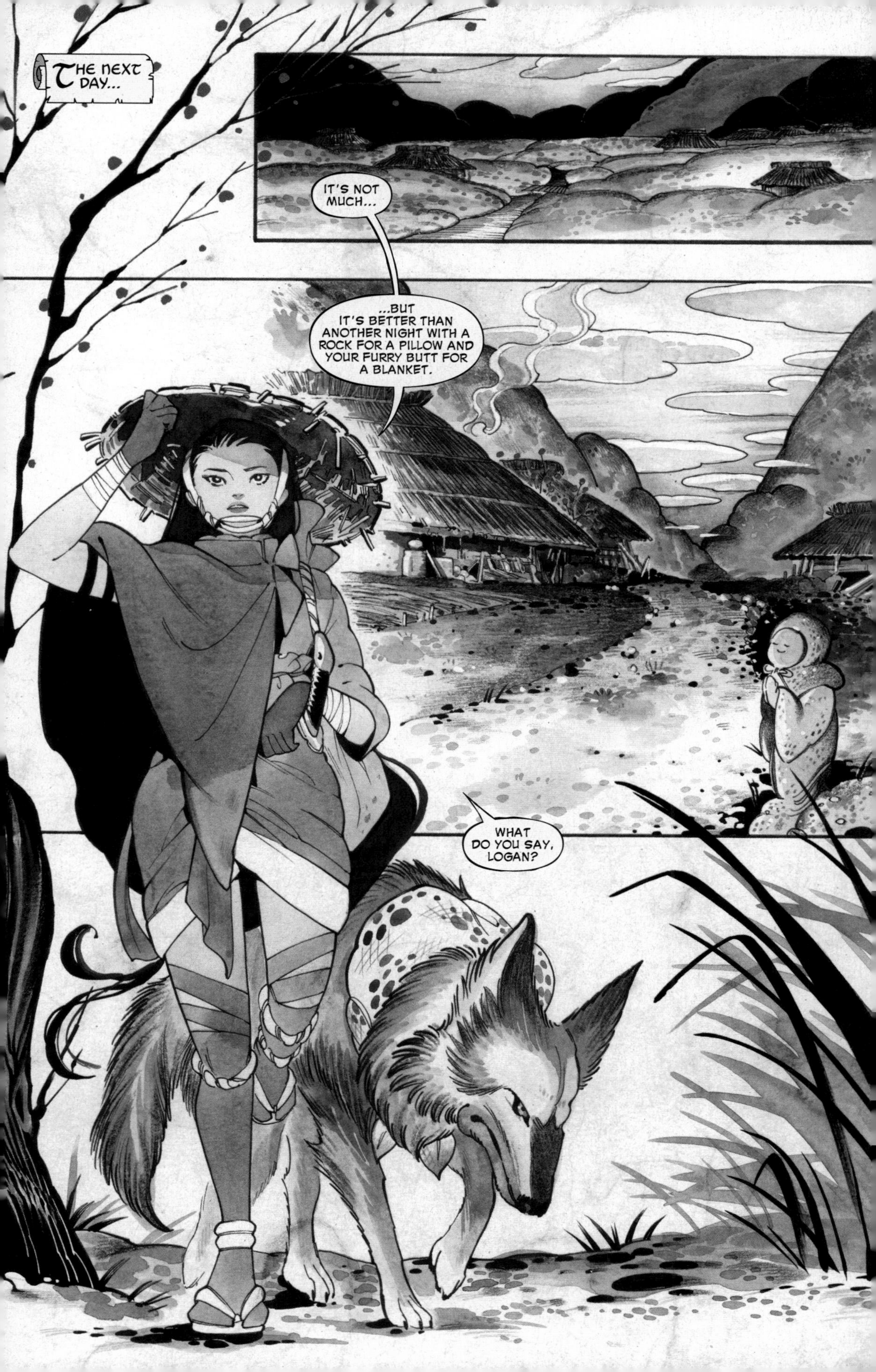
THE NEXT DAY...
IT'S NOT MUCH...
...BUT IT'S BETTER THAN ANOTHER NIGHT WITH A ROCK FOR A PILLOW AND YOUR FURRY BUTT FOR A BLANKET.
WHAT DO YOU SAY, LOGAN?

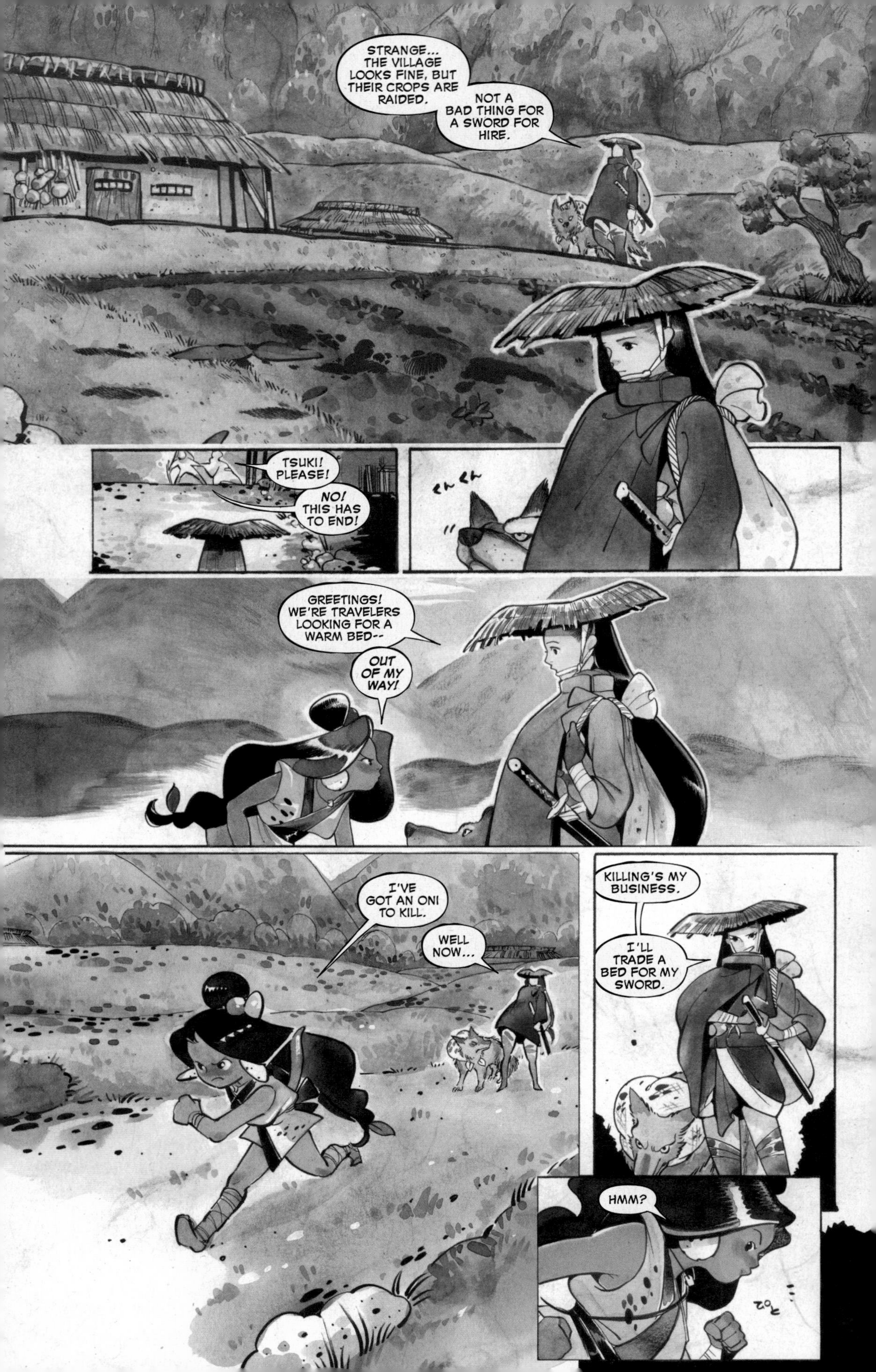
STRANGE... THE VILLAGE LOOKS FINE, BUT THEIR CROPS ARE RAIDED.
NOT A BAD THING FOR A SWORD FOR HIRE.
TSUKI! PLEASE!
NO! THIS HAS TO END!
GREETINGS! WE'RE TRAVELERS LOOKING FOR A WARM BED--
OUT OF MY WAY!
I'VE GOT AN ONI TO KILL.
WELL NOW...
KILLING'S MY BUSINESS.
I'LL TRADE A BED FOR MY SWORD.
HMM?

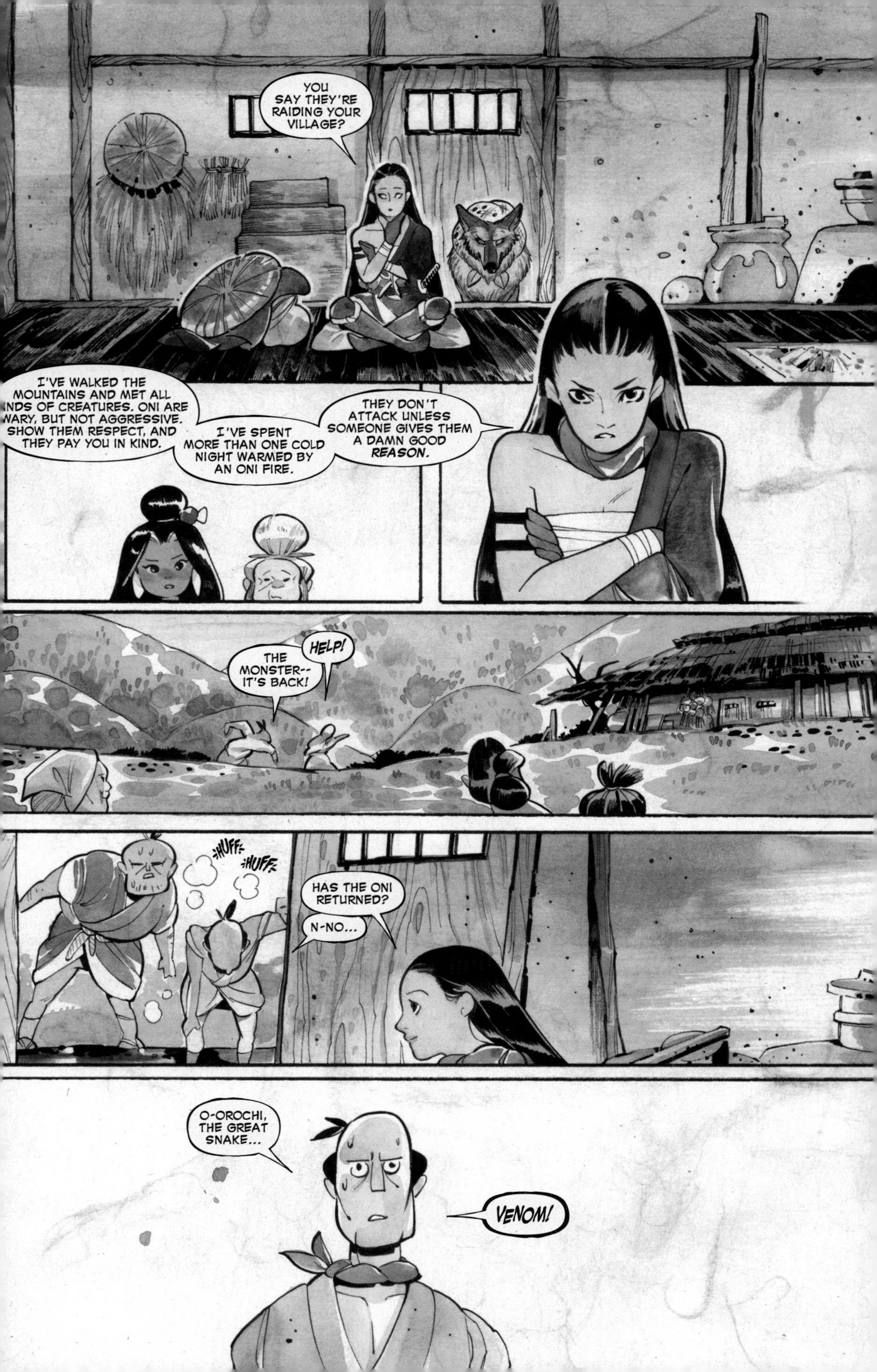
YOU SAY THEY'RE RAIDING YOUR VILLAGE?
I'VE WALKED THE MOUNTAINS AND MET ALL KINDS OF CREATURES. ONI ARE WARY, BUT NOT AGGRESSIVE. SHOW THEM RESPECT, AND THEY PAY YOU IN KIND.
I'VE SPENT MORE THAN ONE COLD NIGHT WARMED BY AN ONI FIRE.
THEY DON'T ATTACK UNLESS SOMEONE GIVES THEM A DAMN GOOD REASON.
HELP!
THE MONSTER-- IT'S BACK!
HUFF
HUFF
HAS THE ONI RETURNED?
N-NO...
O-OROCHI, THE GREAT SNAKE...
VENOM!

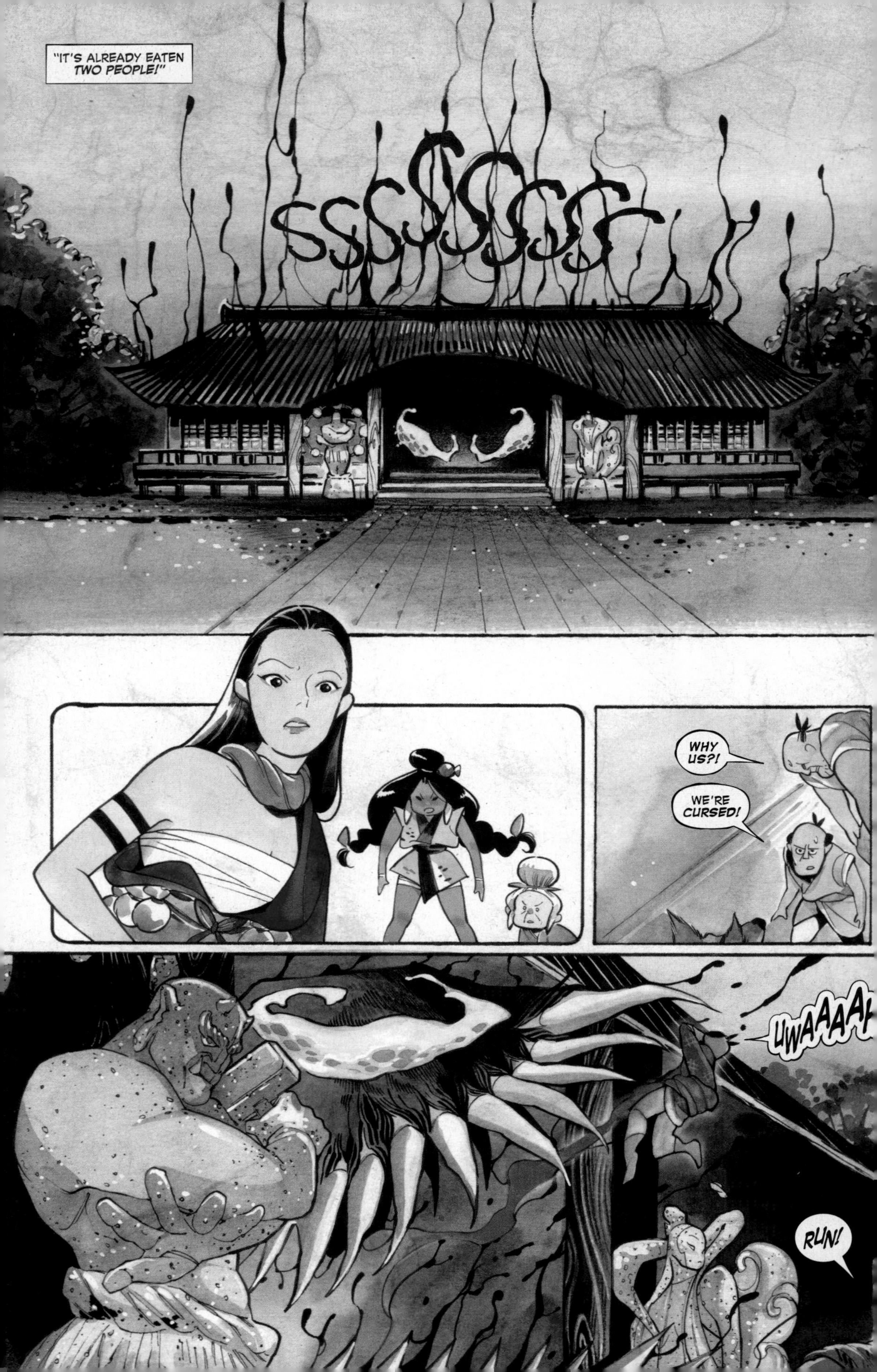
"IT'S ALREADY EATEN TWO PEOPLE!"
SSSSSSSSS
WHY US?!
WE'RE CURSED!
UWAAAA!
RUN!

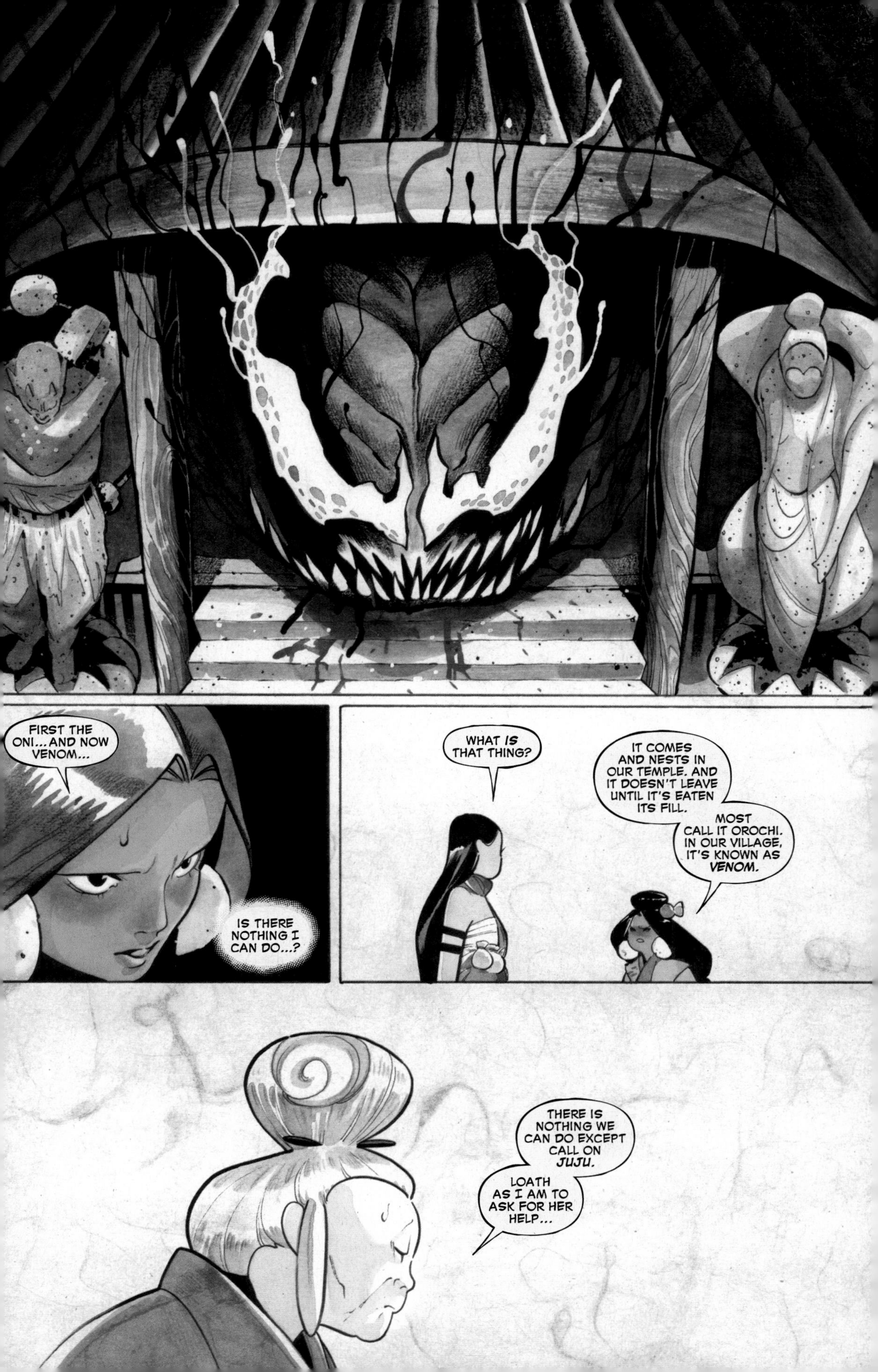
FIRST THE ONI... AND NOW VENOM...
IS THERE NOTHING I CAN DO...?
WHAT IS THAT THING?
IT COMES AND NESTS IN OUR TEMPLE. AND IT DOESN'T LEAVE UNTIL IT'S EATEN ITS FILL.
MOST CALL IT OROCHI. IN OUR VILLAGE, IT'S KNOWN AS VENOM.
THERE IS NOTHING WE CAN DO EXCEPT CALL ON JUJU.
LOATH AS I AM TO ASK FOR HER HELP...

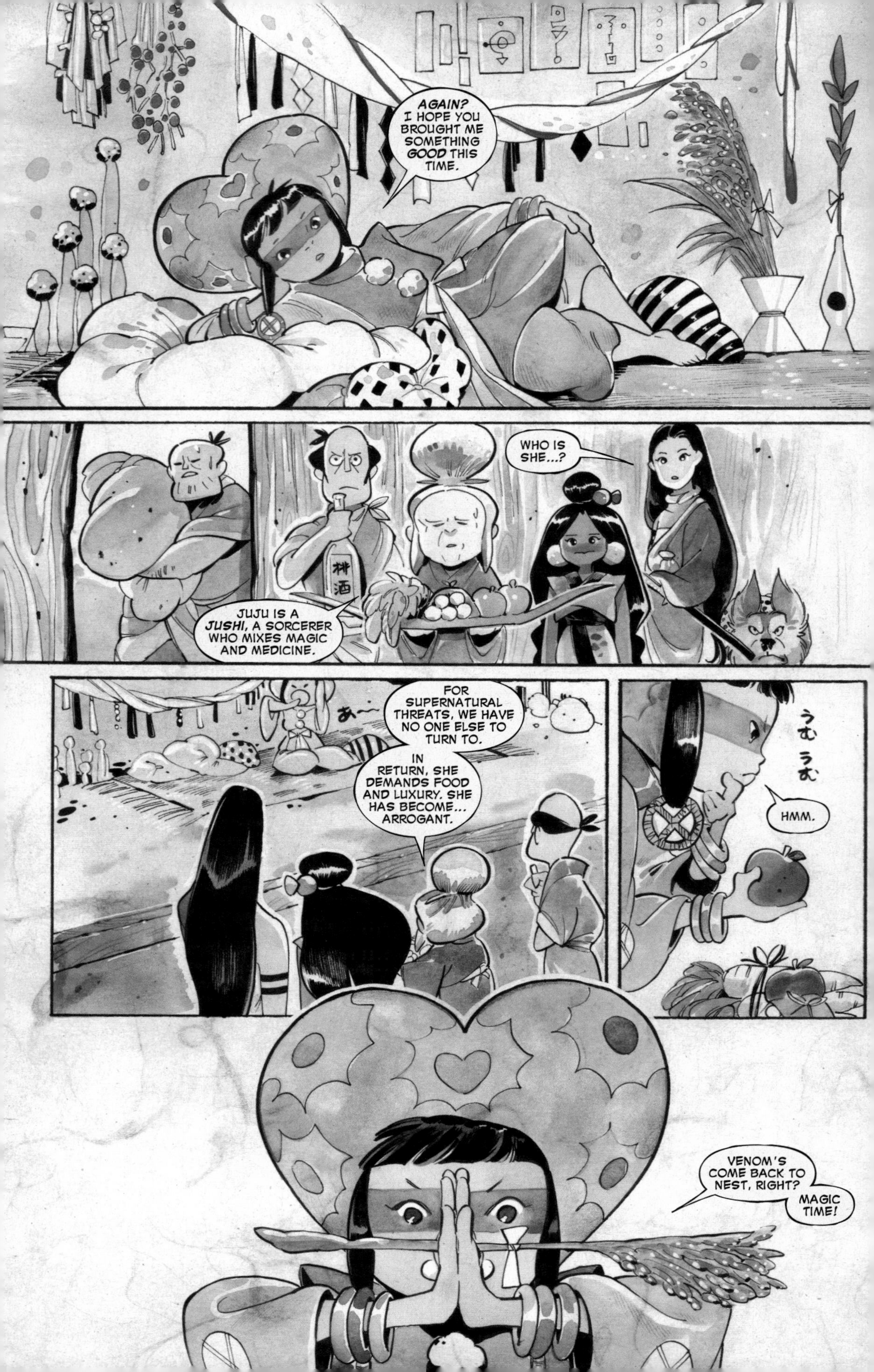
AGAIN? I HOPE YOU BROUGHT ME SOMETHING GOOD THIS TIME.
WHO IS SHE...?
JUJU IS A JUSHI, A SORCERER WHO MIXES MAGIC AND MEDICINE.
あ~~
FOR SUPERNATURAL THREATS, WE HAVE NO ONE ELSE TO TURN TO.
IN RETURN, SHE DEMANDS FOOD AND LUXURY. SHE HAS BECOME... ARROGANT.
うむ うむ
HMM.
VENOM'S COME BACK TO NEST, RIGHT?
MAGIC TIME!

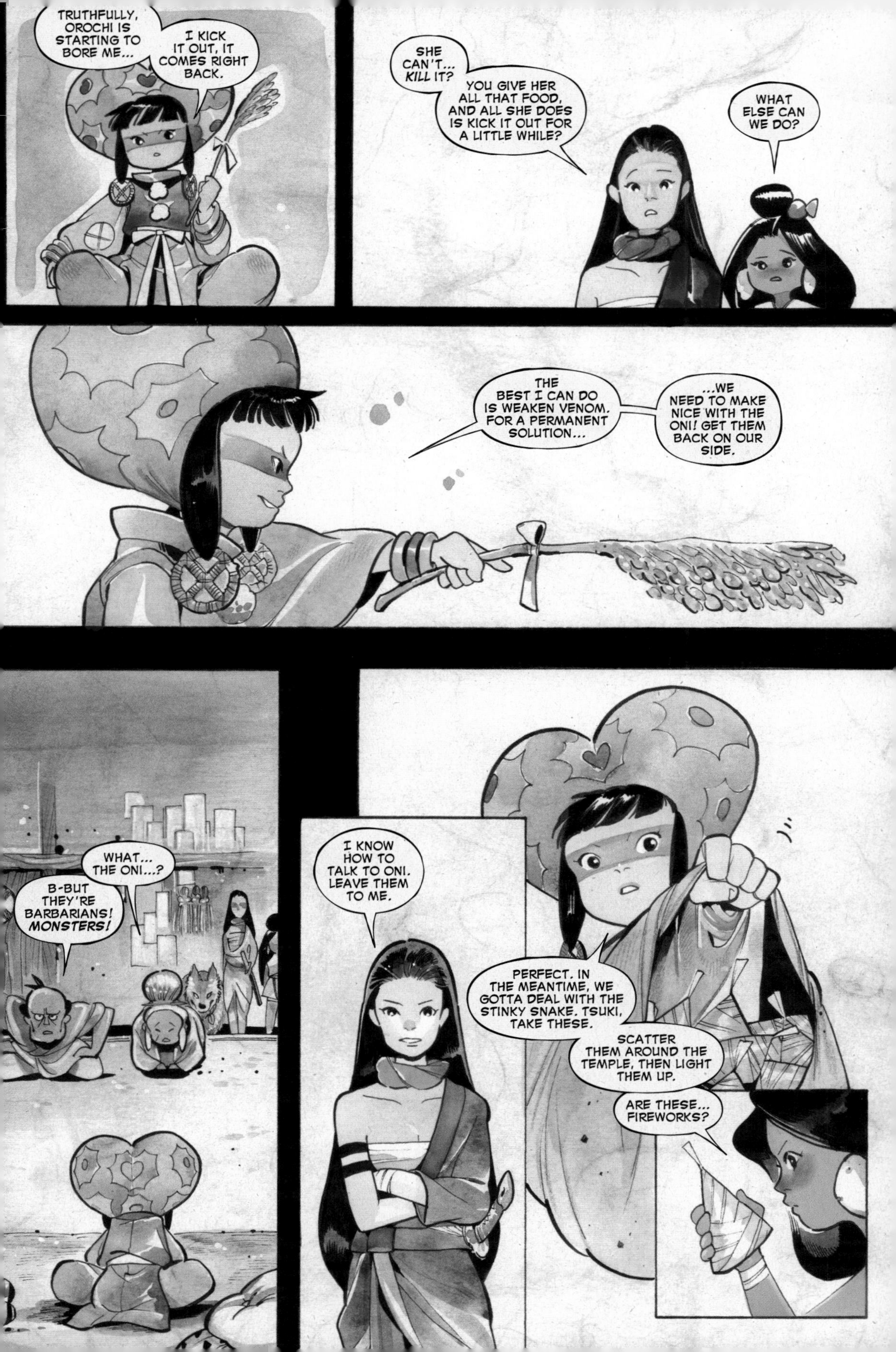
TRUTHFULLY, OROCHI IS STARTING TO BORE ME...
I KICK IT OUT, IT COMES RIGHT BACK.
SHE CAN'T... *KILL* IT?
YOU GIVE HER ALL THAT FOOD, AND ALL SHE DOES IS KICK IT OUT FOR A LITTLE WHILE?
WHAT ELSE CAN WE DO?
THE BEST I CAN DO IS WEAKEN VENOM. FOR A PERMANENT SOLUTION...
...WE NEED TO MAKE NICE WITH THE ONI! GET THEM BACK ON OUR SIDE.
WHAT... THE ONI...?
B-BUT THEY'RE BARBARIANS! *MONSTERS!*
I KNOW HOW TO TALK TO ONI. LEAVE THEM TO ME.
PERFECT. IN THE MEANTIME, WE GOTTA DEAL WITH THE STINKY SNAKE. TSUKI, TAKE THESE.
SCATTER THEM AROUND THE TEMPLE, THEN LIGHT THEM UP.
ARE THESE... FIREWORKS?

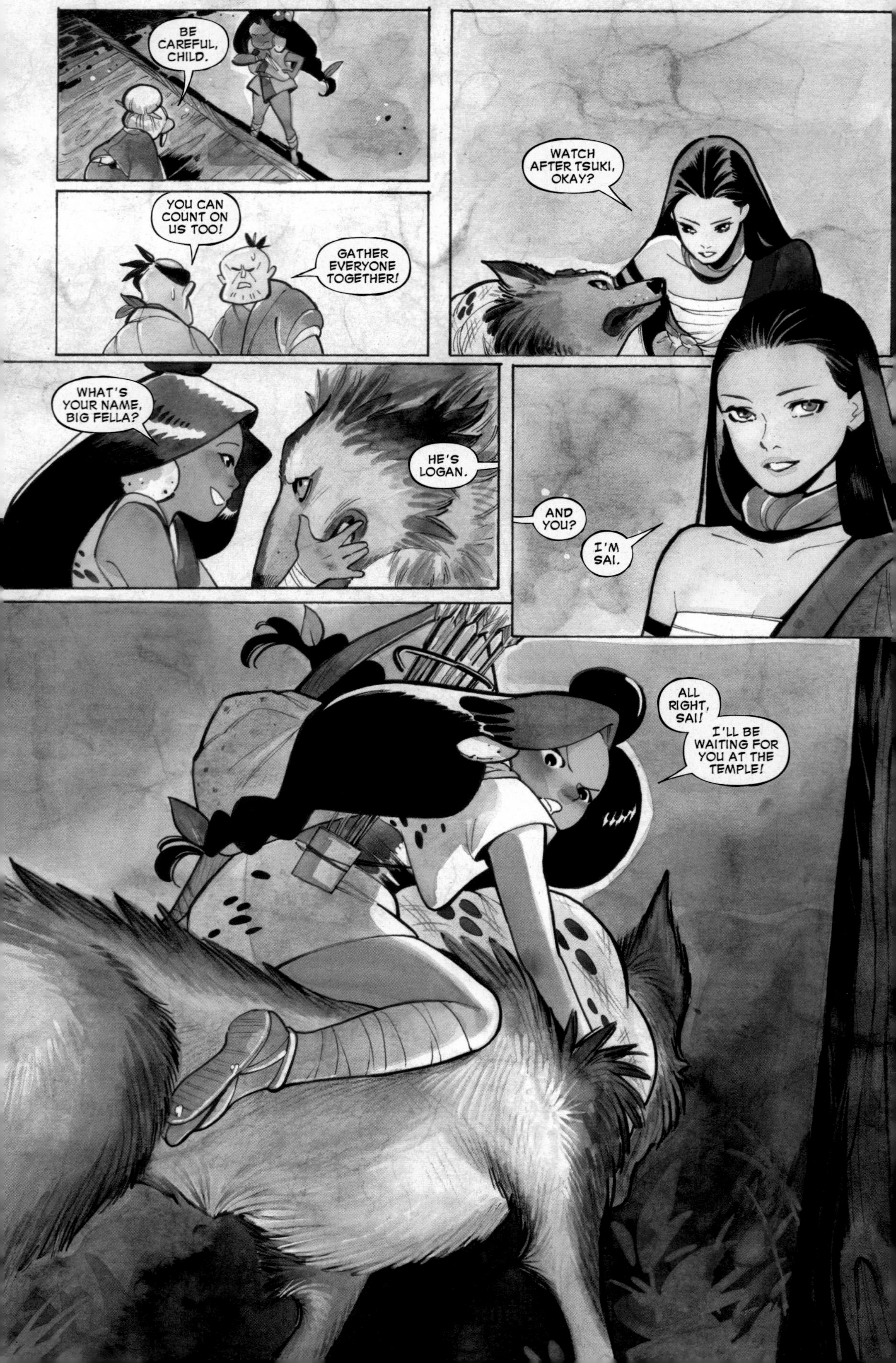
BE CAREFUL, CHILD.
WATCH AFTER TSUKI, OKAY?
YOU CAN COUNT ON US TOO!
GATHER EVERYONE TOGETHER!
WHAT'S YOUR NAME, BIG FELLA?
HE'S LOGAN.
AND YOU?
I'M SAI.
ALL RIGHT, SAI!
I'LL BE WAITING FOR YOU AT THE TEMPLE!

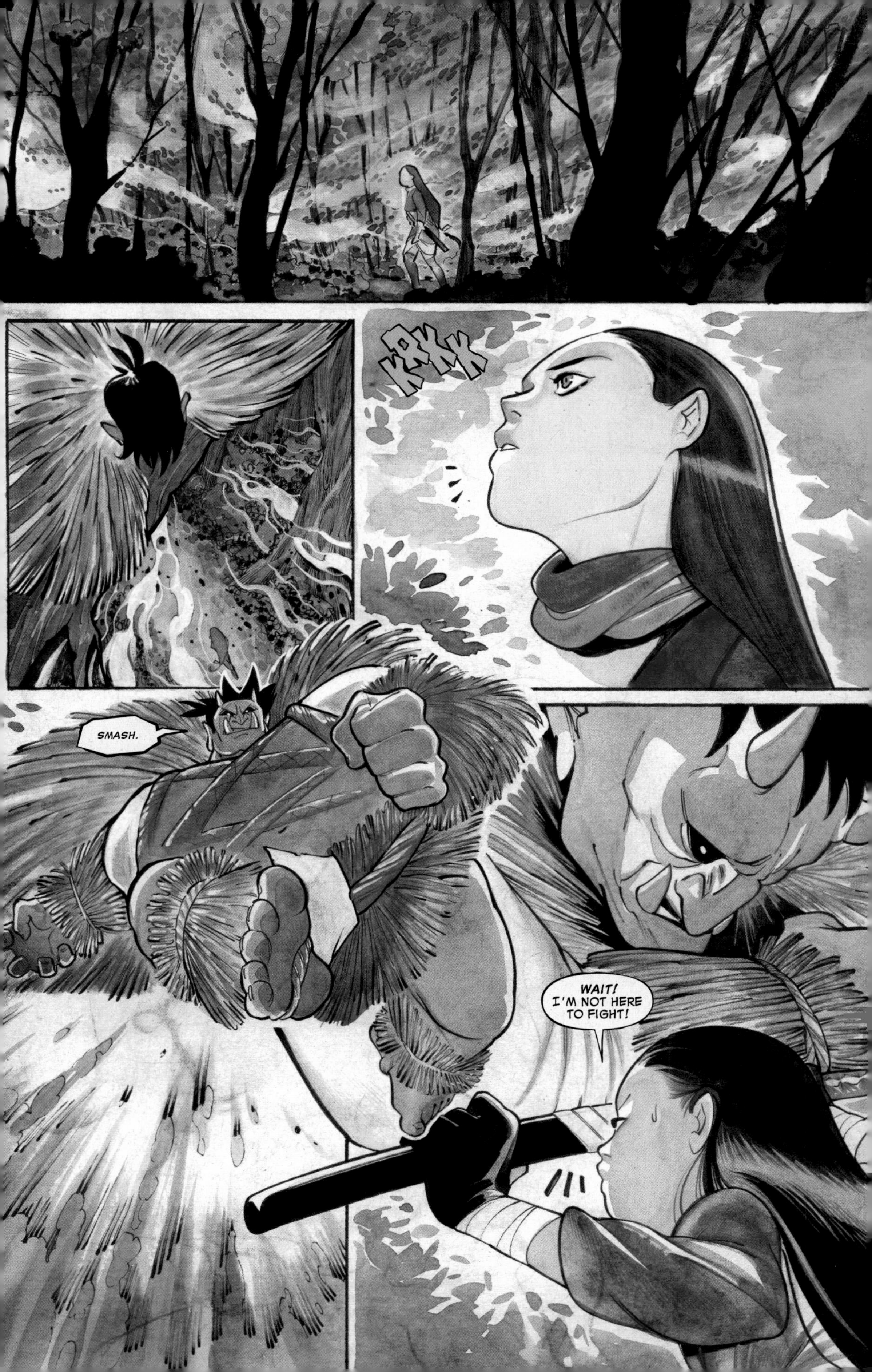
KRKK
SMASH.
WAIT! I'M NOT HERE TO FIGHT!

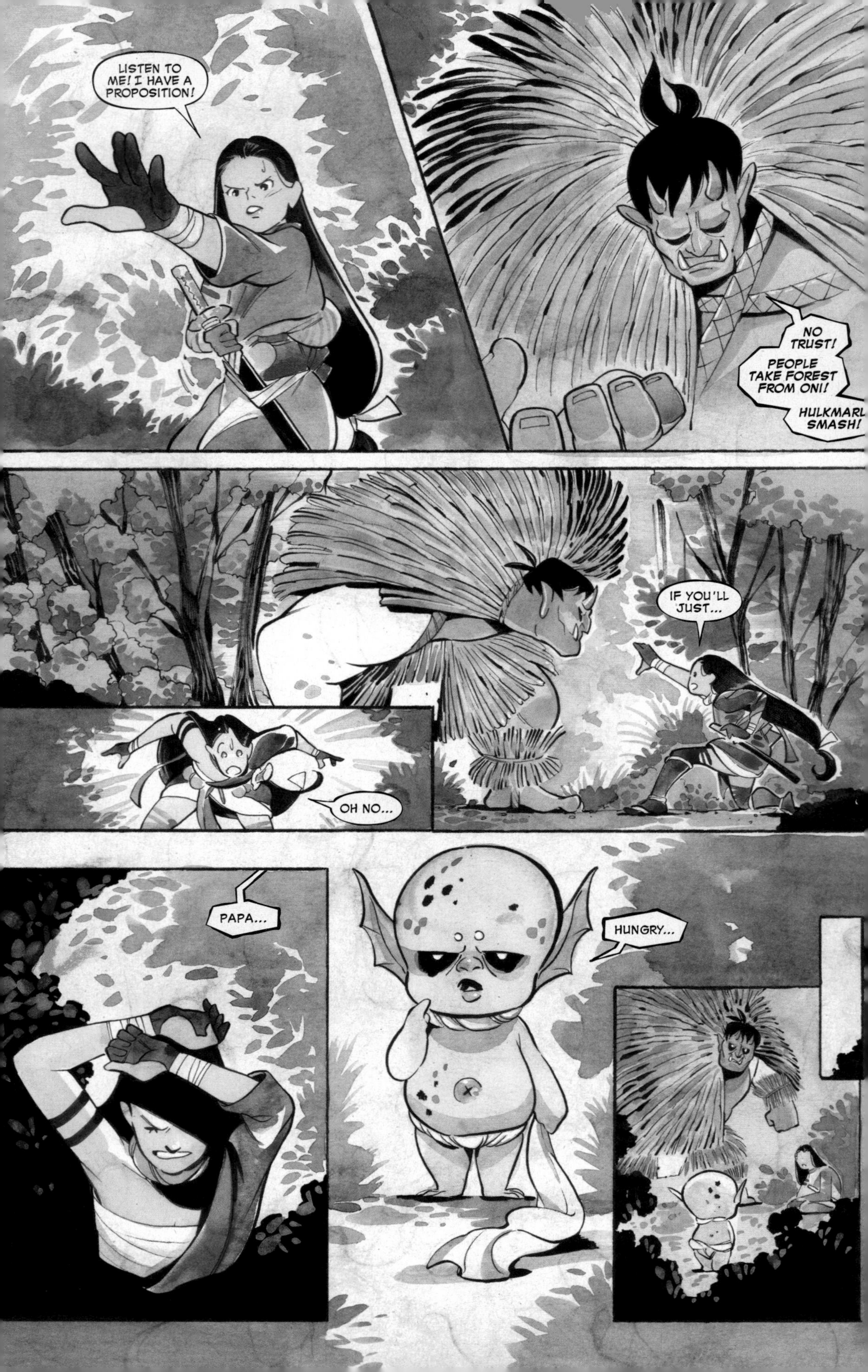
LISTEN TO ME! I HAVE A PROPOSITION!
NO TRUST!
PEOPLE TAKE FOREST FROM ONI!
HULKMARU SMASH!
IF YOU'LL JUST...
OH NO...
PAPA...
HUNGRY...

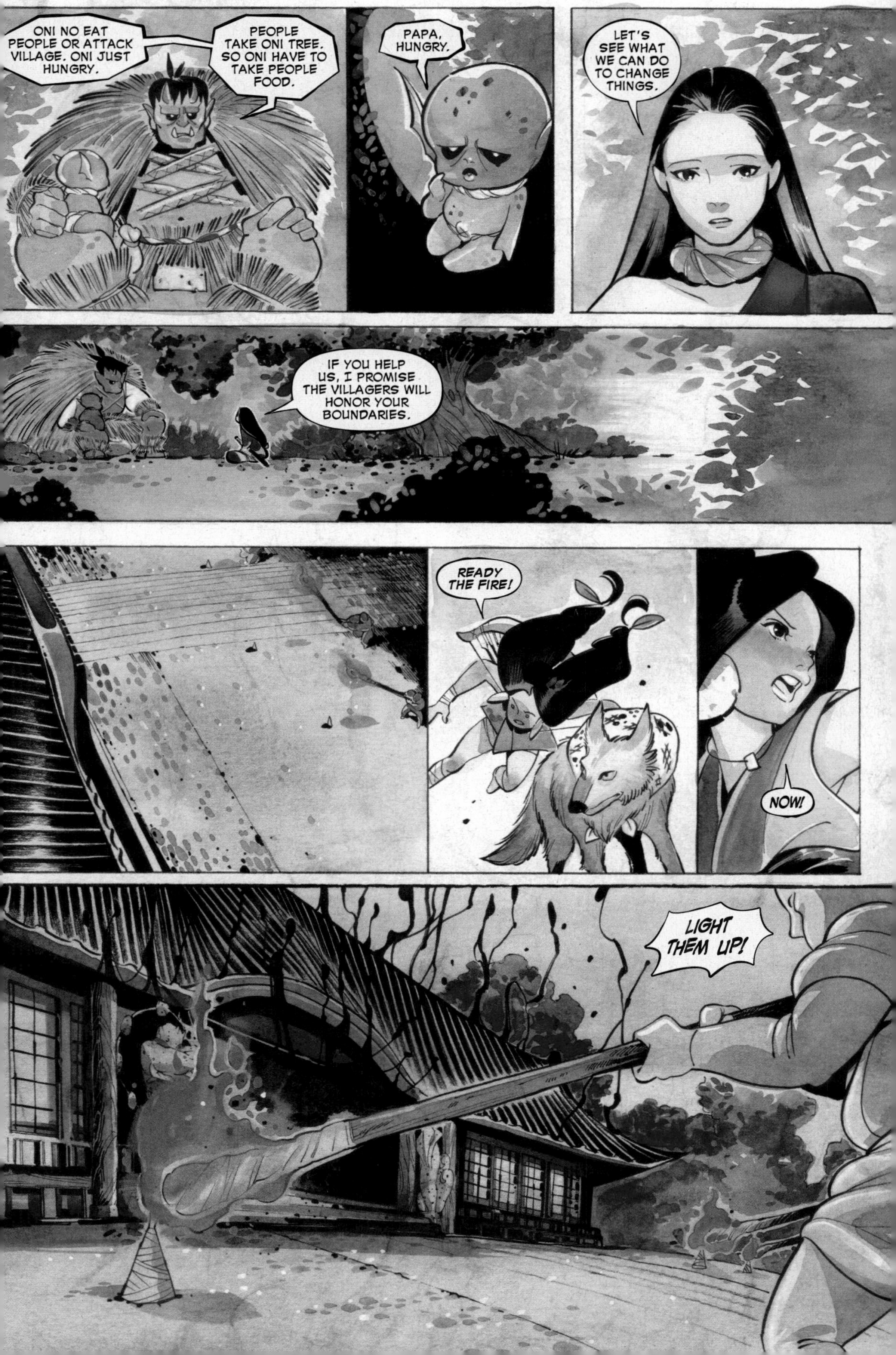
ONI NO EAT PEOPLE OR ATTACK VILLAGE. ONI JUST HUNGRY.
PEOPLE TAKE ONI TREE. SO ONI HAVE TO TAKE PEOPLE FOOD.
PAPA, HUNGRY.
LET'S SEE WHAT WE CAN DO TO CHANGE THINGS.
IF YOU HELP US, I PROMISE THE VILLAGERS WILL HONOR YOUR BOUNDARIES.
READY THE FIRE!
NOW!
LIGHT THEM UP!

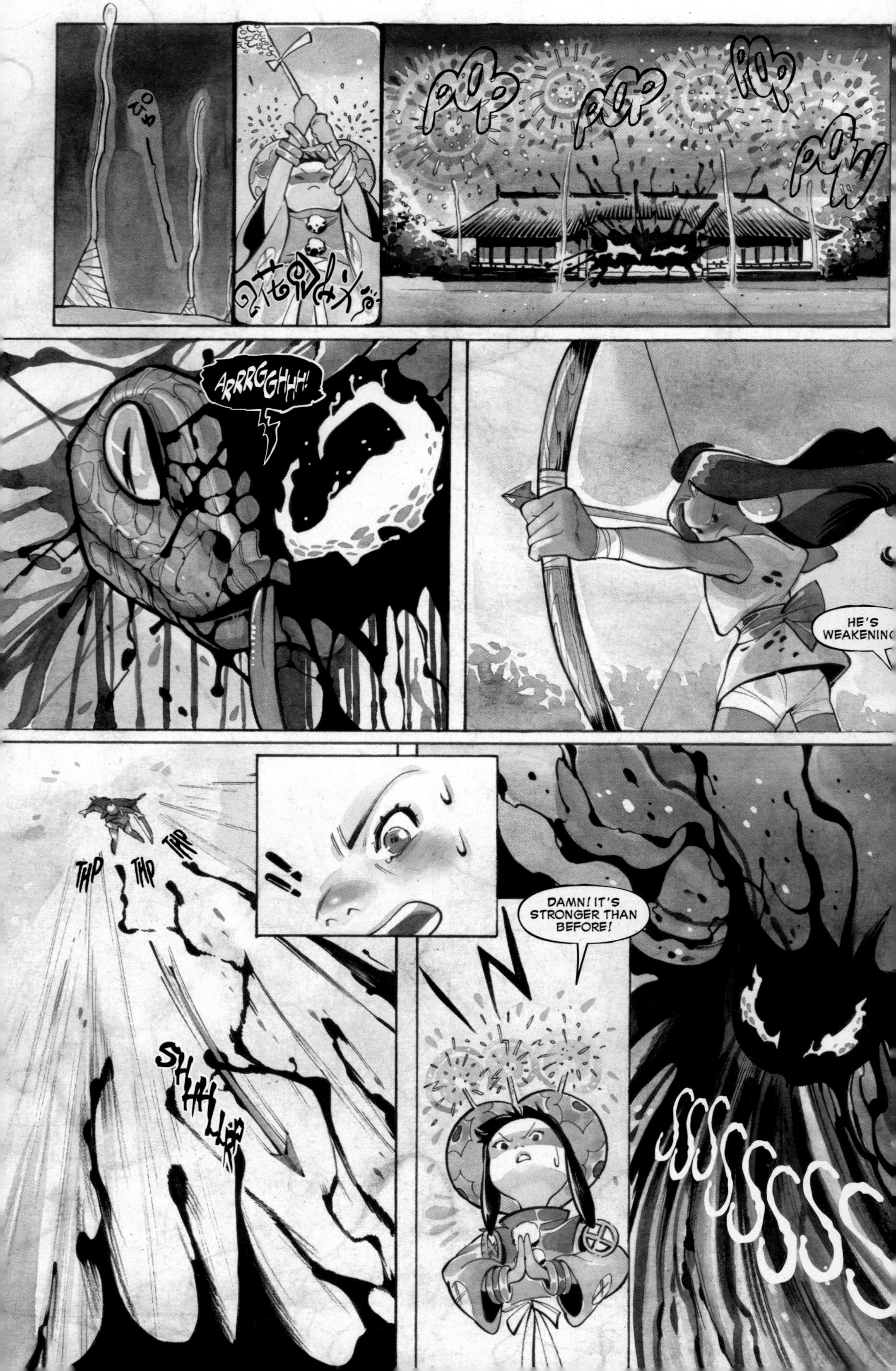

ひゅー
POP
POP
POP
POW
ARRRGGHHH!
HE'S WEAKENING
THP
THP
THP
!!
SHHHLLRR
DAMN! IT'S STRONGER THAN BEFORE!
SSSSSSSSSS

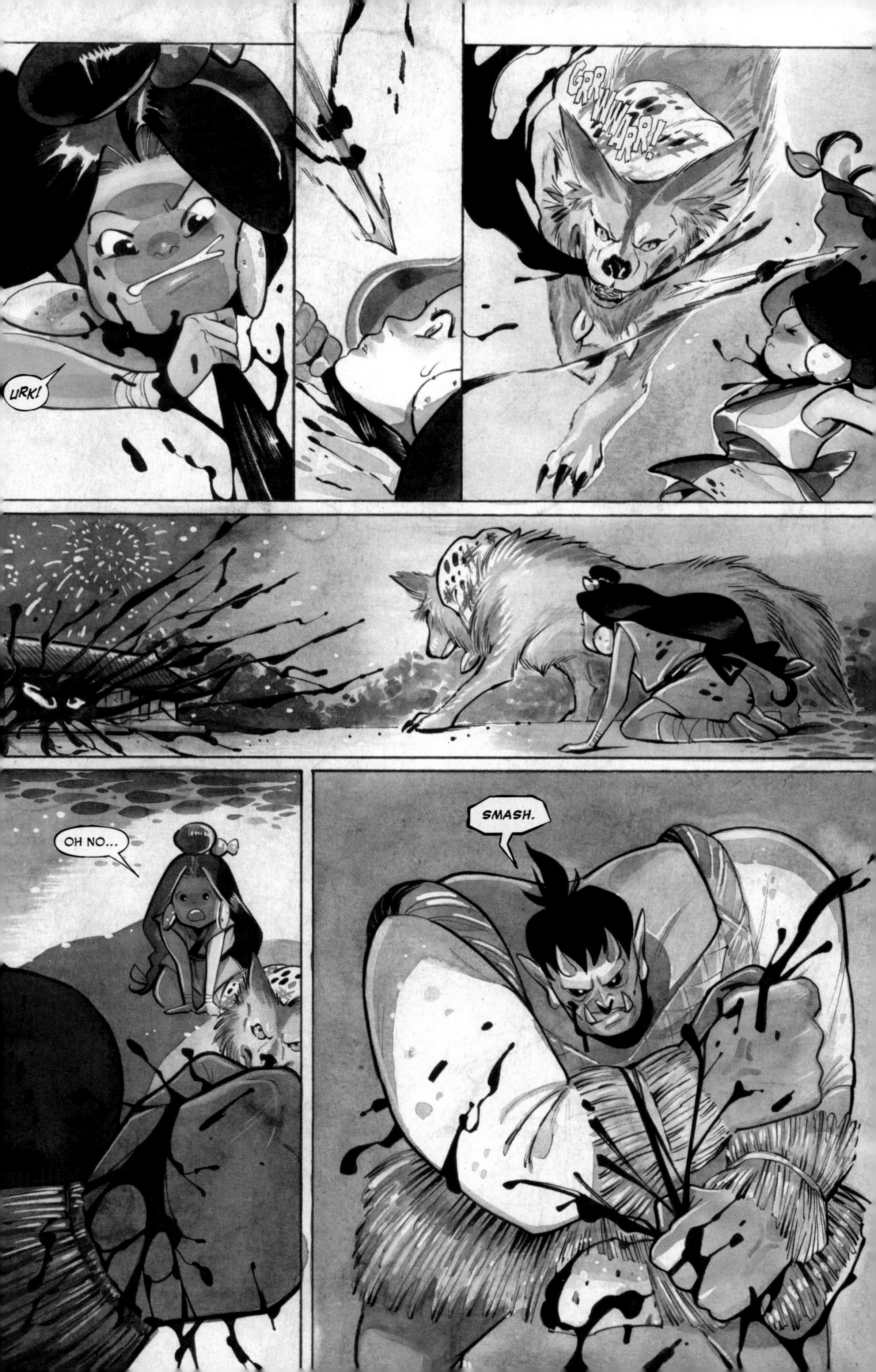
URK!
GRRWWARR!!
OH NO...
SMASH.

HYAH!

I-- --ABJURE THEE.

WE NEED TO PULL VENOM OUT OF THERE!

TSUKI! YOU AND LOGAN GET READY!

WHEN WE'RE CLEAR, TAKE YOUR SHOT!

ON IT!

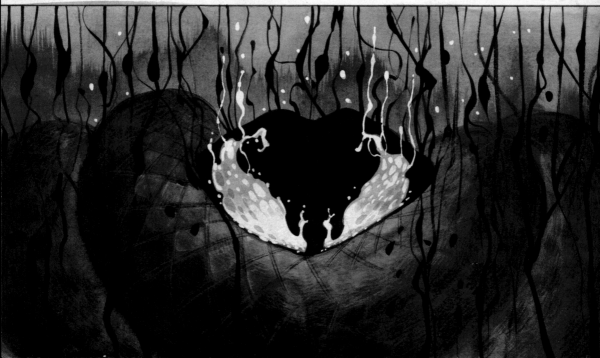

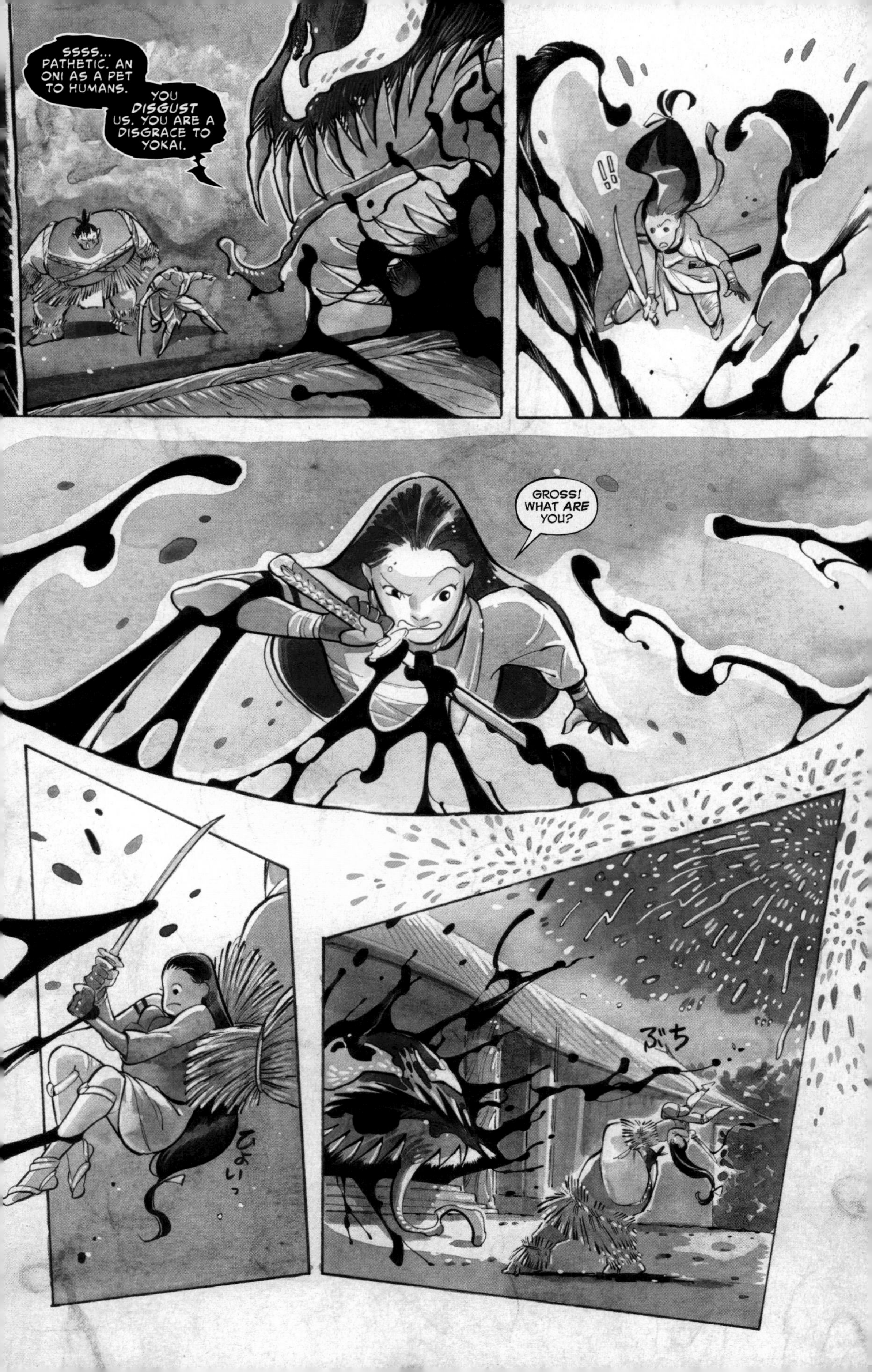
SSSS... PATHETIC. AN ONI AS A PET TO HUMANS.
YOU DISGUST US. YOU ARE A DISGRACE TO YOKAI.
!!
GROSS! WHAT ARE YOU?
ひょいっ
ぶち

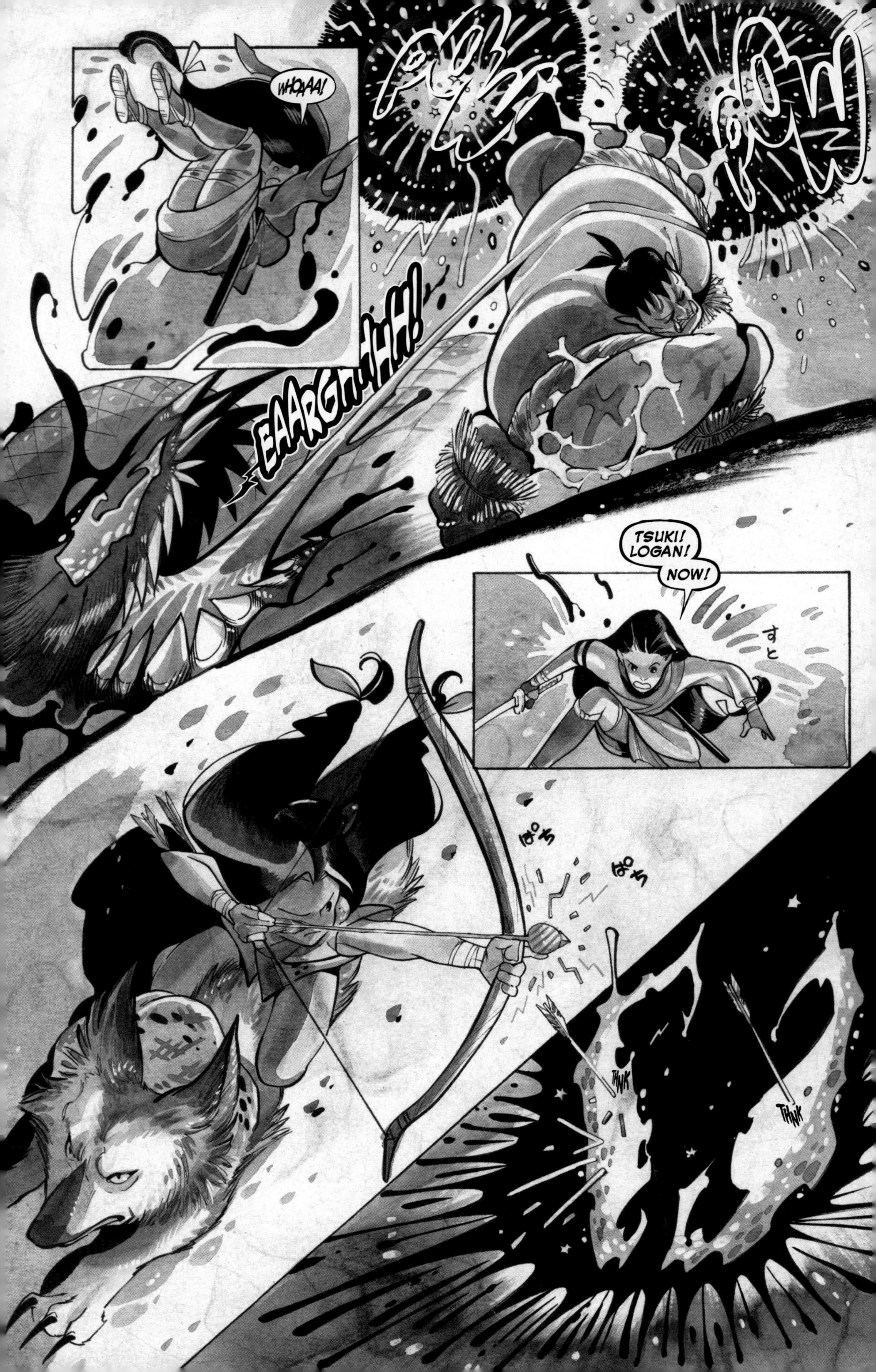
WHOAAA!
POW
POW
EAARGHHHH!
TSUKI! LOGAN!
NOW!
すと
ぽち
ぽち
THNK
THNK

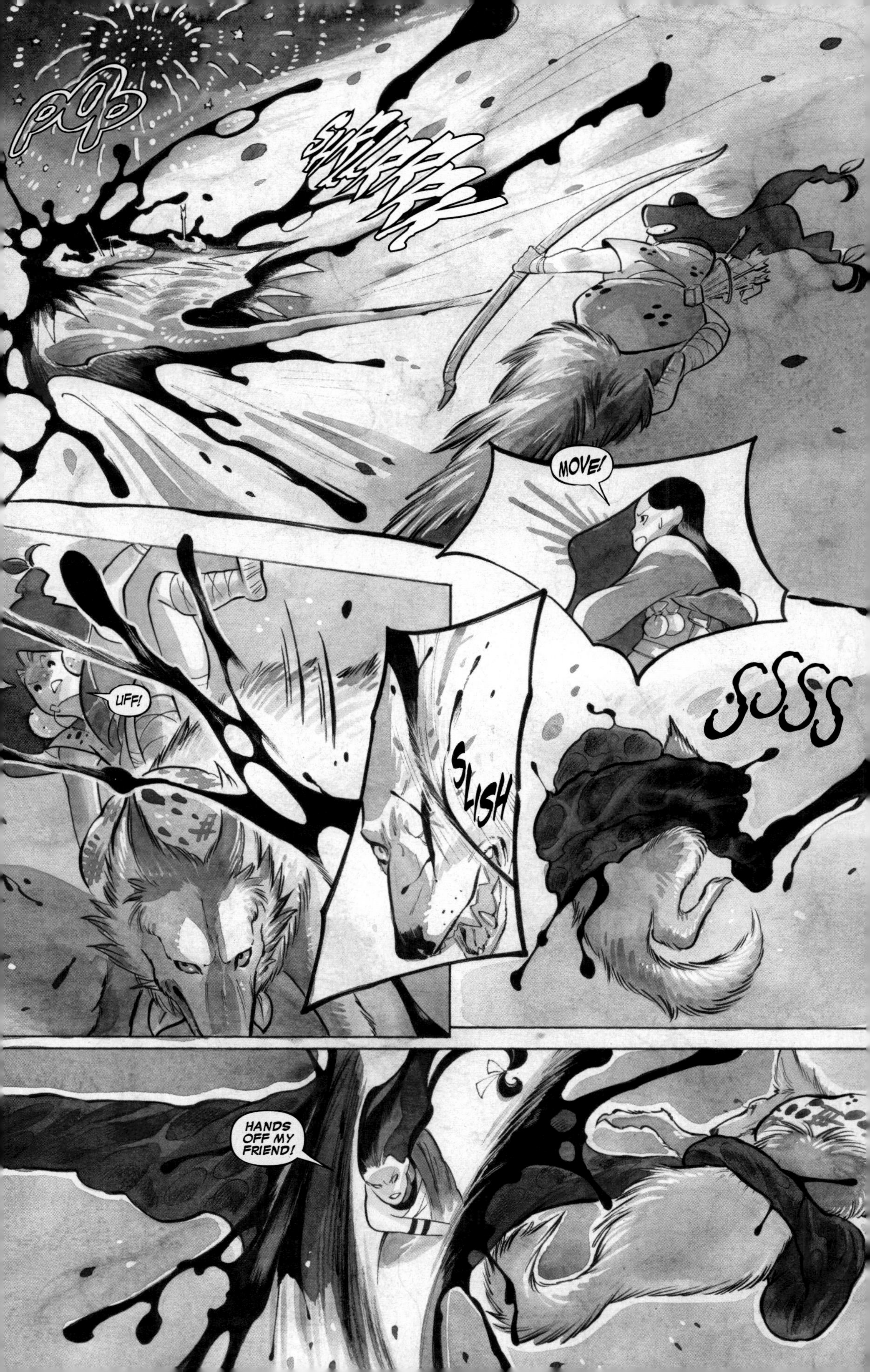
MOVE!
UFF!
SLISH
SSSS
HANDS OFF MY FRIEND!

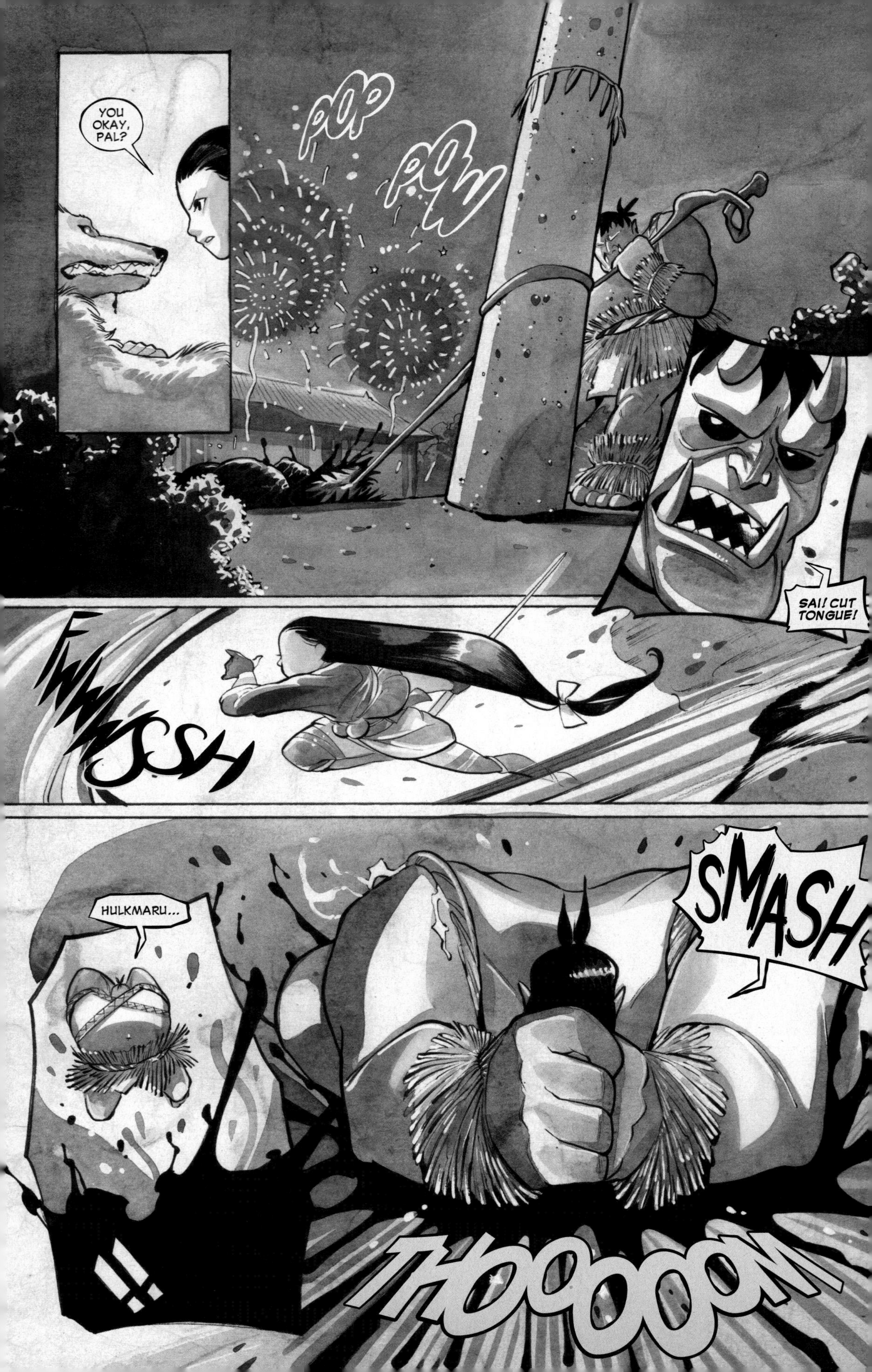
YOU OKAY, PAL?
POP
POW
SAI! CUT TONGUE!
FWWWSSH
HULKMARU...
SMASH
!!
THOOOOOM

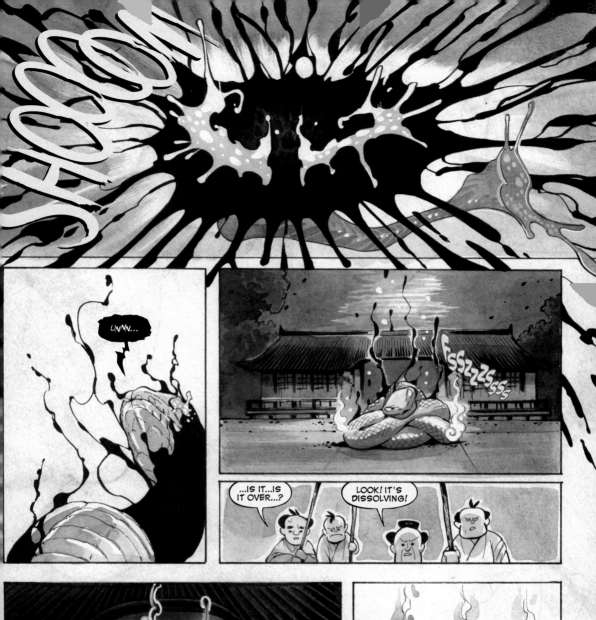

UNNN...

FSSSZZZSSSS

...IS IT...IS
IT OVER...?

LOOK! IT'S
DISSOLVING!

PHEW.

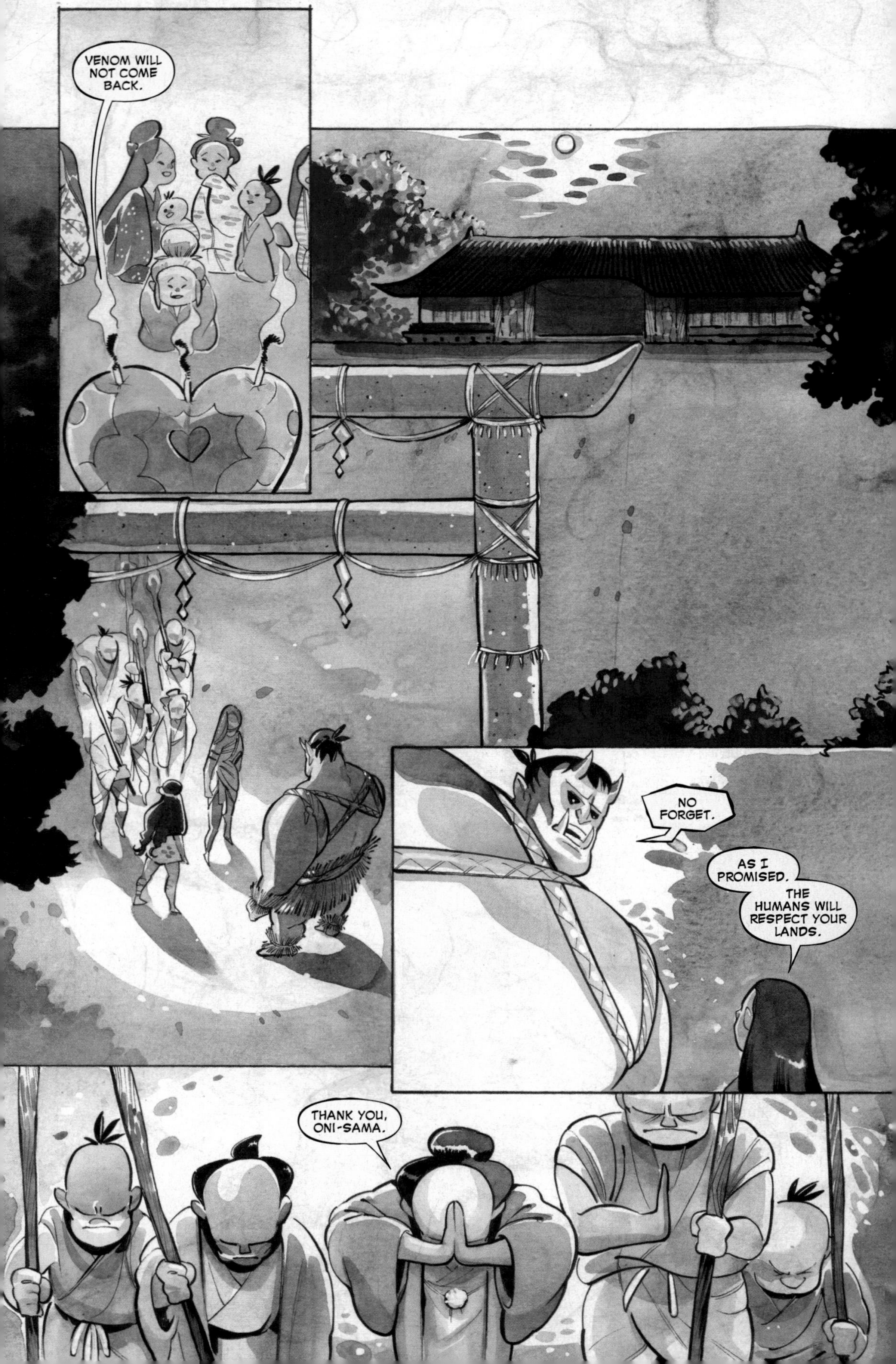
VENOM WILL NOT COME BACK.
NO FORGET.
AS I PROMISED.
THE HUMANS WILL RESPECT YOUR LANDS.
THANK YOU, ONI-SAMA.

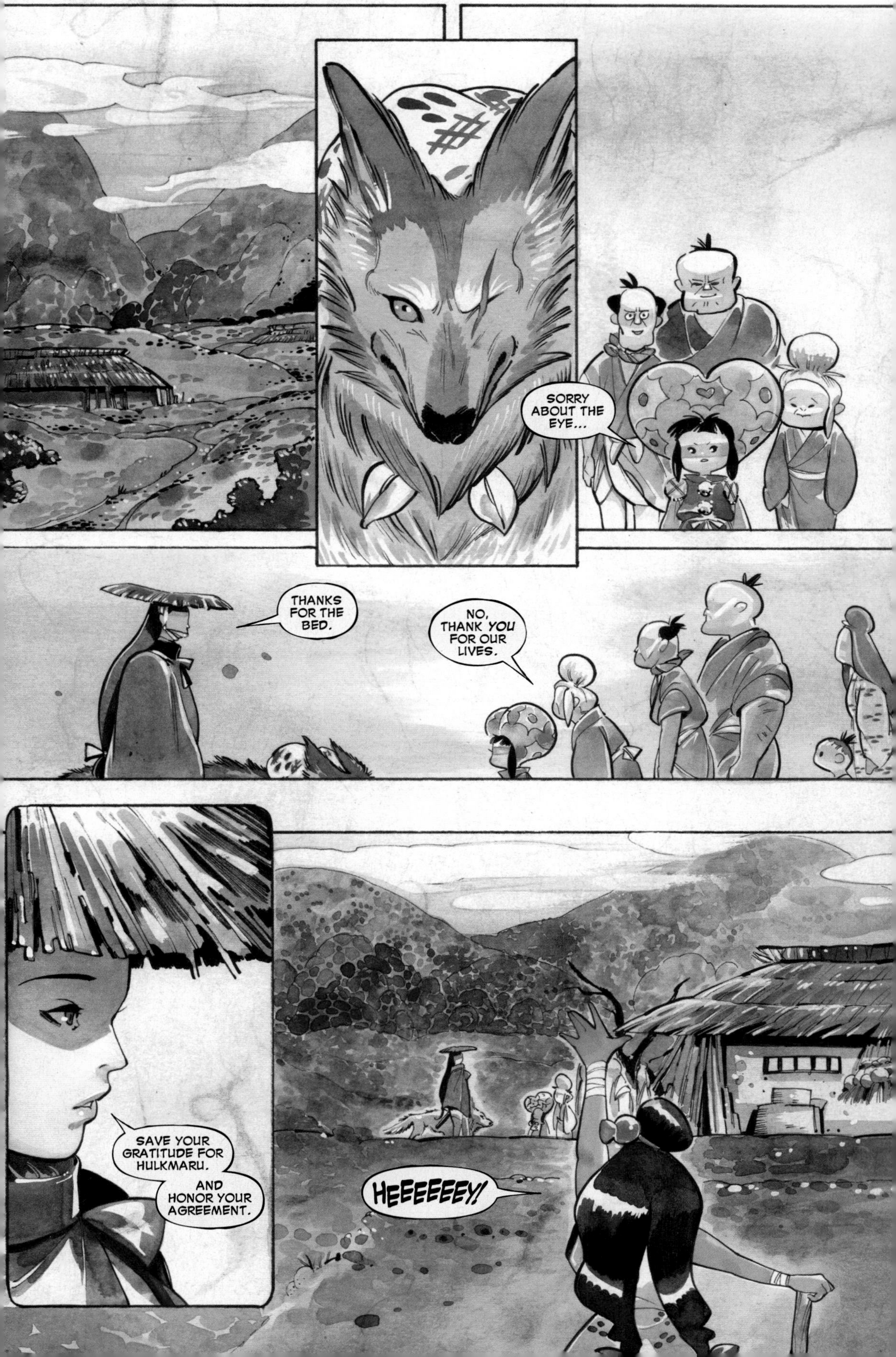
SORRY ABOUT THE EYE...
THANKS FOR THE BED.
NO, THANK YOU FOR OUR LIVES.
SAVE YOUR GRATITUDE FOR HULKMARU.
AND HONOR YOUR AGREEMENT.
HEEEEEEY!

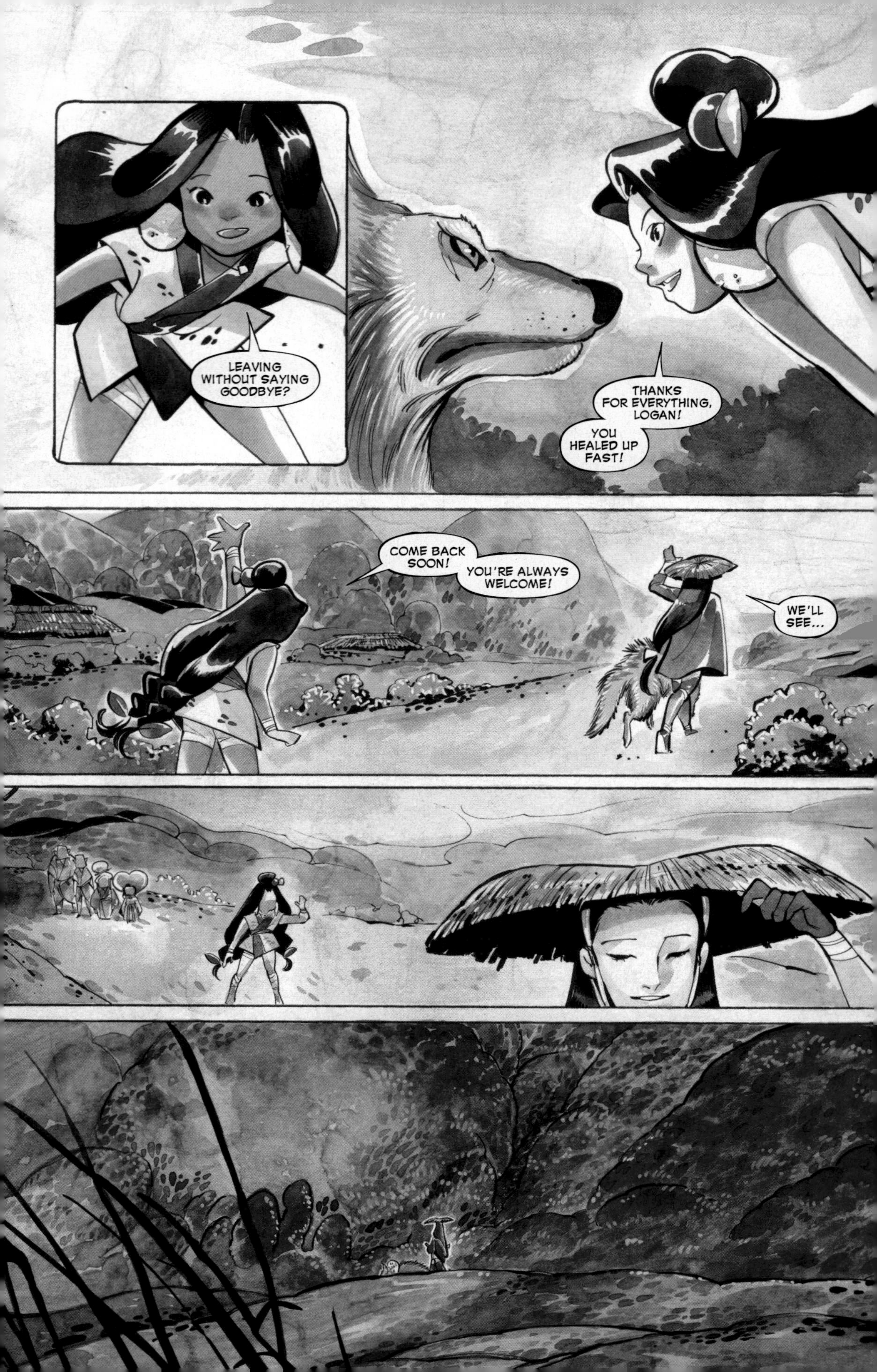
LEAVING WITHOUT SAYING GOODBYE?
THANKS FOR EVERYTHING, LOGAN!
YOU HEALED UP FAST!
COME BACK SOON!
YOU'RE ALWAYS WELCOME!
WE'LL SEE...

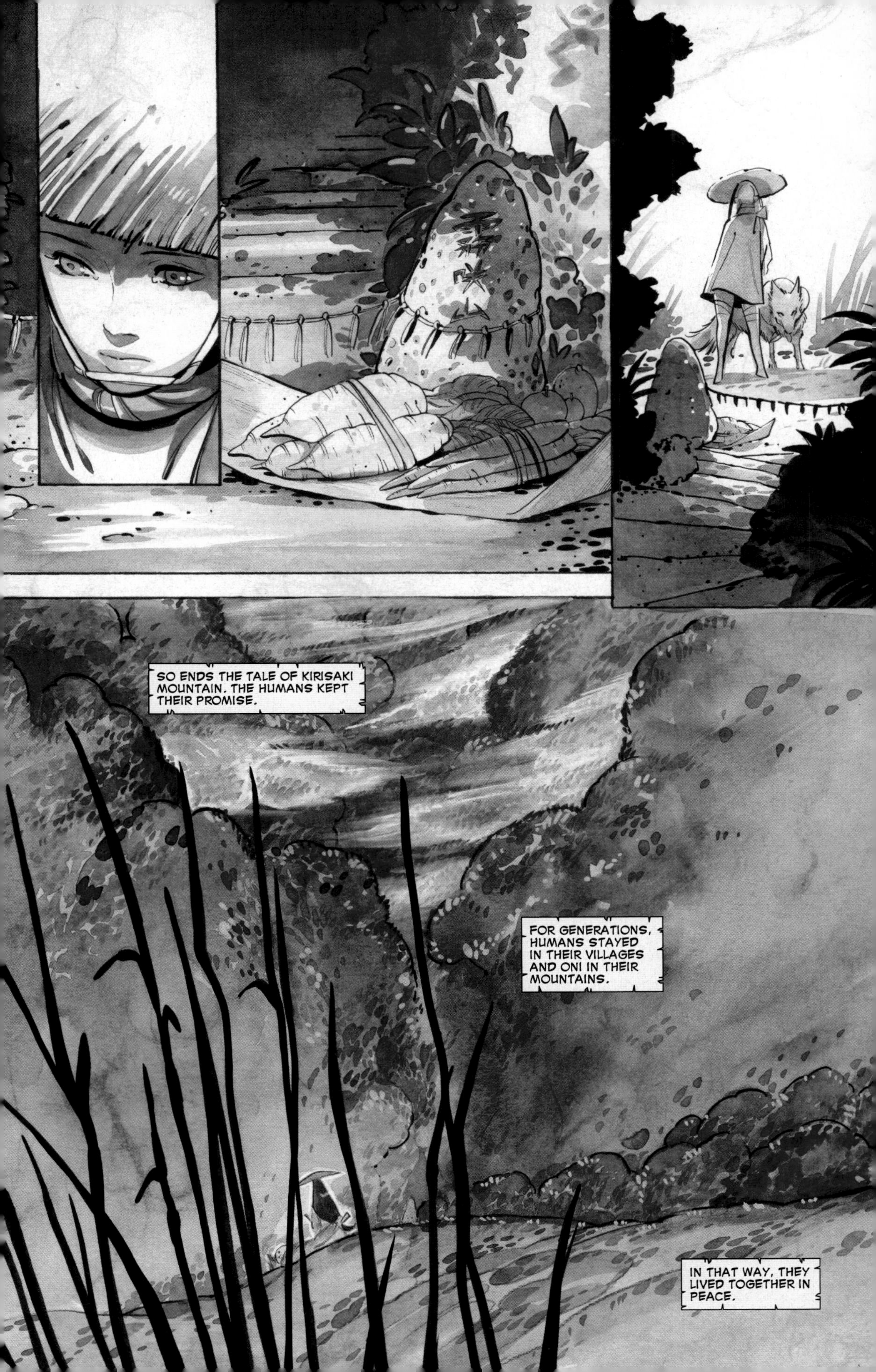
SO ENDS THE TALE OF KIRISAKI MOUNTAIN. THE HUMANS KEPT THEIR PROMISE.
FOR GENERATIONS, HUMANS STAYED IN THEIR VILLAGES AND ONI IN THEIR MOUNTAINS.
IN THAT WAY, THEY LIVED TOGETHER IN PEACE.

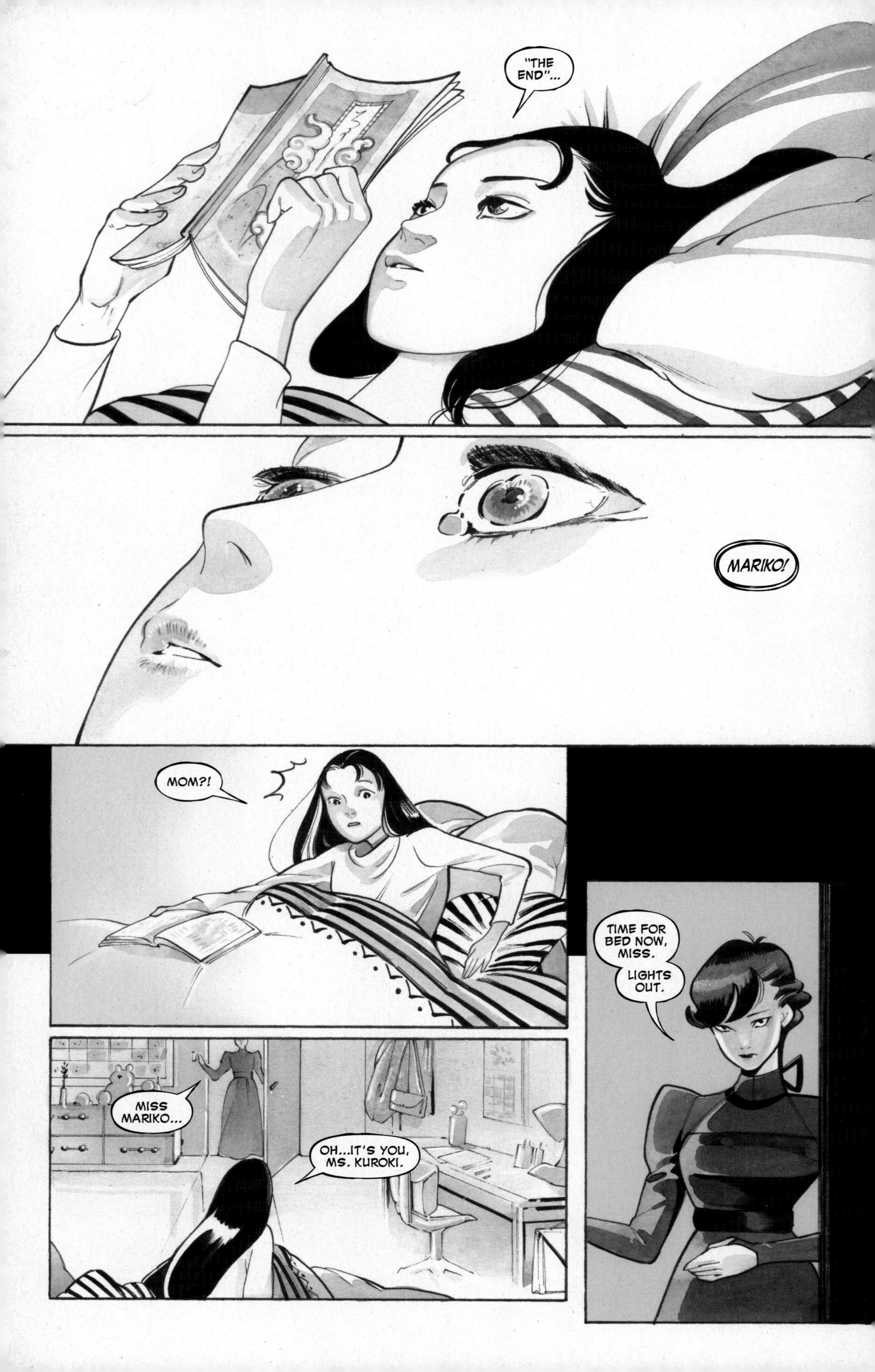
"THE END"...
MARIKO!
MOM?!
TIME FOR BED NOW, MISS.
LIGHTS OUT.
MISS MARIKO...
OH...IT'S YOU, MS. KUROKI.

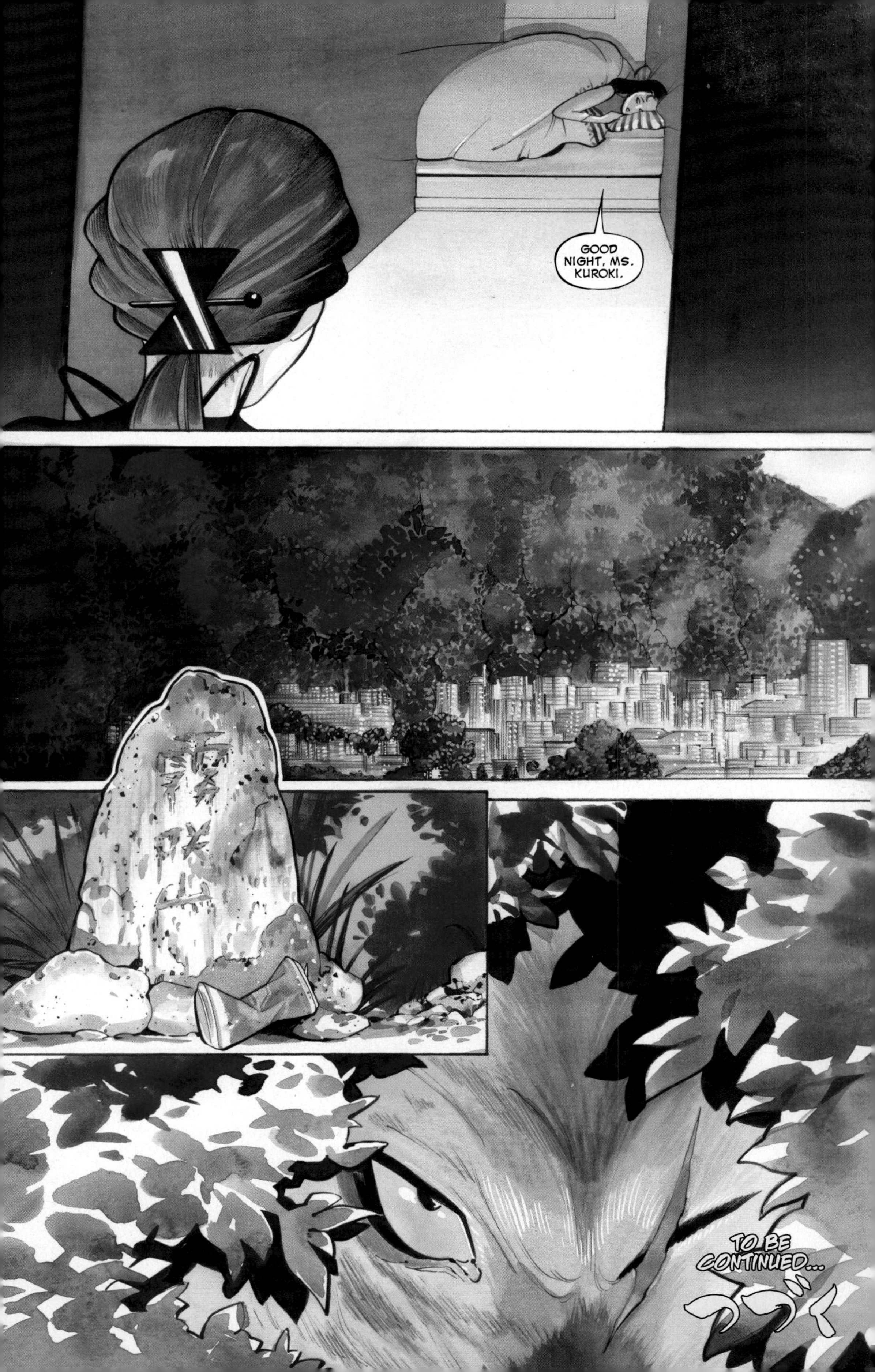
GOOD NIGHT, MS. KUROKI.
TO BE CONTINUED...
つづく

YOKAI FILES

呪師

Jushi (Lit: **Curse Master**)

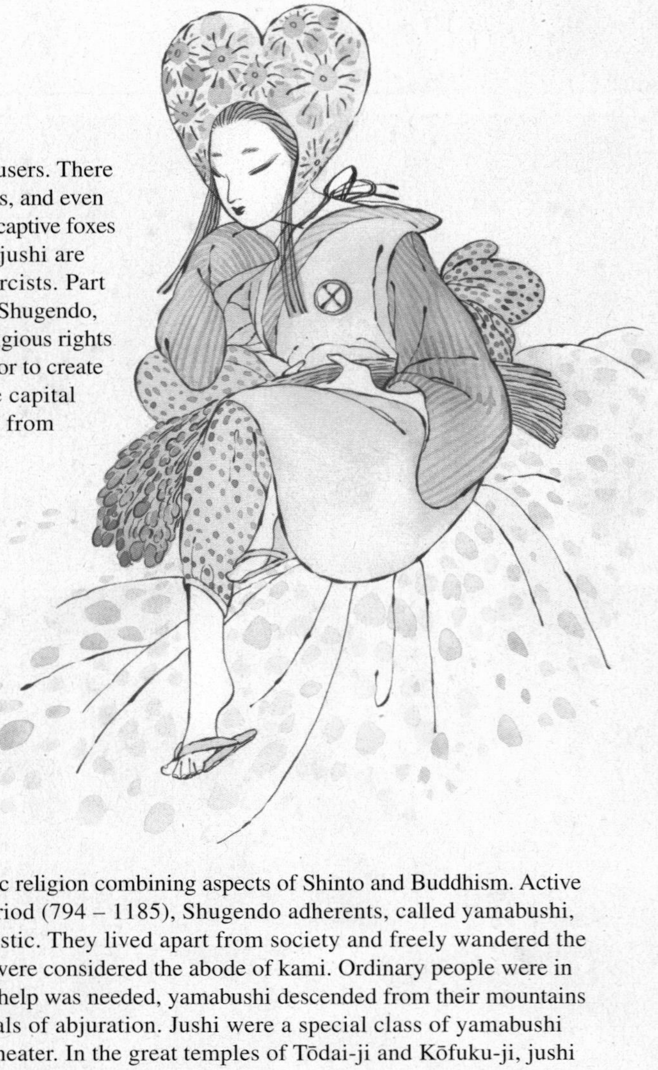

Japan has many magic users. There are magicians, sorcerers, and even a class of wizards who use captive foxes to fuel their powers. But jushi are more properly called exorcists. Part of a religious order called Shugendo, jushi performed yearly religious rights by command of the emperor to create a spiritual shield over the capital and to protect the empire from malevolent spirits.

Shugendo is a syncretic religion combining aspects of Shinto and Buddhism. Active during the Heian period (794 – 1185), Shugendo adherents, called yamabushi, were part priest, part mystic. They lived apart from society and freely wandered the mountains of Japan that were considered the abode of kami. Ordinary people were in awe of Shugendo. When help was needed, yamabushi descended from their mountains to perform complex rituals of abjuration. Jushi were a special class of yamabushi dedicated to dance and theater. In the great temples of Tōdai-ji and Kōfuku-ji, jushi conducted the yearly ceremony of jushi-hashiri, a ritualized performance intended to entertain benevolent kami spirits and invite their protection. As centuries passed, both Shugendo and jushi vanished almost completely from Japanese society. The rituals of the jushi live on only in the dances of Noh theater. ◉

Art by **Peach Momoko** / Text by **Zack Davisson**

大蛇

Orochi (Lit: **Great Snake**)

Orochi's full name describes it well: Yamata no Orochi, the Great Eight-headed Snake. Described as having eight heads and eight tails, Orochi's many eyes were as red as winter cherries. Its length was eight hills and eight valleys, and upon its back grew fir and cypress trees. Orochi is a mythic monster from Japanese folklore who battled the god of storms, Susanoo-no-Mikoto. Their story was first told in the *Kojiki*, or *Record of Ancient Matters*, in the year 680.

According to legend, Susanoo was expelled from heaven for tricking his sister, Amaterasu, the sun goddess. On Earth, he encountered two crying Earth deities who said they had been forced to sacrifice their daughters to the great snake. Susanoo knew he could not beat Orochi in a fight, so he made eight great vats of liquor and left them for each of the serpent's heads to drink. After it had passed out, Susanoo snuck up and cut it to pieces. In one of Orochi's tails, Susanoo found a mighty sword, Kusanagi-no-Tsurugi, or Grass Cutter. This blade became one of the three sacred treasures of Japan and is said to be housed in Atsuta Shrine in Nagoya to this day. ◉

赤鬼

Aka Oni (Lit: **Red Oni**)

Oni are as old as Japan. In ancient times, oni was the word for malevolent energy, the opposing force to benevolent energy called kami. Invisible and formless, oni were blamed for illness and famine, for earthquakes and lightning. With the arrival of Buddhism in Japan in 552, this negative energy merged with Indian demigods called rakshasa and other influences to give oni physical form. This new religion also put Japan's oni to work; reimagined as demons in hell, oni meted out punishment to sinning mortals under the watchful eye of Enma Dai-Ō, judge of the dead.

For centuries oni were the terrors of Japanese imagination. Their reputation changed in 1933 when Hamada Hirosuke wrote the children's book *The Red Oni Who Cried*. This told of a kind red oni who wanted to be friends with humans. But the humans were afraid. So his friend the blue oni pretended to attack some children, allowing the red oni to come to their rescue. He got his wish and the love of humanity, yet at the cost of the blue oni. The red oni cried at the loss of his friend. ◉

AFTERWARD...AND ONWARD

BY GREG PAK

I grew up in the '70s and '80s as a half-Korean kid in Dallas, Texas, which means I grew up gloriously immersed in Ray Bradbury, *Star Wars*, Westerns, comic books and classic film noir double features at the local repertory cinema. But that also means I grew up at a time when it was vanishingly rare to see non-stereotypical Asian or Asian American characters in American pop culture. Yet, there I was, a kid who didn't quite look like anyone else in my suburban neighborhood.

In retrospect, that experience clearly contributed to my lifelong commitment to storytelling. I loved the sheer *escape* that genre stories provided. At the same time, consciously or not, I knew that to carve a safe path through the world, I needed to understand the stories of others and learn how to tell my own. I remember the thrill of finding Toshiro Mifune movies and *Usagi Yojimbo* comics for the first time. The threads came together as I started to grasp that genre storytelling could make people fall in love with characters from completely different backgrounds from theirs.

So I became a writer and filmmaker who eventually started writing comics for Marvel in 2004. At the time, I was trying to raise money for what I hoped would be my second feature film, an American Western with a Chinese hero and a Mexican heroine. But I'd hit a wall. No one I met with money in the film industry seemed to be able to wrap their heads around those leads.

But when I pitched an Asian American point-of-view character for the new *Warlock* book for Marvel, my editors didn't blink. They just dug the story and gave the thumbs-up. The next year, artist Takeshi Miyazawa and I co-created Amadeus Cho, who subsequently co-starred in the *Incredible Hercules* book I co-wrote with Fred Van Lente, popped up in video games and animation, and headlined the *Totally Awesome Hulk* series. After nearly seventeen years, it turns out I've written or co-written over one hundred Marvel comics starring or co-starring Asian or Asian American characters, including classic heroes like Jimmy Woo and brand new characters like Wave and the other stars of the new *Agents of Atlas* series.

So yes, I'm bragging a bit. I'm hugely proud to have been able to add to the pantheon of characters and follow in the footsteps of incredible, inspirational comics creators like Larry Hama, Jim Lee, Janice Chiang, Stan Sakai and so many more.

But the most exciting thing about this stretch of time is that so many *more* brilliant Asian American comics creators, both independent and mainstream, have told countless *more* stories. At Marvel alone, hundreds of books have been published featuring new and old Asian and Asian American characters like Kamala Khan, Cindy Moon, Jimmy

Woo, Shang-Chi, Sword Master and Wave. And I hope that's just the start.

"Pak has found a way to breathe new life into the Hulk franchise." —WeTheNerdy.com
THE TOTALLY AWESOME HULK
PAK • CHO • CHOI
MARVEL
CHO TIME

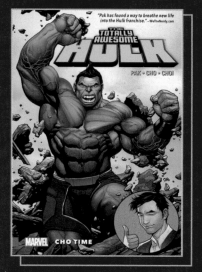

The Totally Awesome Hulk Vol. 1: Cho Time
cover by **Frank Cho** & **David Curiel**

We spend a lot of time in our culture celebrating firsts. And it's been a thrill to personally be part of a few.

But it's time for seconds and thirds and twelfths and twentieths.

I want surfeit and excess. I want so much representation from so many different storytellers that no one character, no single creator has to feel the impossible pressure to represent an entire community in all its diversity. I want so much representation that we can stretch a thousand miles beyond "role model" to revel in heroes and villains and everything in between in every genre conceivable. I want so much representation that countless new creators are building careers and a legacy of work to thrill us for generations.

Right now, we're closer to that dream that we've ever been in my lifetime. The book you're holding in your hands may feel like the most natural and obvious thing in the world — and it should! Marvel has always been about the world outside your window, and these stories — like all the other glorious books that the company's published that explore characters of all different backgrounds — are simply fulfilling that promise.

But sometimes, the most obvious things in the world are still miracles, born from the hard work and passion of countless people. Thank you so much to everyone who's been writing, drawing, coloring, lettering and editing these stories. Thank you so much to everyone who's been fighting for and greenlighting them. And thank you especially to every reader of every background who's supported these characters and stories and is reading this very book right now.

Here's to all of us...and to more and more and more.

GREG PAK
NEW YORK CITY, 2022

GREG PAK is the writer of over five hundred comic books, including *Planet Hulk*, *Darth Vader*, *Agents of Atlas*, *Magneto Testament*, *Mech Cadet Yu* and *Ronin Island*. He co-created the Marvel chara... rs Amadeus Cho (with

MARVEL'S VOICES

ESSAY BY ALYSSA WONG

I've always been drawn to character stories. For me, character *is* story: The deeper and more personal you get, the more interesting and reactive the story becomes. Give me someone with a compelling voice and I'll follow them anywhere. Saving the galaxy? Rad. Baking bread? Also rad. And if you set things up right, maybe the character will do both!

Storytelling is about people. It's about building a fantasy and cracking it open in strategic places so you can see the real-life scaffolding. Those flashes of recognition when someone sees an anxious Stormtrooper with their helmet off or a Super Hero walking into a Korean BBQ joint, and goes, "Oh wait, that person's just like me."

I'll be honest. For most of my life, I had no idea that comics *could* be about people like me. I rarely saw Asian characters in media. Manga was the exception, and I loved everything that it promised — compelling characters, clever dialogue, and dramatic, intense plotlines that hinged on character arcs. So I read a ton of manga, looking for myself in the margins.

I came back to Western comics in my 20s, thanks to Asian American friends who worked in the industry. They were doing really exciting work, and it drew me in. My turning point was a scene in Greg Pak's ***The Totally Awesome Hulk #15***, where a group of Asian and Asian American Super Heroes fight over the check at a restaurant. It was such a familiar scenario, one I'd seen play out in my family many times (minus the stun gun), that it made Super Hero comics finally click for me. It was like catching sight of your reflection in a mirror you didn't know was there.

Those are the moments that make comics so special. They're the anchoring beats of real life and personal vulnerability, amidst the flash and chaos of saving the world, fighting monsters, and outrunning the Empire. In that same comic issue referenced above, that group of Asian and Asian American Super Heroes bonds over food, karaoke, and community outreach. They open up to each other about their lives and the social pressures they share. In ***War of the Realms: New Agents of Atlas #3***, another group of Asian, Asian diaspora, and Pacific Islander heroes are down and out, alienated from each other and facing inevitable defeat. They finally manage to bond over a familiar comfort food — spam. It takes a shared feast of Korean spam fried rice, Filipino spam silog, and Hawaiian spam musubi for them to truly become a team.

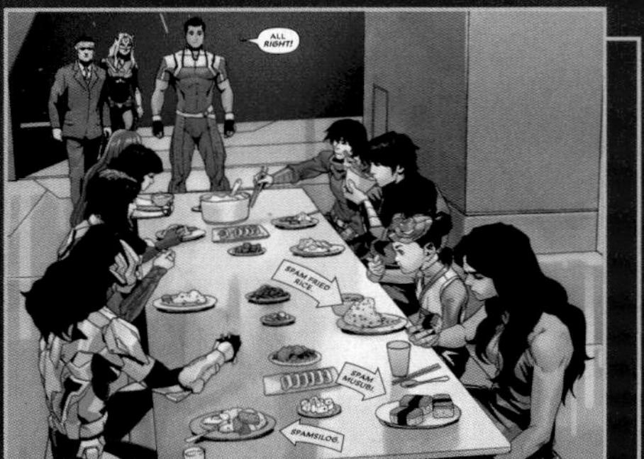
ALL RIGHT!
SPAM FRIED RICE.
SPAM MUSUBI.
SPAMSILOG.

War of the Realms: New Agents of Atlas (2019) #3

In ***Shang-Chi***, Gene Luen Yang explores the characters' relationships with the Chinese and English language. British-Chinese MI-6 agent Leiko Wu can't speak Chinese to save her life. (*Relatable*.) Meanwhile, Shang-Chi navigates several Chinese dialects, including modern Cantonese and ancient Mandarin (due to being raised in a Qing Dynasty-obsessed cult), and reflects on the way Westerners' assumptions shaped the way he speaks English. When he's alone with Leiko, he switches syntax and drops the formal tone. We stan a code-switching king! It's a kind of code-switching that I'm used to seeing in real life, too — a recognizable complexity that adds dimension to the story.

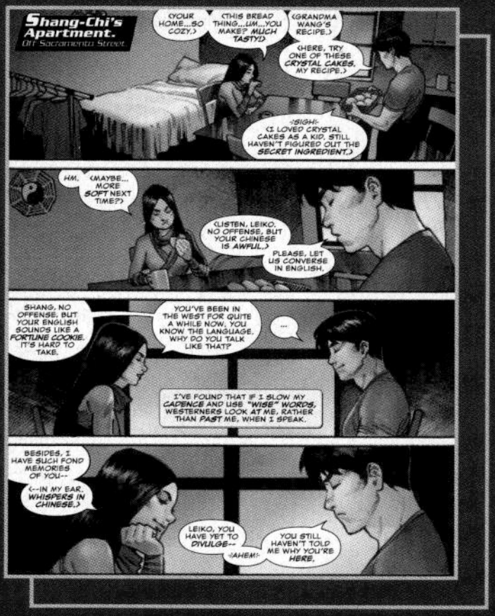
Shang-Chi's Apartment.
Off Sacramento Street
<YOUR HOME...SO COZY.>
<THIS BREAD THING...UM...YOU MAKE? MUCH TASTY!>
<GRANDMA WANG'S RECIPE.>
<HERE, TRY ONE OF THESE CRYSTAL CAKES. MY RECIPE.>
-SIGH-
<I LOVED CRYSTAL CAKES AS A KID. STILL HAVEN'T FIGURED OUT THE SECRET INGREDIENT.>
HM.
<MAYBE... MORE SOFT NEXT TIME?>
<LISTEN, LEIKO. NO OFFENSE, BUT YOUR CHINESE IS AWFUL.>
PLEASE, LET US CONVERSE IN ENGLISH.
SHANG, NO OFFENSE, BUT YOUR ENGLISH SOUNDS LIKE A FORTUNE COOKIE. IT'S HARD TO TAKE.
YOU'VE BEEN IN THE WEST FOR QUITE A WHILE NOW. YOU KNOW THE LANGUAGE. WHY DO YOU TALK LIKE THAT?
...
I'VE FOUND THAT IF I SLOW MY CADENCE AND USE "WISE" WORDS, WESTERNERS LOOK AT ME, RATHER THAN PAST ME, WHEN I SPEAK.
BESIDES, I HAVE SUCH FOND MEMORIES OF YOU--
<--IN MY EAR. WHISPERS IN CHINESE.>
LEIKO, YOU HAVE YET TO DIVULGE--
-AHEM-
YOU STILL HAVEN'T TOLD ME WHY YOU'RE HERE.

Shang-Chi (2020) #1

Comics are a great medium for exploring these complexities. They give us the chance to dive deep into characters who reflect the world and bodies we inhabit, and in doing so, create real, powerful stories. I think comics writing hinges on one of the most important aspects of character: *voice*. Voice tells you who a person is, and whether or not you're going to get along or have fun watching them crash and burn.

I'm so stoked to be writing Doctor Aphra, whose voice seized my attention from the

ambitious, charming, and impossibly clever, Doctor Aphra is a hot mess of a human being. I adore her for it. ***Doctor Aphra Vol. 1***, by Kieron Gillen and Si Spurrier, is a masterclass in character-centric storytelling. Her complicated relationships with her family and loved ones — her dad, her charge Vuulada, and her exes Sana Starros and Magna Tolvan — actively propel her through the story. Aphra's actions are motivated by these relationships versus her own self-interest, and her decisions are rarely the right ones. Every bad choice counts. It keeps her story delightfully feral. I'm looking forward to exploring Aphra's relationships with old flames — especially Sana, who gets a nasty surprise in ***Doctor Aphra Vol. 2, #7***, when Aphra shows up to complicate her life...again. (And without spoilers: They're not the only pair of messy queer exes in this arc.)

I love writing complicated, morally-gray characters, and the fact that Aphra is a queer Asian woman is both icing on the cake and a great honor. To go from seeing no *Star Wars* characters like me, to writing a *Star Wars* comic series with a lead who shares several facets of my identity has been wild. It's the mirror moment — not because I am Aphra or any other character, but because her existence means there's room in comics for stories like mine. Everyone should have that feeling.

Storytelling is about people. The more real you get, the more layered and complex your stories become. I'm excited to continue writing comic characters who reflect the people in my life and the things I've experienced. It's about giving a voice to the stories I've always wanted to see. There will be space battles, double-crossing, and super villain showdowns...but at the heart of the fantastical lies the familiar,

MARVEL'S VOICES

ESSAY BY CHRISTINE DINH

Growing up, I didn't have many heroes that looked like me; I was impacted like many others by "narrative scarcity," a tool white supremacy utilized to deprive BIPOCs of stories that could unite us. When groups of people do not see themselves or others don't see them as part of the story, then it's hard to see us as people.

At Marvel, our stories reflect the world outside our windows, including race, gender, and ethnic diversity. We relate to Marvel super heroes because their lives reflect *our* lives. This includes both the good and the bad. Lately, I've been reflecting on Cindy Moon (Silk)'s origin story and her path to becoming a hero. As a teen, Cindy Moon attended a school field trip with classmate Peter Parker. On that trip, Cindy was bitten by the same radioactive spider that bit Peter, giving her similar powers. Unlike Peter, Cindy and her family, terrified by her newfound powers and to protect her from Morlun and his Inheritors, agreed to have Cindy go underground; *literally*.

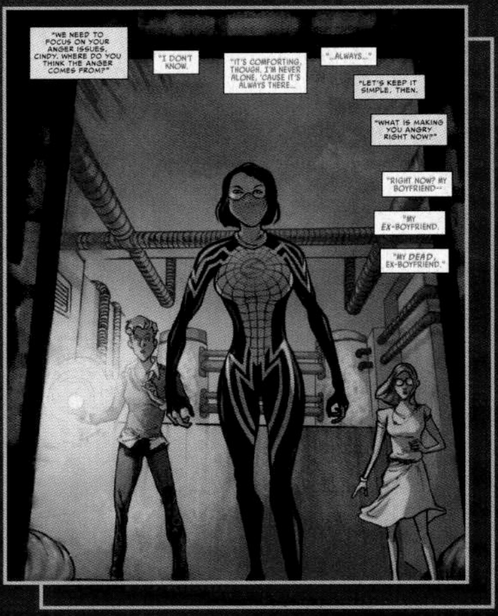

"WE NEED TO FOCUS ON YOUR ANGER ISSUES, CINDY. WHERE DO YOU THINK THE ANGER COMES FROM?"
"I DON'T KNOW.
"IT'S COMFORTING, THOUGH. I'M NEVER ALONE, 'CAUSE IT'S ALWAYS THERE...
"...ALWAYS..."
"LET'S KEEP IT SIMPLE, THEN.
"WHAT IS MAKING YOU ANGRY RIGHT NOW?"
"RIGHT NOW? MY BOYFRIEND--
"MY *EX*-BOYFRIEND.
"MY *DEAD*, EX-BOYFRIEND."

Silk (2015) #11

Hidden away for a decade, Cindy was isolated from loved ones and robbed of a "normal" teenage life. This deprivation and isolation initially became a source of frustration and anger for Cindy, something we are all currently familiar with. Cindy, determined and strong, eventually was able to channel this anger into power on her path to becoming a hero and fighting for what was right. Similar to Cindy, I — like so many of us — have spent the last year in my own secluded bunker of sorts due to the ongoing pandemic. This type of isolation is something I would never have imagined my life paralleling in any capacity, but this reality feels like Cindy's time in that bunker.

Beyond that, this year has given me more and more reasons to be angry at the continuous injustices impacting communities of color. For many Black, Indigenous, and People of Color (BIPOC), the concept of racial injustice and racism is something we have dealt with our whole lives. I was nine the first time I heard the phrase "Go back to China" shouted by a neighbor — I was with my mom unloading groceries into our apartment. As a Vietnamese-American born in the United States, I didn't understand then the vitriol behind those four words, or the very real and sometimes deadly impact that racism and xenophobic rhetoric can have. Now I shun the ingrained desire to deflect and respond with "I'm Vietnamese, not Chinese" — being Asian is not and should never be considered an insult.

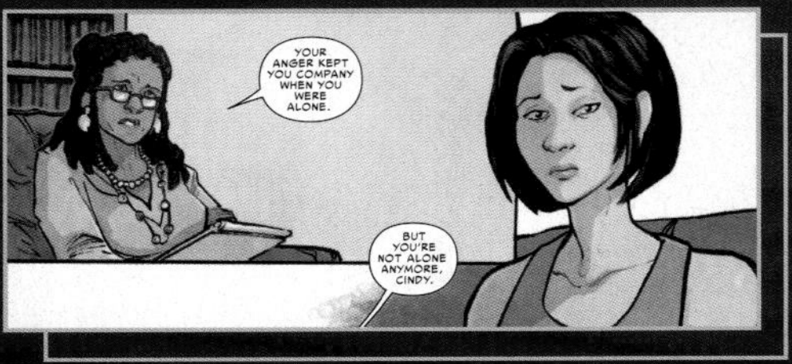

YOUR ANGER KEPT YOU COMPANY WHEN YOU WERE ALONE.
BUT YOU'RE NOT ALONE ANYMORE, CINDY.

Silk (2015) #1

Those devasting impacts resulted in a number of incidents of violence against Asian Americans — Asian American women, specifically, in just the last month,

On March 16, 2021, Stop AAPI Hate released a report revealing Asian Americans reported 3,800 hate-related incidents during the pandemic. On the same day, a gunman targeted three Asian American businesses and murdered eight people, including six Asian women in Atlanta. This comes on the heels of other incidents like the deadly attacks on 84-year-old Vicha Ratanapakdee in San Francisco and 75-year-old Pak Ho in Oakland. As a result of this and other incidents, I'm *angry*. I am *angry* like Cindy.

It isn't difficult to trace these actions back to the xenophobic rhetoric amid the Covid-19 pandemic with labels such as "*China virus*" and "*Kung flu*" used by the government. This type of rhetoric isn't new; Asian Americans have had a long history of facing racism and xenophobia in the US, including the fatal beating of Chinese American Vincent Chin in 1982, because two white men "thought" he was Japanese. In addition, the US imposed actions such as the Chinese Exclusion Act of 1882, the Yellow Peril after WWI, and the Japanese internment during WWII.

So, I am *angry*. Angry that I've been isolated from loved ones because of the pandemic and unable to comfort them or find comfort in my community, angry that our communities live in fear of being attacked for no reason. And personally, I am angry that my mom, a small business owner who came to this country as a refugee, could easily be a target. I'm angry that the institutions meant to protect us are the same ones harming us — resulting in the deaths of George Floyd, Breonna Taylor, Eric Garner, and countless others. This harm echoes when the Cherokee County Sheriff's Department said Soon Chung Park, Hyun Jung Grant, Sun Cha Kim, Yong Ae Yue, Delaina Ashley Yaun Gonzalez, Paul Andre Michels, Xiaojie Tan, and Daoyou Feng, lost their lives, not because of racial motivations, but

"*bad day*." The impact of xenophobia, the continual objectification of Asian women in Western culture, and the erasure of our agency — our "ability" to be angry — can eat away at a person.

Just like the negative impact of the words by the Cherokee County Sheriff, words can have positive power; we can have a positive impact. Today, kids can see themselves through Daisy Johnson, Kamala Khan, Luna Snow, Cindy Moon, and teams like the Agents of Atlas. And, in my role at Marvel, I'm able to elevate the works of our incredible creators such as Alyssa Wong, Maurene Goo, Greg Pak, Preeti Chhibber, Gene Luen Yang, Saladin Ahmed, and so many more.

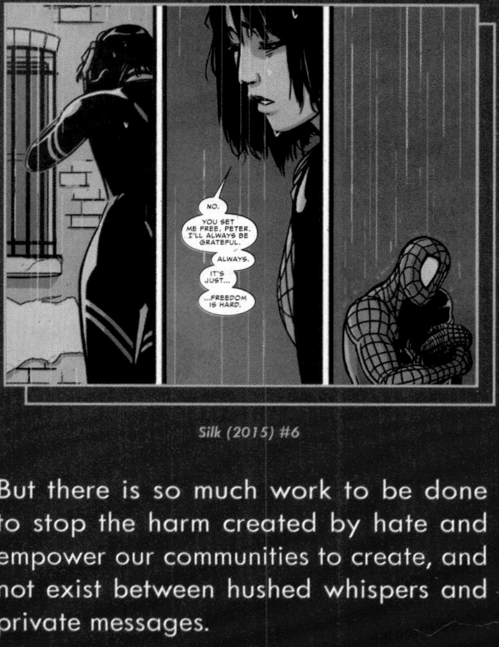
NO.
YOU SET ME FREE, PETER. I'LL ALWAYS BE GRATEFUL.
ALWAYS.
IT'S JUST...
...FREEDOM IS HARD.

Silk (2015) #6

But there is so much work to be done to stop the harm created by hate and empower our communities to create, and not exist between hushed whispers and private messages.

So we must persevere like Cindy. Cindy with her unique path after being bitten by the same spider as Peter Parker, who hid away for a decade, who left that bunker and channeled her anger, stayed alive, and became strong despite her circumstances. In the same way, I believe our anger and our grief will serve us as well. While our story may be different than Peter's, our stories matter and we deserve to exist in

MARVEL'S VOICES

ESSAY BY PREETI CHHIBBER

There's a specific experience that a lot of brown kids go through when we're growing up. It's one of attempted assimilation, of trying to be as much of what we see around us as we can be, but never quite being able to get there.

Not because we aren't exactly as we should be, but because people and society as a whole decide we need a hyphen to quantify what we are — a qualifier to define us, because supposedly we need to be defined. Like most brown kids, I'm immensely proud of my heritage and my cultural background as an American-born Indian, and as a child of immigrants. But, instead of being Indian and American, I was given a hyphenate, a qualifier: Indian-American. And when we were playing make-believe? Indian-Peter Pan (*Hook* was a big deal for us, okay?), Indian-Luke Skywalker, Indian — you get it. Even in the deepest part of our imaginations, our identities were relegated and qualified. The result was that all my heroes were someone I couldn't *just* be.

When Peter Parker, Spider-Man, hit the pages back in 1962, he quickly became a revelation. Here was a relatable teenager, someone who had everyday problems, who dealt with things like having crushes, dealing with bullies and doing homework. The fact that this young, awkward nerd could be a hero was aspirational. When he put on the mask, became Spider (HYPHEN) Man, he pulled together the parts of himself into someone he could just *be*. Still, the fact remained, that Peter was *Peter*. There were pieces of him that reflected us, his marginalized readers, but never the whole. Unlike Spidey's hyphen, mine is one that breaks me apart instead of putting me together.

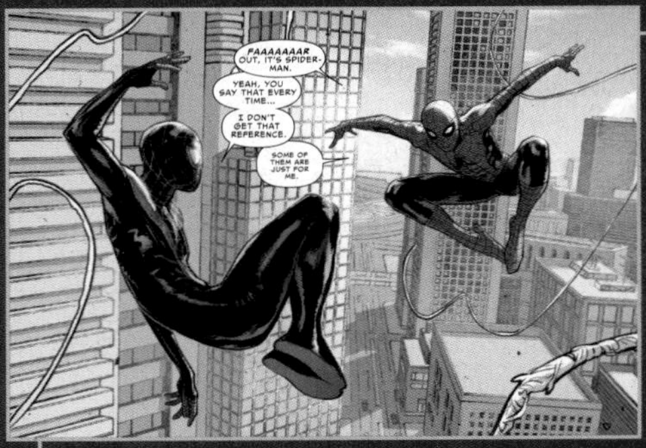
FAAAAAAAR OUT, IT'S SPIDER-MAN.
YEAH, YOU SAY THAT EVERY TIME...
I DON'T GET THAT REFERENCE.
SOME OF THEM ARE JUST FOR ME.

Spider-Men II (2017) #1

But that is the power of the mantle of Spider-Man. It is both Peter and so much more. Spider-Man could literally be *anyone* and at times has been! Marvel has often recognized the importance of costumes as symbols, and when their heroes fall but the symbol needs to go on? Someone else takes up the mantle and it *still matters*. Or if there are other people in the multiverse who wear the mask? They're still Spider-Man and it still matters. In 2011, what Miles Morales brought to the Ultimate universe was a gift we didn't know we were waiting for — it was the implication made explicit. Miles put on the mask and became Spider-Man. This was, of course, lauded wonderfully in 2018's *Spider-Man: Into the Spider-Verse*, where someone tells our burgeoning hero that "anyone can wear the mask." Peter Parker's even hired people to play Spider-Man to keep up the ruse of his own double-identity

So, why does all of this matter?

What matters is that it is affirming. It's not someone assimilating to become the hero, it's the hero assimilating to the person. I grew up never ever seeing someone who looked like me as a hero. I could be a sidekick, or a bit role in someone else's story, but never the lead and certainly *never* the one who saved the day. Never the one who was centered. Spider-Man was aspirational, but never achievable. So, it's affirming to know that it's not just in theory that a Black or brown face can exist behind the mask, but in practice. When a writer has the opportunity with a character like Spider-Man (as I have) — a character who has universally-beloved qualities you want to have and hold — it can help a reader feel seen. This was a step toward *every* Spidey-fan feeling seen.

Let's talk about Spider-Man: India, A.K.A. Pavitr Prabhaker. Created by Jeevan Kang, Suresh Seetharaman, and Sharad Devarajan in 2005, Pavitr was initially given an "Indianized" version of Peter Parker's backstory. Whether it was his Uncle Bhim or Aunt Maya, or his friend Meera Jain — these resulted in them just being facsimiles of the Peter Parker story we already knew, transplanted out of Queens and into Mumbai. The result, Pavitr was hyphenated twice over, qualified by being "Indian-Spider-Man."

It wasn't until a decade later in 2015 that Pavitr started his journey as being his own version of Spider-Man, not Spider-Man: India. In the midst of the first *Spider-Verse* run by writer Dan Slott, Spider-people from all of the Marvel universes are pulled together to fight against their collective greatest threat. For Prabhakar, this meant the identity crisis of seeing his unique story played out by dozens of versions of himself. But Slott wrote a conversation that both recognized the absurdity of a copy, and that the character can exist as Spider-Man, period. No qualifier necessary. And as someone who consistently has that "necessary qualifier" set against her Americanness, her Indianness, her identity, this was a transformative moment. Pavitr is Indian and Spider-Man, and those two parts of his identity speak to each other and exist together authentically. But he doesn't need a descriptor to separate him out. As a writer, the potential of bringing my own lived experience into a character who can embody all those different pieces of me *and* be a Super Hero is not something I'm used to. There just aren't enough of us yet. (If anyone wants to do a solo Pavitr Prabhakar book, I am right here, keyboard ready.)

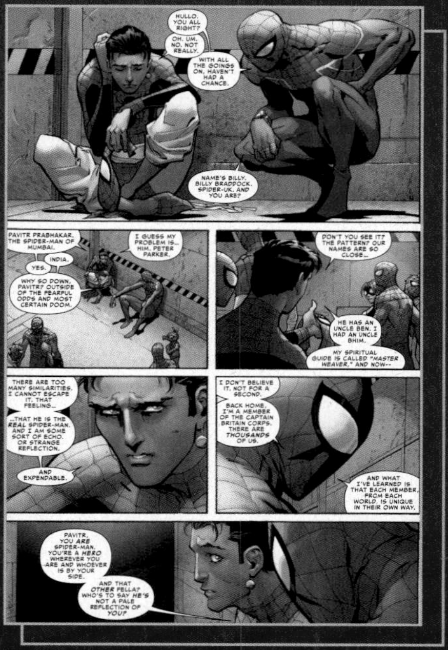
HULLO. YOU ALL RIGHT?
OH. UM. NO. NOT REALLY.
WITH ALL THE GOINGS ON, HAVEN'T HAD A CHANCE.
NAME'S BILLY. BILLY BRADDOCK. SPIDER-UK. AND YOU ARE?
PAVITR PRABHAKAR. THE SPIDER-MAN OF MUMBAI.
INDIA.
YES.
WHY SO DOWN, PAVITR? OUTSIDE OF THE FEARFUL ODDS AND MOST CERTAIN DOOM.
I GUESS MY PROBLEM IS... HIM. PETER PARKER.
DON'T YOU SEE IT? THE PATTERN? OUR NAMES ARE SO CLOSE...
HE HAS AN UNCLE BEN. I HAD AN UNCLE BHIM.
MY SPIRITUAL GUIDE IS CALLED "MASTER WEAVER," AND NOW--
THERE ARE TOO MANY SIMILARITIES. I CANNOT ESCAPE IT. THAT FEELING...
...THAT HE IS THE REAL SPIDER-MAN. AND I AM SOME SORT OF ECHO. OR STRANGE REFLECTION.
AND EXPENDABLE.
I DON'T BELIEVE IT. NOT FOR A SECOND.
BACK HOME, I'M A MEMBER OF THE CAPTAIN BRITAIN CORPS. THERE ARE THOUSANDS OF US.
AND WHAT I'VE LEARNED IS THAT EACH MEMBER, FROM EACH WORLD, IS UNIQUE IN THEIR OWN WAY.
PAVITR, YOU ARE SPIDER-MAN. YOU'RE A HERO WHEREVER YOU ARE AND WHOEVER IS BY YOUR SIDE.
AND THAT OTHER FELLA? WHO'S TO SAY HE'S NOT A PALE REFLECTION OF YOU?

Amazing Spider-Man (2014) #13

I am a *huge* Spider-Man fan, a "superfan" some might say, and to see a desi character inhabit the mantle in his own, unique-to-Pavitr way in multiple series has been nothing short of brilliant. Spider-Man is our everyman. We see ourselves in him, in his shortcomings, and in his desire to do good despite those flaws. And when we make that everyman as inclusive as possible. By truly allowing anyone to pull on that mask and be a hero. It makes heroes of us all, and every part of us a hero.

AN INTERVIEW WITH RONNY CHIENG

BY ANGÉLIQUE ROCHÉ
EDITED FOR BREVITY

Malaysian comedian and actor Ronny Chieng made his U.S. debut as a correspondent on Comedy Central's *The Daily Show* in 2015 and has never looked back. Since then, Chieng has gone on to do a number of projects including *Crazy Rich Asians*, *Doogie Kameāloha, M.D.* on Disney and Marvel Studios' *Shang-Chi and the Legend of the Ten Rings*. I had the opportunity to sit down with him to chat about the U.S. release of his Australian-based comedy, *Ronny Chieng: International Student* on Comedy Central, his career, how he got into comedy and his love of Marvel.

AR: How did you get into Marvel?

RC: The *X-Men Animated Series*. Iconic theme song. Great animation. Really cool storylines. It's like a gateway drug. Then you start to explore more of that world. You start learning about the different characters and wanting to know what happens next.

AR: Is there one character that you really loved?

RC: Spider-Man. My favorite thing about Spider-Man is how resourceful he is. He manages to get so much done with, arguably, a very limited power range. He shoots webs and he can stick to a wall, but he's fighting, literally, everybody from aliens to criminal organizations.

AR: If you could have a super-power, what would it be?

RC: Freezing time. It is super useful because you can prepare for interviews. [Laughs.]

AR: How did you get into comedy?

RC: There was a campus comedy competition. I went to give it a try and it worked out. You never know where opportunities will lead you.

AR: Let's talk about your new show. It's loosely based on your life, right?

RC: It's been out in Australia for a year now. But it's a new comedy — on Comedy Central. *Ronny Chieng: International Student.* A lot of the core of each episode — a lot of the heart of each episode — comes from a very real place.

AR: Why did you want to tell your story?

RC: [Jokingly.] That's the only reason I get out of bed: money and fame. And not even a lot. You can just give me a little bit. I'll get out of bed for like ten dollars.

AR: [Laughs.] That was the only reason?

RC: The Australian Broadcasting Corporation (ABC) asked me to write a series. The pilot did well, so we wrote a whole series. I learned so much writing those seven screenplays with my co-creator Declan Fay. We learned how to write an episode of TV. The kind of energy it takes, the pace, story arcs and keeping things interesting.

AR: How difficult was it to accurately represent multiple cultures without falling into tropes?

RC: No one's really talked about the cross-cultural aspects of Asian people from Asia living in Australia and the layers that come with it. In that sense, any TV trope that we used was

flipped on its head by us being unconventional characters.

AR: Why come to the States?

RC: Everything I loved about creating came out of America. It wasn't even about [money]. I took a pay cut to come here. All my creative heroes — my comic heroes, my movie heroes — came out of America. I wanted to make stuff with them or at least make stuff at that level.

AR: Has the shift been a challenge?

RC: Yes. I started in Australia, and I'm very much a product of the Australian comedy scene. When I moved to America, I had to relearn how to do comedy. I met up with John Oliver when I first moved here to ask him how to be a non-American correspondent on *The Daily Show*. Even he had an adjustment period.

AR: What did he say?

RC: He told me it took him two years to relearn how to really do comedy in America. He was spot on to the day.

Originally Released: October 2018.

Listen to the full interview on the Marvel's Voices podcast, available on Apple Podcasts and anywhere you can listen

AN INTERVIEW WITH SALADIN AHMED

BY ANGÉLIQUE ROCHÉ

EDITED FOR BREVITY

In 2018, Eisner Award-winning author and poet Saladin Ahmed became the first person of color to write an ongoing series for Brooklyn's own Spider-Man, Miles Morales. Almost four years later, Ahmed continues to write the series in addition to working on various other projects and series including his recent run on *Magnificent Ms. Marvel*. A lifelong comics fan, Saladin attributes a lot of his love for storytelling to the comics he read as a kid. I had a chance to sit down with him during the Marvel Creative Summit in 2018, shortly before *Miles Morales: Spider-Man #1* hit shelves.

AR: Did you have any favorite comics as a kid?

SA: I was a big Marvel head in the '80s. I was reading *X-Men, Fantastic Four* and *Secret Wars*. At its core, Marvel was the mythos that came to me immediately as my first introduction to comics. I think that is the reason I'm here telling stories in this world now.

AR: Did you ever think that you were going to write Spider-Man?

SA: I never thought about it as a possibility. I didn't grow up in New York. I was in the Midwest, and it's not like I saw comic book writers. Queens was some bizarre, far-off place.

AR: How did you get into poetry?

SA: My father was very big on the Detroit art scene, and he used to take me to poetry readings. I saw a poet named Kim Hunter perform with my dad. He was just the coolest person on the planet. I wanted to do that. So I went home and wrote my crappy imitations of his poems and focused more on writing.

AR: From poetry, you shifted to sci-fi and fantasy. What caused the shift?

SA: In both cases, it's the ability to imagine different worlds and use that to look at our own. When you go to an alien planet, then you come back to Earth and compare notes, you can learn something about Earth and about our life here that you don't get if you're just doing an office drama or a medical drama. It's a different kind of remove from which you can look at us.

AR: Your family has a rich history and is composed of artists and community organizers and is very politically active; your great-grandmother was even a private detective.

SA: Aliya Hassan was the matriarch of our family and a remarkable woman. She was born in South Dakota in 1910 and married at 15 — not that uncommon back then — but she left him because he was abusive. It's astonishing that she lived on her own terms in an era when it was unheard of to do so. She educated herself, studied and eventually got a private detective's license. She was also a union organizer. Someday, I'll write her story.

AR: Can you tell me a little bit about your upcoming *Miles Morales: Spider-Man* series?

SA: He's been to different universes, he's been a major player on a super-team and

he is all those things, but he's also a teenager. This book — at least the first arc or two — is about taking Miles back to being a teenager. He's going to be dealing with romance. There's going to be a menacing assistant principal figure, because these super heroes are always skipping class and the consequences never catch up with them. I'm also very much trying to respect the world. The world we live in now is not the world from when I was a teenager. It's a world with a lot of scary, heavy stuff happening, and I'm trying to speak to some of those issues.

AR: Do you have a dream project, what would it be?

SA: Oh gosh, I think I'm doing it right now. Before coming into comics, I used to think that way, "I want to write this character." To me, it's become less about I have to write this guy and more about I'm just excited to be telling these stories. I mean, I would love someday to do my run on Cap. But I could live my whole life happily not doing that too.

Originally Released: November 2018.

Listen to the full interview on the Marvel's Voices podcast, available on Apple Podcasts and anywhere you can listen to podcasts.

AN INTERVIEW WITH KIMIKO GLENN

BY ANGÉLIQUE ROCHÉ

EDITED FOR BREVITY

Shortly after the release of *Spider-Man: Into the Spider-Verse*, I had the opportunity to sit down with actress Kimiko Glenn who plays the Super Hero Peni Parker, A.K.A. SP//dr, in the film. Created by Gerard Way and Jake Wyatt, Peni Parker is a 14-year-old super hero from Earth-14512, originally appearing in *Edge of the Spider-Verse #5* (2014). I chatted with Glenn about her career, pushing back against stereotypes and what inspired the Phoenix native to become a performer.

AR: What was it about Peni Parker, A.K.A. SP//dr, that you felt you connected with?

KG: She's an unlikely hero because she's small, she's cute and she's very expressive. She is the type of character who you'd think couldn't fight crime. But she does and she does it super well. She's smart, strong-willed and she has this awesome super-power of being able to telepathically communicate with this robot. I think I related to her because I'm small and I feel kind of like an unlikely hero in my own book.

AR: What was that thing that made you decide on this path as a performer?

KG: It was singing. I loved doing impressions, grabbing my dad's camcorder and making commercials about furniture or recording myself doing the news with a cup of tea. I called it Happy Cup News. This was just me alone with my dad's camcorder just for fun, for me. I think my parents thought they should scoot me in a direction where this might be beneficial. My dad suggested I audition

for a musical. I was so happy and I felt like I was expressing myself in a way that I felt like I couldn't before.

AR: When considering a role, especially as a woman of color, what is that thought process like?

KG: The industry has changed so much since I started — there wasn't a conversation happening around why diversity is important. I was auditioning for stereotypical Asian parts and I felt really uncomfortable. Not to say I don't connect with Japanese culture, but I'm half white, half Japanese and I grew up in Phoenix. When there were Asian people in the media, they would be playing into a stereotype or the butt of an ethnic joke. Thankfully, I'm able to voice my opinions about that sort of thing.

AR: What has been the major shift between your stage, screen and voiceover work?

KG: It's so different. Being a cartoon character, you can be as outrageous as you want. I love that. Theater, you have to just be able to turn it on right

away. With film, you have to sit around for hours and just bring it in the moments that you're doing it. There might be chaos ensuing, but you have to ride through it. Theater is the same thing, but the audience is in on the joke with you.

AR: Do you have a favorite role you've played?

KG: It's hard to say. I find the fun in a lot of the roles, even if they're serious. I feel like *Waitress*, playing Dawn, was one of the more fun ones because she was really in my wheelhouse. She was so goofy. And I had a great scene partner, Chris Fitzgerald. I also really liked playing Yoshimi in *Yoshimi Battles the Pink Robots*. It was the world premiere of a musical based on the album *Yoshimi Battles the Pink Robots* by the Flaming Lips.

Originally Released: January 2019.

Listen to the full interview on the Marvel's Voices podcast, available on Apple Podcasts and anywhere you can listen to podcasts.

AN INTERVIEW WITH JACINDA CHEW

BY ANGÉLIQUE ROCHÉ

EDITED FOR BREVITY

Insomniac Games Senior Art Director Jacinda Chew has been working in the gaming industry for over two decades. From sports games to zombie adventures, Chew has credits on almost two dozen games including the award-winning Marvel's *Spider-Man* for Playstation released in 2018. I sat down with her at the Electronic Entertainment Expo (E3) in Los Angeles to chat about her love for video games, diversity in the gaming industry and how she brings her lived experiences to game design.

AR: Folks are getting a chance to play *Spider-Man* for Playstation for the first time. How does it feel?

JC: It's awesome. The fans are so supportive. I've been reading the first impressions of the gameplay. It's overwhelming how people are responding to the game. *Spider-Man* was an absolute joy to work on and it's an absolute joy to play.

AR: Have you always wanted to work in the gaming industry?

JC: Yes. I've been drawing since I can remember and playing video games since I was a little kid. My dad is an electrical engineer, so we've always been surrounded by PC games. I went to a traditional art school because I wanted to explore what it meant to be an artist. Afterward, I was like, it would be really cool to make video games. At the time, there was no major for it, but I was lucky enough to have a friend who knew somebody in the industry. That person gave me some advice and that's how I learned how to mod games. My first portfolio was me modding a PC game. That got me my first job.

AR: What games did you love as a kid?

JC: I loved *Gabriel Knight*. It was a story-driven PC game series. One of the things I love about the series is that it was created by a woman, Jane Jensen, and it featured a really strong partner to Gabriel Knight, his assistant Grace Nakimura. She was Asian like me. That game inspired so many things because I never thought I couldn't do video games because of Jane Jensen and I never thought I couldn't be in a video game because of Grace Nakimura.

AR: How important is a person's personal story to the thing they create?

JC: It's everything. I was thinking about what Marvel means to me, and one of the things I love about Marvel is that — ultimately — everyone in the Marvel Universe is "human." They're just human beings who have extraordinary things happen to them. They have relationship problems. They have issues with their families. Maybe they have self-esteem problems. Marvel characters are very relatable in that way.

AR: How does having an inclusive team impact your work?

JC: On *Spider-Man* we have this whole city filled with New Yorkers. It was really important to me that they reflected the diversity of New York City, and that even people in the background of the cinematics or people that Spider-Man interacts with were equally diverse. It's our responsibility, especially if we have a voice in new media like video games to carry the torch for future generations so that they can see themselves in the media that they're playing or digesting. When they see themselves even in the developers, that's how you get more diversity into the industry and into the world.

AR: What inspires you?

JC: Life. I always tell this to my artists, don't sit at your computer all day. Go out and live your life. Until you live your life, you can't really put any of that into your work. I've traveled all over the world. Traveling the world opens your eyes. Bringing that kind of thoughtfulness and mindfulness back into your work is really important to me. So living your life is the biggest inspiration you can give to yourself.

Originally Released: August 2018.

Listen to the full interview on the Marvel's Voices podcast, available on Apple Podcasts and anywhere you can listen to podcasts.

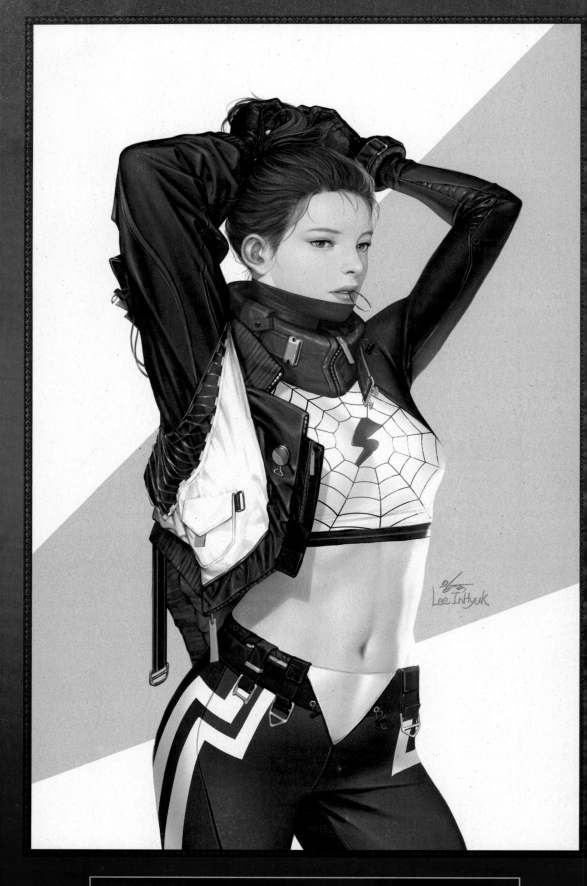

AMAZING SPIDER-MAN #72 ASIAN VOICES VARIANT BY INHYUK LEE

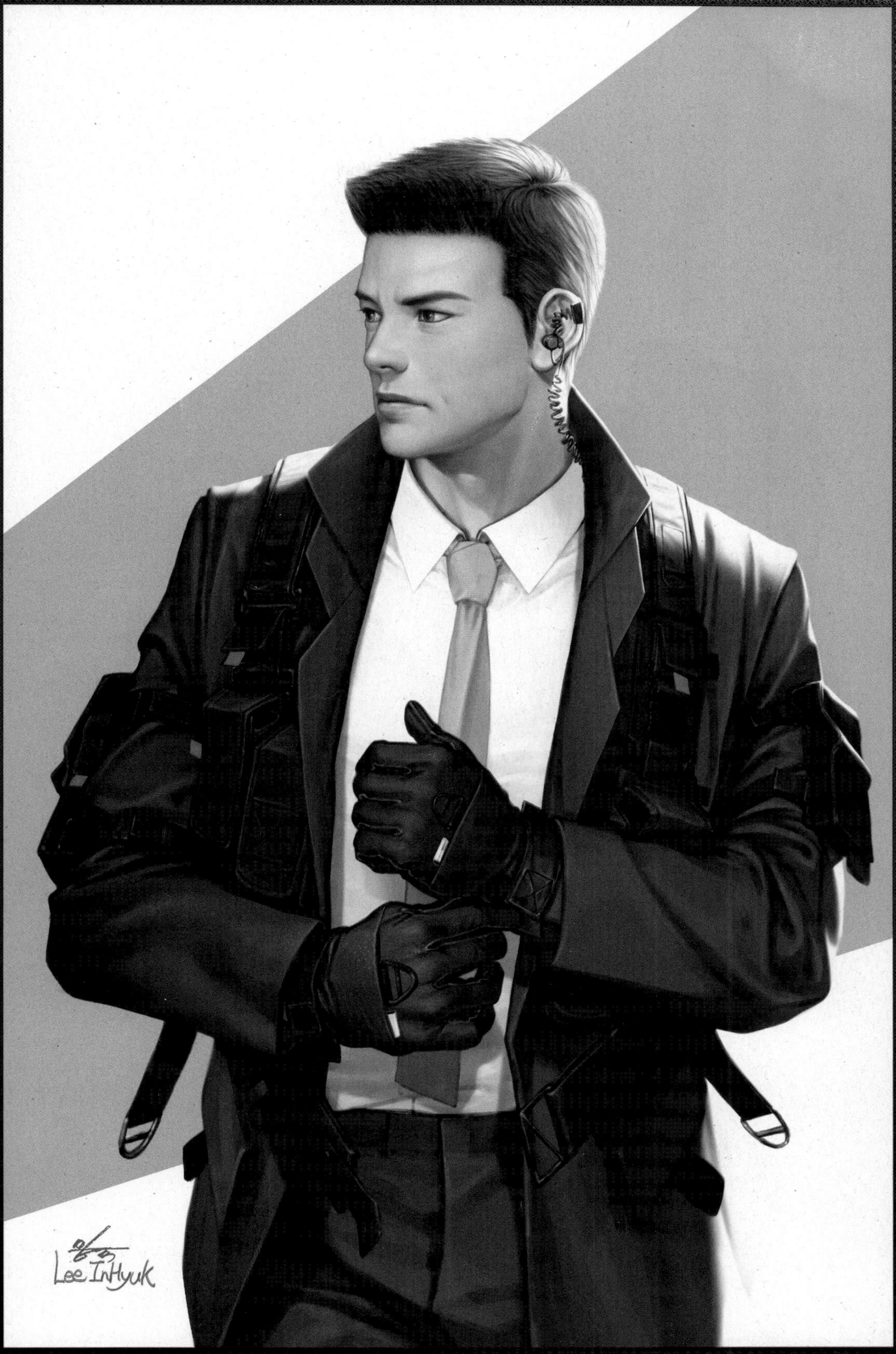
Lee InHyuk

AVENGERS #47 ASIAN VOICES VARIANT BY **INHYUK LEE**

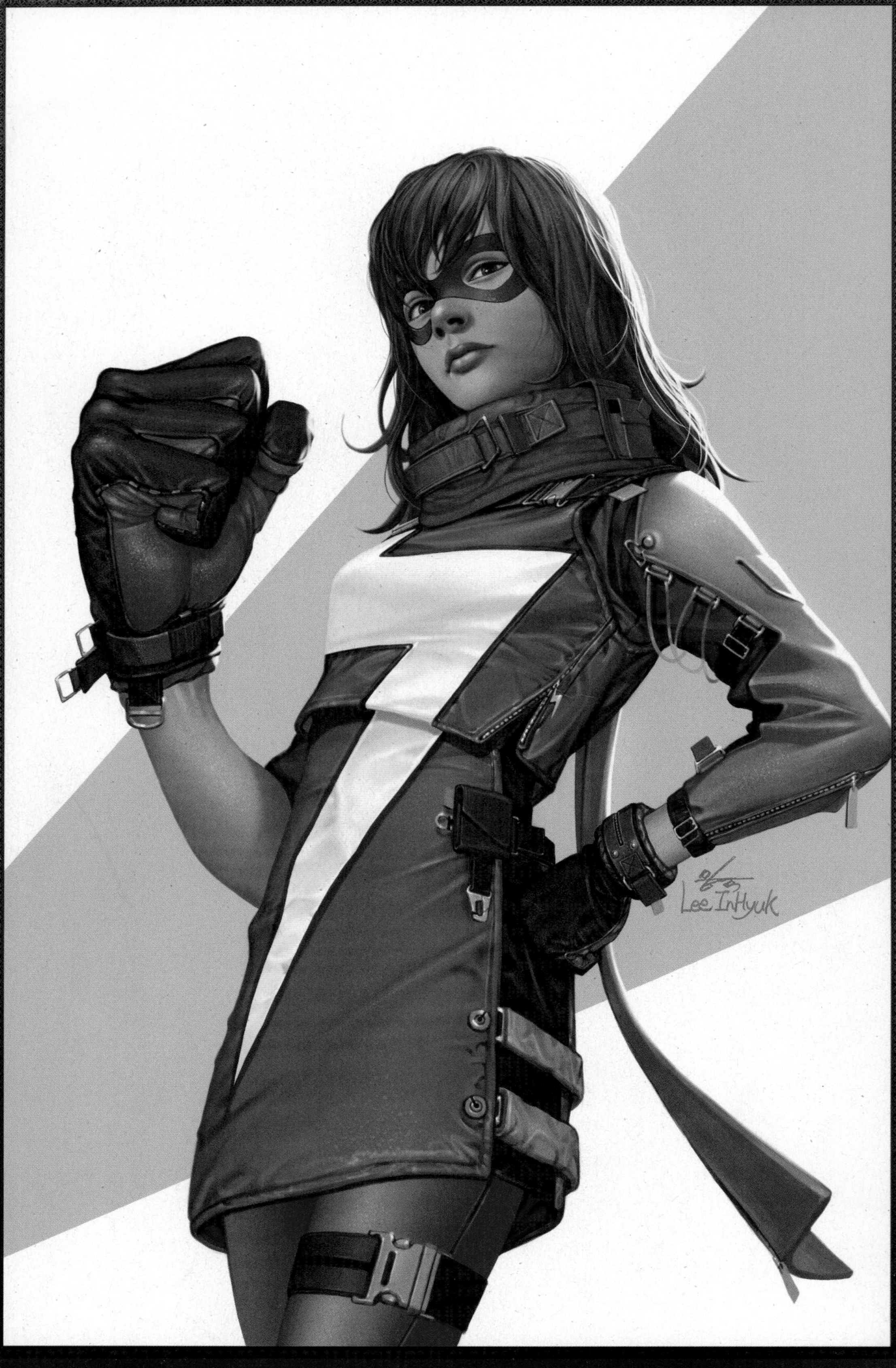
Lee InHyuk

CAPTAIN MARVEL #31 ASIAN VOICES VARIANT BY **INHYUK LEE**

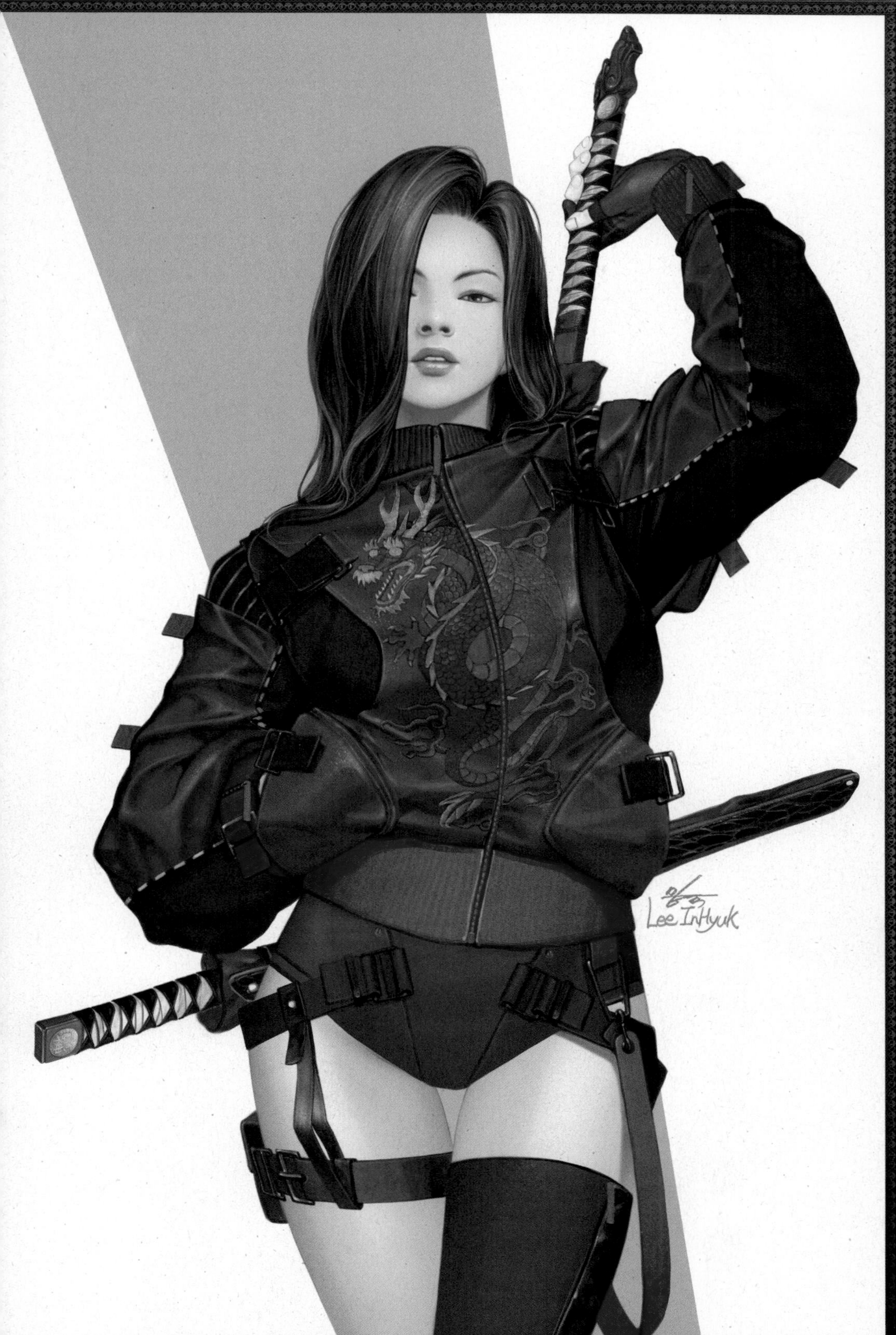
Lee InHyuk

HELLIONS #14 ASIAN VOICES VARIANT BY **INHYUK LEE**

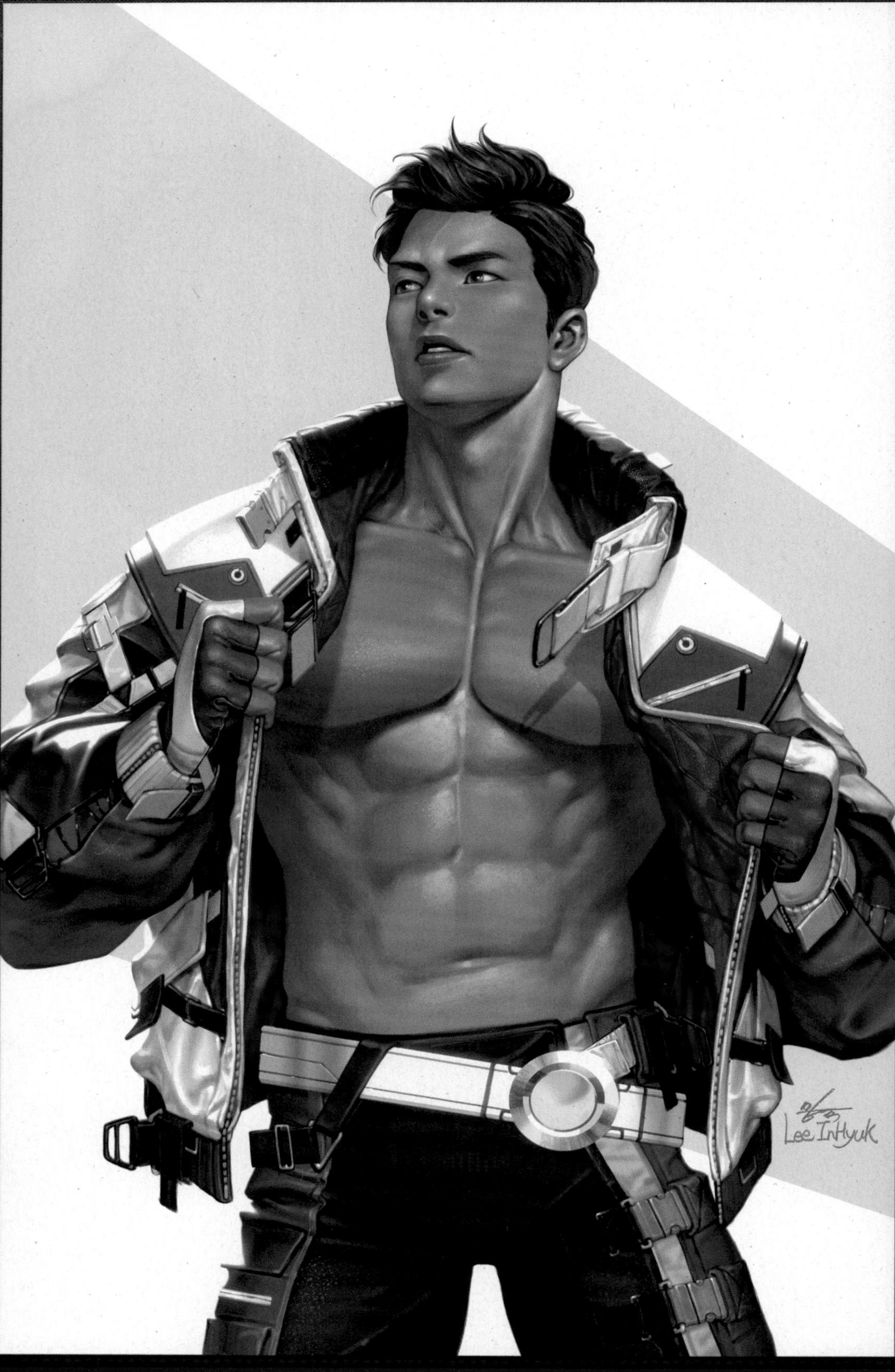
Lee InHyuk

IMMORTAL HULK #49 ASIAN VOICES VARIANT BY **INHYUK LEE**

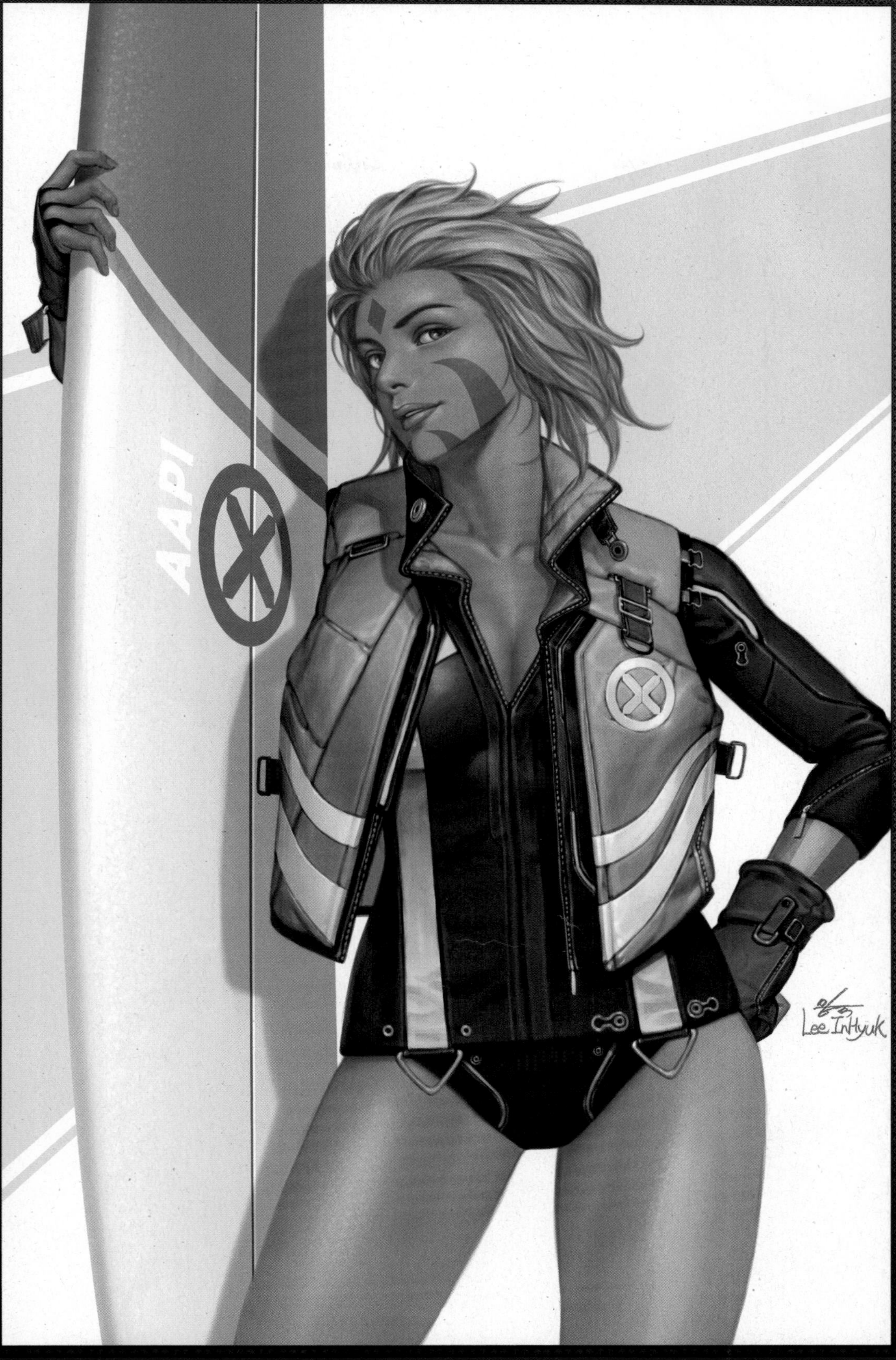
AAPI
Lee InHyuk

WAY OF X #5 ASIAN VOICES VARIANT BY **INHYUK LEE**

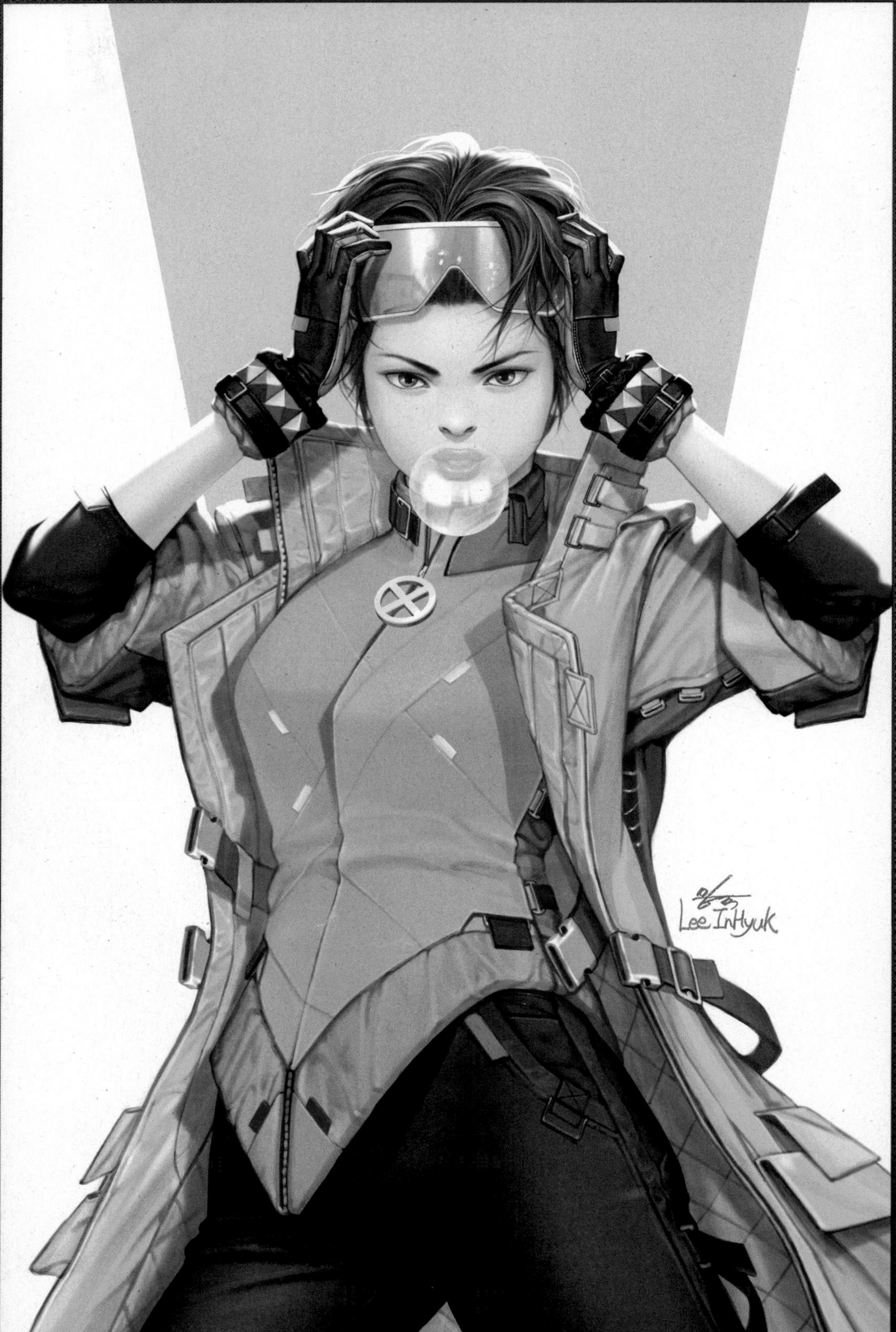
Lee InHyuk

WOLVERINE #15 ASIAN VOICES VARIANT BY **INHYUK LEE**

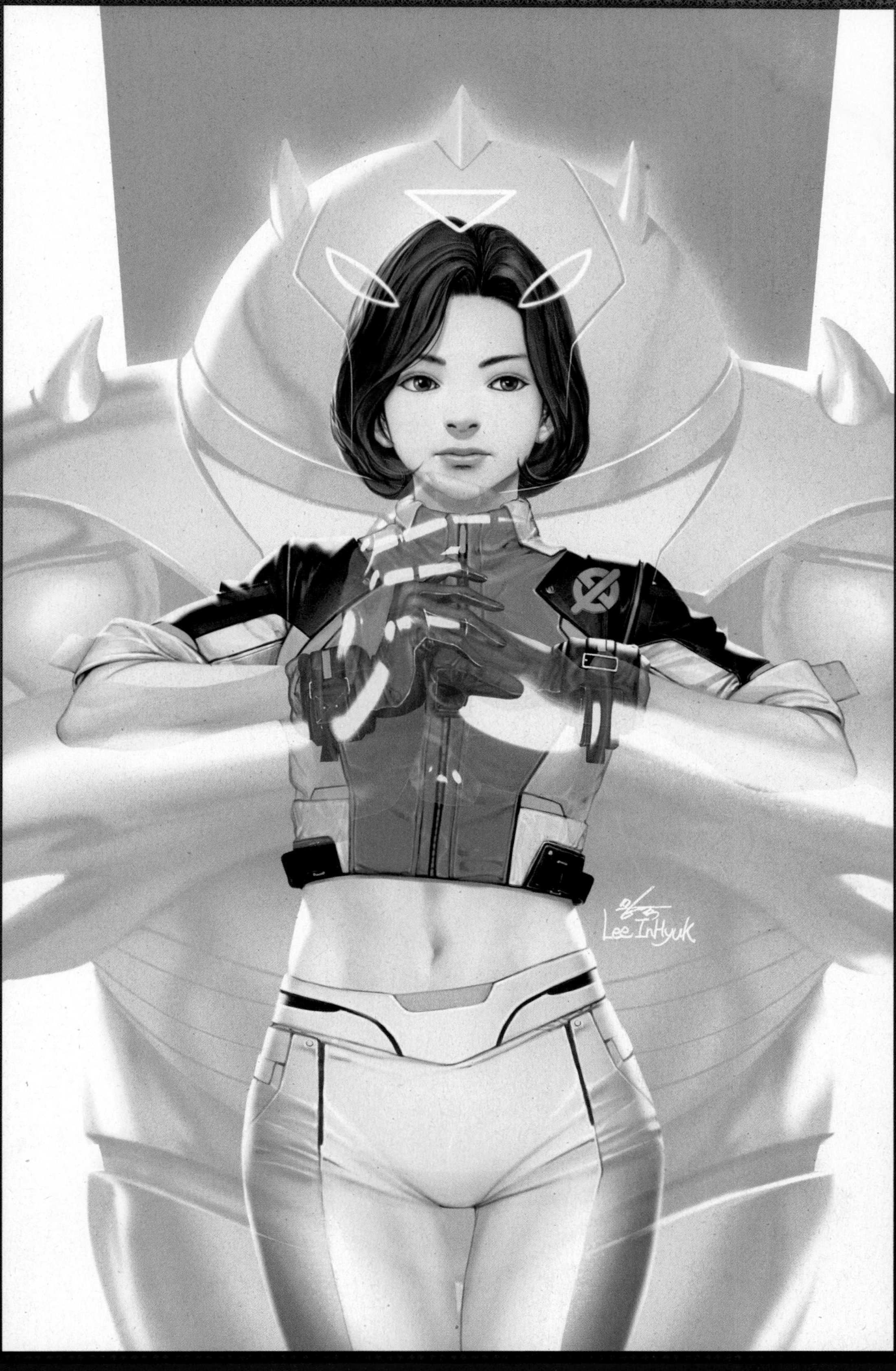
Lee InHyuk

***X-MEN* #2** ASIAN VOICES VARIANT BY **INHYUK LEE**

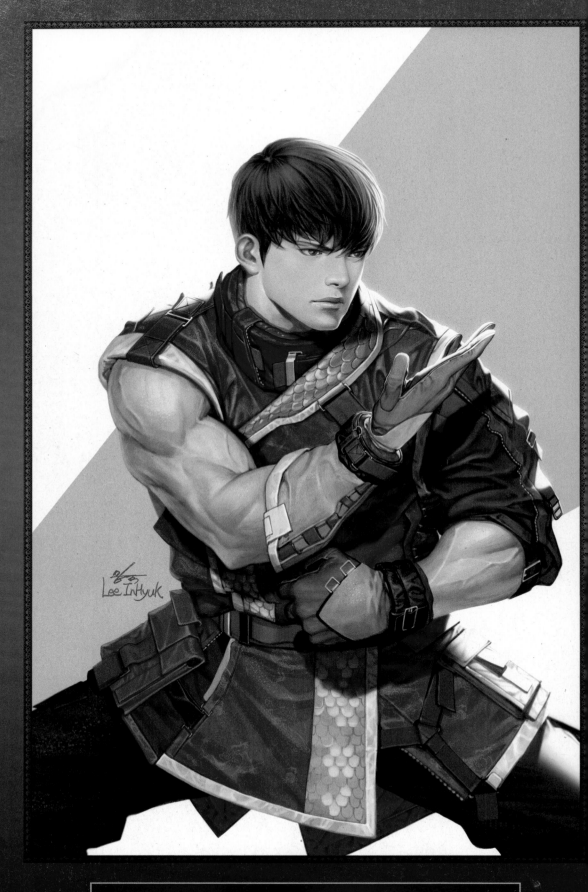

MARVEL'S VOICES: *IDENTITY* ASIAN VOICES VARIANT BY **INHYUK LEE**

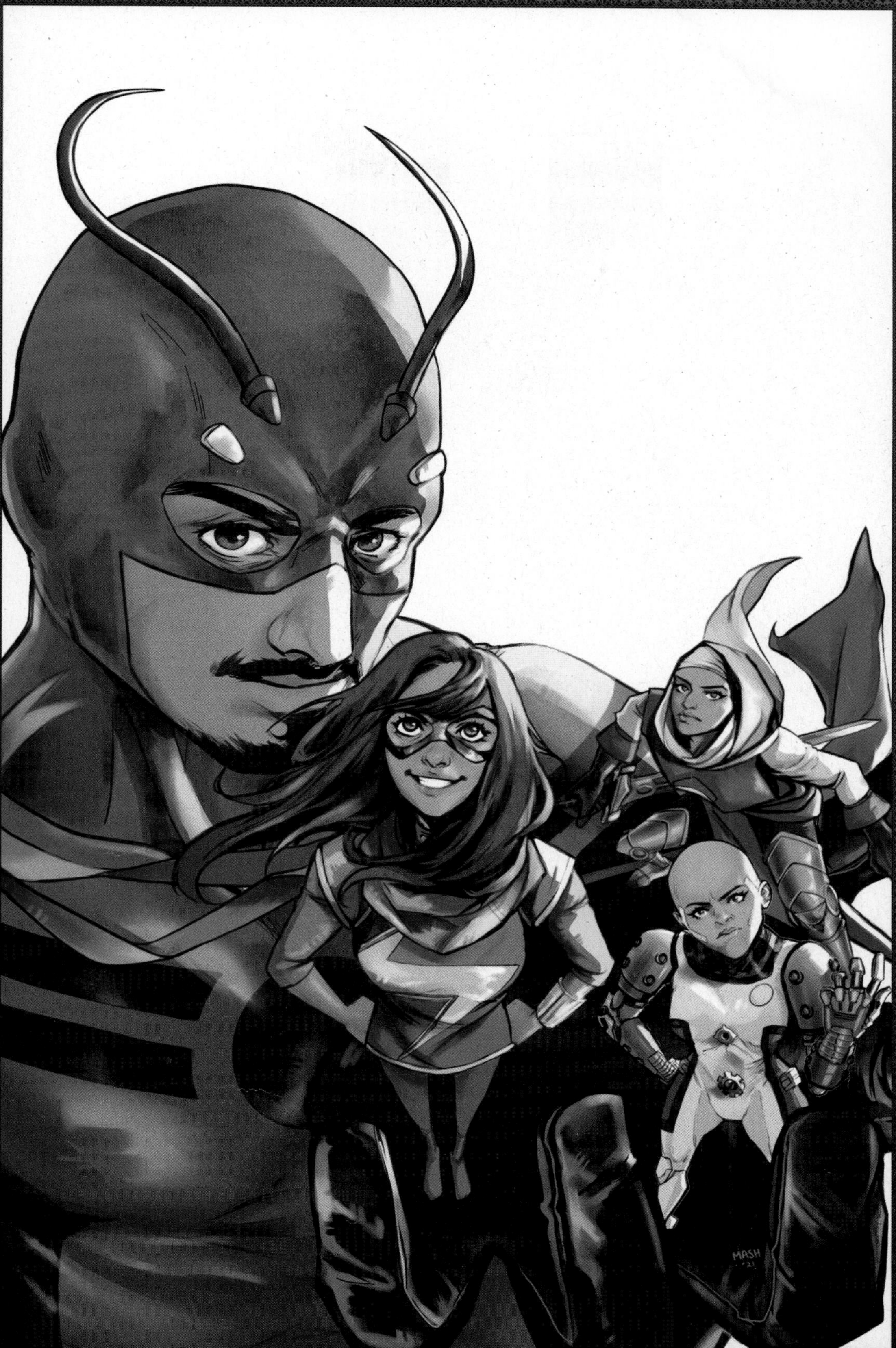
MASH '21

MARVEL'S VOICES: IDENTITY VARIANT BY **MASHAL AHMED**

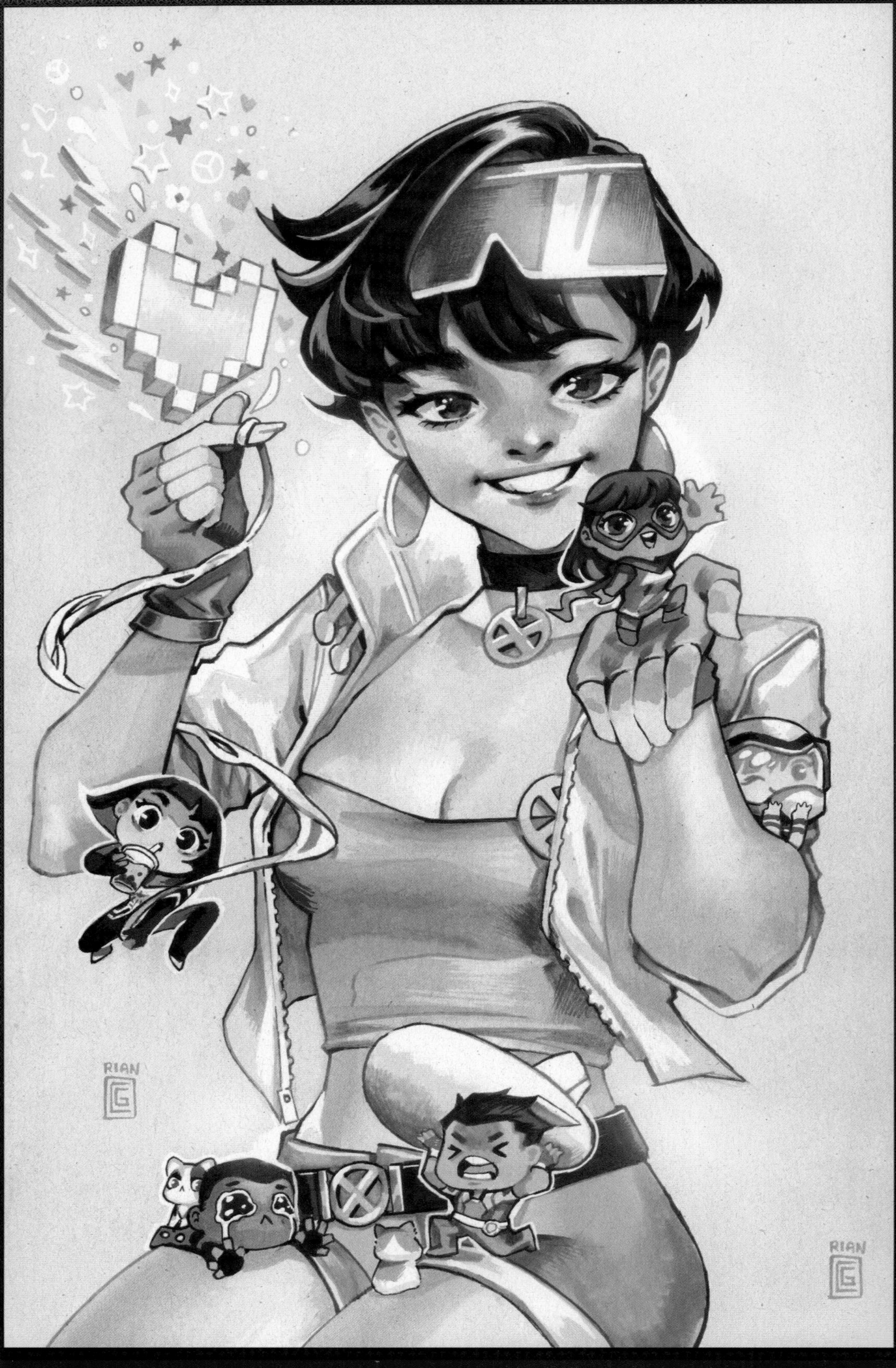
RIAN
RIAN

MARVEL'S VOICES: IDENTITY **VARIANT BY RIAN GONZALES**

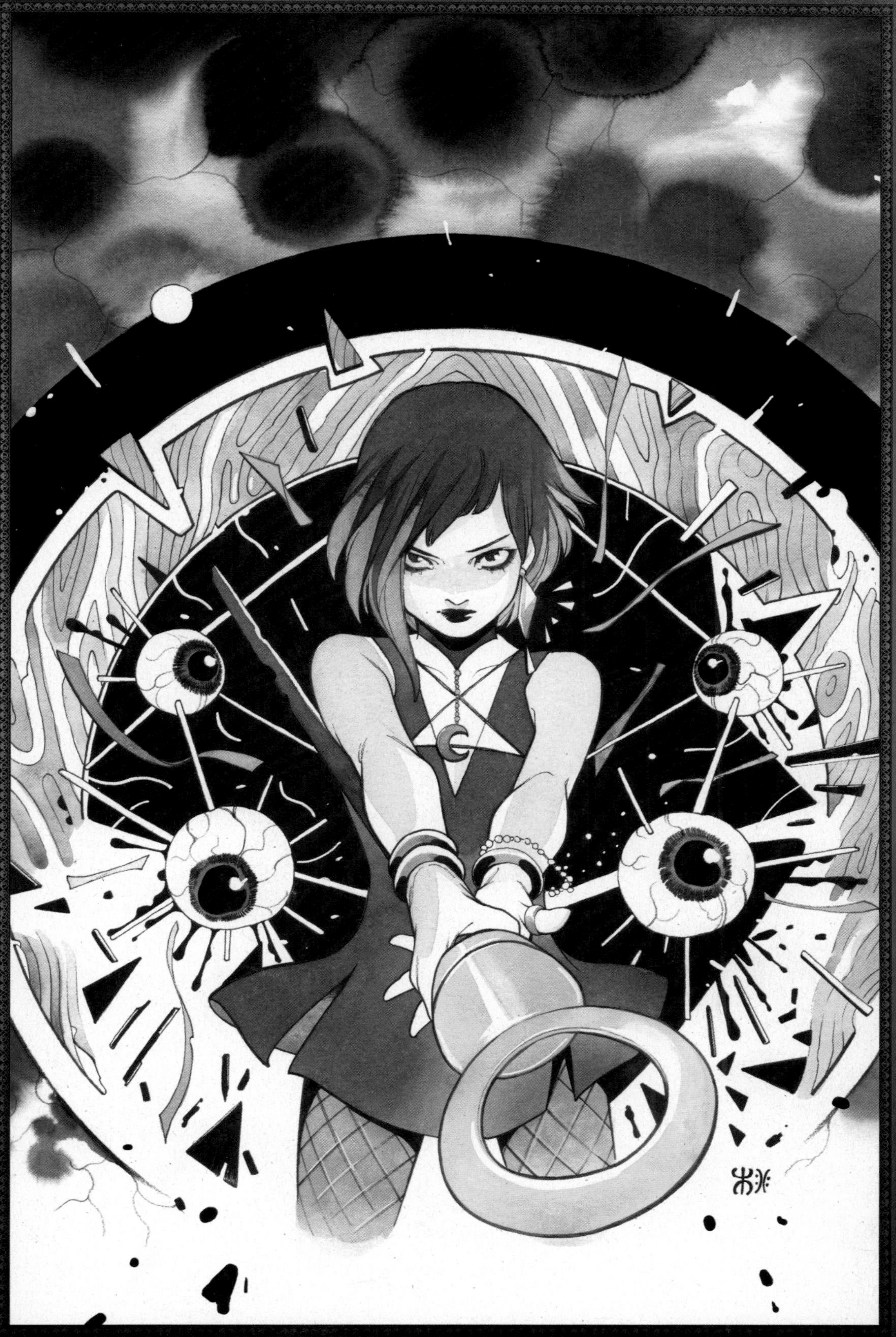

MARVEL'S VOICES: IDENTITY VARIANT BY **PEACH MOMOKO**

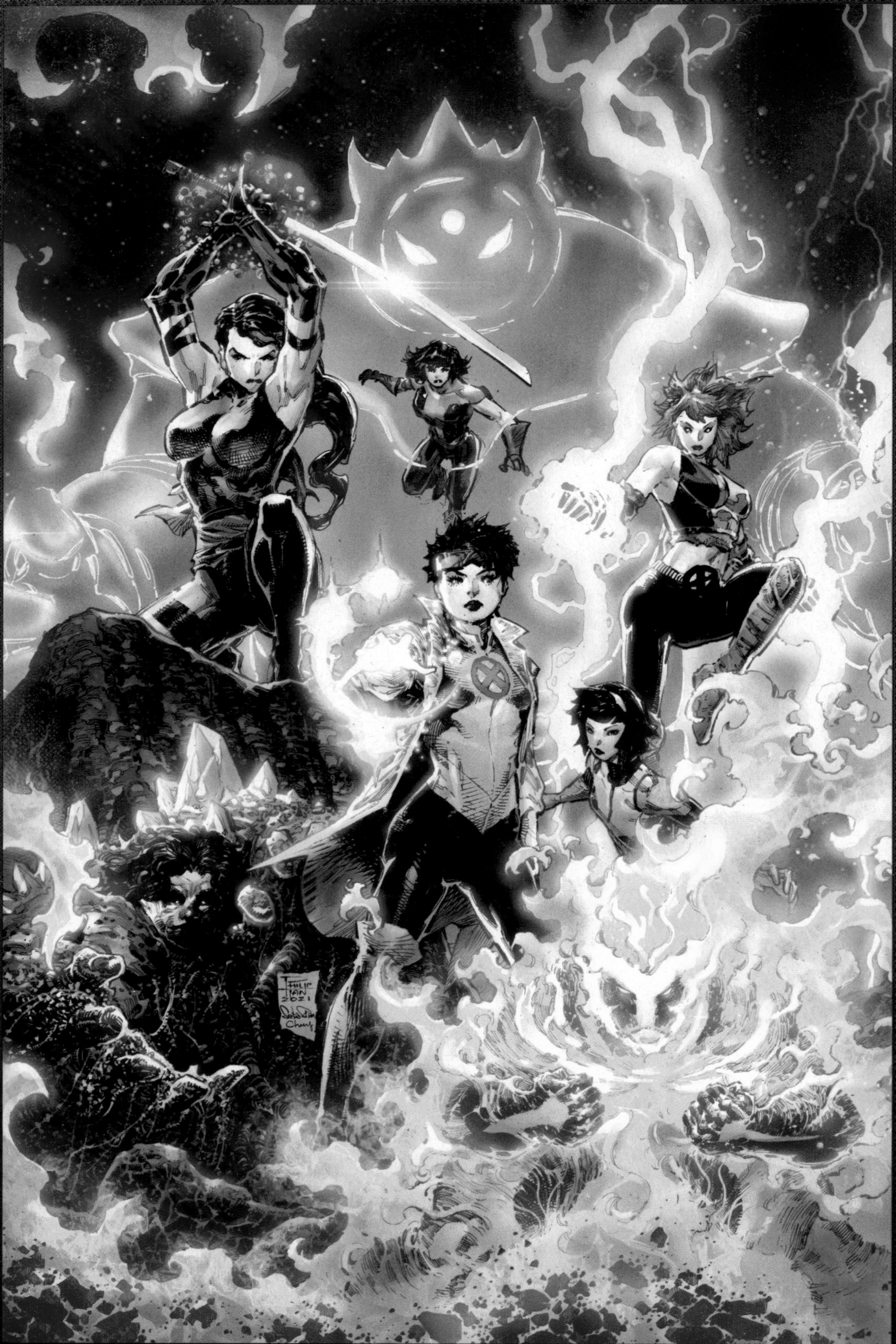

MARVEL'S VOICES: IDENTITY VARIANT BY **PHILIP TAN & SEBASTIAN CHENG**